D0982934

EVERYMAN, I will go with thee,

and be thy guide,

In thy most need to go by thy side

GIORGIO VASARI

Born at Arezzo in 1511
Died in Florence 1574

GIORGIO VASARI

The Lives of the Painters, Sculptors and Architects

IN FOUR VOLUMES · VOLUME TWO

TRANSLATED BY
A. B. HINDS

EDITED WITH AN INTRODUCTION BY
WILLIAM GAUNT, M.A.

DENT: LONDON
EVERYMAN'S LIBRARY
DUTTON: NEW YORK

NO. 785

ISBN: 0 460 0785 8

CONTENTS OF VOLUME TWO

PART II—*continued*

PART III

CONTENTS

LIONARDO DA VINCI

PART II—*Continued*

Frà Filippo Lippi, Painter of Florence
(?1406 – 1469)

Frà Filippo di Tommaso Lippi, the Carmelite, who was born in Florence in a side street called Ardiglione, under the Canto alla Cuculia, behind the convent of the Carmelite friars, was left at the age of two in great poverty by the death of his father Tommaso, and with no one to care for him, as his mother had died shortly after his birth. Accordingly he remained in the charge of his aunt, Mona Lapaccia, his father's sister, who, after rearing him with great difficulty until he attained the age of eight, could no longer maintain him, and made him a friar in the convent of the Carmine. Here he showed himself as dexterous and ingenious in all manual exercises as he was clumsy and ill-fitted to learn letters, for he would never apply his mind or take kindly to them. The boy, who was called Filippo, the name which he had borne in the world, being with others in the noviciate under the discipline of the master of grammar, in order that it might be seen what he was fit for, instead of studying did nothing but cover his books and those of the others with caricatures. Accordingly the prior determined to give him every opportunity to learn to paint. The chapel in the Carmine had just been newly painted by Masaccio, and being very beautiful, greatly delighted Frà Filippo, who frequented it every day, and was always practising in the company of many youths who spent their time in drawing there. These he far surpassed in skill and knowledge, so that all agreed that he ought to do something wonderful in times to come. But in his early as well as in his mature years he produced such admirable works that he was a miracle. Thus a short time after he painted in *terra verde* in the cloister near the Consecration of Masaccio a pope confirming the rule of the Carmelites,

I

and painted in fresco on several walls in many parts of the church, notably a St. John the Baptist and some incidents of his life. And so making progress every day, he had so far acquired the manner of Masaccio, making his things in a similar manner, that many declared that the spirit of Masaccio had entered into the body of Frà Filippo. On a pilaster in the church he made the figure of St. Martial, near the organ, which brought him great renown, as it would bear comparison with the paintings of Masaccio. Then hearing himself so greatly praised by the general cry, he boldly discarded the habit at the age of seventeen. But one day, while he was in the March of Ancona on a pleasure excursion with some of his friends, they were all taken while in a small boat by the light galleys of the Moors which scoured those parts, and being put into chains they were carried off as slaves to Barbary, where they remained for eighteen months, enduring great hardships. One day Filippo, who was on very good terms with his master, had the happy fancy to draw him, and picking up a burnt coal from the floor he drew his portrait on a white wall, with his Moorish clothes. The other slaves told the master of this, since it appeared a miracle to them, painting and design being unknown in those parts, and this led to Filippo's release from the chains in which he had been bound for so long a time. It is indeed a glorious tribute to this faculty that one who has the legal power to condemn and punish should do the contrary, and instead of punishment and death should give caresses and liberty. After Filippo had done some things in colours for his master, he was taken in safety to Naples, where he painted a panel in tempera for King Alfonso, then Duke of Calabria, in the castle chapel where the guard now is. He afterwards became anxious to return to Florence, remaining there for some months, painting a fine picture for the nuns of S. Ambruogio at the high altar.[1] This procured for him the favour of Cosimo de' Medici, who became his fast friend. He did another picture in the chapter-house of S. Croce, and another which was placed in the Chapel of the Casa Medici, representing the Nativity of Christ.[2] For the wife of Cosimo he made a picture of the Nativity and St. John the Baptist,[3] to be placed in the hermitage of the Camaldolites in one of their cells, which she caused to be built for her devotions, and dedicated to St. John the Baptist. He also did some small scenes to be sent by Cosimo as a gift to Pope Eugenius IV., the

[1] A Coronation of the Virgin, now in the Uffizi, painted in 1447.
[2] Now in the Uffizi.　　　　[3] Now in the Uffizi, Florence.

Venetian. By this work Filippo acquired great favour with the Pope. He is said to have been so amorous that when he saw a woman who pleased him he would have given all his possessions to have her, and if he could not succeed in this he quieted the flame of his love by painting her portrait. This appetite so took possession of him that while the humour lasted he paid little or no attention to his work. Thus, on one occasion when Cosimo de' Medici was employing him, he shut him up in the house so that he might not go out and waste time. He remained so for two days, but overcome by his amorous and bestial desires, he cut up his sheet with a pair of scissors, and, letting himself down out of the window, devoted many days to his pleasures. When Cosimo could not find him he caused a search to be made for him, until at length Filippo returned to his labours. From that time forward Cosimo gave him liberty to go and come as he chose, repenting that he had shut him up, and thinking of his folly and the danger which he might run. For this reason he ever after sought to hold Filippo by the bonds of affection, and was thus served by him with greater readiness, for he said geniuses are celestial forms and not pack asses. Filippo did a picture in the church of S. Maria Primerana on the piazza of Fiesole containing an Annunciation, most carefully finished, the figure of the angel exhibiting a truly celestial beauty. For the nuns of the Murate he did two pictures, one of an Annunciation placed at the high altar, containing stories of St. Benedict and St. Bernard, and in the palace of the Signoria he painted an Annunciation on a panel over a door, and he also made a St. Bernard [1] there over another door. In the sacristy of S. Spirito at Florence he made a Madonna surrounded by angels, with saints at the side, a rare work which has always been held in the highest veneration by our masters here.

In the chapel of the wardens at S. Lorenzo Filippo made another Annunciation and yet another for the Stufa, which is unfinished. In a chapel in S. Apostolo in the same city he painted some figures about Our Lady on a panel, and for M. Carlo Marsuppini he did the altar-piece of the chapel of St. Bernard in the convent of the monks of Monte Oliveto at Arezzo representing the Coronation of the Virgin, surrounded by many saints, so well preserved that it looks as if Frà Filippo had just painted it. Here M. Carlo warned him to take care what he painted, because many of his things were blamed. For this reason Frà Filippo painted nearly all

[1] Painted in 1447, now in the National Gallery, London.

his figures from that time forward either covered with draperies or with other inventions, in order to escape such censure. In this work he drew the portrait of this same M. Carlo. For the nuns of Annalena, at Florence, he painted a picture of the Manger, and some of his pictures may still be seen at Padua. He sent to the Cardinal Barbo at Rome two small scenes of tiny figures which were most excellently done and very carefully finished. He certainly worked with marvellous grace, giving his things a wonderful finish, so that they are always valued by artists and highly esteemed by modern masters; indeed, he will be held in veneration by every age so long as time will permit his works to remain extant. In Prato, near Florence, where he had some relations, he remained for many months in the company of Frà Diamante of the Carmine, for they had been companions and novices together, doing a number of things in all that district. After this the nuns of S. Margherita employed him to do the picture of the high altar.[1] While at work there he chanced one day to see a daughter of Francesco Buti, a Florentine citizen, who was there either as a ward or as a nun. Frà Filippo cast his eyes upon Lucrezia, for that was the girl's name, for she was very graceful and beautiful, and persuaded the nuns to allow him to paint her as the Virgin for their work. Becoming more enamoured of her by this work, he subsequently contrived to take her away from the nuns on the very day that she was going to see the exhibition of the girdle of Our Lady, an honoured relic of that city. By this mishap the nuns were covered with shame, while a perpetual gloom settled upon her father Francesco, who made every effort to recover her. But whether through fear or some other cause, she would never return, and remained with Filippo, who had a boy by her, also called Filippo,[2] who afterwards became a great and famous painter like his father. In S. Domenico at Prato there are two pictures and a Madonna on the screen of S. Francesco. This was removed from its original position to the place it now occupies, by cutting away the wall and making a wooden framework. In the Ceppo of Francesco di Marco there is a small panel by the same hand, with a portrait of the said Francesco, the originator and founder of that pious house, over a well in a courtyard.[3] In the Pieve of the town he painted on a small panel over the side door leading to the staircase the death of St. Bernard, who is healing a number of lame folk who touch

---

[1] About 1450. [2] Born in 1457 and known to fame as Filippino Lippi.
[3] Now in the Municipal Gallery at Prato.

the bier.[1] Here also are the friars weeping for their master, the heads being truly admirable, the grief of the weeping men being finely represented. Some of the folds of the friars' hoods are excellent, and deserve the highest praise for their good design, colouring and composition, and for the grace and proportion displayed by the most delicate hand of Frà Filippo. The chapel of the high altar of the Pieve was assigned to him by the wardens, who wished to have a memorial of him.[2] This enabled him to display his skill, the draperies and heads being admirable, not to speak of the general excellence and artistic qualities of the whole. In this work he made the figures greater than life-size, thus introducing the modern method of doing things on a large scale. Some of the figures are dressed in a manner not common at that time, when men began to emerge from that simplicity which deserves to be called old-fashioned rather than ancient. The work contains incidents from the life of St. Stephen, patron saint of the Pieve, arranged on the right-hand wall, to wit, the disputation, stoning and death of the proto-martyr, the scene in which he is disputing with the Jews displaying such zeal and fervour that it is difficult to imagine and much more so to describe the hatred, rage and anger depicted in the faces and attitudes of the Jews at seeing themselves conquered by him. Filippo has been even more successful in depicting the brutality and fury of those who are killing him with stones, some picking up large ones and some small, and grinding their teeth in a horrible manner in their cruelty and fury. And yet, in the midst of this terrible assault, Stephen, with the utmost calmness, lifts his eyes to heaven and with the greatest charity and fervour prays to the Eternal Father for the very men who are killing him. These are fine ideas, and show the inestimable value to painting of invention and an ability to depict feeling. The artist has observed this in making the attitudes of those who are burying Stephen so sorrowful, and some so afflicted and distressed in their mourning, that it is hardly possible to look at them without emotion. On the other side he did the Nativity, the preaching, the baptism, the banquet of Herod, and the beheading of St. John the Baptist, the face of the preacher displaying the divine spirit, while the divers movements of the crowd are expressive of joy and sorrow, in the women as well as the men, all of them hanging on the ministrations of St. John. The baptism shows beauty and excellence, and the banquet of Herod the majesty of the occasion, the address of

[1] Now in the Duomo   [2] Begun in 1456.

Herodias, the astonishment and the excessive sorrow of the
guests at the presentation of the head on the charger. About
the table are a number of figures in fine attitudes, and well
executed as regards the draperies and expressions on the faces.
Among these Filippo drew his own portrait with the aid of a
mirror, clothed in black in a prelate's habit, together with his
pupil, Frà Diamante, in the scene of the mourning for St. Stephen.
Indeed, this work was the most excellent which he produced,
for the reasons given above, or because he made the figures
somewhat larger than life-size, a thing which encouraged those
who came after to work on a larger scale. He was so highly
esteemed for his abilities that many blameworthy things in
his life were covered over by his excellencies. In this work he
drew the portrait of M. Carlo, natural son of Cosimo de' Medici,
then provost of the church, upon which he and his house
conferred many benefits. After the completion of this work
Filippo painted in tempera, in 1463, a picture for the church
of S. Jacopo at Pistoia, containing a fine Annunciation, for M.
Jacopo Bellucci, whose most life-like portrait is drawn there.
The house of Pulidoro Bracciolini contains a picture of the
Nativity of the Virgin by him, and the magistracy of the Eight
at Florence have a round Madonna and Child in tempera. In
the house of Ludovico Capponi is a most beautiful Madonna;
and in the possession of Bernardo Vecchietti, a Florentine gentleman of great virtue and respectability, is a remarkably fine small
picture by the same hand of St. Augustine in this study. Far
better even than these is a St. Jerome, in penance, of the same
size, in the wardrobe of Duke Cosimo. Remarkable in all his
paintings, Frà Filippo surpassed himself in the small ones,
making them so graceful and so beautiful that nothing better
could be desired, as we see by the predellas of all his paintings.
Indeed, such was his excellence that no one surpassed him in
his day, and but few in our own, while Michelagnolo has never
tired of singing his praises and has frequently imitated him.
For the old church of S. Domenico at Perugia Filippo did a
picture of Our Lady, with St. Peter, St. Paul, St. Louis and
St. Anthony the abbot, afterwards placed at the high altar.
M. Alessandro degli Alessandri, a knight of that time, and his
friend, employed him to do a St. Laurence and other saints for
his church at Vincigliata on the hill of Fiesole, introducing
portraits of the knight and his two sons.

Filippo loved to surround himself with cheerful companions
and lived with gaiety. He taught the art of painting to Frà

Diamante, who did a number of pictures in the Carmine at Prato, and by imitating his master's style won much honour, attaining to the highest perfection. Among those who studied with Filippo in his youth were Sandro Botticello, Pisello, Jacopo del Sellaio of Florence, who painted two pictures in S. Friano and one in the Carmine, in tempera, and countless other masters to whom he taught his art with unfailing kindness. He lived in honour on his labours, and incurred very heavy expenses on love intrigues, in which he continued to indulge until his death. Through Cosimo de' Medici he was requested by the community of Spoleto to decorate the chapel in the principal church of Our Lady.[1] Working in conjunction with Frà Diamante he had made good progress with this when death prevented him from completing it. It is said that in one of his everlasting intrigues the relations of the lady had poisoned him. Frà Filippo finished his career at the age of fifty-seven, in 1438, and by his will left his son Filippo to the care of Frà Diamante. The boy being then ten years of age, learned the art from Frà Diamante and returned with him to Florence, the monk taking with him 300 ducats which were due to him by the community. With this money the friar bought some property for himself, and gave but little to the child. Sandro Botticello, then considered a most excellent master, took Filippo into his workshop. The father was buried in a tomb of white and red marble set up by the people of Spoleto in the church which he painted for them. His death caused great sorrow to his friends, particularly to Cosimo de' Medici and Pope Eugenius,[2] who had endeavoured to legitimatise the union between Filippo and Lucrezia di Francesco Buti, but the former refused, because he wished to be able to give full rein to his appetite. During the lifetime of Sixtus IV., Lorenzo de' Medici, being ambassador of Florence, went by way of Spoleto to ask for the body of Frà Filippo which he wished to place in S. Maria del Fiore at Florence, but they answered that they were badly provided with things of note, and especially with men of eminence, and asked leave to possess Filippo as a favour, because Florence had countless distinguished men, indeed almost a superfluity, so that they could spare this one, and so Lorenzo failed to carry his point. It is true that, it being decided to honour him in the best possible way, Lorenzo sent Filippo the son to the Cardinal of Naples at Rome, to make a chapel. When the Cardinal passed through Spoleto, he caused a marble tomb to be made under the organ and above the sacristy, by commission of

[1] 1467-9. [2] Both were dead before Frà Filippo.

Lorenzo, on which he expended 100 gold ducats, paid by Nofri
Tornaboni, director of the bank of the Medici. He further
obtained the following eprigram from M. Agnolo Poliziano,
which was inscribed on the tomb in antique letters·

> Conditus hic ego sum picturae fama Philippus
> Nulli ignota meae est gratia mira manus,
> Artifices potui digitis animare colores
> Sperataque animos fallere voce diu,
> Ipsa meis stupuit natura expressa figuris
> Meque suis fassa est artibus esse parem,
> Marmoreo tumulo Medices Laurentius hic me
> Condidit, ante humili pulvere tectus eram.

Filippo designed excellently, as may be seen in our book of the
drawings of the most famous painters, and especially in some
sheets containing his designs for the picture of S. Spirito, and in
others of the chapel of Prato.

PAOLO ROMANO and MAESTRO MINO, Sculptors, and
CHIMENTI CAMICIA, Architect
(fl. 1460; fl. 1462; 1431–alive 1495)

WE now go on to speak of Paolo Romano[1] and Mino del Regno,
contemporaries, and of the same profession, but very different
in the nature of their habits and their art, for Paolo was modest
and of considerable ability, whereas Mino, though much less
talented, was so presumptuous and arrogant that he always
absurdly exaggerated his own achievements. When Pius II.
employed Paolo to make a figure, Mino, out of envy, pestered
him so much that Paolo with all his good nature and modesty
could not help resenting it, whereupon Mino proposed a bet of
1000 ducats as to who would make the better statue, a most
presumptuous and impertinent thing, for he knew that Paolo
would not incur unnecessary trouble, and did not think that he
would accept the challenge. In this he was deceived, and Mino
half repented, and would only wager 100 ducats. When the
figures were made the award was given to Paolo as a rare and
excellent artist, and it became clear that Mino was a better hand
at talking than at performing. There is a tomb by Mino's hand
at Monte Cassino, a place of the black monks in the kingdom of
Naples, and some things in marble at Naples. In Rome he made
the St. Peter and St. Paul which are at the foot of the staircase of
St. Peter, and the tomb of Pope Paul II. in S. Pietro. The figure

[1] Paolo di Mariano.

made by Paolo in competition with Mino was the St. Paul which may be seen at the entry of the Ponte S. Angelo on a marble pedestal which stood for a long time unrecognised before the chapel of Sixtus IV. It happened afterwards that Pope Clement VII. cast his eyes upon the figure one day, and having a good knowledge and judgment of such things, it pleased him greatly. He therefore determined to have a St. Peter of the same size, and to put them side by side at the entrance of the Ponte Sant' Angelo, where two little marble chapels stood dedicated to the Apostles, removing the chapels which obstructed the view from the south, and putting the statues in their place.

We read in the work of Antonio Filarete that Paolo was not only a sculptor but a clever goldsmith, who did a part of the twelve Apostles in silver which stood on the altar of the papal chapel before the sack of Rome. Paolo's pupils, Niccolo della Guardia and Pietro Paolo da Todi, were also engaged upon this work, and they afterwards became meritorious masters in sculpture, as we see by the tombs of Pius II. and Pius III., which contain the effigies of these popes. By the same hands are the three emperors and other great persons on medals. Paolo also made a statue of an armed man on horseback which is now on the floor of S. Pietro near the chapel of St. Andrew. Iancristoforo, a Roman, was a pupil of Paolo and a sculptor of merit, some of his works being in S. Maria Trastevere and elsewhere.

Chimenti Camicia, of whose origin nothing is known except that he was a Florentine, while in the service of the King of Hungary, made for him palaces, gardens, fountains, temples, fortresses, and many other buildings of importance, with ornaments, carvings, coats of arms and other things executed with much diligence by Baccio Cellini. After these works Chimenti returned to Florence, for he loved his country, and sent to Baccio, who remained behind, telling him to give the king some paintings by the hand of Berto, the flax-seller, which were considered very fine in Hungary, and greatly admired by the king. This Berto, of whom I will take the opportunity to speak, after executing many pictures in his fine style, now in the houses of various citizens, died in the flower of his age, thus disappointing the hopes which had been entertained for him. But to return to Chimenti: he had not been long in Florence before he returned to Hungary, where in going to the Danube to design some mills for the king he contracted an illness through over-fatigue, which in a few days terminated his life. The works of these masters were about 1470.

At the same time there lived in Rome, under Pope Sixtus IV.,
one Baccio Pintelli,[1] a Florentine, who was deservedly employed
by the Pope for every construction undertaken by him, on
account of his skill in architecture. Thus it was from his design
that the church and convent of S. Maria del Popolo were constructed,[2] and some chapels there with much ornamentation,
particularly that of Domenico della Rovere, cardinal of S.
Clemente, and the Pope's nephew. The same Pope constructed a
palace in the Borgo Vecchio from Baccio's design, which was
then considered a fine and well-planned edifice. The Pope also
made the large library under the apartments of Niccola and the
so-called Sistine chapel in the palace, which is adorned with fine
paintings.[3] He further rebuilt the new hospital of S. Spirito in
Sassia, which was burned down in 1471 almost to its foundations,
adding a long loggia to it with all the most useful and desirable
accessories. Inside the length of the hospital he had scenes
painted of the life of Pope Sixtus from his birth until the completion of the building, and indeed until the end of his life. He also
made the Ponte Sisto, called after him, which was considered an
excellent work, because Baccio had made the ribs so strong, and
had distributed the weights so well, that it is a most firm and
excellent structure. Similarly in the year of jubilee, 1475, he
erected a number of small churches in Rome, to be recognised
by the arms of Pope Sixtus, notably S. Apostolo, S. Pietro in
Vincula, and S. Sisto. For the Cardinal Guglielmo, bishop of
Ostia, he made the model of his church and of the façade and
staircases in their present form. Many affirm that the design
of the church of S. Pietro a Montorio at Rome was by Braccio,
but I cannot truthfully say that I have found this to be so. This
church was built at the expense of the King of Portugal, almost
at the very time that the Spaniards were building the church of
S. Jacopo at Rome. The worth of Baccio was so highly valued
by the Pope that he would never undertake any building without
his advice. Thus when in 1480 he heard that the church and
convent of S. Francesco at Assisi were in danger of falling, he
sent Baccio there, who made a strong buttress on the side of the
plain, and rendered the whole of that marvellous fabric perfectly
safe. On a spur he placed the statue of the Pope, who not many
years before had built in that same convent many rooms and
halls which, besides their magnificence, may be recognised by
the arms of the Pope displayed there. In the courtyard is

[1] Pontelli.   [2] 1477–80.
[3] Carried out in 1473 by Giovanni de' Dolci.

one much larger than the others, with some Latin verses in honour of Pope Sixtus, who showed in many ways how highly he reverenced that holy place.

ANDREA DAL CASTAGNO of Mugello and DOMENICO VINI-ZIANO, Painters
(?1410 – 1457; c. 1400 – 1461)

WHAT words can express the vileness of the vice of envy in distinguished men, bad in any person? How dreadful and horrible a thing it is to endeavour, under the guise of a false friendship, to extinguish not only the fame and glory of others, but their very life, for the baseness of the act surpasses all the resources of the tongue, however eloquent it may be. Without going any further into this matter, I will content myself with saying that those who do such things are not only inhuman and cruel, but altogether diabolical, so far removed from every trace of virtue that the offenders are inhuman, inferior to the brutes, and unworthy to live. Just as loyal emulation and competition, which aim at progress rather than at glory and honour, are worthy and valuable, being necessary and useful to the world, so on the contrary such villainous envy is infamous and odious. For when it is unable to bear that honour and rewards should be given to others, it proposes to take the life of those whom it cannot deprive of glory, as did the vile Andrea dal Castagno. His painting and design were indeed excellent, but far greater were the rancour and envy which he bore to the other painters, so that the darkness of his sin has obscured the splendour of his genius. Born in a small township called Il Castagno in the Mugello, in the territory of Florence, Andrea took it as his surname when he came to live in Florence, and this happened in the following manner. Left without a father in his earliest childhood, he was adopted by an uncle, who kept him for many years to look after cattle, for he found him so ready, wide-awake and capable that he was able to manage not only the animals but the pastures and everything that concerned his interests. Such was his occupation when one day he happened to take refuge from the rain in a house where one of those country painters, who work for very little, happened to be painting a tabernacle for a rustic. Andrea, who had never seen the like, was struck with wonder, and attentively looked on, observing

the method of the work, so that he immediately became possessed of the desire to practise the art. Without losing any time
he began on the wall with a piece of coal or the point of his
knife, scratching and drawing animals and figures so well that
he aroused no small wonder in those who saw him. The fame of
this new study of Andrea began to spread about the country,
and, as chance willed, came to the ears of a Florentine nobleman called Bernardetto de' Medici, who had property there,
and who wished to see the child. After seeing him and hearing
him speak with much intelligence, he asked the boy if he would
like to be a painter. Andrea replied that he desired nothing
better. In order that he might be perfected in the art, Bernardetto took the lad to Florence, and put him to work with one
of the masters then most in repute. In this way Andrea studied
the art of painting, and by devoting himself entirely to it he
showed the greatest intelligence in the difficulties of the art,
and especially in design. He did not make equal progress in the
colouring of his works, which, being somewhat crude and hard,
detracted considerably from the excellence and grace of his
pictures, chiefly because it lacks a certain charm. The movements
of his figures were bold and the heads of the men and women
striking, of grave aspect, and correctly drawn. In his early youth
he painted in the cloister of S. Miniato al Monte, as one descends
from the church to the convent, the parting of St. Miniato and
St. Cresci from their parents, in fresco. In St. Benedetto, a fine
monastery outside the Pinti gate, there were many paintings
by Andrea's hand in a cloister and in the church, which it is
not necessary to describe, as they were knocked down during
the siege of Florence. Inside the city, in the monastery of the
monks of the Angeli, in the first cloister opposite the principal
door, he painted the Crucifixion, which is still there, Our Lady,
St. John, St. Benedict and St. Romuald. At the end of the cloister
above the garden he made another like it, with variations in
the heads and a few other details. In S. Trinità, beside the
Chapel of Maestro Luca, he made a St. Andrew. At Legnaia he
painted for Pandolfo Pandolfini a number of illustrious men in
a hall,[1] and a standard for the company of the Evangelist,
considered very fine, to be carried in procession. For the Servites
of that city he decorated three flat niches in some chapels, one
containing events from the life of St. Julian, with a good number
of figures, and a dog foreshortened, which has been much
admired. Above this, in the chapel dedicated to St. Jerome, he

[1] Now in S. Apollonia, Florence.

painted that saint, shrivelled and clean-shaven, with good design and much care. Over this he made a Trinity with a foreshortened crucifix, so well done that Andrea deserves high praise for it, because he made the foreshortening in a much better and far more modern style than his predecessors. But his painting can no longer be seen because a picture has been placed over it by the family of Montaguti. In the third, which is beside the one below the organ, erected by M. Orlando de' Medici, he painted Lazarus, Martha and the Magdalene. For the nuns of S. Giuliano he did a Crucifixion in fresco over the door, a Madonna, St. Dominic, St. Julian and St. John. All artists agree in admiring this painting, which is one of his best. In the chapel of the Cavalcanti at S. Croce he did a St. John the Baptist and St. Francis, considered excellent figures. But the work which excited the greatest admiration of the artists was a Christ at the Column in the new cloister of that convent, at the end opposite the door, where he introduced a loggia with columns in perspective, the crossing of the vaults diminishing and the walls with their oval compartments depicted with such art and so much study that it is clear that he was as completely master of the difficulties of perspective as of design. In the same scene the attitudes of those who are scourging the Christ are free and bold, displaying hatred and fury in their faces, while the Christ is all patience and humility. In the attitude of His body bound to the column with the ropes Andrea seems to have attempted to show the suffering of the flesh, and the divinity hidden in the body preserving a certain splendour of nobility which move Pilate, who is seated among his councillors, to seek some means of setting Him free. In short, this picture is so fine that if it had not been scratched and damaged, owing to the neglect of those in charge, by children and other simple persons, who have scratched all the heads and arms, and almost every other part of the Jews, as if to avenge the sufferings of the Saviour upon them, it would certainly be the most beautiful of Andrea's works. If Nature had only given him a tenderness of colouring comparable to his invention and design, he would truly have been a marvel. In S. Maria del Fiore he painted the effigy of Niccolo da Tolentino on horseback,[1] and because a child in passing shook the ladder while he was at work, he fell into such a rage that, like the brutal man he was, he got down and chased him as far as the corner of the

---

[1] Niccolo died in 1434; a monument was voted in 1435; the fresco was painted in 1456.

Pazzi. In the cemetery of S. Maria Nuova, below the charnel-house, he did a St. Andrew, which gave such satisfaction that he was afterwards employed to paint the Last Supper in the refectory [1] where the servants and other ministers eat. By this work he found favour with the house of the Portinari and with the master, being employed to paint a part of the principal chapel, the remainder being allotted to Alesso Baldovinetti, and to the then very celebrated painter Domenico Viniziano, who had been invited to Florence because of his new method of colouring in oil. Thus each of them attended to his section, but Andrea was most envious of Domenico, because although he knew that he excelled him in design, yet it offended him that a foreigner should be caressed and entertained by the citizens, and so strong was his anger and rage that he began to plot to get rid of Domenico by some means. Now Andrea was not less skilful in dissimulating than in painting, could make his face appear merry at will, was quick of tongue and proud in spirit, and resolute in every action both of the body and of the mind. He was animated by the same spirit towards other artists as well as Domenico, and used to scratch their works secretly with his nails if he found a fault. In his youth, when his works were blamed, he would be even with his critics by blows and insults, to show them that he was always both able and willing to vindicate himself.

But before coming to the work of the chapel I will first speak of Domenico. Previous to his visit to Florence he had painted some things with much grace in the sacristy of S. Maria di Loreto in conjunction with Piero della Francesca. These things, together with his works in other places, such as a chamber in the house of the Baglioni in Perugia, now destroyed, had made him known at Florence by repute. Being invited to Florence, the first thing which he did there was to paint a Madonna in fresco in a tabernacle surrounded by other saints on the side of the Carnesecchi, at the junction of the two ways, one leading to the new and the other to the old piazza of S. Maria Novella. Because this work gave great satisfaction and was much admired by the citizens and artists of the time, the envy and wrath in the vile mind of Andrea only increased against poor Domenico. Accordingly he determined to accomplish by deceit and treason what he could not do openly without manifest danger. He feigned himself to be friendly to Domenico, who, being a good fellow and amiable, who sang and was fond of playing the lute, received him willingly

[1] In 1457.

into his friendship, thinking Andrea a clever and amusing companion. This friendship, real on one side but feigned on the other, went on so that they were together every night, making good cheer and serenading their loves. This gave great pleasure to Domenico, who unfeignedly loved Andrea and taught him the method of colouring in oils, which was not then known in Tuscany. But to take things in order: Andrea did an Annunciation on the front of the chapel of S. Maria Nuova, which was considered very beautiful because he painted the angel in the air, which had not been customary before. But a much finer work is his Virgin ascending the steps of the Temple, representing many poor people, and among others one who hits another on the head with a tankard; not only this figure but all the others being entirely admirable, for he devoted great labour to them out of emulation with Domenico. Here also may be seen in perspective in the middle of a piazza an octagonal temple, standing alone and full of pilasters and niches, beautifully adorned on its façade with marble figures, and a number of fine buildings round the piazza on which the sun is throwing the shadow of the temple, the whole beautifully and artistically contrived. On the other side Maestro Domenico did the meeting of Joachim and Anna his wife, with the Nativity of the Virgin below, representing a very ornate chamber and a boy knocking at the door of the room, with much grace. Below this he made the Marriage of the Virgin, with a good number of portraits comprising M. Bernardetto de' Medici, constable of the Florentines, in a red cap, Bernardo Guadagni the gonfaloniere, Folco Portinari, and other members of that family. He also introduced a dwarf breaking a staff with much animation, and some women in uncommonly delightful and graceful draperies, such as were in use at the time. But this work was left unfinished for reasons which will be related below. Meanwhile Andrea on his wall had painted in oils the Death of Our Lady, on which, owing to his rivalry with Domenico and because he wished to show his capabilities, he bestowed great diligence in foreshortening the bier on which the dead Virgin rests. It seems to be three braccia long, although it is no more than one and a half. About her are the Apostles, their faces displaying joy at seeing their Madonna carried to heaven by Jesus Christ, but at the same time their sorrow at remaining on the earth without her. Among the Apostles are some angels holding burning lights, their heads so finely executed that it is clear that Andrea could employ the medium of oils as successfully as his rival Domenico. In these paintings Andrea drew the portraits of M. Rinaldo degli Albizzi, Puccio Pucci, Il Falgavaccio, who was the instrument of the release of Cosimo de' Medici, together with Federigo Malevolti, who kept the keys of the inn. He also drew there M. Bernardo di Domenico della Volta, master of that place, kneeling, who seems to breathe, and in a medallion at the head of the work he painted himself as Judas Iscariot, whom he resembled in appearance and in deed. Having brought this work to a good stage, but blinded by envy and by the praises which he heard bestowed upon Domenico, Andrea determined to rid himself of his rival, and after thinking upon many ways, he effected his purpose in the following manner. One summer evening, according to his custom, Domenico took his lute and went out of S. Maria Nuova, leaving Andrea drawing in his room, as he would not accept the invitation to go out with him to enjoy themselves, pretending that he had some designs of importance to make. Accordingly, when Domenico had gone out alone to his pleasures, Andrea, unknown to him, laid in wait for him round a corner, and when Domenico reached the spot in returning home Andrea smashed both his lute and his stomach with some lead. But not feeling certain that he had been killed, he also struck him on the head, and, leaving him on the ground, returned to his apartments at S. Maria Nuova, and after fastening the door continued drawing just as Domenico had left him. Meanwhile the alarm was raised and the servants came to tell the bad news to the murderer and traitor himself. Andrea hastened to where they were standing about Domenico, and would not be comforted, repeating, "Alas! my brother." At length Domenico expired in his arms, and in spite of every effort it was never known who had killed him, and it would never have been discovered had not Andrea confessed it on his deathbed.[1] In S. Miniato, between the towers of Florence, Andrea painted a picture containing an Assumption of Our Lady, with two figures, and a Madonna in a tabernacle in the nave at Lanchetta outside the Croce gate.[2] He also painted in the house of the Carducci, now of the Pandolfini, the portraits of some famous men, partly imaginary and partly from life. Among these are Filippo Spano degli Scolari, Dante, Petrarch, Boccaccio, and others.[3] Over the door of the vicar's palace at the Scarperia in Mugello he painted a very fine nude Charity,

---

[1] The difficulty in the way of accepting this story is that Andrea died four years before Domenico. Another painter, Domenico di Matteo, was murdered in Florence in 1448.

[2] In 1449.

[3] The same as those referred to above at page 12, now in S. Apollonia.

which was afterwards ruined. In the year 1478, when Giuliano de' Medici was killed in S. Maria del Fiore by the family of the Pazzi and their adherents and fellow-conspirators, and his brother Lorenzo wounded, the Signoria resolved that all those who had taken part in the conspiracy should be painted upon the wall of the Podesta palace. This work was offered to Andrea, and he accepted it willingly, being the servant of the house of the Medici and under obligations to them.[1] He made the figures so well that the people were amazed, it being impossible to exaggerate the art and judgment displayed in the most natural portraits of these men hung up (*impiccati*) by their feet in extraordinary attitudes, all different and very fine. This thing pleased all the city, and especially those who took an interest in painting, and ever afterwards they called the artist not Andrea dal Castagno, but Andrea degl' Impiccati. Andrea lived sumptuously, but as he spent a great deal, especially in clothing himself and in maintaining his house, he left little property when he died at the age of seventy-one. As his wickedness to his friend Domenico became disclosed after his death, he was buried with ignominious obsequies in S. Maria Nuova, where his victim had been laid at the age of fifty-six, his work begun in S. Maria Nuova remaining incomplete. But he finished shortly before the picture of the high altar of S. Lucia de' Bardi, in which a Madonna with the Child in her arms is executed with great diligence, and so are St. John the Baptist, St. Nicholas, St. Francis and St. Lucy.[2] The pupils of Andrea were Jacopo del Corsi, a meritorious master, Pisanello, Il Marchino, Piero del Pollaiuolo and Giovanni da Rovezzano.

GENTILE DA FABRIANO and VITTORE PISANO of Verona, Painters

(?1370–1450; ?1397–1455)

VERY great are the advantages of the man who at the outset of his career inherits from the dead who have obtained honour and renown, because he need only follow in the footsteps of his master to attain to an honourable station, which would have cost him much toil and labour if obtained by his own unaided effort. This is proved by many instances, among others by

---

[1] This is a mistake; the persons executed were the Albizzi and their followers in 1434.
[2] Now in the Uffizi.

Pisano or Pisanello, painter of Verona, who remained many
years in Florence with Andrea dal Castagno, finished the works
he left at his death, and acquired so much credit by means of
Andrea's name that, when Pope Martin V. came to Florence,[1]
he took Vittore with him to Rome. Here he painted some scenes
in fresco in S. Giovanni Lateran [2] of great charm and beauty,
because he freely introduced a kind of ultramarine blue given
to him by the Pope, so fine and so rich that it has never been
equalled. In competition with Vittore, Gentile da Fabriano
painted some other scenes beneath the first-named, which are
mentioned by Platina in the Life of the Pope. He relates that, having restored the pavement, the ceiling and the roof of S. Giovanni
Lateran, Gentile painted many things, and among other figures
in chiaroscuro between the windows he did some prophets, which
are considered the best part of the whole work. This same Gentile
did a great number of things in the March and especially at
Agobbio, where some may still be seen, and also for all the
state of Urbino. He worked in S. Giovanni at Siena, and for the
sacristy of S. Trinità at Florence he painted the story of the
Magi, introducing his own portrait.[3] In S. Niccolo at the S.
Miniato gate, he did the picture of the high altar for the family
of the Quaratesi, which appears to me to be indubitably the
best of all the works of this artist which I have seen, because,
besides the Madonna and the saints about her, which are all
well made, the predella is full of events from the life of St. Nicholas
in small figures, and could not have been more exquisitely done
by anyone.[4] At S. Maria Novella in Rome he painted Our Lady
with the Child between St. Benedict and St. Joseph in an arch
over the tomb of the Cardinal Adimari, a Florentine and Archbishop of Pisa, which is beside that of Pope Gregory IX. This
work was prized by the divine Michelagnolo, who, in speaking
of Gentile, used to say that his hand in painting corresponded
to his name. In Perugia the same man made a very fine picture
in S. Domenico and a crucifix in S. Agostino di Bari, the cross
being surrounded by three very fine half-size figures, which are
over the choir doorway.

But to return to Vittore Pisano. The things which I said about
him above were written without any addition when this book
was printed for the first time, because I had not then the knowledge and estimate of this excellent artist which I have since

---

[1] He came to Florence on 1 November, 1419.   [2] In 1427.
[3] Painted in 1423; now in the Uffizi, Florence.
[4] Painted 1425; probably identical with a picture now in the Uffizi.

acquired. In the opinion of the Very Rev. and learned Frà Marco
de' Medici of Verona, of the order of the Friars Preachers, as
Il Biondo of Forli also relates when he speaks of Verona in his
Italia Illustrata. Vittore was equal in excellence to any of the
painters of his age, as many of his works which may be seen
in Verona will abundantly testify, in addition to those mentioned above, although they are partially damaged by time.
As he took especial pleasure in making animals, he painted a
St. Eustace in the chapel of the Pellegrini family in S. Anastasia
at Verona, who is caressing a white and tan dog, whose fore-
paws rest on the saint's leg, and he turns his head back as if
he had heard a noise, the action being delightfully natural.[1]
Under this figure Pisano painted his name. He used to call
himself sometimes *Pisano* and sometimes *Pisanello*, as may be
seen in the paintings and medals by his hand. After this St.
Eustace, which is among the best of his works and very fine
indeed, he painted all the outside front of that chapel, representing St. George in white armour made of silver, according to the
custom of all the painters of that age, and not of himself alone.
This St. George, after having killed the dragon, is about to sheath
his sword, and raises his right hand to put in the point while
he lowers the left. The distance between the hands in sheathing
this long sword gives a graceful effect and is in such excellent
style that it could not be improved. Michele Sanmichele, architect of Verona, and well versed in the fine arts, was often seen
contemplating this picture of Vittore with admiration, and would
say that there were few better things to be seen than the St.
Eustace with the dog and this St. George. Over the arch of the
chapel, St. George after the slaying of the dragon is represented
freeing the king's daughter, who is near the saint in a long
garment, such as was worn in those days. Here again the figure
of St. George is admirable. He is armed as before, and stands
with his body and face turned towards the spectator, one foot
in the stirrup and his left hand on his saddle in the action of
jumping on to his horse, which has its tail turned towards the
spectator, and is excellently foreshortened in a small space. To
sum up in one word: the design, grace and judgment displayed
in this work cannot be contemplated without the greatest
admiration. The same Pisano painted, in S. Fermo Maggiore at
Verona (a Franciscan conventual church, in the Brenzoni Chapel
on the left-hand side on entering by the principal door, over the
tomb of the Resurrection, a work in sculpture and a beautiful

[1] Now in the National Gallery, London.

thing for its time) an Annunciation, the two figures, which are touched with gold according to the habit of the time, being very beautiful, as are some very well-drawn buildings and small animals and birds scattered about the work, which are at once as natural and full of life as can be imagined. This same Pisano made a large number of portraits of the prominent men of his day in cast medals, and of others whose portraits have since been painted from them. Monsignor Giovio in a letter in the vernacular written to Duke Cosimo, which has been printed with many others, says these words in speaking of Vittore Pisano: "He was also most excellent in making bas-reliefs, which are considered most difficult by artists, because they are midway between the flat level of painting and the full relief of sculpture. And many much-admired medals of great princes by his hand may be seen, made in the large size of the same dimensions as the reverse which Il Guidi has sent me of the armed horse. Among these I have one of King Alfonso with a shock of hair, the reverse being a captain's helmet; that of Pope Martin, with the Colonna arms on the reverse; one of the Sultan Mahomet who took Constantinople, with himself on horseback in Turkish costume and a scimitar in his hand; Sigismondo Malatesta, the reverse being Madonna Isotta of Rimini; and Niccolo Piccinino with an oblong cap on his head, and the reverse of Il Guidi, which I am returning. Besides these I also have a very fine medal of John Paleologus, Emperor of Constantinople, in that peculiar Greek cap which the emperors used to wear, made by Pisano in Florence at the time of Eugenius's council, and on the reverse is the cross of Christ held up by two hands, namely the Latin and the Greek." So far Giovio. Pisano also made portraits on medals of Filippo de' Medici, Archbishop of Pisa, Braccia da Montone, Giovanni Galeazzo Visconti, Carlo Malatesta, lord of Arimini, Giovanni Caracciolo, seneschal of Naples, Borso and Ercole da Este, and many other lords and men distinguished in arms and in letters. Pisano earned by his fame and reputation in this art the appreciative notices of very great men and rare writers, because besides what Biondo wrote he was much praised in a Latin poem by Guerino the elder, his compatriot, a very distinguished man of letters and writer of the day, of which poem Biondo makes honourable mention, the poem being entitled *Pisano del Guerino*. He was also celebrated by the elder Strozzi, that is to say by Tito Vespasiano, father of the other Strozzi, both accomplished poets in the Latin tongue. The father wrote a very fine epigram in celebration of the memory of

Vittore Pisano, which is printed with the others; such are the fruits of ability. Some say that when Vittore was a young man, studying art in Florence, he painted in the old church of the Temple the story of the pilgrim to the shrine of St. James of Galicia, into whose pocket the daughter of an innkeeper put a silver cup in order that he might be punished as a thief, but whom St. James aided and brought back in safety to his house. In this work Pisano gave promise of what an excellent painter he would become. Finally, at a good old age, he passed to a better life. Gentile also, after having done many things in Città di Castello, became paralytic, so that he could no longer produce good work. At last, being worn out by old age, he died in his eightieth year. I have not been able to find a portrait of Pisano anywhere. Both these painters designed very well, as may be seen in our book.

PESELLO and FRANCESCO PESELLI,[1] Painters of Florence (1367 – 1446; 1422 – 1457)

IT is very rare that the pupils of distinguished masters do not themselves become excellent if they follow their precepts, and even if they do not surpass them they are found to equal them in every respect. This is because an ardent imitation and assiduous study enable them to equal the ability of those who show the true methods of working. Thus the pupils make such progress that they afterwards compete with their masters and easily surpass them, because it is always less difficult to add to what has been found by others. As an illustration of this, Francesco di Pesello imitated the style of Frà Filippo, so that if death had not unhappily removed him he would have far surpassed his model. It is further known that Pesello imitated the style of Andrea dal Castagno, and took such pleasure in drawing animals, keeping live specimens of every species in his house, that no one in that age could rival him in that branch. He was under Andrea until the age of thirty, learning from him, and he became an excellent master. Thus, as he had given proofs of his abilities, the Signoria of Florence employed him to paint a picture in tempera of the Magi offering gifts to Christ, which was placed half-way up on the staircase of their palace.[2] By this work Pesello acquired great fame, especially as he had introduced

---

[1] Giuliano Pesello; Francesco was his grandson. Vasari confounds the names, works and relationship of these artists.
[2] This picture seems to be identical with one now in the Uffizi

some portraits into it, and among others that of Donato Acciaiuoli. At the Chapel of the Cavalcanti in S. Croce, beneath
the Annunciation of Donato, he made a predella with small
figures containing events from the life of St. Nicholas.[1] In the
Medici palace he made a very fine espalier of animals and some
coffers with small scenes of jousting on horseback. To this day
there are some canvases by his hand in the same palace representing lions looking through bars, which are most realistic. He did
others at liberty, one fighting with a serpent. On another canvas
he painted an ox and a wolf with other animals, with great
animation and movement. In S. Pier Maggiore, in the Chapel of
the Alessandri, he did four scenes in small figures of St. Peter,
St. Paul, St. Zanobius raising the widow's son, and St. Benedict.
In S. Maria Maggiore, also in Florence, he did a Madonna in the
Chapel of the Orlandini, and two other beautiful figures. For the
children of the company of St. George he made a Crucifixion,
St. Jerome and St. Francis. In the church of S. Giorgio he did an
Annunciation on a panel.[2] In the church of S. Jacopo at Pistoia
he made a Trinity, St. Zeno and St. James,[3] and there are many
of his pictures both round and square in private houses at
Florence. Pesello was an affable and gentle man, and always
helped his friends as much as he could, both graciously and
readily. He married a young girl who bore him a son, Francesco,
called Pesellino, who was a painter, and closely imitated the
methods of Frà Filippo. If he had lived longer he would, so far
as one can judge, have made great progress, because he studied
his art, designing night and day without rest. A marvellous
predella of small figures, which looks like a work of Frà Filippo,
now in the chapel of the noviciate of S. Croce, is his.[4] He made
a number of small pictures with figures for Florence, and thus
acquired his name. He died at the age of thirty-one, to the great
grief of his father, Pesello, who followed him not long after at
the age of seventy-seven.

[1] This predella is perhaps that in the Casa Buonarotti, but the ascription
has been thought doubtful. Berenson considered it a work of Pesellino.
[2] Now in the Uffizi.
[3] Now in the National Gallery; painted by Pesellino in 1457.
[4] Painted about 1440; the predella is now in the Uffizi, Florence, and
the Louvre.

Benozzo, Painter of Florence
(1420-1498)

He who travels toilsomely by the road of virtue will indeed find it stony and full of thorns, as is reported, but at the end of his climb he will emerge in a broad plain, replete with every desired happiness. And as he looks back and sees the difficult passes which he has perilously traversed, he will thank God, who has brought him safely through, and will gratefully bless the labours which have won him such advantages. Thus the joy of present well-being obliterates past vexations, and for the future he will have no further care than to endeavour to show others how the cold, the frost, the sweat, hunger, thirst and other inconveniences which are endured to acquire skill, liberate men from indigence, and bring them to that assured and tranquil condition enjoyed by Benozzo Gozzoli. He was a pupil of Frà Giovanni Angelico, deservedly loved by his master, and considered by those who knew him to be a man of fertile invention and prolific in animals, perspective, landscapes and ornaments. He worked exceedingly hard, taking but little pleasure in other diversions, and although he was not of great excellence as compared with many who surpassed him in design, yet he distanced all the others of his age by his perseverance, because among the multitude of works produced by him some are necessarily good. In his youth he painted in Florence the altar-picture for the company of St. Mark,[1] and a Death of St. Jerome in S. Friano, which has been destroyed in repairing the side of the church along the street. In the chapel of the palace of the Medici he painted in fresco the story of the Magi, and in the Chapel of the Cesarini at Araceli at Rome he did scenes from the life of St. Anthony of Padua, introducing portraits of the cardinal, Giuliano Cesarini and Antonio Colonna.[2] Again, over a door in the tower of the Conti, he did a Madonna in fresco, with many saints. In S. Maria Maggiore, in a chapel on the right-hand of the principal doorway on entering, he did many meritorious figures in fresco. Returning to Florence from Rome, Benozzo went to Pisa, where, in the cemetery beside the Duomo, called the Campo Santo, he did the whole of one side, painting scenes from the Old Testament, and displaying the greatest invention.[3] This may indeed be called a stupendous work, seeing that he represents all the events in

---

[1] Painted in 1461; now in the National Gallery.
[2] In 1459.   [3] Begun in 1468.

the Creation of the world day by day. After this he did Noah's
ark and the Flood, with fine composition, and a quantity of
figures. Then follow the proud building of the tower of Nimrod,
the burning of Sodom and the neighbouring cities, the history
of Abraham, many things being finely expressed. For although
Benozzo was not very remarkable in drawing figures, yet he
displayed his art effectively in the sacrifice of Isaac, representing an ass foreshortened in such a manner that it faces every
point of view, and is greatly admired. Then come the birth of
Moses, with all his signs and wonders, until he led his people
out of Egypt, and fed them so many years in the wilderness. To
these Benozzo added the history of the Jews to the time of David
and Solomon. His courage was marvellous, for a work of such
magnitude might well have dismayed a whole legion of painters,
yet he completed it single-handed, thus acquiring the highest
praise and earning the following epigram, which was placed in
the midst of his work:

> Quid spectas volucres, pisces, et monstra ferarum,
> Et virides silvas aethereasque domos ?
> Et pueros, juvenes, matres, canosque parentes,
> Queis semper vivum spirat in ore decus ?
> Non haec tam variis, pinxit simulacra figuris
> Natura ingenio factibus apta suo :
> Est opus artificis, pinxit viva ora Benoxus :
> O superi vivos fundite in ora sonos.

Scattered about the work are a multitude of portraits, but as I
do not know them all, I will only mention such as are important,
and with which I am acquainted through some record. The scene
of the Queen of Sheba visiting Solomon contains portraits of
Marsilio Ficino among various prelates, Argiropolo, a most
learned Greek, Battista Platina, whose portrait was first drawn
at Rome, and the artist himself on horseback, represented as an
old man clean-shaven, a black cap on his head, in which a piece
of paper is stuck, perhaps as a sign, or possibly because he
intended to write his name on it. In the same city of Pisa, Benozzo painted the whole of the life of St. Benedict for the nuns of S.
Benedetto on the Arno, and in the company of the Florentines,
where the monastery of S. Vito now stands, he did the altar-
picture and many other paintings. Behind the archbishop's
throne in the Duomo he painted a small panel in tempera of St.
Thomas Aquinas, with a countless number of learned men
disputing over his works.[1] Among these is a portrait of Sixtus
IV., with several cardinals and the heads and generals of various

---

[1] Now in the Louvre.

orders. This is the best and most complete work that Benozzo
ever produced. In S. Caterina of the Friars Preachers, in the
same city, he did two panels in tempera, which may easily be
recognised by the style, and in the church of S. Niccola he did
another, and two in S. Croce, outside Pisa. When he was a young
man he also did the altar of St. Sebastian in the Pieve of S.
Gimignamo, in the middle of the church over against the principal chapel.[1] In the Sala del Consiglio there are figures, some by
his hand, and some old ones restored by him. For the monks of
Monte Oliveto, in the same country, he did a crucifix and other
paintings, but his best work in that place was in the principal
chapel of St. Agostino, being events in the life of St. Augustine
from his conversion to his death, painted in fresco.[2] I have
all his drawings for this work in my book, as well as many
sketches for the scenes in the Campo Santo at Pisa. At Volterra
again he did some works, which it is not necessary to mention.

While Benozzo was working at Rome there was another artist
there, called Melozzo,[3] who came from Forli, so that many, who
are not better informed, on finding the name Melozzo, and
observing the time, have concluded that Benozzo was meant.
But they are wrong, because Melozzo flourished at the same
time, and was a zealous student of art, especially of foreshortening, as may be seen in S. Apostolo at Rome in the tribune of the
high altar,[4] where a frieze for the ornamentation of that work,
drawn in perspective, contains some figures gathering grapes,
and a cask, possessing considerable merit. But this is more clearly
shown in a choir of angels in an Ascension of Christ leading him
to heaven, the figure of Christ being so well foreshortened that
it seems to be passing through the vault, as do the angels, who
are flying about in the airy space with varied movements.
The Apostles also, on the earth, are so well foreshortened in their
different attitudes that Melozzo was much praised then, and has
been since, by artists who have greatly profited by his labours. He
was very skilful in perspective as the buildings shown here prove.
The work was done for the Cardinal Riario, nephew of Pope
Sixtus IV., by whom he was liberally rewarded. But to return
to Benozzo. Being at length worn out by years and toil, he went
to his true rest, at the age of seventy-eight, in the city of Pisa,
where he lived in a little house in Carraia di S. Francesco, which
he had bought during his long stay there. This house he left to
his daughter when dying, and amid the universal mourning of

---

[1] In 1465.   [2] Done in 1465.   [3] 1438–94.
[4] Portions are in the inner sacristy of St Peter's, Rome.

the city he was honourably buried in the Campo Santo, with this epitaph, which may still be read:

Hic tumulus est Benotii Florentini, qui proxime has pinxit historias ; hunc sibi Pisanor. donavit humanitas MCCCCLXXVIII.

Benozzo always lived most temperately and like a good Christian, spending his whole life in worthy employments, thus winning the esteem of the Pisans for his virtues as well as by his abilities. He left behind him as pupils Zanobi Machiavelli of Florence, and others, whom it is not necessary to mention.

FRANCESCO DI GIORGIO, Sculptor and Architect, and LORENZO VECCHIETTO, Sculptor and Painter, both of Siena.

(1439–1502; ?1412–1480)

FRANCESCO DI GIORGIO of Siena, who was an excellent sculptor and architect, made the two bronze angels upon the high altar of the Duomo of that city.[1] They are a truly fine cast, and were afterwards polished by him with the utmost possible diligence. He was enabled to do this, being no less endowed with rich property than with rare genius, so that he worked to please himself and not for gain, hoping to leave an honoured name. He also practised painting and did some things, but not equal to his sculptures. In architecture his judgment was excellent, showing a thorough grasp of the profession. This is amply displayed in the palace which he built at Urbino for the Duke Federigo Feltro,[2] the distributions being made in a beautiful and convenient manner, while the staircases are remarkable and more pleasing than any erected before that time. The halls are large and magnificent, and the apartments useful and exceptionally noble. To sum up in a word, the entire palace is as fine and well built as any other that has been erected up to the present. Francesco was a noted engineer, especially of engines of war, as is shown by a frieze painted by him in the palace of Urbino, full of rare things pertaining to war. He designed some books full of such implements, the best of which are among the choicest possessions of Duke Cosimo de' Medici.[3] He was so curious in endeavouring to understand the warlike machines of the ancients, and devoted so much time to investigating the method

[1] 1497-9.
[2] The architect was Luciano di Laurana; the palace was begun in 1447.
[3] His *Trattato d'architettura civile e militare* was published in 1841.

of ancient amphitheatres and similar things that he neglected his sculpture, though these studies did not bring him less honour than sculpture would have done. All these things rendered him very agreeable to Duke Federigo, whose portrait he made both in a medal and in a picture, so that when he returned to his native Siena he was no less honoured than enriched. For Pope Pius II. he made all the designs and models of the palace and Vescovado of Pienza, the Pope's native place, originally called Corsignano.[1] These were of the utmost possible magnificence and nobility for that place. He also devised the form and fortification of the city, as well as the palace and loggia for the same Pope. Thus he always lived in honour and was rewarded with the supreme magistracy of the Signori in his city.[2] But having attained the age of forty-seven years, he died. His works were executed about 1480. He left behind him his dear friend and companion Jacopo Cozzerello,[3] who practised sculpture and architecture and made some wooden figures at Siena. In architecture he did S. Maria Maddalena outside the Tufi gate, left unfinished through his death. But we owe him this much, that he left a portrait by his own hand of Francesco. This Francesco deserves our regard because he smoothed the difficulties of architecture and did more for that art than anyone from the days of Filippo di ser Brunellescho to his own time.

Another Sienese and highly esteemed painter was Lorenzo di Piero Vecchietto,[4] who, after being a much-valued goldsmith, finally turned his attention to sculpture and to casting in bronze. To these arts he devoted so much study that he became highly proficient, and was employed to make the bronze receptacle for the Host of the high altar of the Duomo in his native Siena, decorating it with the marble ornamentation which may still be seen.[5] This truly marvellous cast brought him fame and renown for the proportion and grace which reign in every part. All who study the work will perceive the excellence of its design and the judgment and talent of the artist. For the chapel of the Sienese painters in the great hospital of the Scala he made a fine metal cast of a nude Christ carrying the cross in his hands, of life-size. This work was cast finely and polished with equal care and diligence.[6] The Pilgrimage in this same house contains a scene painted in colours by Lorenzo, and over the door of S. Giovanni the tympanum is painted in fresco with figures.[7] As the bap-

---

[1] Bernardo Rossellino was the architect.
[2] He was one of the Priors in 1485 and again in 1493.
[3] 1453-1515. [4] Lorenzo di Lando.
[5] 1465-72. [6] In 1441. [7] In 1450.

tistery was not finished, he made some small bronze figures for
it, and completed a bronze bas-relief begun by Donatello. In
this place Jacopo della Fonte had also done two bronze bas-
reliefs, and Lorenzo always imitated his style as closely as
possible. The same Lorenzo brought this baptistery to its final
completion, introducing further some bronze figures cast by
Donato, but finished by himself, and considered very beautiful.
For the Loggia degli Ufficiali in Banchi Lorenzo made a St. Peter
and a St. Paul in marble of life-size,[1] enriched with the utmost
grace and carried out with finished skill. His treatment of the
things which he did deserves high praise as he made the dead
alive. He was a melancholy and solitary man, continually
brooding, and this may perhaps be the reason why he did not
live longer, for he died at the age of fifty-eight. His works were
executed about the year 1482.

Galasso Galassi, Painter of Ferrara
(1423–1473)

The presence of foreign artists at work in some town that possesses none of its own, always acts as a stimulant upon someone
there to learn the art and exert himself so that his native place
may no longer be dependent upon outsiders and tributary to
them, and that he may win for himself those gains which seemed
to him too much to go abroad. This was clearly the case with
Galasso. The sight of the rewards received by Pietro dal Borgo
a San Sepolcro from the duke for his works at Ferrara, and his
honourable reception there, moved him so strongly to devote
himself to painting, that he won the reputation of a good and
accomplished master in that city. This rendered him the more
acceptable to that place because he learned colouring in oils on
a visit to Venice and introduced it to Ferrara.[2] Thus he made
a countless number of figures in this medium for various churches
in Ferrara. Being invited subsequently to Bologna by some
Dominican friars, he painted in oils a chapel in S. Domenico,
which served to increase his name and reputation. Accordingly
he worked afterwards at S. Maria del Monte, a place of the black
monks outside Bologna,[3] and did many pictures in fresco outside
the S. Mammolo gate. In addition he painted in fresco the whole

[1] In 1458 and 1460.
[2] It was introduced at Ferrara by Rogier van der Weyden, who taught
Galasso and others.
[3] In 1455.

of the Casa di Mezzo church on the same road,[1] with scenes from the Old Testament. He was a man of even temper, always courteous and amiable, from being accustomed to live more abroad than at his native place. It is true that he did not enjoy a long life, being rather irregular in his habits. He passed to the other life at the age of fifty or thereabouts. A friend celebrated his memory in this epitaph:

Galassus Ferrarien.
Sum tanto studio naturae imitatus et arte
Dum pingo rerum quae creat illa parens;
Haec ut saepe quidem non picta putaverit a me,
A se crederit sed generata magis.

At this same time Cosme [2] also lived at Ferrara, of whom we may see a chapel in S. Domenico of that city and two organ doors in the Duomo. He was better at drawing than at painting, and, so far as I can gather, he cannot have painted much.

ANTONIO ROSSELLINO, Sculptor of Florence, and BERNARDO his brother
(1427–1479; 1409–1461)

MODESTY is indeed praiseworthy and virtuous at times, and so are the amiability and the rare talents which adorned the life of Antonio Rossellino the sculptor. He practised his art with such grace that he was valued as something more than a man by those who knew him, who well-nigh adored him as a saint for those pre-eminent qualities which he possessed in addition to his talents. Antonio was called il Rossellino del Proconsolo because his workshop was in a place of that name in Florence. His works were so soft and delicate, the finesse and polish so perfect, that his style may justly be called true and really modern. For the palace of the Medici he made the marble fountain which is in the second court, containing children who hold dolphins spouting water, finished with the utmost skill and diligence.[3] In the church of S. Croce by the holy-water vessel he made the tomb of Francesco Neri with a Madonna in bas-relief above, and another Madonna in the house of the Tornabuoni, as well as many other things sent to divers parts, such, for example, as a marble tomb for Lyons in France. At S. Miniato al Monte, a monastery of the white monks outside the walls of Florence, he was employed to

[1] S. Maria di Mezzaratta. [2] Cosimo Tura,1420–95.
[3] Probably the one now at Castello.

make the tomb of the Cardinal of Portugal,[1] which was executed
so marvellously and with such diligence and art that no artist
can ever expect to see anything to surpass it for finish and grace.
To anyone looking at it, it seems not difficult but impossible
that it should have been made so. It contains angels which
in their grace and beauty, with their draperies and attitudes,
seem not marble creations but living beings. One of them holds
the cardinal's crown of virginity, as he is said to have died chaste;
another raises the palm of victory which he won against the
world. Among the many charming things there is a macigno arch
supporting a marble curtain hooked up, so that with the white
of the marble and the grey of the stone it is much more like real
cloth than marble. On the sarcophagus are some really lovely
children, and the deceased prelate himself with a Madonna, in a
circle very finely worked. The sarcophagus resembles the porphyry one on the Piazza della Rotonda at Rome. This tomb was
set up in 1459,[2] and so pleased the Duke of Malfi, nephew of
Pope Pius II., who was equally delighted with the architecture
of the chapel, that he caused another to be made for his wife at
Naples, similar in every respect except the effigy of the deceased.
Antonio further made a bas-relief of the Nativity of Christ in
the Manger, with angels dancing on the thatch, singing with
open mouth,[3] so that with the sole exception of breath Antonio
endowed them with every movement and gesture, and with
such grace and finish that steel and genius could produce no
more out of marble. For this reason his works have been highly
praised by Michelagnolo and by every other artist of distinction.
For the Pieve of Empoli he made a marble St. Sebastian which
is much admired,[4] his design for it being in our book, together
with those for the architecture and figures of the chapel of St.
Miniato in Monte, already mentioned, as well as his own portrait.
Antonio died in Florence at the age of forty-six, leaving his
brother Bernardo, an architect and sculptor. Bernardo made in
S. Croce the marble tomb of M. Leonardo Bruni of Arezzo,[5] who
wrote the history of Florence, and was a very learned man, as
everyone knows. This Bernardo was highly valued as an architect
by Pope Nicholas V., who thought much of him, and employed
him on many of the works carried out during his pontificate.
He would have done more had not death interrupted the works
which the Pope had in his mind. Thus, if we may believe Giannozzo Manetti, he restored the piazza of Fabriano, where he

remained for some months on account of the plague, enlarging it and improving its shape where it was narrow and ill-made, and surrounding it with rows of shops at once useful, commodious and beautiful. He then restored the church of S. Francesco in the same place, which was falling to ruin. At Gualdo he may be said to have rebuilt, with the addition of some fine structures, the church of S. Benedetto. In Assisi he strengthened the foundations and repaired the roof of the church of S. Francesco, which was in ruins in some places and threatened to fall. At Cività-vecchia he made many fine and magnificent buildings. At Cività-castellana he restored more than a third of the wall in a fine style. At Narni he restored and enlarged the fortress with strong walls. At Orvieto he made a large fortress with a magnificent palace, a work as costly as it was splendid. At Spoleto he enlarged and strengthend the fortress, making the dwellings inside so fine, so convenient and so well arranged that nothing better could be desired. He restored the baths of Viterbo at a great expense and in regal style, making apartments suitable not only for the sick, who daily go there to bathe, but worthy of the greatest princes. All these works were carried out by the Pope outside the city from Bernardo's designs. In Rome he restored and in many places rebuilt the city walls, which were for the most part in decay, adding some towers and including in them a new fortress which he made outside the Castle S. Angelo, with many apartments and ornaments within. The Pope further conceived and in great part executed a project for restoring and rebuilding, so far as was necessary, the forty churches of the stations established by St. Gregory I. called the Great. He also restored S. Maria Trastevere, S. Prassedia, S. Teodoro, S. Pietro ad Vincola, and many others of less importance. In six of the largest and most important he carried this out with greater spirit, ornament and diligence, namely in S. Giovanni Lateran, S. Maria Maggiore, S. Stefano on the Celian Mount, S. Apostolo, S. Paolo and S. Lorenzo *extra muros*. I do not include S. Pietro because that was a separate undertaking. It was this Pope again who thought of converting the Vatican into a fortress, making it like a separate city, and designing three ways leading to S. Pietro, I fancy where the old and new Borgo now are. These he covered with loggias here and there, and convenient shops separating the nobler and richer arts from the lesser, and putting each in a street by itself. He had previously made the round tower, still known as the tower of Nicholas. Over these shops and loggias were magnificent and convenient dwellings in beautiful architecture, so contrived as to be sheltered from all the pestiferous winds of Rome, all the impediments of water or refuse which engender bad air being removed. Nicholas would have finished it all if only he had lived a little longer. This pontiff was bold and resolute and so well informed that he guided and controlled the artists no less than they did him, an arrangement which brings about the speedy completion of great undertakings, the patron being skilled in the subject and capable of making up his mind quickly, whereas an irresolute and ignorant man would lose much time in wavering between yes and no, and between various designs and opinions, the work standing still meanwhile. Of this design of Nicholas it is unnecessary to say more than that it was not carried out. He also wished to build the papal palace with such magnificence and grandeur, united to convenience and beauty, that it would have been the finest building in Christendom. He desired that it should serve not only the pontiff and head of Christendom, with the sacred college of cardinals, which advised and assisted him and which he wished to be always about him, but also that all affairs, expeditions, and judgments of the court should take place there; and this gathering together of all the offices and courts would have made a magnificent and grand edifice with incredible pomp, if the word is permissible in this connection, and what is of infinitely more importance, it was to receive emperors, kings, dukes and other Christian princes who visited the Most Holy Apostolic See either to make their devotions or on their affairs. It seems incredible that he even intended to erect a theatre for the coronation of the Pope, and gardens, loggias, aqueducts, fountains, chapels, libraries, and a separate conclave hall, of great splendour. In short this (I know not whether to call it palace, castle or city) would have been the most superb creation since the beginning of the world so far as we know. What greatness would have belonged to the Holy Roman Church had its chief pontiff and head gathered together all the ministers of God inhabiting Rome into a kind of famous and sacred monastery, there to live as in a new earthly paradise, a celestial, angelical and holy life, affording an example to all Christendom and kindling the minds of unbelievers to the true worship of God and of Jesus Christ! But this great work was left unfinished as it was barely begun at the time of the Pope's death. The little that was done may be recognised by the Pope's arms, or what he used as arms, namely two keys in saltire on a red field. The last of the five things which he intended to do was the church of S. Pietro, which he wished to make so large, so rich and so ornate that I shall do better to keep silence than to attempt to depict that which is utterly indescribable, especially as the model was afterwards destroyed and others were made by other architects. If anyone desires to know fully the great mind of Pope Nicholas V., let him read what Giannozzo Manetti, a noble and learned citizen of Florence, has written in detail upon the life of that pontiff. In all these designs Nicholas employed the abilities and industry of Bernardo Rossellino, as well as others, as I have said. Antonio, the brother, to return to the point where I started, produced his sculptures about the year 1490. The extraordinary diligence and mastery of difficulty displayed in his work have excited general wonder, so that he merits fame and honour as being the best example from whom the moderns have been able to learn how statues should be made, to win praise and fame overcoming difficulties. After Donatello he added a certain polish and completeness to the art of sculpture, seeking to turn his figures so that they should appear entirely round and finished, a matter which had not been previously perfected. As he was the first to introduce this style, it appeared marvellous in the following age, and does so even in our own day.

DESIDERIO DA SETTIGNANO, Sculptor
(1428–1464)

THOSE men who create without fatigue, with a certain grace, what others cannot produce by toil and imitation, owe a great debt to Nature. But this is a truly heavenly gift which bestows upon their works such a light and graceful appearance that they attract not only those who understand the profession, but also many others. This arises from the facility with which they are produced, being free from the hardness and crudity so frequent in things produced with effort and difficulty. This grace and simplicity, which give universal pleasure and are felt by every-one, are characteristic of the work of Desiderio. Some say that he came from Settignano, a place two miles from Florence, others consider him a Florentine, but this is of little importance where the distance is so slight. He imitated the style of Donato, being naturally endowed with gracefulness and lightness in the treatment of heads. His women and children possess a soft, delicate and charming manner, due as much to Nature as to art. In his youth he made the pedestal of Donato's David, which is in the duke's palace at Florence, introducing some fine harpies and vine-tendrils all in bronze, very graceful and well contrived. On the façade of the house of the Gianfigliazzi [1] he made a large escutcheon with a magnificent lion, as well as other things in stone in that city. In the Brancacci Chapel in the Carmine he made an angel of wood, and in S. Lorenzo he finished the marble chapel of the Sacrament, completing it with great diligence. It contained a marble child in relief, which was taken away, and is placed to-day on the altar at Christmas-time as being a marvellous thing. To replace it Baccio da Montelupo made another, also of marble, which stands upon the tabernacle of the Sacrament. In S. Maria Novella he made the marble tomb of the Blessed Villana,[2] with some graceful little angels, drawing the saint from life, so that she does not seem dead but asleep. For the convent of the nuns of the Murate he made a small Madonna upon a column in a tabernacle, in a light and graceful style, for both of which works he is greatly valued and esteemed. In S. Piero Maggiore he made the tabernacle of the Sacrament in marble, with his usual finish, and although it contains no figures, it displays the grace and style distinctive of his work. He made a marble bust of Marietta degli Strozzi,[3] from life, and, as she was very beautiful, it proved most successful. He made the tomb of M. Carlo Marsuppini of Arezzo,[4] in S. Croce, which not only amazed the artists and clever men of his day, but those who see it now also marvel, for on the sarcophagus he has intro-duced foliage which, although somewhat hard and dry, as not many antiquities had been discovered then, was considered very beautiful at the time. Among other portions of the work there are some wings attached to a scallop-shell at the foot of the sarcophagus which seem to be really feathers and not marble, a great achievement, seeing that the chisel cannot easily repro-duce hair and feathers. The large marble scallop-shell there is marvellously realistic. There are also some children and angels executed in a lively and beautiful style, while the effigy of the dead man, taken from life, is of the highest excellence and art. A medallion of a Madonna done in bas-relief, in the manner of Donato, possesess wonderful judgment and grace, as do many other of his marble bas-reliefs,some being in the wardrobe of Duke Cosimo, notably the heads of Our Lord Jesus Christ and John the Baptist as a child, in a medallion. At the foot of the tomb

[1] On the lung Arno, between the Trinità and Carraia bridges.
[2] The tomb is by Bernardo Rosselino.
[3] Now in the Berlin Museum.
[4] Who died 1455.

of M. Carlo he made a large slab for M. Giorgio, a famous doctor and secretary of the Signoria of Florence, with a very fine bas-relief containing the portrait of M. Giorgio, in the doctor's robes of the time. If death had not so soon removed this spirit who worked with such excellence, he might with experience and study have surpassed in art all those whom he excelled in grace. But death cut the thread of his life at the age of twenty-eight, causing great sorrow to all who expected to see the perfection of his mind in his old age, who were dazed by such a loss. He was carried to the church by his relations and numerous friends, while for a long time epigrams and sonnets were affixed to his tomb. Out of a large number I content myself by selecting the following only:

Come vide natura
Dar Desiderio ai freddi marmi vita
E poter la scultura
Agguagliar sua bellezza alma e infinita
Si fermo sbigottita
E disse : omai sara mia gloria oscura
E piena d'alto sdegno
Tronco la vita a cosi bell'ingegno.
Ma in van, che se costui
Die vita eterna ai marmi e i marmi a lui.

Desiderio's sculptures were executed in 1485. He left a sketch of St. Mary Magdalene in penitence, afterwards finished by Benedetto da Maiano, and now in S. Trinità at Florence, on the right-hand as one enters the church. It is a marvellously fine figure. In our book there are some fine designs by Desiderio's hand, and his portrait, which I had from some of his relations at Settignano.

MINO DA FIESOLE, Sculptor
(1431–1484)

WHEN artists have no other aim in their works but to imitate the style of their master or some other excellent man, whose methods of work, posture of figures, carriage of the heads or folds of the draperies please them, and if they seek no more than this, then, although they may produce similar works by dint of time and study, yet they will never attain to the perfection of art by this means alone, and it is naturally a most rare thing for one who is always following to get in front, because the imitation of Nature is arrested in the style of the artist with whom long practice has developed a set manner. Imitation is the art of reproducing things exactly, taking the most beautiful things Nature affords in their purity, without adopting the master's style or that of others, who infuse their personality into the things which they take from Nature. For although the works of excellent artists appear natural and real, yet no one can display such diligence as to make his things like Nature itself, nor even by selecting the best can a composition be made so perfect that art will surpass Nature. It therefore follows that the things taken from Nature constitute perfect paintings and sculptures, and whoever closely studies the methods and habits of artists alone, and not natural bodies and objects, produces works inferior to those of Nature and also of the artists from whom he borrows his style. Thus it may be observed that many of our artists have studied nothing but the works of their masters, neglecting Nature, from which they have learned nothing whatever, while they have not surpassed their masters, but have done the greatest injury to their talents. If they had studied both his style and Nature as well they would have produced better works. We see this in Mino da Fiesole the sculptor, whose genius was equal to any task, but being dazzled by the style of Desiderio da Settignano, his master, by the beauty and grace of the heads of his women, children and all other figures, which seemed to him to be better than Nature, he followed Desiderio, abandoning natural things as useless, so that his art was rather graceful than well grounded.

On the hill of Fiesole, a very ancient city near Florence, was born Mino di Giovanni the sculptor. Placed as stone-cutter with the young and clever sculptor, Desiderio da Settignano, and feeling drawn to that profession, he learned while thus engaged to make clay imitations of the marble works of Desiderio, so like them that when the master happened to see them he took the boy and set him to work on marble in his own shop. By keen observation Mino endeavoured to profit by his position, and before long he became quite skilful and gave great satisfaction to Desiderio. Mino was even more delighted at his kindness, being persistently taught to avoid the errors which may be made in that art. Whilst he was on the road to excellence he had the misfortune to lose Desiderio. This was a great blow to him, and in despair he left Florence and went to Rome, where he assisted the masters engaged upon works in marble and the tombs of the cardinals about S. Pietro, at Rome, now demolished for the new building. He thus became known as a skilful master, and as his style pleased the Cardinal d'Estouteville, he was employed by that dignitary to make the marble altar in the church of S. Maria Maggiore, where the body of St. Jerome is, with scenes from the saint's life in bas-relief. These he completed and introduced the cardinal's portrait. Afterwards, when the Venetian Pope Paul II. built his palace to S. Marco,[1] Mino was employed to make some arms there. After the Pope's death his tomb was given to Mino, who finished it in two years, building it in S. Pietro. It was considered at the time to be the richest tomb in ornamentation and figures ever erected to any pope. Bramante pulled it down when S. Pietro was destroyed, and it remained buried for several years among the rubbish until 1547, when it was again set up by some Venetians in S. Pietro, in the old part near the Chapel of Pope Innocent. Although some think that this tomb is by the hand of Mino del Reame, who flourished about the same time, it is undoubtedly the work of Mino da Fiesole. It is indeed true that Mino del Reame [2] made some small figures for the pedestal which may be recognised, if indeed his name was Mino and not Dino as some affirm.

But to return to our subject. Having acquired a reputation in Rome by this tomb and by a sarcophagus which he made in the Minerva with the marble effigy of Francesco Tornabuoni upon it from life, which is a good deal admired, and by other works, Mino returned to Fiesole with his gains, which were considerable, and took a wife. Not long after he made a marble tabernacle in half-relief for the nuns of the Murate to receive the Sacrament.[3] It was executed with all the diligence of which he was capable. He had not finished this when the nuns of S. Ambruogio, hearing of his powers, and desiring a similar ornament but more richly decorated for themselves, to hold the miracle of the most holy Sacrament, employed him on that work, which he finished with such diligence that the nuns paid him all that he asked. Shortly afterwards he undertook to make a small half-relief, with the figures of the Madonna and Child between St. Laurence and St. Leonard,[4] to serve for the priests or chapter of S. Lorenzo, at the instance of M. Dietisalvi Neroni, but it has remained in the sacristy of the Badia at Florence. For those monks he made a marble medallion, containing Our Lady and the Child in relief, which is placed over the principal entrance to the church. As this afforded great satisfaction to all, Mino was commissioned to make a tomb for the magnificent M.

---

[1] The Palazzo di Venetia was begun in 1455.
[2] See the Life of Paolo Romano above.
[3] Begun in 1481.   [4] Rather before 1470.

Bernardo de' Giugni, knight,[1] who, being a man greatly honoured
and esteemed, merited this memorial from his brethren. Besides
the sarcophagus and the fine effigy of the dead man upon it,
Mino introduced a Justice, closely following the style of Desiderio, except that the draperies are rather cut up by the
carving. This work induced the abbot and monks of the Badia
at Florence, where the tomb was set up, to employ Mino to
make the tomb of the Count Hugh, son of the Marquis Hubert
of Magdebourg, who left a good deal of property and many
privileges to that Badia.[2] Thus, as they desired to give him the
highest possible honour, they employed Mino to make a tomb
of Carrara marble. This was the finest work which he ever
produced, containing as it does some boys supporting the count's
arms, standing with spirit and childish grace. In addition to
these he made the effigy of the dead count upon the sarcophagus,
and above this a Charity with children in half-relief executed
with great diligence and finely grouped. The same remark applies
to a Madonna with the Child in a half-circle made by Mino, as
nearly like the style of Desiderio as he could. Had he but aided
himself by the study of Nature, he would doubtless have made
very great progress in art. This tomb cost altogether 1600 lire,
and was finished in 1481. Mino acquired great fame by it, and
was employed to make another tomb in a chapel in the Vescovado at Fiesole on the right-hand side near the principal one.
This was for Leonardo Salutati, bishop there. Here he introduced
the prelate's effigy in his pontificals, a wonderful likeness. For
the same bishop he made a head of Christ in marble of life-size
and finely executed. Together with many other things of his it
was left to the hospital of the Innocents, and is now in the hands
of the Very Rev. Don Vincenzio Borghini, prior of the hospital,
among his choicest possessions, for he is inexpressibly fond of
the arts. In the Pieve of Prato Mino made a pulpit entirely of
marble,[3] containing stories of Our Lady, executed with great
diligence, and so well joined that it seems to consist of a single
block. This pulpit is at the side of the choir, almost in the midst
of the church, above some ornaments of Mino's own handiwork.
He made very natural and life-like portraits of Piero di Lorenzo
de' Medici and his wife.[4] These two heads stood for many years
in lunettes over two doors in Piero's room in the Medici palace.
Together with a number of other portraits of illustrious men of

[1] Who died 1466; this tomb was commissioned in 1468.
[2] Allotted in 1469, finished 1481.
[3] Completed 1473.
[4] Now in the Bargello, Florence.

the house, they were afterwards removed to the wardrobe of
Duke Cosimo. Mino also made a Madonna of marble, now in the
audience-chamber of the art of the builders, and sent a marble
picture to Perugia to M. Baglione Ribi, which was set up in the
chapel of the Sacrament in S. Piero.[1] It consists of a tabernacle
with St. John and St. Jerome on either side, two good figures in
half-relief. In the Duomo at Volterra there is another tabernacle
of the Sacrament by his hand,[2] with an angel on either side,
executed with such skill and finish that the work deserves the
praise of every artist. At length Mino over-exerted himself in
endeavouring to move some stones, not having the help which
he needed, so that he caught a chill of which he died, and was
honourably buried by his friends and relations in the cloister of
Fiesole in the year 1486. Mino's portrait, by whose hand I know
not, is in our book of drawings. It was given to me with some of
his designs in black lead of considerable merit.

LORENZO COSTA,[3] Painter of Ferrara
(c. 1460–1535)

ALTHOUGH men have always practised the arts of design in
Tuscany more than in any other province of Italy and perhaps
of Europe, yet the other provinces have also produced rare and
excellent spirits in that profession at all epochs, as has been
already shown in a number of Lives, and will be further demonstrated in the future. It is indeed true that, where men are not
habitually inclined to study, it is not possible to make such
rapid progress or to become so excellent as it is in those places
where artists are continually practising and studying in competition. But so soon as one or two begin, it seems that many
others invariably follow, so great is the force of genius, endeavouring to pursue the same road with honour to themselves
and to their country. Lorenzo Costa of Ferrara, being naturally
inclined to painting, and hearing the praises of Frà Filippo,
Benozzo and others in Tuscany, came to Florence to see their
works. Arrived there he was greatly attracted by their style, and
he remained in the city for many months, endeavouring to
imitate them so far as he could, especially in drawing from life,
in which he was most successful. Returning to his native place
he produced many admirable works there, in spite of a somewhat

[1] In 1473.   [2] Done in 1471.
[3] Vasari confuses this artist with Francesco Cossa, 1435–99.

dry and hard style, for instance in the choir of S. Domenico at Ferrara, which is entirely by his hand, where the diligence and study which he devoted to his works are well displayed. In the wardrobe of the Duke of Ferrara there are numerous portraits by his hand, very finely done and most life-like. A large number of his works in the houses of noblemen are equally valued. He painted in oils the picture of the chapel of St. Sebastian in the church of S. Domenico at Ravenna,[1] as well as some much-admired scenes in fresco. Being invited to Bologna, he painted for the Chapel of the Mariscotti in S. Petronio a St. Sebastian at the Column, with many other figures. This was the best work in tempera produced in that city up to that time. Another work of his was the picture of St. Jerome in the Chapel of the Castelli, and the St. Vincent, also in tempera, in the Chapel of the Grifoni, the predella of which he left to a pupil [2] who succeeded far better than himself, as I shall relate in the proper place. In the same city and in the same church Lorenzo did a picture for the Chapel of the Rossi, containing Our Lady, St. James, St. George, St. Sebastian and St. Jerome.[3] This work is the best and the smoothest that he ever produced. Entering the service of Francesco Gonzaga, Marquis of Mantua, he painted a number of scenes for him in a room in the palace of S. Sebastiano, partly in water-colours and partly in oils.[4] One contains the portrait from life of the Marchioness Isabella, accompanied by a number of ladies singing sweetly. Another has the goddess Latona turning peasants into frogs, according to the legend. The third has the Marquis Francesco led by Hercules in the path of virtue to the top of a mountain dedicated to Eternity. In another picture the marquis is seen on a pedestal in triumph with a baton in his hand, while about him are many lords and servants bearing standards in their hands, all full of joy and delight in his greatness, among them being a number of portraits. At each end of the great hall containing the triumphs by Mantegna, Lorenzo painted a picture. The first is in water-colour, and contains several nude figures offering fire and sacrifices to Hercules, and includes portraits of the marquis himself with his three sons, Federigo, Ercole and Ferrante, who afterwards became great and illustrious lords. There are also portraits of great ladies. The second picture, painted in oils many years after the first, and one of the very best things which Lorenzo did, contains the Marquis Federigo as a man with a baton in his hand as general of the Holy Church under Leo X. About him are a number of lords, being portraits drawn from life by Costa. In the palace of M. Giovanni Bentivogli at Bologna Lorenzo painted some apartments in competition with many other masters, of which I will not speak, because they perished in the destruction of the palace. I will not, however, omit to state that of the works which Lorenzo did for the Bentivogli,[1] the only one which remains is the chapel which he did for M. Giovanni in S. Jacopo, where he painted two Triumphs in two scenes, containing many portraits and much admired. In S. Giovanni in Monte he did a picture for Jacopo Chedini in the year 1497 in the chapel, where he desired to be buried, containing a Madonna, St. John the Evangelist, St. Augustine and other saints. In S. Francesco he painted in another picture the Nativity, St. James and St. Anthony of Padua. For Domenico Garganelli, a gentleman of Bologna, he began a very fine chapel in S. Piero, but whatever the cause, he left it unfinished and indeed barely begun, after making some figures on the ceiling. Besides the works which he executed for the marquis at Mantua, of which I have already spoken, he painted a Madonna on a panel for S. Salvestro, with St. Silvester on one side of her, pleading for the people of the city, and on the other St. Sebastian, St. Paul, St. Elizabeth and St. Jerome.[2] So far as is known, this picture was placed in the church after Costa's death. He died at Mantua, where his descendants have continued to reside, and desired to have a tomb in that church for himself and his family. He painted many other pictures, of which I will make no further mention, it being enough to speak of the best. I have had his portrait in Mantua from Fermo Ghisoni, an excellent painter, who assures me that it is by Costa himself. He designed fairly, as may be seen by a sheet of parchment in our book containing the Judgment of Solomon and a St. Jerome, in grisaille, which are excellent.

Among Lorenzo's pupils were his countryman, Ercole da Ferrara, whose Life will be given below, and Ludovico Malino,[3] also of Ferrara, who did many works in his native place and elsewhere. But the best thing which he did there was a panel for the church of S. Francesco at Bologna in a chapel near the principal door, containing the dispute of Christ at the age of twelve with the doctors in the Temple. Dosso of Ferrara, the elder, also learned the first principles from Costa, but his works will be referred to in another place. And this is all that can be related of the life and works of Lorenzo Costa of Ferrara.

[1] These works were done by Cossa.   [2] Now in S. Andrea.   [3] Mazzolino.

Ercole, Painter of Ferrara [1]

ALTHOUGH Ercole of Ferrara, the pupil of Lorenzo Costa, was in good repute long before his master's death, and was invited to work in many places, yet he would never leave his master, a very rare occurrence, but preferred to remain with him, gaining but little money or praise, to working by himself with more profit and credit. Such gratitude is a rare virtue in the men of to-day, and it deserves the greater praise in Ercole, who, recognising his debt to Lorenzo, subordinated his own interests to his master's wishes, and behaved to him like a brother and a son to the very end of his life. Being a better designer than Costa, he painted below his master's picture in the chapel of St. Vincent in S. Petronio some scenes of small figures in tempera, in such a fine style that it would be hard to wish for better, or to realise the pains and diligence which Ercole bestowed upon them. Thus the predella is a far better performance than the picture itself, and both were produced at the same time during the life of Costa. After the death of the latter, Ercole was set by Domenico Garganelli to finish the chapel in S. Petronio, which, as I have already said, Lorenzo had begun, doing a small portion. Domenico gave him four ducats a month, all his expenses and those of a boy, as well as all the colours used in the work, and Ercole laboured to such purpose that he far surpassed his master in design and colouring as well as in invention. In the first part or front is the Crucifixion of Christ, made with great judgment, because besides the figure of Christ, who is already dead, the rabble of the Jews who have come to see the Messiah on the cross is admirably expressed, the diversity of the heads being marvellous. We see here how Ercole sought carefully to make them all different, so that they should not be alike in any particular. Some other figures display their grief in weeping, and show how carefully he tried to imitate the truth. The fainting of the Madonna is most moving, but much more so are the Maries near her, their appearance being eloquent of almost inconceivable grief at seeing their dearest Lord lying dead before them and being in danger of losing another dear one. Among the other notable things there is a Longinus mounted on a lean beast

[1] There were two painters of this name, Ercole di Roberti (?1440–1513), and Ercole di Giulio Grandi (1465–1535). All the works mentioned here are by the former, with the possible exception of the Grifoni altarpiece, which is by Cossa, the master of Ercole di Roberti. Costa was the master of Ercole di Giulio Grandi.

foreshortened and standing out wonderfully. We see his impiety in piercing the side of Christ, and his repentance and conversion on coming to himself. Ercole further represented in curious attitudes some soldiers who are gaming for the garments of Christ, grotesque both in countenance and dress. The thieves on the cross again are well depicted with good invention. Ercole delighted in foreshortening, which is effective when well done, and into this work he introduced a soldier on horseback, the animal raising its fore-legs so that it appears to be in relief, while the wind unfurls a banner which the man holds in his hand, executed with great power. He also made a St. John fleeing away, wrapped in a sheet. The soldiers in this work are also excellently done, with the most natural and appropriate movements, better than any figures seen before that time. All these postures and this power prove that Ercole possessed a thorough knowledge of his art and had studied deeply.

On the wall opposite Ercole made the Passing of Our Lady, surrounded by the Apostles in remarkable attitudes, among them being six portraits so well done that those who knew the originals declare them to be most life-like. In the same work he drew his own portrait and that of Domenico Garganelli, the patron of the chapel, who gave him 1000 lire of Bologna on the completion of the work, from the love which he bore Ercole and for the praise which he heard bestowed upon the painting. It is said that Ercole devoted twelve years to this work, seven in doing it in fresco and five in retouching it *a secco*. It is indeed true that he did other things in the meantime, notably, as we know, the predella of the high altar of S. Giovanni in Monte, containing three scenes from the Passion of Christ.[1] Being very eccentric, especially because, when at work, he would allow no one to see him, Ercole was much disliked by the painters of Bologna, who have always been envious of the foreigners who have been invited to labour there, and even exhibit the same animosity in their rivalry among themselves, although this is perhaps the besetting sin of our art everywhere. Some painters of Bologna accordingly bribed a carpenter, and with his assistance they shut themselves up in a church near the chapel where Ercole was at work. On the following night they broke into it, and not content with seeing the work, which ought to have satisfied them, they stole all the drawings, sketches, and everything else of value. So disgusted was Ercole at this treatment that he left Bologna the

[1] Probably painted in 1482. Two portions of the predella are in the Dresden Gallery, while the Walker Art Gallery appears to possess the third.

moment he had finished the work, taking away with him il duca Tagliapietra,[1] a sculptor of repute, who carved for the painting of Ercole those lovely marble leaves which are on the parapet before the chapel, and who afterwards made all the handsome stone windows of the duke's palace at Ferrara. Ercole, tired of remaining away from home, established himself finally at Ferrara with this sculptor, and executed many works there.

He was inordinately fond of wine, and his frequent debauches shortened his life. Having attained to the age of forty without any mishap, he was one day seized by an apoplexy which in a short time deprived him of his life. He left behind his pupil Guido Bolognese, a painter, who, in 1491, painted in fresco a crucifix, with the Maries, the thieves, the horsemen and other figures of merit, under the portico of S. Piero at Bologna, where he put his name. As he was extremely anxious to win fame in that city, as his master had done, he studied so earnestly and underwent so many hardships that he died at the age of thirty-five. Had Guido been put to learn art as a child, instead of beginning when eighteen, he would not only have equalled his master without trouble, but have far surpassed him. Our book of designs contains some excellent examples by Ercole and Guido, executed gracefully and in a good style.

JACOPO, GIOVANNI and GENTILE BELLINI, Painters of Venice

(c. 1400 – c. 1464;   1428 – 1516;   1426 – 1507)

WHERE there is a foundation of ability, no matter how vile or base the beginning may appear, steady progress is invariably made until the zenith of glory is attained, without any pause by the way. This is clearly shown in the base and humble origin of the house of the Bellini, and in the rank to which they after-wards attained by means of painting. Jacopo Bellini, painter of Venice, was a pupil of Gentile da Fabriano. In comparison with that same Domenico who taught oil-painting to Andrea del Castagno, although he took great pains to achieve excellence in the art, he did not acquire fame in it until after the departure of Domenico from Venice. Being then left without a rival in that city, his credit and renown steadily increased, and he became so excellent that he was the most famous in his profession. To

[1] Variously conjectured to be Frisoni or Foscardi.

preserve this renown in his house, and to augment it, he had two sons, devoted to the arts and possessing great ability, the one Giovanni, the other Gentile, named after Gentile da Fabriano, his dear master, who had been like a loving father to him. When these boys were grown, Jacopo himself taught them the principles of design with all diligence. But it was not long before they both far surpassed him, to the delight of their father, who incited them to endeavour to surpass each other, competing as the Tuscans did, so that Giovanni should beat him, then Gentile both of them, and so on. The first things which brought fame to Jacopo were the portraits of Giorgio Cornaro and of Catherine, Queen of Cyprus; a picture which he sent to Verona of the Passion of Christ with many figures, including his own portrait, and a Story of the Cross, said to be in the Scuola of S. Giovanni Evangelista. All these and many others were painted by Jacopo with the aid of his sons. The last one was painted on canvas, the almost invariable practice in that city, where they seldom employ wood panels of poplar as is done elsewhere. This wood, which grows along rivers or other waters, is extremely soft and excellent for painting upon, as it holds firmly together when joined with glue. But in Venice they do not make panels, or, if they do, they are of fir, which is abundant there, being brought down from Germany by the River Adige in great quantities, while a great deal also comes from Sclavonia. It is thus the custom of Venice to paint on canvas, either because it does not split and is not worm-eaten, or because pictures can be made of any size desired, or else for convenience, as is said elsewhere, so that they may be sent anywhere with very little trouble or expense. Whatever the cause, Jacopo and Gentile, as I have said above, made their first works on canvas, and afterwards Gentile by himself added seven or eight pictures to the Story of the Cross,[1] representing the Miracle of the Cross of Christ, which the Scuola keeps as a relic. This miracle was as follows: The cross having fallen by some accident from the Ponte della Paglia into the canal, many men threw themselves into the water to recover it, owing to their reverence for the wood of the True Cross, but it was the will of God that no one was found worthy to take it except the warden of the school. In treating this story, Gentile represented the Grand Canal in perspective, with many houses, the Ponte della Paglia, the Piazza of S. Marco, and a long procession of men and women following the clergy. He also represented

[1] Gentile only did three of them, which are all in the Accademia, Venice. The Miracle of the Cross was painted in 1500.

many in the water, others ready to jump in, several half-immersed and other fine and varied attitudes, including the warden who recovers it. Great pains and diligence were displayed by Gentile in this work, as we see by the countless figures, the numerous portraits, the foreshortening of the distant figures and the portraits notably of almost all the members of the Scuola or company at that time. He finished by doing the restoration of the Cross to its place, including many fine incidents; all these pictures, painted on canvas, greatly increasing his reputation. After this Jacopo retired, and each of the brothers devoted himself to his art. I will say no more about Jacopo, because his works were not remarkable compared with those of his sons, and not long after they left him he died, so that I consider it best to speak at length of Giovanni and Gentile only. Although the brothers lived apart, they bore such a respect for each other and for their father that each one declared himself to be inferior to the other, thus seeking modestly to surpass the other no less in goodness and courtesy than in the excellence of art. The first works of Giovanni were some portraits which gave great satisfaction, especially that of the Doge Loredano, although some say that it is Giovanni Mozzenigo, brother of that Piero who was doge long before Loredano.[1] Giovanni next made a large picture for the altar of St. Catherine of Siena in the church of S. Giovanni,[2] representing Our Lady seated, with the Child, St. Dominic, St. Jerome, St. Catherine, St. Ursula and two other Virgins, with three beautiful children standing at the Madonna's feet and singing from a book. Above them he represented the inside of the vaulting of a building, which is very fine. This work was among the best which had been produced in Venice up to that time. In the church of S. Jobbe he painted the altar-picture with excellent design and fine colouring, representing the Virgin seated somewhat higher in the midst, with the Child, St. Job and St. Sebastian, both nude figures, and St. Dominic, St. Francis, St. John and St. Augustine hard-by.[3] Below are three children playing various instruments with much grace. This picture not only excited great admiration when it was new, but it has always been praised as a most beautiful work.

Moved by these admirable works, it occurred to some noblemen that it would be well to employ such rare masters to decorate the hall of the great council with paintings descriptive

[1] Mocenigo was doge 1478–85, Loredano 1501–21.
[2] i.e. Zanipolo. The picture was destroyed by fire in 1867 together with Titian's St. Peter Martyr.
[3] Now in the Accademia, Venice.

of the magnificence and greatness of their marvellous city, its achievements in war, its enterprises, and other matters worthy of such celebration, as a reminder to succeeding generations, who would derive both pleasure and instruction from scenes appealing alike to the eye and to the mind. Here they would see representations of illustrious lords made by skilful hands as well as the notable deeds of men worthy of undying renown. Accordingly the Government allotted this task to Giovanni and to Gentile, whose reputation increased daily, with instructions to begin as soon as possible.[1] It is only right to mention, however, that long before this Antonio Viniziano had begun to paint the same hall, as I have said in his Life, and had finished a large scene, but was forced to abandon it by the envy of some malignant persons, and so he never carried out that honourable task. Now Gentile, being more accustomed to paint on canvas than in fresco, or for some other cause, so contrived it that the work should not be painted in fresco but on canvas. The first thing which he did was the Pope presenting to the doge a candle to be carried in a solemn procession then about to take place. In this work Gentile pictured the whole of the exterior of S. Marco, and represented the Pope in his pontificals, followed by numerous prelates, the doge standing, and accompanied by a number of senators. In another part he first did the Emperor Barbarossa graciously receiving the Venetian envoys, and then where he is angrily preparing for war, containing many fine perspectives and countless portraits executed with the utmost grace. In the following scene he painted the Pope exhorting the doge and Venetian senators to arm thirty galleys at the common expense to go and fight with Frederick Barbarossa. The Pope is seated on a pontifical throne in his rochet, with the doge at his side and many senators below. In this scene also Gentile drew the piazza and façade of S. Marco, but in another manner, and the sea with such a multitude of men upon it as to be a veritable marvel. The same Pope occurs again standing in his robes and blessing the doge, who appears armed, with many soldiers behind him, ready to set out. Behind the doge is a long line of nobles, and in the same part the palace and S. Marco are drawn in perspective. This is among the best works of Gentile, although there is another representing a naval battle which is more remarkable for invention and for the countless number of galleys, where multitudes of men are fighting, showing that

[1] Gentile began the work in 1474 and Giovanni carried it on in 1479, when his brother went to Constantinople. It was destroyed by fire in 1577.

he was no less acquainted with naval warfare than with painting. In this work he depicted a number of galleys involved together with the soldiers fighting, boats drawn in perspective, with the fury, force and strength of the soldiers in fighting, men dying in various ways, the cleaving of the water by the galleys, the confusion of the waves and every kind of naval armament. This endless variety shows the boldness, skill, invention and good judgment of Gentile, everything being excellent in its kind while the whole forms an admirable composition. In another scene he represented the joyful reception accorded by the Pope to the doge on his return after the victory, presenting him with a gold ring to espouse the sea, as his successors have done every year, and still do in sign of the true and perpetual lordship over it which they have earned. In this he made a portrait of Otto, the son of Frederick Barbarossa, kneeling before the Pope; the doge having many armed men behind him, while cardinals and nobles stand behind the Pope. Only the poops of the galleys appear in this scene, and over the admiral's galley is a gilded Victory seated, wearing a gold crown on her head, and holding a sceptre in her hand.

The paintings on the other side of the hall were allotted to Gentile's brother Giovanni, but as his arrangement depends on work already begun there by Vivarino and left unfinished, I must say something of this artist. The portion of the hall not given to Gentile was partly entrusted to Giovanni and partly to Vivarino, in order that competition might induce them to do better. Accordingly Vivarino began his section,[1] starting next to the last scene of Gentile, where Otto offers his services to the Pope and the Venetians to go and procure peace between them and his father Frederick, and this being granted, sets out, dismissed on his parole. In this scene, besides many noteworthy things, Vivarino painted an open church in perspective, with steps and many persons. In the foreground is seated the Pope surrounded by senators, while Otto kneels before him and pledges his honour. Next to this Vivarino did the arrival of Otto and his father's joyful reception, with a fine perspective of buildings. Barbarossa is seated, while his son kneels and holds his hand, a number of Venetian nobles hard-by being portraits from life, showing how well the artist imitated Nature. Poor Vivarino would have completed the remainder of his section with great praise, but it pleased God that he should die, worn out by his toil and by bad health, so that he did no more, and even what he had done

[1] Alvise Vivarini, in 1488.

was not completed, and it was necessary for Giovanni Bellini to retouch it in some places.

Giovanni had himself begun four scenes which followed those just mentioned. In the first he made the Pope in S. Marco, drawing the church as it then was, offering his foot to Frederick Barbarossa to kiss. But whatever the cause, this first scene of Giovanni was treated much more forcefully and incomparably better by the master Titian. Giovanni then represented the Pope saying Mass in S. Marco, and then standing between the emperor and the doge and granting a plenary and perpetual indulgence to all who visit that church at a certain time, notably at the Ascension. He made the interior of the church, the Pope standing on the steps leading to the choir, dressed in his pontifical robes, and surrounded by a multitude of cardinals and nobles, composing a full, rich and beautiful scene. In the painting beneath this the Pope stands in his rochet, and is giving a canopy to the doge, after having presented one to the emperor and reserved two for himself. In the last scene painted by Giovanni he represents the arrival at Rome of Pope Alexander, the emperor and the doge. Outside the gates the clergy and all the Roman people have come to present eight standards of various colours and eight silver trumpets, which are handed by the Pope to the doge, that he and his successors may preserve them as a memento. Here Giovanni drew Rome in perspective, taken some distance off, a large number of horse and foot, with banners and other signs of joy floating from the castle of S. Angelo. As these works of Giovanni gave great satisfaction, and they are truly excellent, he was immediately employed to paint all the rest of the hall, when his death took place, for he was then an old man.

As I have spoken of nothing hitherto except this hall, so as not to interrupt the narrative, I will retrace my steps somewhat and speak of other works. Among them is a picture now on the high altar of S. Domenico[1] at Pesaro. In the chapel of St. Jerome in the church of S. Zaccaria at Venice there is a picture of Our Lady with many saints, executed with great diligence, containing a building painted with great judgment. In the sacristy of the Minorites, called Ca grande,[2] in the same city, there is another by his hand of good design and manner. Yet another is in S. Michele, at Murano, a monastery of the Camaldoline monks; and in the old church of S. Francesco della Vigna, of the barefooted friars, there was a picture of a dead Christ. This was so beautiful that Louis XI. of France took a great fancy to it, and

[1] S. Francesco. [2] Now known as the Frari.

as he made an earnest request to have it, the owners were
obliged to gratify him, though they did so unwillingly. Another
work of Giovanni was put in its place, but not so good or so well
executed as the first one. Some, indeed, believe that it was
painted by Giovanni's pupil, Girolamo Mocetto. In the brotherhood of S. Girolamo there is a much-admired work of small
figures by the same Bellini, while the house of M. Giorgio Cornaro
contains a similar fine picture, with Christ, Cleophas and Luke.
In the hall already spoken of, but at another time, he painted
the scene where the Venetians discover some pope in the monastery della Carita, who had taken refuge in Venice, and had long
served the monks as a cook. Into this scene he introduced a
number of portraits and other fine figures. Not long after this
the Grand Turk happened to see some portraits brought by an
ambassador, which filled him with wonder and amazement, and
although paintings are prohibited by the Mahommedan laws
he gladly accepted them, ceaselessly praising the artist and his
work and, what is more, requesting that the master should be
sent for. The senate, reflecting that Giovanni was of an age at
which he could ill support hardships, and unwilling to deprive
their city of such a great man, especially as he was at the time
employed upon the hall of the great council, decided to send his
brother Gentile, who would, they thought, do as well.[1] Accordingly Gentile was safely taken in their galleys to Constantinople,
and on being presented by the ambassador of the Signoria to
Mahommed, he was received graciously and highly favoured as
being something novel, especially as he presented the prince with
a lovely picture, which he greatly admired, wondering how a
mortal man could possibly possess such divine talent as to be
able to express natural things so vividly. Gentile had not long
been there before he painted the emperor himself so well that
it was considered a miracle. After the emperor had seen many
examples of his art he asked Gentile if he would like to paint
his own portrait. Gentile replied in the affirmative, and in a few
days he had made a wonderful likeness of himself with the aid
of a mirror. When the portrait was shown to the prince he was
amazed, feeling convinced that the artist had been assisted by
some divine spirit, and if such things had not been forbidden
among the Turks by their laws, he would never have allowed
Gentile to go. Whether he feared that murmurs might arise,
or for some other reason, the emperor sent for Gentile one day,

[1] 1479. But Gentile was the elder and it was he who was first engaged
upon the Great Hall.

and after thanking him and praising his excellence, he asked him to name any favour which he desired, and it would immediately be granted to him. Gentile, being a modest and worthy man, asked for nothing but a letter of recommendation to the senate and government of his native Venice. This was written in the warmest possible terms, after which Gentile was dismissed with noble gifts and the honour of knighthood. Among other gifts and privileges accorded to him by the lord of the country, a golden chain worked in the Turkish fashion and weighing 250 gold crowns was placed on his neck, and it is still in the possession of his heirs at Venice. Leaving Constantinople,[1] Gentile enjoyed a prosperous voyage back to Venice, where he was joyfully received by his brother Giovanni and almost all the city, everyone being delighted at the honour rendered to his skill by Mahommed. When he went to pay his respects to the doge and the senate he was graciously received and commended for having accomplished their wish in giving so much gratification to the emperor. In order to show their consideration for that prince's letter of recommendation, they decreed to him a provision of 200 crowns a year, which was paid to him until the end of his life. After his return Gentile produced but few more works. At length, when nearly eighty years of age, and after having executed the above-mentioned works and many others, he passed to the other life, and was honourably buried by his brother in S. Giovanni e Paolo in the year 1501.

Giovanni, who had always loved his brother tenderly, being thus left alone, still continued to work, old as he was, and as he was employed to paint portraits, it became a practice in that city that every man of any note should have his portrait painted either by Giovanni or by some other. Hence all the houses of Venice contain numerous portraits, and several nobles have those of their ancestors to the fourth generation, while some of the noblest go even farther back. The custom is an admirable one, and was in use among the ancients. Who does not experience the utmost satisfaction in seeing the likeness of his ancestors, especially of those who have been distinguished in politics, for worthy deeds in war and peace, in letters or other honourable employments; moreover the portraits are in themselves ornamental. To what other end did the ancients place the images of their great men in public places, with laudatory inscriptions, except to kindle those who come after to virtue and to glory! Giovanni painted for M. Pietro Bembo, before he went to visit

[1] November 1480.

Pope Leo X., a portrait of his mistress so finely that he earned a mention in the verses of this second celebrated Venetian, just as Simon of Siena had been celebrated by Petrarch, as in the sonnet:

O imagine mia celeste and pura,

where at the beginning of the second quatrain he says:

Credo che'l mio Bellini con la figura, etc.

And what greater reward can our artists desire for their labours than to be celebrated by the pens of illustrious poets. Thus Titian has been sung by the learned M. Giovanni della Casa in the sonnet beginning:

Ben veggo io Tiziano, in forme nuove;

and in the other:

Son quest Amor le vaghe treccie bionde.

And was not Bellini numbered among the best painters of his age by the renowned Ariosto at the beginning of Canto XXXIII. of the *Orlando Furioso*? But to return to the works of Giovanni, that is to say to the chief ones, for it would take too long to mention all the pictures and portraits which are in the houses of the Venetian nobles and in other places of that state. In Rimini he made a Pieta for Sig. Sigismondo Malatesta, borne by two children, a large picture now in S. Francesco in that city.[1] Among other portraits he drew that of Bartolommeo da Liviano,[2] a captain of the Venetians.

Giovanni had many pupils, because he taught all with pleasure. Among them, sixty years ago, was Jacopo da Montagna, who closely imitated his style, as his works in Padua and Venice show. But the one who imitated him most and who did him the greatest honour was Rondinello da Ravenna, of whom he made great use in all his works. This pupil painted a picture in S. Domenico at Ravenna and another in the Duomo, which is considered a fine example of that style. But his best work was that in the Carmelite church of S. Giovanni Battista in the same city, where, besides a Madonna, he painted a St. Albert of that order, the head being very fine, and the whole figure much admired. Benedetto Coda of Ferrara was also with Giovanni, though he did not profit much by the association. He lived at Rimini, where he painted many pictures, and left a son Bartolommeo, who did the same. It is said that Giorgio da Castelfranco

---

[1] Now in the Gallery, Rimini.   [2] Alviano.

began by studying art with Giovanni, as well as many others, of the Trevisano and Lombardy, whom I need not mention.

At length, when Giovanni had attained to the age of ninety years, he died of old age, leaving an immortal name by the works which he produced in his native Venice and elsewhere. He was buried in the same church and in the same tomb where he had previously laid his brother Gentile. There was no lack at Venice of those who endeavoured to honour him when dead with sonnets and epigrams, just as he had honoured his country when alive.

At the time, when the Bellini were at work or shortly before, Giacomo Marzone [1] painted a number of things in Venice, and among others one in the chapel of the Assumption in S. Elena, representing the Virgin with a palm, St. Benedict, St. Helena and St. John, but in an old-fashioned style, the figures standing on the tips of their toes, after the manner of the painters who lived in the time of Bartolommeo da Bergamo.

COSIMO ROSSELLI, Painter of Florence
(1439–1507)

MANY men take an ignoble pleasure in deriding and scorning others though this most frequently recoils upon themselves, just as Cosimo Rosselli returned scorn upon the heads of those who endeavoured to minimise his efforts. This Cosimo, although not a very rare or excellent painter, produced some very meritorious works. In his youth he painted a picture for the church of S. Ambruogio at Florence,[2] on the right as one enters, and three figures over the arch of the nuns of S. Jacopo dalle Murate. In the church of the Servites, also at Florence, he did the altarpiece of the chapel of St. Barbara,[3] and in the first courtyard in front of the entrance to the church he painted in fresco the Blessed Philip receiving the habit from Our Lady. For the monks of Cestello he painted the picture of the high altar, and another for another chapel of the same church, as well as the one in a small church above the Bernardino, beside the entrance of Cestello. He painted the banner for the children of the company of Bernardino and also that of the company of St. George, containing an Annunciation. For the same nuns of S. Ambruogio he did the chapel of the Miracle of the Sacrament,[4] quite a good work,

---

[1] It should be Morazzoni.   [2] In 1498.
[3] Now in the Accademia.   [4] In 1486.

considered his best in Florence, in which he represented a procession in the piazza of the church. The bishop is carrying the tabernacle of the miracle, accompanied by the clergy and a throng of citizens and women in the costumes of the day. Besides many other portraits, it contains one of Pico della Mirandola, so excellent that he seems alive. In the church of S. Martino at Lucca, on the right-hand side on entering by the smaller door of the principal façade, he painted Nicodemus carving the statue of the Holy Cross and its transport in a ship to Lucca.[1] This work also contains many portraits, notably one of Paolo Guinigi, taken from a clay model made by Jacopo della Fonte when he was engaged upon the tomb of the wife. In the chapel of the cloth-weavers in S. Marco at Florence he made a picture containing the cross in the middle, and at the sides St. Mark, St. John the Evangelist, St. Anthony, Archbishop of Florence, and other figures.

Being summoned with other painters to the work carried on by Sixtus IV., in the chapel of the palace, he worked in conjunction with Sandro Botticello, Domenico Ghirlandajo, the abbot of S. Clemente, Luca da Cortona and Piero Perugino, painting three scenes, namely the drowning of Pharaoh in the Red Sea, the preaching of Christ to the people by the Sea of Tiberias, and the Last Supper.[2] In the last of these he represented an octagonal table in perspective, the roof above being likewise octagonal, the whole very well foreshortened and showing that he understood this art as well as others did. It is said that the Pope had offered a prize to the painter who in his judgment should acquit himself the best. When the scenes were finished His Holiness went to see them and judge how far the painters had striven to earn the reward and the honour. Conscious of his weakness in invention and design, Cosimo had endeavoured to cover these defects by using the finest ultramarine and other bright colours, illuminating the whole with a quantity of gold, so that there was not a tree, a blade, a garment or a cloud which was not illuminated, in order that the Pope, who knew very little of art, might be convinced that he ought to award the prize to him. When the day came for uncovering all the works, the artists laughed at Cosimo and chaffed him, making jokes at his expense instead of pitying him. But the event proved that they were deceived, for, as Cosimo had expected, the Pope, being ignorant of such matters, though he took great delight in them, judged that Cosimo had done much better than all the rest. Accordingly he received

[1] Usually known as the "Volto Santo."   [2] Painted in 1482.

the prize, while the Pope directed the others to cover their pictures with the best ultramarine which they could find, and touch them up with gold so as to make them resemble that of Cosimo in richness and colouring. The poor painters, in despair of trying to please so foolish a pope, set themselves to spoil their own good work. Cosimo, however, had the laugh of those who had been laughing at him shortly before.

Returning afterwards to Florence with some money, he continued to work as usual, though living very comfortably, having with him that Piero who has always been known as Piero di Cosimo, his pupil, who assisted him with his work at the Sistine Chapel in Rome, painting, among other things, a landscape for the Sermon of Christ, considered the best thing there. Andrea di Cosimo, who was also with him, devoted himself chiefly to grotesques. At length, when Cosimo had lived sixty-eight years, and after enduring a long illness, he died in 1484 and was buried in S. Croce by the company of the Bernardino. He was very fond of alchemy, and wasted much time upon it, like all others who are attracted to that study. Owing to this he was reduced from comfortable circumstances to great poverty. Cosimo designed very well, as may be seen in our book, not only in the sheet containing the drawing for the preaching in the Sistine Chapel, but in many others in pencil and in grisaille. We have his portrait in this book by the hand of Agnolo di Donnino, a painter and close friend of his. This Agnolo was a diligent worker, as we see by his drawings as well as in the loggia of the hospital of Boniface, which contains a Trinity in fresco by his hand, on the keystone of the vaulting. Beside the door of the hospital, where the abandoned ones are laid, there are some poor people, painted by him, being received by the master, and some women, all very well done. He lived thus, wasting all his time in making designs which he never carried out, and at length died in the utmost poverty. Cosimo, to return to him, only left one son, who was a meritorious builder and architect.

Il Cecca,[1] Engineer of Florence
(1447–1488)

If necessity had not forced men to display all the resources of their intellect for their own benefit and convenience, architecture would never have developed to such an extent in the minds of

[1] Francesco d' Angelo.

those who, in order to acquire fame and profit, have produced works which win the daily homage of connoisseurs. This necessity originally produced buildings, then their ornamentation, and finally the dispositions, statues, gardens, baths, and all those other sumptuous accessories which everyone desires and few possess, so that emulation has not only produced buildings, but has rendered them luxurious. In this way artists have been compelled to display their industry in methods of traction, in machines of war, in hydraulic apparatus, and in all those employments by which engineers and architects render the world beautiful and luxurious, and provide the means for annoying their adversaries and accommodating their friends. All who have excelled the rest in such things not only escape hardship for themselves, but are highly praised and valued, as was Cecca of Florence in the days of our fathers. Many things of great importance passed through his hands, and he served his country so well, to the benefit and satisfaction of his fellow-citizens, that his ingenious labours have rendered him famous and distinguished among other excellent and admirable artists.

It is said that Cecca was an excellent carpenter in his youth, and having employed all his ingenuity in finding a means to convey to military camps scaling ladders, battering-rams, defences for the combatants and everything which could injure an enemy and assist his friends, he was a most useful man to his country, and deserved the provision made for him by the Government of Florence. Thus in time of peace he toured about the territory examining fortresses, city walls and castles which were weak, and directed the methods of repairing them and for doing everything else necessary. It is said that the clouds used in the procession at Florence at the feast of St. John, a most ingenious and beautiful thing, were his invention, and were much used in those days when the city indulged in frequent festivities. To-day such spectacles have almost entirely died out, but then they used to be very sumptuous. Hardly a company or brotherhood, not to speak of private gentlemen, but had its feasts and assemblies, meeting at certain seasons, there being always a number of clever artists who set their wits to work to make the apparatus for such feasts. Four of these, one for each quarter, of peculiar solemnity, were publicly celebrated practically every year, namely, S. Maria Novella that of St. Ignatius; S. Croce that of St. Bartholomew, called il Baccio; S. Spirito that of the Holy Spirit; il Carmine that of the Ascension and the Assumption of Our Lady. The feast of St. John was a thing apart and celebrated by a most

solemn procession, as will be related. I shall describe the feast
of the Ascension because the others have already been described
or will be. It was very fine. Christ was raised upon a mountain
admirably made of wood by a cloud full of angels and carried
into heaven, leaving the Apostles on the mountain. This was
marvellously done, especially as the heaven was somewhat
larger than that of S. Felice in Piazza, though with almost the
same apparatus. As the church of the Carmine, where this was
enacted, is considerably broader and loftier than S. Felice,
another heaven, besides the one which received Christ, was
arranged over the principal tribune, in which large wheels like
windlasses moved ten circles representing the ten heavens, from
the centre to the circumference, full of lights representing the
stars, arranged in copper lanterns and so fixed that when the
wheel turned they always remained in position, as some lanterns
do which are in common use to-day. From this heaven, which
was a truly beautiful thing, issued two large cables connected
with the gallery or rood-loft of the church. Each was supplied
with a small bronze pulley supporting an iron bar, fixed to a
plane upon which stood two angels bound at the waist, counter-
poised by a lead weight beneath their feet, and another at the
base of the plane on which they stood. The whole was covered
with cotton wool, forming a cloud full of cherubim and seraphim,
and other angels in divers colours and very well arranged. These
being let down by ropes to the top of the screen, announced to
Christ His Ascension to heaven, or performed other offices. As
the iron to which they were bound by the girdle was fixed in the
plane where their feet were set, they could turn round, issuing
out and returning, making reverences and turning themselves at
need. Thus in mounting upwards they faced the sky, and they
were drawn up by the same means by which they had descended.
These machines and contrivances were the work of Cecca, who
added many things to the devices invented by Filippo Brunelleschi, with great judgment. It afterwards occurred to him to
make the clouds which go through the city in procession
every St. John's Eve, as well as other beautiful things. This
was entrusted to him, because he was, as I have said, in the
public service.

This will be a good opportunity to relate what was done at
this feast and in the procession, in order to preserve the memory
of things which have mostly gone out of use. Firstly, the Piazza
of S. Giovanni was covered all over with blue cloth full of large
lilies worked in yellow thread and sewn on. In the middle were

large cloth medallions, ten braccia across, containing the arms of the people and commune of Florence, those of the captain of the Guelph party and others. All round the edges of this canopy, covering this large area, hung small flags painted with various devices, with the arms of the magistrates and the arts and with many lions, which are among the insignia of the city. The sky or covering thus formed was about twenty braccia from the ground and supported by strong ropes attached to iron hooks which may still be seen about the church of S. Giovanni, on the façade of S. Maria del Fiore and on the houses about the piazza. Between the ropes were smaller cords, the whole being made very strong and so well contrived that nothing better could be desired. What is more, it was so well constructed that even in a high wind, such as is frequent there at all seasons, as everyone knows, the sails would belly out but could not be carried away or disarranged. These coverings were in five pieces so that they could be more easily managed, but when set up they were all fastened together and looked like one piece. Three of the pieces covered the piazza and the space between S. Giovanni and S. Maria del Fiore, and the middle one had the circles bearing the arms of the Commune already mentioned to the right of the principal doors, and the other two pieces covered the sides, one towards the Misericordia and the other towards the Canonicata and the Opera of S. Giovanni. The clouds, which were differently made by the various companies, were usually of this fashion: A square piece of canvas was made on a framework about two braccia high, with four strong legs at the corners, to serve as supports, and these were tied together. Over this web two frames were placed crosswise, of a braccia each, having in the middle a hole of half a braccia in which was a post supporting a *mandorla*. This was covered with cotton wool and filled with cherubim, lights and other ornaments, and pierced by an iron bar supporting a person, seated or standing as was desired, representing the saint who was honoured by the company as their protector, or else a Christ, a Madonna, St. John or some other, the draperies covering the iron so that it should not be seen. Irons were fixed which passed beneath the *mandorla*, making four branches, more or less like those of a tree, and at the end of each was a little child dressed as an angel. These were able to turn about, as the supports were hinged. By means of such branches two or three rows of angels or saints were sometimes arranged, according to the needs of the representation. The entire structure sometimes formed a lily, sometimes a tree, and frequently a cloud or something similar, being covered with cotton wool, as I have said, and filled with cherubim, seraphim, golden stars and other ornaments. Inside were the workmen who carried it on their shoulders, who were disposed about what we have called the web, bearing the weight on their shoulders on a cushion of feathers, cotton-wool or some soft material. All these machines were covered over with cotton-wool, which made them beautiful to look at, and they were all called clouds. Behind them came cavalcades of men and foot serjeants of various kinds as required by the scene represented, just as nowadays they follow the cars or other things which have replaced the clouds. I have in my book some admirable and truly ingenious ideas for these things, designed by Cecca, full of excellent notions. It was by his invention that saints were carried in procession, either dead or tortured in various ways, some transfixed by a lance or a sword, some with a dagger in the throat, and so forth. It is now well known that this is done by using a broken sword or lance united by a piece of curved iron arranged so as to make it appear to be wounding the person struck, but I only wish to say that these things were mostly the invention of Cecca.

The giants who took part in these feasts were made in this manner. Men skilled in the use of stilts made some which raised them five or six braccia from the ground, and putting on huge masks and other clothes to make their members appear to be those of a giant, they mounted, and by a dexterous use of the stilts, they looked like veritable giants. They carried a prop upon which they rested, but in such a manner that it looked like a weapon, a mace or a lance, such as Morgante used to carry, according to the romantic poets. In the same way as the giants, giantesses were made, who were a truly fine and marvellous sight. The spirits were arranged differently, being nothing more than an ordinary person mounted on stilts, five or six braccia high, and carrying a prop upon which to lean. It is said that some were able to go about without any such assistance. And anyone who is acquainted with Florentine wit will not marvel at these things. To say nothing of Montughi of Florence, who surpassed everyone yet seen in his performances on a rope, we have known Ruvidino, who died not ten years ago, who could mount any height on a rope and descend from the walls of the city to the ground, and who used stilts much higher than those mentioned above, walking as easily as others do on level ground. Thus it is no wonder that the men of that day could do such things, and even greater ones, seeing that they practised them frequently for reward or otherwise.

I will not speak of some candles painted in various guises, but so rudely that they have given a name to common painters, so that bad pictures are called "Candle puppets," things of no account. In the time of Cecca these had nearly gone out of use, being replaced by cars like the triumphal ones used to-day. The first of those was that of the Mint, which was brought to its present state of perfection, being sent out every year by the masters and lords of the mint with a St. John at the top, and many other saints and angels below represented by living persons. Not long ago it was decided that each district should offer a candle, and as many as ten were made to adorn the feast, but it did not take place on account of the events which supervened. The first then, that of the Mint, was made under Cecca's direction by Domenico, Marco and Giuliano del Tasso, then among the best master joiners in Florence. The lower wheels in particular are especially admirable, being so arranged that the whole structure shall turn easily with the least derangement possible out of consideration for those bound above. He also made a scaffolding for the cleaning and repairing of the mosaics of S. Giovanni. This could be turned, raised, lowered and directed at will with such ease that two men could manage it, and it greatly increased Cecca's reputation.

When the Florentines were besieging Piancaldoli, Cecca contrived a mine by means of which the soldiers entered the city without striking a blow. But when the army proceeded to other places he was killed, as bad fortune would have it, in endeavouring to measure some altitudes from a difficult point. For he put his head out to let down a string, and a priest on the side of the enemy, who were more afraid of Cecca's ingenuity than of all the opposing forces, discharged a quarrel at him, which passed through his head, so that the poor fellow fell dead on the spot. His death was a great loss to the army and to his fellow-citizens, but there being no remedy, they brought the body back to Florence, where he was buried by the sisters in S. Piero Scheraggio. Beneath his portrait in marble the following epitaph was placed:

Fabrum magister Cicca, natus oppidis vel obsidendis vel tuendis,hic jacet. Vixit an. XXXXI. mens. IV. dies XIV. Obiit pro patria telo ictus. Piæ sorores monumentum fecerunt MCCCCXCIX.

DON BARTOLOMMEO,[1] ABBOT OF S. CLEMENTE, Illuminator and Painter

IT rarely happens that a man of good and exemplary life is not provided by Heaven with the best friends and an honourable abode, and is not greatly revered for his blameless character when alive, and lamented after his death by those who have known him. Such a man was Don Bartolommeo della Gatta, abbot of S. Clemente at Arezzo, who excelled in many things, and was a man of exemplary character. He was a monk of the Angioli at Florence, of the Camaldoline order, and in his youth, perhaps for the same reasons that have been related in the Life of Don Lorenzo, he proved himself a remarkable illuminator, and very skilful in design, as is shown by the illuminations which he did for the monks of S. Fiore and Lucilla in the abbey of Arezzo, and particularly in a missal given to Pope Sixtus, where the first page for private prayers contains a most beautiful Passion of Christ. Those also which are in the Duomo of S. Martino at Lucca are by his hand. Soon after this he was employed to do the abbey of S. Clemente at Arezzo by Mariotto Maldoli, an Aretine, general of the Camaldolines, a member of the same family as that Maldolo who gave to St. Romuald, the founder of the order, the place and site of Camaldoli, at that time called the field of Maldolo. Bartolommeo, as if grateful for this favour, afterwards did many things for the general and for his order. On the outbreak of the plague of 1468, the abbot, like many others, remained in his house, and devoted himself to making large figures, and, finding himself successful, he began to do more important things. The first was a St. Roch which he painted on a panel for the rectors of the fraternity at Arezzo, and which is now in their audience-chamber, the figure interceding with Our Lady for the people of Arezzo.[2] He introduced the piazza of the city, and the house of the fraternity, with some gravediggers burying the dead. He did yet another St. Roch like it for the church of S. Pietro, representing Arezzo as it then was, very different from its present form, and a third, which was far better than the other two, in a panel which is in the Lippi Chapel in the Pieve of Arezzo. This last St. Roch is a very fine and remarkable figure, and probably the best that he ever produced, it

---

[1] Professor Venturi gives reasons for the conclusion that there was no such person. The facts given here seem to apply to one Pietro Dei.
[2] Now in the Pinacoteca, Arezzo; painted about 1479.

being impossible to imagine a finer head or hands. In the same city of Arezzo he painted a panel of the Archangel Raphael in S. Piero, where the Servite friars are, and in the same place he drew the portrait of the Blessed Jacopo Filippo of Piacenza. Being invited to Rome, he did a scene in the Sistine Chapel in conjunction with Luca of Cortona and Pietro Perugino.[1] Returning to Arezzo, he did for the Chapel of the Gozzari in the Vescovado a St. Jerome in penance, the figure being lean and clean-shaven, with his eyes fixed intently upon the crucifix, while he strikes his breast, and shows the force of his struggle against the passions. For this work he made a large rock with some caves, the openings of which he filled with stories of the saint in very graceful small figures. After this he did a Coronation of the Virgin in fresco in a chapel of S. Agostino, for the nuns of the third order, it is said, which has been much admired, and is very well done. Below this, in another chapel, he has done an Assumption, with some angels in delicate draperies, forming a large picture. It has been much admired as a work in tempera, and indeed it shows good design, and was executed with extra-ordinary diligence. In the tympanum above the door of the church of S. Donato, in the citadel of Arezzo, he painted in fresco Our Lady with the Child, St. Donato and St. John Gualbert, all very fine figures. In the abbey of S. Fiore, in the same city, there is a chapel by his hand near the principal door, containing St. Benedict and other saints executed with much grace, skill and sweetness. He also painted a dead Christ in a chapel for Gentile of Urbino, bishop of Arezzo,[2] his close friend, with whom he passed nearly all his time in the episcopal palace. In a loggia he drew the bishop himself, his vicar, and Ser Matteo Francini, the bishop's notary of the bench, who is reading a bull to him, as well as his own portrait, and some canons of the city. For the same bishop he designed a loggia connecting the palace and the Vescovado, and on the same level as they are. The bishop wished to have his tomb constructed here in the form of a chapel, and Bartolommeo therefore worked hard at it, but at his death it was left unfinished, for though he instructed his successor to complete it he did nothing, as is usually the case when works are thus left. For the same bishop the abbot made a large and beautiful chapel in the old Duomo, but as it had a short life I will say no more about it. Besides this he worked in many places in the city, as, for example, three figures in the Carmine and the chapel of the nuns of S. Orsina, and a picture in tempera in the chapel of the high altar in the Pieve of S. Giuliano at Castiglione of Arezzo, containing a lovely Madonna, St. Julian and St. Michael, all excellent figures, particularly the St. Julian, who steadfastly regards the Christ in His Mother's arms, and seems greatly distressed at having killed his father and his mother.[1] In a chapel slightly below this there is a small door by him which used to belong to an old organ, on which is painted a St. Michael, considered remarkable, with a baby in a woman's arms, which seems alive. For the nuns of the Murate at Arezzo he did the chapel of the high altar, a much-admired painting. At Monte S. Savino he did a tabernacle opposite the palace of the Cardinal di Monte, which was considered very fine, and in Borgo S. Sepolcro, where the Vescovado now is, he did a chapel which won him great honour and profit. Don Clemente possessed a mind capable of all things, and, besides being a good musician, he made lead organs, and one of paper in S. Domenico, which has always remained sweet and good. There was another by his hand in S. Clemente, raised on high, with the keyboard below on a level with the choir. This was a good idea, for the place had but few monks, and he wished the organist to sing as well as play. This abbot was devoted to religion, being a true minister and not a squanderer of Divine things, and he greatly improved that place with buildings and paintings, restoring the principal chapel of his church and painting it all, and in two niches on either side he put St. Roch and St. Bartholomew, which have perished with the church. But to return to the abbot. He was a good and pious monk, and left as his pupil in painting Matteo Lappoli of Arezzo, who was a worthy and skilful artist, as is seen by his works in the chapel of St. Sebastian in St. Agostino, that saint being represented in a niche, made in relief. About him are painted St. Blaise, St. Roch, St. Anthony of Padua and St. Bernardino. In the arch of the chapel there is an Annunciation, while the four Evangelists are smoothly represented in fresco on the vaulting. There is another chapel in fresco by the same hand, on the left as one enters the side door, containing the Nativity and an Annunciation, the angel being a portrait of Giuliano Bacci, then a beautiful youth. Over this door, on the outside, he did an Annunciation, between St. Peter and St. Paul, the Madonna being a portrait of the mother of M. Pietro Aretino, the famous poet. In the chapel of St. Bernardino in St. Francesco he painted a life-like figure of the saint, which is the best figure that he ever did. In the Chapel of the Pietramaleschi in the Vescovado he did

[1] 1486. For this saint, see note vol. i., page 265.

a very fine St. Ignatius in tempera, and at the door opening on to the piazza in the Pieve he did St. Andrew and St. Sebastian. For the company of the Trinity he displayed great power of invention in the execution of a work done for Buoninsegna Buoninsegni of Arezzo, which may be numbered among the best which he ever did. This is a crucifix upon the altar between St. Martin and St. Roch, who are both kneeling. The one is a poor, shrivelled, hungry and ill-clothed man, from whom issue rays towards the wounds of the Saviour, whom he regards intently; the other is richly clothed in purple and fine linen, rubicund and joyful of countenance, and his rays, although they issue from his heart like those of the other, do not go straight to the wounds of Christ, but spread and enlarge through a country full of corn, wheat, cattle, gardens and other like things, while others descend towards the sea upon some vessels laden with merchandise, and others again to some benches where money is changed. All these were executed by Matteo with judgment, skill and diligence, but were destroyed not long afterwards to make a chapel. In the Pieve below the pulpit he made a Christ with the Cross for M. Lionardo Albergotti.

Another pupil of the abbot of S. Clemente was an Aretine friar of the Servites, who painted in colours the front of the house of the Belichini of Arezzo, and two chapels in fresco in S. Piero, next each other. Another pupil was Domenico Pecori of Arezzo, who did three figures in tempera at Sargiano, and a fine banner in oils for the company of St. Mary Magdalene, to be carried in procession, and a picture of St. Apollonia for M. Presentino Bisdomini in the chapel of St. Andrew in the Pieve, like the one mentioned above. He finished many things which his master had left, as, for instance, the picture of SS. Sebastian and Fabian, with the Madonna, for the family of the Benucci,[1] and in the church of S. Antonio he painted the picture for the high altar, containing a very devout Madonna, with some saints. The Madonna is adoring the Child, who is in her lap, and he has introduced a little angel kneeling, who holds up Jesus on a cushion, the Virgin not being able to support Him, as she has her hands folded in adoration. In the church of S. Giustino he painted a chapel of the Magi in fresco for M. Antonio Roselli, and a large picture in the Pieve for the company of the Madonna, representing Our Lady in the air, with the people of Arezzo beneath, comprising a number of portraits.[2] He was assisted in this work by a Spanish painter who worked skilfully in oils,

[1] Now at Campriano, near Arezzo.   [2] Pinacoteca, Arezzo.

Domenico not being so skilled in oils as in tempera. The same artist helped him with a picture for the company of la Trinità, containing the Circumcision of Our Lord,[1] considered very good, and a *Noli me tangere* in fresco in the garden of S. Fiore. Finally, he painted in the Vescovado for M. Donato Marinelli, the dean, a picture [2] containing many figures of good invention and design, and in high relief, which brought him much honour at the time, and has done since. As he was an old man, he called to his assistance il Capanna, a painter of Siena and a meritorious master who had done a number of walls in grisaille and many panels at Siene. If he had lived he would have won great honour in the art, to judge from the little which he did accomplish. For the fraternity of Arezzo Domenico had made a baldachino, painted in oils, a rich and costly thing, but a short while ago it was lent for a representation of St. John and St. Paul in S. Francesco to adorn a Paradise near the roof of the church, and the large number of lights caused a fire [3] which burned the picture, as well as the representative of God the Father, who, being bound, was unable to escape as the angels did, and there was a great loss of ecclesiastical adornments and injury to the spectators, who were panic-stricken and rushed to the door, about eighty of them being crushed, a most lamentable circumstance. The baldachino was subsequently restored with more richness and painted by Giorgio Vasari. Domenico next devoted himself to making windows, and there were three by his hand in the Vescovado, but they were destroyed by the artillery during the wars. Another pupil of the abbot was Angelo di Lorentino, painter,[4] who possessed no mean talent. He also worked at the door of S. Domenico, and with assistance he might have become an excellent master. The abbot died at the age of eighty-three, leaving the church of Our Lady of the Tears unfinished, after making the model. The edifice was afterwards completed by various masters. The abbot thus deserves praise as an illuminator, architect, painter and musician. His monks buried him in his abbey of S. Clemente, and his works have always been held in high repute in the city, where these lines may be read upon the tomb:

> *Pingebat docte Zeusis, condebat et ædes*
> *Nicon Pan capripes, fistula prima tua est.*
> *Non tamen ex vobis mecum certaverit ullus*
> *Quæ tres fecistis, unicus hæc facio.*

---

[1] Now in S. Agostino.   [2] Pinacoteca, **Arezzo**.
[3] In 1556.   [4] Who died 1527.

He died in 1461, after having enriched the art of illuminating with the beauties which characterise all his works. Some of his sheets in our book may serve as an example. His style was afterwards imitated by Girolamo Padoano in the illuminations in some books at S. Maria Novella, Florence, and by Gherardo, a Florentine illuminator, also called Vante, who is spoken of elsewhere, and whose works are mostly at Venice. I have inserted a notice upon him sent to me by some Venetian nobles. I have copied this exactly to satisfy those who have taken such pains to collect the information here given, adopting their own words, for as I have not seen the things myself I am unable to give an independent judgment.

GHERARDO, Illuminator of Florence
(1445-1498)

TRULY of all work in colours nothing resists the wind and weather longer than mosaics. This was recognised by Lorenzo de' Medici in his day, and being a man of understanding and one who inquired into ancient things, he endeavoured to reintroduce the art which had long been neglected, for, being so devoted to painting and sculpture, he naturally took delight in mosaics. Perceiving that Gherardo, then an illuminator and an ingenious spirit, was seeking to overcome the difficulties of this work, Lorenzo showed him great favour, for he always assisted those in whom he perceived the seeds of ability. Accordingly he associated him with Domenico del Ghirlandajo, inducing the wardens of S. Maria del Fiore to assign the chapels of the transepts to him.[1] Gherardo began on the chapel of the Sacrament, where the body of St. Zanobius is. Deriving great benefit from this, he would have accomplished the most remarkable things in conjunction with Domenico, as may be surmised from his uncompleted work there, had not death supervened. Besides his work in mosaic, Gherardo was a most delicate illuminator, while he also made large figures on the wall. Outside the S. Croce gate there is a tabernacle of his in fresco, and another in Florence, at the top of the via Larga, which has been much admired. On the wall of the church of S. Gilio at S. Maria Nuova, below the scenes of Lorenzo di Bicci, representing the consecration of the church by Pope Martin V., he painted the scene where the Pope

[1] In 1491.

invests the master with a habit and grants many privileges. This scene contained many figures which were smaller than seemed necessary, as they were cut across by a tabernacle containing a Madonna. This has at length been removed by Don Isidoro Montaguto, the present master, to restore a principal door of the house, and the remainder of the scene has been repainted by Francesco Brini, a young Florentine artist.

But to return to Gherardo. No master who was not very skilful could possibly have achieved what he did in fresco without the greatest diligence. For the same hospital Gherardo illuminated a large number of books, and did others for S. Maria del Fiore at Florence, and for Matthias Corvinus, King of Hungary. These last, after the king's death, were bought for a great sum by Lorenzo the Magnificent, together with some by Vante and other masters who worked for the king in Florence, and added to the renowned library which was afterwards built by Pope Clement VII., and is now made public by order of Duke Cosimo. Gherardo, having taken up painting from being an illuminator, composed a large sheet containing the four Evangelists, which were to be executed in mosaic in the chapel of St. Zanobius. Before this chapel was entrusted to him by Lorenzo the Magnificent, in order to show that he could work without an associate, he made a head of St. Zanobius of life-size, which is still in S. Maria del Fiore, and is placed on the altar of the saint or some other place on festival days as a remarkable work. While Gherardo was engaged upon these things some prints were brought to Florence, done in the German style by Martin [1] and Albert Dürer. As this style of engraving greatly pleased his fancy, Gherardo took it up, and copied some of them admirably with the burin, some good examples being in our book together with drawings by his hand. Gherardo painted a number of pictures which were sent abroad, one being in the chapel of St. Catherine of Siena in S. Domenico, at Bologna, containing a finely painted picture of the saint.[2] Over the Table of Indulgences in S. Marco, at Florence, he painted the lunette, full of graceful figures. But though he gave great pleasure to others, he never satisfied himself, except in mosaic. In that branch of art he was rather the rival than the colleague of Domenico Ghirlandajo. Had he lived longer he would have attained to great excellence in it, because he was willing to take great pains, and had discovered most of its secrets. Some insist that Attavante or Vante, the Florentine illuminator mentioned above, was, like Stefano, another Floren-

---

[1] Martin Schongauer.　　　　[2] Now Pinacoteca, Bologna.

tine illuminator, a pupil of Gherardo, but I think it is clear that as they were contemporaries, Attavante was rather the friend, companion and colleague of Gherardo than his pupil. Gherardo died well advanced in years, leaving all his artistic affairs to Stefano.[1] This Stefano shortly after took up architecture, and left illuminating and all its concerns to Boccardino the elder, who did most of the books in the Badia of Florence. Gherardo died at the age of sixty-three, his works dating about the year 1470.

DOMENICO GHIRLANDAJO,[2] Painter of Florence
(1449–1494)

DOMENICO DI TOMMASO DI GHIRLANDAJO, who for the excellence, size and multitude of his works deserves to be considered one of the best masters of his age, was meant by Nature to be a painter, and despite the opposition of his guardian, a thing which frequently spoils the best fruits of our great minds by diverting them from the things for which they are best fitted, he followed his natural bent and won great honour at his art for himself and his house, enriching and charming his age. His father put him with a goldsmith, in which trade he himself possessed considerable merit, the greater part of the silver votive offerings in the treasury of the Nunziata being by his hand, as well as the silver lamps of the chapel, destroyed in the siege of 1529. Tommaso was the first to invent and make fashionable the head ornament worn by Florentine girls called garlands (*ghirlande*), and from this circumstance he obtained the name of Ghirlandajo, not only because he was the original inventor, but because he had made a large quantity of rare beauty, so that everyone must needs have those which came from his shop. Being put with a goldsmith, but discontented with that trade, Domenico did nothing but design. Endowed by Nature with great ability, admirable taste and good judgment in painting, he always studied design, goldsmith as he was at first, and succeeded in becoming so facile that many relate that even while he was with the goldsmith he would draw everyone who passed the shop, making extraordinary likenesses, a story which is largely borne out by the number of excellent portraits which he produced. His first paintings were in the Chapel of the Vespucci at Ognissanti, representing a dead Christ and some saints, and a Misericordia over an arch, contain-

---

[1] Stefano Lunetti.   [2] Domenico Bigordi.

ing a portrait of Amerigo Vespucci, who navigated the Indies, while in the refectory he painted a Last Supper in fresco.[1] On the right-hand of the entrance to S. Croce he painted the story of St. Paulinus. Having thus acquired fame and credit, he did a chapel in S. Trinità for Francesco Sassatti with stories of St. Francis,[2] an admirable work, remarkable for its grace, finish and delicacy. In it he represented the Ponte S. Trinità with the palace of the Spini, the first scene showing the appearance of St. Francis in the air to raise a child of that family, with the women who see him arise, the grief at his death while they are carrying him to burial, and their joy and wonder at his resurrection. Here also are the friars issuing from the church, with the gravediggers following the cross for the purpose of burial, all very life-like, as are the other figures, who are marvelling and rejoicing at the miracle, affording no little pleasure to the rest of us. Among them are portraits of Maso degli Albizzi, M. Agnolo Acciaiuoli, M. Palla Strozzi, notable citizens and prominent in the history of Florence. Another scene shows St. Francis in the presence of the vicar, renouncing the inheritance of his father, Pietro Bernardone, and assuming the habit of penitence with its rope girdle. In the middle is his visit to Rome to obtain the confirmation of his order from Pope Honorius, presenting a rose to that pontiff in January. In this scene Domenico represented the consistory hall, the cardinals seated about it, and some steps approaching it on which are figures standing, among them being a portrait of Lorenzo de' Medici the Magnificent, the elder. He further painted there St. Francis receiving the stigmata, and finally his death and the lamentation of the friars, one of them represented kissing his hand, an act which could not be better presented than it is here. A bishop in his habit, wearing spectacles, is singing the vigil, and is shown to be merely a painting only because one does not hear him. In two pictures on either side he painted Francesco Secca kneeling, and Madonna Nera, his wife and her children, the latter being in the scene above where the boy is raised to life, with some beautiful maidens of the same family whose names I have not been able to find, all wearing the costumes of the day and making a pleasing picture. Besides this he did four sibyls in the vaulting, and outside the chapel an ornamentation on the front arch, showing how the Tiburtine sibyl caused the Emperor Octavian to adore Christ. This is a very skilfully executed fresco, the colouring being bright and attractive. He painted in tempera, as a companion to this work,

[1] 1480. [2] 1483-6.

a Nativity of Christ [1] which must excite the wonder of every thinking man, introducing his own portrait and some heads of shepherds, which are considered divine. The drawings for this sibyl and other parts of this work, notably the perspective of the Ponte S. Trinità in grisaille, are in our book. For the high altar of the Jesuit friars he painted a picture containing the following saints, kneeling: St. Just, bishop of Volterra, to whom the church was dedicated; St. Zanobius, bishop of Florence; the Angel Raphael; a St. Michael in magnificent armour, and others.[2] In truth, Domenico deserves praise, for he was the first to imitate the colours of ornaments of gold and other materials, and he did away in a great measure with those borders made by gilding over plaster or gypsum, which are more suited for cloth hangings than for the works of good masters. The most beautiful figure is the Madonna with the Child, surrounded by four little angels. This picture, which is of the highest merit for a work in tempera, was then placed in the church of those friars, outside the Pinti gate, but it was subsequently damaged, as will be said elsewhere, and it is now in the church of S. Giovannino, inside the S. Pier Gattolini gate, where the Jesuit convent stands. In the church of Cestello Domenico painted a picture, finished by his brothers David and Benedetto, containing the Visitation of Our Lady and some very beautiful heads of women.[3] In the church of the Innocenti he painted in tempera [4] a much-admired picture of the Magi, containing some fine heads and varied physiognomies of people both young and old, notably a head of the Virgin, displaying all the modesty, beauty and grace which art can impart to the Mother of God. On the screen of S. Marco he did another picture, and a Last Supper in the guest-chamber, both carefully finished. In the house of Giovanni Tornabuoni he did a round picture of the Magi, painted with care; and a scene of Vulcan forging thunderbolts for Jove at the Spedaletto for the Lorenzo de' Medici the elder, containing a number of nude figures. In the church of Ognissanti at Florence he painted a St. Jerome [5] surrounded by a quantity of books and instruments, in competition with Sandro Botticelli, now placed beside the door leading into the choir. This painting, as well as that of Sandro Botticelli, was removed without injury and set up in the middle of the church at the very time when these Lives were being printed for the second time, the friars having decided to remove the position of the choir. Domenico also painted the

<hr />

[1] Accademia, Florence; painted 1485. [2] Uffizi Gallery; painted 1480.
[3] Louvre; painted 1491. [4] In 1488, Uffizi. [5] In 1480.

tympanum of the door of S. Maria Ughi, and a small tabernacle for the art of the flax merchants. In Ognissanti he also did a fine St. George slaying the Serpent. He was, indeed, well versed in the methods of painting walls, and worked with great facility, though his compositions were finely finished. Being invited by Pope Sixtus IV. to Rome to paint his chapel with other artists,[1] he represented Christ calling Peter and Andrew from their nets, and the Resurrection of Christ, the greater part of which is now destroyed, for it was above the door, and it became necessary to replace a falling architrave.

There was in Rome at this time a rich merchant and great friend of Domenico named Francesco Tornabuoni. His wife having died in child-birth, as is related in the Life of Andrea Verocchio, Francesco caused her to be buried in the Minerva, as became her rank, and he wished Domenico to paint the entire front of the tomb and also to do a small picture in tempera there. Accordingly the artist did four scenes, two of St. John the Baptist and two of Our Lady, which were then much admired. Francesco treated Domenico so well that when the latter returned to Florence with honour and money he brought with him a letter to his patron's kinsman, Giovanni, describing how well he had done his work and how highly the Pope was delighted with his paintings. When Giovanni heard this he immediately resolved to employ Domenico on some great work which would do honour to himself and bring fame and riches to the artist. It happened that the principal chapel of S. Maria Novella, the convent of the Friars Preachers, had been already painted by Andrea Orcagna, but the roof of the vaulting being badly protected, it was almost entirely destroyed by the damp. Many citizens had wished to have it restored or newly painted, but the family of the Ricci, who were the patrons, had never been able to make up their minds, as they could not bear the expense themselves and would not grant the task to others from fear of losing their rights and their armorial bearings left them by their ancestors. Giovanni, being anxious that Domenico should paint this memorial for him, tried various expedients, and at last promised the Ricci that he would bear the entire cost, would recompense them in some way, and would have their arms put up in the most prominent and honourable part of the chapel. This was accepted, and a strictly worded agreement having been drawn up of the tenor indicated above, Giovanni entrusted the work to Domenico, who was to follow the original subjects, arranging that the price

[1] In 1481.

should be 1200 gold ducats, and if it should give satisfaction, 200 more. Domenico set to work, and never rested until in four years he had completed the task. This was in 1485, and it gave the utmost satisfaction to Giovanni, who frankly admitted that the 200 ducats had been fairly won, but intimated that he would prefer to keep to the first price. Domenico, who thought more of glory than of wealth, at once forgave him the extra amount, declaring that he was better pleased at having satisfied him than he could be with any payment that he might receive. After this Giovanni caused two large coats of arms to be carved in stone, those of the Tornaquinci and the Tornabuoni, and placed on pilasters outside the chapel, and on the arch other arms of the same family, namely those of the Giachinotti, Popoleschi, Marabottoni and Cardinali, as well as the first two. When Domenico afterwards did the altar-picture he caused a fine tabernacle of the Sacrament to be placed in a gilt ornament under an arch, as a finish to the picture, introducing the arms of the patrons, that is the Ricci, on a shield a quarter of a braccia high. But the best was to come, for when the chapel was un-covered the Ricci looked everywhere for their arms, and when they could not see them they went off to the magistracy of the Eight, taking their contract. But the Tornabuoni were able to show that the arms had been placed in the most honoured situa-tion, and if the Ricci could not see them it was their own fault, because they ought to be satisfied that their arms were placed near the Sacrament, than which no place was more holy. Ac-cordingly it was decided that things should remain as they were, and so they stand to this day. If anyone objects that this is outside my subject, I beg him to excuse me, because it was at the point of my pen, and serves to show, if nothing else, that poverty is at the mercy of wealth, and that wealth united to prudence may attain its ends without censure.

To return to the fine works of Domenico. In the first place, the vaulting of this chapel contains the four Evangelists, larger than life-size, and the wall with the window has St. Dominic, St. Peter Martyr, St. John going into the desert, the Annunciation, with many of the patron saints of Florence kneeling; above the windows, and at the bottom, a portrait of Giovanni Tornabuoni on the right-hand and of his wife on the left, which are said to be very life-like. On the right wall the scenes are divided into seven compartments, six large ones below occupying the width of the wall, and one above in the arch of the vaulting, twice the size of the others. The left wall has an equal number of spaces, and these scenes relate to St. John the Baptist. The first scene on the right represents Joachim being driven from the Temple, his own face exhibiting patience and those of the Jews contempt and hatred of those who, being childless, came to the Temple. This scene on the side towards the window contains four portraits. One of these, the old, clean-shaven man in a red cap, is Alesso Baldovinetti, Domenico's master in painting and mosaic. Another, standing bareheaded, his hand at his side, in a red mantle, with a blue vest beneath, is Domenico himself, drawn with the help of a mirror. The man with black hair and thick lips is Bastiano da S. Gemignano,[1] the artist's pupil and brother-in-law, and the other, with his back turned and wearing a cap, is Davidde Ghirlandajo, his brother, the painter. All these are said to be most excellent likenesses by those who knew the originals. The second scene is the Nativity of the Virgin, executed with great diligence. Among other remarkable things it contains a window which lights the chamber and actually deceives the beholder. Again, while St. Anne, stretched on her bed, receives the visit of some ladies, he introduced women washing the Infant with great care, pouring out water, drying, and other like services, and while each is attentive to her own duty, one of them holds the Child in her arms and makes it laugh by smiling, with a feminine grace truly worthy of a work of this great genius, each figure being distinguished in its various expressions. The third, which is above the first, represents the Virgin mounting the steps of the Temple, and contains a building diminishing correctly as it recedes from the eye, as well as a nude figure, which gave great satisfaction then, because such things were not common, although it is not so perfect as the more excellent ones of to-day. Besides this is the Marriage of the Virgin, the youths angrily breaking their rods, which did not flower like that of Joseph. This scene contains many figures and a good building. The fifth shows the Coming of the Magi to Bethlehem with a number of men, horses, dromedaries and other things, a very well-arranged scene. Next to this is the cruel crime of Herod against the Innocents, showing finely the struggles of the women, and the soldiers and horses striking and driving them. Of all his subjects this is the best, being carried out with judgment, ingenuity and great art. Here we see the cruelty of those who at Herold's command kill the poor children without pity for their mothers; one of the babes may be seen still at the breast and dying of a wound in the throat, so that it is sucking, or rather

---

[1] Bastiano Mainardi.

drinking, as much blood as milk, a sight that might well arouse pity even where the emotion has become extinct. Here again is a soldier who has taken a child by force, and as he is pressing it to him to kill it, the mother tears his hair with fury, forcing him to bend backwards. This displays three emotions very finely: first the death of the child who is cut open, then the cruelty of the soldier who is avenging himself on the babe for the pain which he is suffering, and third the mother, beholding her dead child, in her fury and grief seeking to stop the murderer from escaping scot-free, the whole for its remarkable judgment rather the work of a philosopher than a painter. Many other emotions are also represented, so that no beholder can doubt the excellence of the master. The seventh scene, in the top of the arch, is the Passing of Our Lady and her Assumption, with troops of angels, a number of figures, landscapes and other ornaments, in which Domenico's easy and skilful style usually abounds. The other wall contains the history of St. John; the first represents Zacharias sacrificing in the Temple, the appearance of the angel, and his dumbness because he would not believe. Wishing to show that the most notable persons came to these sacrifices, Domenico introduced a goodly number of Florentine citizens, who were then members of the Government, and especially all the members of Tornabuoni family, both young and old. In order to show that his age abounded in every kind of virtue, and particularly in letters, he introduced in a circle four half-figures talking together, at the bottom of the scenes. These were the most learned Florentines of the day, namely M. Marsilio Ficino in a canon's dress; Cristofano Landino next, in a red mantle and a black ribbon round his throat; Demetrius the Greek [1] in the middle, turning round and lifting his hand slightly; M. Angelo Poliziano, all full of life and energy. The next scene, on a level with the last, is the Visitation of Our Lady and St. Elizabeth, accompanied by women wearing the costumes of the day, among them a portrait of Ginevra de' Benci, a most beautiful girl of the time. The third scene, above the first, is the birth of St. John, with a beautiful idea that, while Elizabeth is in bed and visited by her neighbours and a nurse is suckling the child, a woman is eagerly calling the attention of the visitors to the wonder that has come to her mistress in her old age; and lastly there is a woman bringing fruit and wine from the city, in conformity with the Florentine custom. This is very fine. In the fourth scene, next to this, Zacharias, still dumb, is marvelling

---

[1] The figure is Gentile de' Becchi, bishop of Arezzo.

that a son has been born to him, and as they ask him what the
name shall be, he writes on his knees, regarding the child all the
while, whom a woman is holding, kneeling reverently before
him, making the words "His name shall be John," to the wonder
of many other figures who appear to question whether it be true
or no. The fifth contains the preaching to the multitudes, showing
the attention of the people in hearing new things, notably the
scribes listening to John who seem to be mocking, so much do
they hate him; many men and women being here both standing
and sitting in various fashions. The next scene shows John
baptising Christ, his reverential attitude displaying the belief
which he had in that sacrament, and as this led to the most
important results he represented a crowd of naked and bare-
footed figures waiting to be baptised, their faces displaying faith
and desire, one especially who is taking off his shoe being energy
itself. The last scene, in the arch next the vaulting, is the sumptuous banquet of Herod, with the dancing of Herodias,[1] and a
troop of servants performing their various duties. It contains
a large building shown in perspective, and in conjunction with
the paintings displays Domenico's skill. He did the altarpiece,
which stands alone, in tempera, and the other figures which are
in the six pictures. Besides a Madonna, who is seated in the air
with the Child, surrounded by the other saints, there are St.
Laurence and St. Stephen, figures full of life, as well as the St.
Vincent and St. Peter Martyr, who only lack the power of speech.[2]
It is true that a part of the picture was left unfinished owing to
his death, but he had done so much that it only wanted the
finishing touches to some figures in the background of the
Resurrection of Christ, and three figures in the square spaces,
afterwards finished by Benedetto and Davidde Ghirlandajo, his
brothers. This chapel was reputed a most beautiful, grand, ornate
and lovely work for the brightness of the colouring, the skill and
finish of the wall painting, and because there are few retouches
a secco, not to speak of the powers of invention and composition
displayed. Certainly Domenico deserves the highest praise from
every point of view, but especially for the life he has infused into
the heads, which are really the portraits of many distinguished
people. For the same Giovanni Tornabuoni he painted a chapel
at the Casa Maccherelli, his villa, not far from the city, on the
River Terzolle, which is now half in ruins owing to its being near
the stream, and has stood roofless for many years, watered by
the rains and scorched by the sun. Nevertheless, the painting

has stood as if it had been protected, such is the quality of fresco-work when well done and not retouched *a secco*. In the hall of the palace of the Signoria, which contains the marvellous clock of Lorenzo della Volpaia, Domenico painted a number of Florentine saints [1] richly adorned. So fond was he of work and so anxious to please that he directed his pupils to accept whatever commissions should be brought to his workshop, even though it were hoops for the women's baskets, declaring that if they would not paint them he would do it himself, and that no one should leave his shop dissatisfied. When household cares were laid upon him he complained bitterly, and for this reason he entrusted all expenditure to his brother David, saying: "Leave me to work while you make provision, because, now that I have begun to master my art, I feel sorry that I am not employed to paint the entire circuit of the walls of Florence," thus displaying his determined and resolute spirit. For S. Martino at Lucca he did a picture of SS. Peter and Paul.[2] He did the front of the principal chapel of the abbey of Settimo outside Florence in fresco, and two panels in tempera on the screen of the church. In Florence he did many pictures, both round and square, which are not to be seen because they are in private houses. He decorated the niche at the high altar in the Duomo of Pisa, and worked at many places in that city, representing on the front of the opera the scene when King Charles, a portrait from life, protects the city.[3] In S. Girolamo he did two panels in tempera for the Jesuits, one of them for the high altar. In the same place there is a picture by him of St. Roch and St. Sebastian,[4] given to the fathers by some member of the Medici family, for which reason they have decorated it with the arms of Pope Leo X.

It is said that when Domenico was drawing antiquities at Rome, such as arches, baths, columns, colosseums, amphi-theatres, aqueducts, etc., his drawing was so exact that he was able to work with his eye unaided by rule or compass, and that the dimensions were as accurate as if he had measured them. When he drew the colosseum he introduced a figure to scale which, when it was tested by the masters after his death, proved most correct. Over a door in the cemetery at S. Maria Nuova he painted in fresco a St. Michael armed, the reflection on the armour being excellent, an effect little practised before his day. At the abbey of Passignano of the monks of Vallombrosa he did

---

[1] 1482-4.   [2] In 1479.
[3] Probably by David Ghirlandaio, as Charles VIII. of France was not there until 1495, a year after Domenico's death.
[4] Now in the Museo Civico, Pisa.

some things in conjunction with his brother David and with
Bastiano da S. Gimignano. Before he arrived the monks entertained the others badly, and they requested the abbot to cause
them to be better served, as it was not right that they should
be treated like workmen. The abbot promised, and excused
himself on the ground that it was due to the ignorance of the
monks in charge, and not through malice. Domenico arrived,
and there was no alteration, so that David, meeting the abbot
one day, complained again, saying that he did not do this for
his own sake, but on account of the merits and talents of his
brother. The abbot, like a fool, could make no reply. That
evening, when they sat down to supper, the forestarius came in
with a tray full of porringers and coarse pastry, just as he had
done before. At this David rose in a rage, emptied the soup on
the friar's head, and, taking the bread off the table, struck him
with it, so that he was carried half-dead to his cell. The abbot,
who was already in bed, ran down on hearing the noise, believing
that the monastery was falling. On finding the friar in such
a sorry plight, he began to rail at David. Infuriated at this,
David replied, telling him to be gone and that Domenico was
worth more than all the swinish abbots who had ever lived
in the monastery. The abbot, thinking better of the matter,
endeavoured from that moment to treat the artists more according to their worth. When this work was completed, Domenico
returned to Florence and painted a picture for the Sig. di Carpi,
and sent another to Rimini to Carlo Malatesta, who put it in
his chapel in S. Domenico.[1] This painting was in tempera, representing three figures, and small scenes beneath, and bronze-
coloured figures behind, executed with great art. He did two other
pictures for the Camaldolite abbey of S. Giusto outside Volterra,
at the command of Lorenzo the Magnificent, very beautiful
works.[2] This was because the Cardinal Giovanni de' Medici,
Lorenzo's son, who afterwards became Leo X., held the abbey
in commendam. This abbey was restored a few years ago by the
Very Rev. M. Gio. Battista Bava of Volterra, who also held it
in commendam to the congregation of Camaldoli. By Lorenzo's
influence Domenico afterwards went to Siena, the prince giving
security for the 20,000 ducats required for doing the façade of
of the Duomo in mosaic.[3] Domenico set to work with good

[1] Now in the Palazzo del Comune. The figures are SS. Vincenzio, Ferrario, Sebastian and Roch.
[2] There is a Christ in Glory in the Municipio, Volterra, painted in 1492.
[3] The work was done by David Ghirlandaio, the contract being signed in 1493.

courage and in his best style. But, being cut off by death, he
left it unfinished just as the chapel of St. Zanobius at Florence
was interrupted by the death of Lorenzo, after Domenico had
begun to decorate it with mosaics,[1] with the assistance of
Gherardo the illuminator. Over the side door of S. Maria del
Fiore leading to the Servites there is a very fine Annunciation
in mosaic by Domenico, and nothing better has been produced
by modern masters. Domenico used to say that painting was
design, but that the true painting for eternity was mosaic.
Bastiano Mainardi of S. Gimignano remained with him to learn,
and became a very skilful master in fresco. He accompanied
Domenico to S. Gimignano, and there they painted the beautiful
chapel of St. Fina.[2] Pleased with the submissiveness and good
behaviour of Bastiano, Domenico considered him worthy to
marry one of his sisters, and thus their friendship was converted
into relationship, the liberality of the master rewarding the skill
acquired by the pupil through his labours. From a cartoon prepared by Domenico, Bastiano painted in the Chapel of the Baroncelli and Bandini in S. Croce Our Lady ascending into heaven
with St. Thomas beneath receiving her girdle, a beautiful work
in fresco. The two together painted a number of scenes with
small figures in a chamber of the palace of the Spannocchi at
Siena; and at Pisa, besides the niche in the Duomo already
mentioned, they did the arch of that chapel, filling it with angels,
painted the organ shutters and began to gild the ceiling.[3] When
they were about to do some very considerable works at Pisa
and Siena Domenico fell sick of a fever, which carried him off
in five days. Whilst he lay ill, the Tornabuoni sent him a gift of
100 ducats of gold, showing their friendship and good-will, and
a sense of the services which Domenico had rendered to their
house. He lived forty-four years, and was lamented deeply by
his brothers David and Benedetto and his son Ridolfo. They
buried him in S. Maria Novella, the loss being deeply felt by his
friends. When his death became known many noted foreign
artists wrote letters of sympathy to his relations. He left as his
pupils David and Benedetto Ghirlandai, Bastiano Mainardi of
S. Gimignano, Michelagnolo Buonarroti of Florence, Francesco
Granaccio, Niccolo Cieco, Jacopo del Tedesco, Jacopo dell'
Indaco, Baldino Baldinetti, and other masters, all Florentines.
He died in 1493. Domenico enriched the modern art of working
in mosaic infinitely more than any other Tuscan, as his works,

[1] Also by David, begun in 1491.
[2] In 1475. [3] In 1473.

though few, amply demonstrate. On this account he deserves high rank and honour in his profession and more than customary praise after his death.

ANTONIO and PIERO POLLAJUOLO, Painters and Sculptors of Florence

(1432–1498; 1443–1496)

MANY men timidly begin with base things, but, their courage increasing with their ability, they attack more formidable tasks, rise into the heavens with their soaring ideas, and, aided by fortune, frequently obtain the favour of some prince who, being well served, is bound to reward their labours, so that their descendants profit richly from their efforts. Thus they proceed through life, always winning fresh renown and filling the world with wonder. Such was the career of Antonio and Piero di Pollajuolo, who were much valued in their day for the great talents which they had acquired by their industry and labour. They were born at Florence within a few years of each other, their father being a man of low birth and not in very easy circumstances. Perceiving the keen intelligence of his sons by many signs, and being without the means to have them taught letters, he put Antonio with the goldsmith Bartoluccio Ghiberti, then a famous master of the craft, and Piero with Andrea dal Castagno, then the best painter in Florence. Antonio, being instructed by Bartoluccio, learned to set jewels and prepare silver enamelwork, and was considered the most skilful workman with his tools that the art possessed. Thus Lorenzo Ghiberti, being then busy with the doors of S. Giovanni, and happening to see Antonio's work, employed him as well as many other youths. Antonio, being set to work on one of the festoons which may still be seen there, made a quail so finely that it lacks nothing but the power of flight. Antonio had not spent many weeks at that employment before he surpassed all his fellows in design and patience, as well as in ingenuity and diligence. His talents and fame increasing, he left Bartoluccio and Lorenzo, and opened a magnificent goldsmith's shop of his own in the Mercato nuovo. He practised this art for many years, designing and making wax models and other fancies in relief, so that he soon gained the well-merited reputation of being the first man in his trade.

At this time there lived another goldsmith named Maso Finiguerra, with an extraordinary but well merited reputation. In engraving and niello no one could put so many figures into small or large spaces as he, as may be seen by some patines done by him in S. Giovanni at Florence, with tiny scenes relating to the Passion of Christ. He designed excellently, and our book contains a number of sheets of his drawings of draped and nude figures and water-colour sketches. In competition with him Antonio did some scenes which equalled Maso's for diligence and surpassed them in design. The consuls of the art of the merchants, recognising the worth of Antonio, proposed to employ him to do some patines in silver for the altar of S. Giovanni, such as had been executed by various masters at different times. This was done, and his work proved so excellent that they may be recognised as the best among all the others. They represented the banquet of Herod and the dancing of Herodias (*sic*), but the most beautiful of all is the St. John [1] in the middle of the altar, entirely chiselled, and greatly admired. After this the wardens allotted to him the silver candelabra to do, three braccia each, and the cross in proportion. [2] He executed these with such elaborate carving, and finished them so beautifully that they have always been considered marvellous by strangers as well as by natives. He spared no pains in his work, whether in gold, silver or enamel. Among them there are some fine patines in S. Giovanni, so well coloured that it would hardly be possible to make better ones with the brush; while the churches of Florence and Rome and other places in Italy contain some marvellous enamels by him. He taught his art to Mazzingo [3] of Florence, and to Giuliano del Facchino, both meritorious masters, and to Giovanni Turini of Siena, who easily surpassed his companions. From the days of Antonio di Salvi, who did many good things, including a large silver cross in the Badia at Florence, until now, no work of extraordinary merit has been seen in that art. Many of the works of these men and of the Pollajuoli have gone into the melting-pot for the requirements of the city during the war.

Antonio foresaw that his art did not promise a lasting fame to his labours, and resolved to take up something else. As his brother Piero was a painter, he went to him to learn the art of manipulating colours. He found this art so different from that

---

[1] Done in 1452 by Michelozzo Michelozzi; now in the Opera del Duomo.
[2] The cross is by Betto Betti.
[3] Antonio de' Mazzinghi.

of the goldsmith, that if he had not resolved entirely to abandon his former pursuit he would probably have returned to it. But being impelled onwards by a sense of shame, he learned the art of colouring in a few months, and became an excellent master. He identified himself completely with Piero, and in conjunction they produced a quantity of pictures. Among these was an oil-painting for the cardinal of Portugal, a great lover of painting, placed upon the altar of his chapel in S. Miniato al Monte, outside Florence.[1] It represented St. James the Apostle, St. Eustace and St. Vincent, and has been much admired. Piero, who had learned oil-painting from Andrea dal Castagno, painted in that medium the wall spaces under the architrave below the vaulting, doing some prophets, and an Annunciation with three figures in a lunette. For the captains of the Parte he did a Madonna and Child in a lunette surrounded by a border of cherubim, all in oils. On a pilaster of S. Michele in Orto they painted in oils on canvas the Angel Raphael with Tobias,[2] and did some Virtues[3] in the Mercatanzia of Florence, in the place where the magistrate sits in judgment. He drew the portrait of M. Poggio, secretary of the Signoria of Florence, who continued the history of Florence by M. Leonardo d'Arezzo, and M. Giannozzo Manetti, a learned and notable person in the Pro consolo, where portraits of the Florentine poet Zanetti da Strada Domenico Acciaiuoli, and others, had been done by other masters. In the Chapel of the Pucci at S. Sebastiano of the Servites he did the altarpiece, a fine work, containing some remarkable horses, nude figures and perspectives, with St. Sebastian, a portrait of Gino di Ludovico Capponi.[4] This work was the most admired of all that Antonio did. He always copied Nature as closely as possible, and has here represented an archer drawing the bowstring to his breast and bending down to charge it, putting all the force of his body into the action, for we may see the swelling of his veins and muscles and the manner in which he is holding his breath. This was not the only figure executed with such considerations, but all the others are alike in their varied attitudes, showing the ingenuity and thought which he bestowed upon the work. This was fully recognised by Antonio Pucci, who gave him 300 crowns for it, declaring that he was barely paying him for the colours. It was finished in

[1] Painted 1465; now in the Uffizi. Berenson considers it entirely the work of Piero.
[2] Painted in 1469; now in the Turin Gallery.
[3] Now in the Uffizi.
[4] Painted 1475; now in the National Gallery, London.

1475. Encouraged by his success, Antonio painted a St. Christopher[1] at S. Miniato between the towers, outside the gate, ten braccia high, done so well and in such a modern style that it was the best-proportioned figure of its size produced up to that time. He then painted a crucifix on canvas, with St. Antonino, now placed in his chapel in S. Marco. In the palace of the Signoria of Florence he did a St. John the Baptist at the Catena door, and in the Casa Medici he did for the elder Lorenzo three Hercules in three pictures, each five braccia high, the one where he crushes Antæus,[2] a very fine figure, with a splendid representation of the force of the hero, the muscles and nerves being all braced for the effort, while the grinding of the teeth and the attitude of the head accord with the tension of the other members. The figure of Antæus is no less remarkable, as all life is being crushed out of him by the grasp of Hercules, and he expires with open mouth. In the next Hercules is killing the lion, with his left knee on its chest, forcing apart the creature's jaws with his hands, setting his teeth and bracing his arms the while, the animal clawing at his arms in self-defence. The third, in which he is killing the hydra, is truly marvellous, especially as the colouring of the creature is of the brightest and most effective hue. Here we perceive the venom, the fire, the fury, all represented with a vigour worthy of admiration and imitation by all good artists. For the company of S. Angelo at Arezzo he painted a banner with a crucifix on one side and on the other St. Michael fighting the dragon, of remarkable excellence. St. Michael is boldly confronting the serpent, grinding his teeth and frowning, so that he actually seems to have come down from heaven for the purpose of wreaking the vengeance of God upon the pride of Lucifer. It is really a marvel. Antonio's treatment of the nude is more modern than that of any of the masters who preceded him, and he dissected many bodies to examine their anatomy, being the first to show how the muscles must be looked for to take their proper place in figures. He engraved a battle scene on copper of all these, surrounded by a chain, and followed this up by a number of engravings far superior to any done by his predecessors. Having become famous among artists, he was invited to Rome on the death of Pope Sixtus IV. by his successor Innocent. There he made a metal tomb for Innocent, representing him seated and in the act of benediction, which

---

[1] Now in the Metropolitan Museum, New York. Berenson considers it the work of Piero.

[2] These large paintings have disappeared. The Uffizi possesses two small panels by Antonio of Hercules and Antæus and Hercules and the Hydra.

was placed in S. Pietro, and he did another very sumptuous tomb for Pope Sixtus, set up in the chapel named after him,[1] richly decorated and standing alone. It contains a fine recumbent effigy of that pope. The tomb of Innocent stands in S. Pietro next the chapel containing the lance of Christ. It is said that Antonio designed the Belvedere Palace for Pope Innocent, though the building was carried out by others, because he had no great experience in such work. Both brothers, having become rich, died in 1498, within a short time of each other, and were buried by their relations in S. Piero ad Vincula. Their portraits in two marble medallions were set up by the middle door on the left-hand side as one enters the church, with the following epitaph:

Antonius Pullarius patria Florentinus pictor insignis, qui duor. pont. Xisti et Innocentii aerea moniment. miro opific. expressit re famil. composita ex test. hic se cum Petro fratre condi voluit. Vixit an. LXXII. Obiit an. sal. M.IID.

Antonio also made a metal bas-relief representing a fight between nude figures, which went to Spain. There is a plaster cast of this fine work in the possession of the artists at Florence. After his death a model was discovered for an equestrian statue of Francesco Sforza, Duke of Milan, which he did for Ludovico Sforza. There are two versions of this design in our book: in the one Verona is represented beneath, in the other the figure is in full armour, and on a pedestal full of battle scenes he makes the horse tread upon an armed man. I have not yet been able to discover why these designs were not carried out. He also made some fine medals, one especially of the conspiracy of the Pazzi, with the heads of Lorenzo and Giuliano de' Medici, and on the reverse the choir of S. Maria del Fiore and the whole incident just at it happened. He also made the medals of some of the popes, and many other things well known to artists.

Antonio was seventy-two at his death and Piero sixty-five. He left many pupils, amongst them Andrea Sansovino. During the course of a most fortunate life Antonio came into contact with very rich popes, while his native city was at the height of her artistic appreciation. Thus he was greatly valued, but if he had lived in unprosperous times he would not have succeeded so well, because they are very unfavourable to the sciences in which men take delight. From his design two dalmaticas, a chasuble and a cope were made for S. Giovanni at Florence of

[1] Pope Sixtus died in 1484; the tomb was made 1490-93.

double brocade, all of one piece without any seam, the borders and ornamentation consisting of scenes from the life of St. John embroidered by Paolo da Verona, a marvellous master at such work, the most skilful to be found, who executed the figures with the needle no less finely than Antonio did them with the brush, so that the patient sewing of the one was not less useful than the skilful designing of the other. The production of this work took twenty-six years, and it looks like a piece of colouring, though it is far more durable. This art is now all but lost, the stitches being now made much longer, rendering the work at once less durable and less pleasing to the eye.

SANDRO BOTTICELLO, Painter of Florence

(1444–1510)

IN these same days of Lorenzo de' Medici the Magnificent, which was a veritable golden age for men of genius, flourished Alessandro, called Sandro according to our custom, and di Botticello, for reasons which I shall give presently. He was the son of Mariano Filipepi, a citizen of Florence, who brought him up with care, teaching him everything which children are usually set to learn before the age when they are first apprenticed to trades. Although Sandro quickly mastered anything that he liked, he was always restless and could not settle down at school to reading, writing and arithmetic. Accordingly his father, in despair at his waywardness, put him with a goldsmith who was known to him called Botticello, a very reputable master of the craft. Very close and friendly relations then existed between the goldsmiths and the painters, so that Sandro, who was an ingenious lad and devoted to drawing, became attracted to painting, and resolved to take it up. When he had told his wish to his father, the latter, who knew his whims, took him to Frà Filippo of the Carmine, an admirable painter of the day, and it was agreed that he should teach Sandro, as the boy desired. Devoting himself heart and soul to his art, Sandro followed and imitated his master so well that Frà Filippo became very fond of him and taught him so carefully that he soon attained to an excellence that no one would have thought possible. While still young he painted for the Mercatanzia of Florence a Fortitude for the series of the Virtues done by An-

tonio and Piero del Pollajuolo.[1] In the Chapel of the Bardi in
S. Spirito, Florence, he painted a panel [2] which is diligently
executed and well finished, containing some olives and palms
produced with whole-hearted delight. For the Convertite nuns
he did a panel, and another for those of S. Barnaba.[3] On the screen
of Ognissanti, by the door leading into the choir, he painted a
St. Augustine [4] for the Vespucci, in which he endeavoured to
surpass all his contemporaries, but especially Domenico Ghirlandajo, who had done a St. Jerome on the other side. This
work proved very successful, the head of the saint being expressive of profound thought and quick subtlety, such as are usually
possessed by those who are always examining into difficult and
abstruse questions. As I have said in the Life of Ghirlandajo, this
painting was removed without suffering damage in 1564. Having
thus won name and fame, Sandro was employed by the art of
Porta S. Maria to do a Coronation of the Virgin [5] for S. Marco,
with a choir of angels, and he executed this commission admirably. In the Casa Medici he did many things for Lorenzo the
Magnificent, the elder, notably a life-size Pallas [6] above a design
of vine-branches flaming fire, and also a St. Sebastian. In
S. Maria Maggiore, at Florence, there is a fine Pieta [7] of small
figures beside the Chapel of the Panciatichi. For various houses
in the city he did round pictures, and a goodly number of nude
female figures, two of which are now at Castello, a villa of Duke
Cosimo. One is a Birth of Venus [8] wafted to land by the breezes,
with cupids; the other is also a Venus in company with the
Graces and flowers, denoting Spring,[9] expressed by him with
much grace. In the house of Giovanni Vespucci in the via de'
Servi, now Piero Salviati's, he did a number of pictures round
a room, framed in an ornamental border of walnut, and figures
full of life and beauty. In the Casa Pucci he did Boccaccio's
story of Nastagio degli Onesto,[10] in small figures, the series
consisting of four pictures of great beauty and grace. He further

[1] Done about 1468, now in the Uffizi.
[2] A Madonna between St. John the Baptist and St. John the Evangelist,
now in the Berlin Gallery.
[3] Now in the Uffizi, Florence.
[4] In 1480.
[5] Probably painted in 1481; now in the Uffizi, Florence.
[6] This seems to be the picture discovered in the Pitti palace in 1895,
painted in 1490, and now in the Uffizi.
[7] Now in the Pinakothek, Munich.
[8] Uffizi.
[9] Uffizi, Florence, painted about 1478.
[10] Decameron Day 5, Novello 8.

did a round picture of the Epiphany. In a chapel of the monks
of Cestello he did an Annunciation.[1] By the side door of S. Piero
Maggiore he did a panel for Matteo Palmieri, with a large
number of figures representing the Assumption of Our Lady,[2]
with zones of patriarchs, prophets, apostles, evangelists, martyrs,
confessors, doctors, virgins, and the orders of angels, the whole
from a design given to him by Matteo, who was a worthy and
learned man. He executed this work with the greatest mastery
and diligence, introducing the portraits of Matteo and his wife
on their knees. But although the great beauty of this work
might well have silenced envy, some evil-disposed persons, who
could find no other fault with it, said that Matteo and Sandro
were guilty of grave heresy. Whether this be true or not, I cannot
say, but I know that Sandro's figures are admirable for the pains
which he has taken and the manner in which he has made the
circles of the heavens, introducing foreshortening and spaces
between the groups of angels, while the general design is excellent.
At this time Sandro was commissioned to paint a small panel,
with figures three-quarters of a braccia high, which was placed
in S. Maria Novella on the main wall of the church between the
two doors, on the left-hand side of the middle door on entering.
The subject is the Adoration of the Magi,[3] remarkable for the
emotion of the elderly man, who overflows with love as he
kisses the foot of Our Lord, clearly showing that he has attained
the end of his long journey. This king is a portrait of Cosimo
de' Medici, the elder, and is the finest of all that are now extant
for its life and vigour. The second is Giuliano de' Medici, the
father of Pope Clement VII., doing reverence with absorbed
devotion and offering his gift. The third, who is also kneeling
and appears to be adoring and giving thanks while he confesses
the true Messiah, is Cosimo's son Giovanni. The beauty of the
heads in this scene is indescribable, their attitudes all different,
some full-face, some in profile, some three-quarters, some bent
down, and in various other ways, while the expressions of the
attendants, both young and old, are greatly varied, displaying the
artist's perfect mastery of his profession. Sandro further clearly
shows the distinction between the suites of each of the kings.
It is a marvellous work in colour, design and composition, and
the wonder and admiration of all artists. It brought Sandro
such a reputation in Florence and abroad that Pope Sixtus IV.

[1] About 1490.
[2] Painted about 1472, now in the National Gallery, ascribed to Botticini.
[3] Uffizi, painted 1477.

entrusted him with the direction of the painting of the chapel which he was building in his palace at Rome. Here Sandro painted the following subjects: Christ tempted by the devil; Moses slaying the Egyptian and receiving drink from the daughter of Jethro the Midianite; the sacrifice of the sons of Aaron and the fire from heaven which consumed them, with some of the canonised popes in the niches above.[1] By these he won yet greater renown among many rivals who were working with him, Florentines and natives of other cities, and he received a goodly sum of money from the Pope. But he spent all during his stay at Rome in his usual thoughtless way, and after finishing his section of the work he uncovered it, and straightway left for Florence.[2] Being of a sophistical turn of mind, he there wrote a commentary on a portion of Dante and illustrated the *Inferno*,[3] which he printed, spending much time over it, and this abstension from work led to serious disorders in his living. He printed many other drawings, but in an inferior style, because the plates were badly engraved, his best work being the triumph of the faith of Frà Girolamo Savonorola of Ferrara. Of this sect he was an adherent, and this led him to abandon painting, and, as he had no income, it involved him in the most serious trouble. But remaining obstinate in his determination and becoming a Piagnone, as they were called, he gave up work, and owing to this he became so poor in his old age that if Lorenzo de' Medici the Magnificent, while he lived, had not assisted him, for he had done many things for that prince at the Spedaletto at Volterra, and if he had not been helped by friends and many wealthy men who admired his genius, he would practically have died of hunger. In S. Francesco, outside the S. Miniato gate, there is a circular picture by Sandro of a Madonna and angels, of life-size, which was considered very beautiful.

Sandro was a merry fellow and played many pranks on his pupils and friends. It is related that he once had a pupil named Biagio, who made a picture for sale like the one just mentioned, and Sandro disposed of it to a citizen for six gold florins. Finding Biagio, Sandro said, "I have sold your picture at last, but the purchaser wants it set up this evening to have a better view of it. Go to the citizen's house to-morrow, taking it with you, so that when he has seen it well placed he may pay you

[1] Commissioned in 1481. Vasari is at fault in some of the subjects; he misconstrues the gallantry of Moses, and the "sacrifice of the sons of Aaron" really represents the purification of a leper as prescribed in Leviticus xiv. 2-7.
[2] In 1482.
[3] The drawings were done between 1492 and 1497.

the price." Biagio was delighted, and thanked his master, and hastened to the workshop, setting the picture fairly high up, and departed. Thereupon Sandro and another pupil called Jacopo made eight hoods of paper, such as the citizens use, and fastened them with white wax to the heads of the angels surrounding the Madonna. The next morning up came Biagio with the citizen who had bought the picture and who was aware of the joke. When Biagio entered the shop and looked up, he saw his Madonna seated not in the midst of angels, but of the Signoria of Florence, with their hoods. He was about to excuse himself to his patron, but as the latter said nothing but praise of the picture, he kept his counsel. Finally Biagio went home with the citizen and received the payment of six florins as settled by his master. Meanwhile Sandro and Jacopo had removed the paper hoods, and on Biagio's return he saw his angels were as they should be and no longer hooded citizens. Lost in amazement, he knew not what to say. At length he turned to Sandro and said, "Master, I do not know if I am dreaming or awake. When I came here these angels had red hoods on their heads and now they have none; what does it mean?" "You must be mad, Biagio," said Sandro; "this money has turned your brain. If they had been like that do you think the citizen would have bought it?" "That is true," replied Biagio, "he said nothing to me about it, and I certainly thought it strange." All the other boys in the shop surrounded him, and together they succeeded in making him believe that his head had been in a whirl.

A cloth-weaver once came to live next door to Sandro, and put up eight looms, which made such a noise when they were at work as to deafen poor Sandro, making the whole house shake, the walls not being so strong as they might have been, so that for one reason and another he was unable to work or remain in his house. He several times begged his neighbour to remedy this nuisance, but the man declared that he could and would do what he pleased in his own house. This aroused Sandro's ire, and his wall being higher than his neighbour's, he balanced a huge stone upon the top of it, which looked as if it would fall at the slightest movement and break the roofs, ceiling and looms of the man below. Terrified by this danger, the weaver had recourse to Sandro, who, adopting his own phrase, replied that he would do as he pleased in his own house. Unable to obtain any fuller satisfaction, the man was forced to come to terms and to act like a good neighbour. It is also related that for a jest Sandro accused a friend of his of heresy to the vicar. The friend appeared and demanded who accused him and of what. Learning that it was Sandro who said that he held the opinion of the Epicureans that the soul dies with the body, he asked to see his accuser before the judge. When Sandro arrived he said, "It is true that I hold this opinion of this man, for he is a brute. Do not you yourselves think him a heretic, since without any education, and scarce knowing how to read, he writes a commentary on Dante, taking his name in vain?"

It is said that Sandro was extraordinarily fond of those whom he knew to be students of the arts, and that he made a good deal, but wasted all through his carelessness and want of control. Having become old and useless, he fell to walking with two crutches, as he could not stand straight, and in this state of decrepitude he died at the age of seventy-eight, being buried in Ognissanti in 1515. There are two female heads in profile by his hand in the wardrobe of Duke Cosimo, one of whom is said to be the mistress of Giuliano de' Medici, Lorenzo's brother, and the other Madonna Lucrezia de' Tornabuoni, Lorenzo's wife.[1] The same place has a Bacchus of Sandro raising a cask with both hands and putting it to his lips, a very graceful figure. In the Chapel of the Impagliata, in the Duomo of Pisa, he began an Assumption, with a choir of angels, but as it did not please him he left it unfinished. In S. Francesco at Montevarchi he did the picture of the high altar and two angels in the Pieve of Empoli, on the same side as Rossellino's St. Sebastian. He was one of the first to find a way of making standards and other draperies by joining pieces together, so that the colours do not run, and show on both sides. He also did the baldachino of Orsanmichele, full of Madonnas, all different and beautiful. It is clear that this method of making standards is the must durable, as they do not suffer from acids, which quickly eat them away, although the latter method is most often used because it is less costly. Sandro's drawing was much beyond the common level, so much so that artists strove to obtain examples for some time after his death, and there are some in our book done with great judgment and skill. He was prodigal of figures in his scenes, as may be noticed in the embroidery of the frieze of the processional cross of the friars of S. Maria Novella, all by his design. Sandro then deserves high praise for his paintings, into which he threw himself with diligence and ardour, producing such works as the Adoration of the Magi in S. Maria Novella already described,

---

[1] The first "la bella Simonetta" is now in the Pitti Gallery, the second at Berlin, and represents the wife of Piero de' Medici.

which is a marvel. Another very remarkable work is a small round picture in the chamber of the prior of the Angeli at Florence, the figures being small but very graceful and beautifully composed. A Florentine gentleman, M. Fabio Segni, has a picture of the same size as the Magi, representing the Calumny of Apelles,[1] of the utmost beauty. He gave this picture to his close friend Antonio Segni, with the following lines of his own composition beneath it:

> *Indicio quemquam ne falso laedere tentent*
> *Terrarum reges, parva tabella monet.*
> *Huic similem Aegypti regi donavit Apelles*
> *Rex fuit et dignus munere, munus eo.*

BENEDETTO DA MAIANO, Sculptor and Architect of Florence
(1442–1497)

BENEDETTO DA MAIANO, sculptor of Florence, began as a woodcarver, and was considered the most skilful master of that craft who ever held tools. He was also the best artist of the method introduced, as is said elsewhere, in the time of Filippo Brunelleschi and Paolo Uccello, of joining small pieces of coloured wood together to make perspectives, foliage and other fantasies. He was thus pre-eminent in his youth, as his numerous works in various parts of Florence show, notably the presses of the sacristy of S. Maria del Fiore, most of which he did after the death of his uncle Giuliano, full of figures and foliage, and other works executed at great cost with much art. Having acquired a great reputation, owing to the novelty of these arts, he did a number of works for various places and princes, among them being a writing-desk for Alfonso, King of Naples, made by the direction of Benedetto's uncle[2] Giuliano, who served that king in architectural matters. Benedetto himself went thither, but as his sojourn there did not please him he returned to Florence, where he did two coffers for Matthias Corvinus, King of Hungary, who had many Florentines at his court and was very fond of all rare things, the work showing a fine mastery of its difficulties. The king sent him a courteous invitation, and, as he was anxious to go, he took the coffers with him in the ship and departed for Hungary. Having paid his respects to the king, by whom he was graciously received, he sent for the coffers and

---

[1] Now in the Uffizi Gallery.   [2] Brother.

caused them to be unpacked in the presence of the king, who was very anxious to see them. But the damp sea air had exercised such an effect on the glue that when the case was opened almost all the inlaid work fell out. It may well be imagined how astonished and dumbfounded Benedetto stood in the presence of that distinguished company. However, he put the pieces together as best he could, so that the king was quite satisfied. But from that time he conceived an aversion for that profession on account of the shame which it had brought him. Accordingly he boldly devoted himself to sculpture, in which he had already some experience, having made a marble basin with angels for the sacristy[1] while he was with his uncle at Loreto. By this means he was able before he left Hungary to show the king that, although he had begun in an unfortunate manner, the fault lay in the baseness of his art and not in his genius, which was high and soaring. After having produced some things in clay and marble which greatly delighted the king, he returned to Florence. No sooner had he arrived than the Signoria employed him to make the marble ornamentation of the door of their audience-chamber, where he did some children bearing festoons very beautifully.[2] But the most beautiful figure of all is that of a youthful St. John in the middle, two braccia high, which is considered remarkable. In order that the whole might be by his hand, he himself did the woodwork, making marquetry portraits of Dante on one side and Petrarch on the other. These alone would prove the excellence of Benedetto's workmanship, even to those who had seen nothing else by his hand. In our own day Duke Cosimo has caused this chamber to be painted by Francesco Salviati, as will be said in the proper place. Benedetto next made a black marble tomb in S. Maria Novella at Florence,[3] where Filippinio painted the chapel, containing a Madonna in a circle and some angels, for Filippo Strozzi the elder, whose portrait in marble, now in his palace, he also made. Lorenzo de' Medici the elder also employed Benedetto to make the portrait of Giotto the painter,[4] for S. Maria del Fiore, and he placed t above the epitaph as related in Giotto's Life. It is considered meritorious as a marble work.

His uncle Giuliano being dead, Benedetto, being left his heir, went to Naples, and besides works done for the king there he did an Annunciation[5] in the monastery of Monte Oliveto for

[1] 1484-7.
[2] In 1481; some fragments are preserved in the Bargello.
[3] In 1491. Strozzi's bust is now in the Louvre.
[4] In 1490.   [5] In 1489.

the Count of Terranuova, on a marble slab, surrounded by saints and by children bearing festoons, while the predella consists of bas-reliefs in good style. In Faenza he made a magnificent marble tomb for the body of St. Savino,[1] representing six scenes from the saint's life in bas-relief, with much invention and design in the buildings and figures alike, so that both works proclaimed him to be a remarkable sculptor. Before he left the Romagna he was employed to make the portrait of Galeotto Malatesta. Whether after or before this, I do not know, he did that of Henry VII. of England, having received a drawing of him from some Florentine merchants. The sketches for these two portraits were found in his house after his death, with many other things. Returning to Florence, he did the present marble pulpit of S. Croce[2] for Pietro Mellino, a citizen and wealthy merchant, considered a work of rare merit, the very best of its kind. It contains in small marble figures stories of St. Francis, executed with such skill and diligence that nothing better could be desired, as he has carved there trees, rocks, houses, landscapes and other things marvellously. There is a repetition of these on a slab beneath the pulpit, executed with such good design that it is impossible to praise it too highly. It is said that while this work was in progress he had difficulties with the wardens, for he wished the pulpit to stand against one of the columns which bear the arches supporting the roof, and to cut away the column to make the steps and entrance to the pulpit, and they would not consent, fearing that this would so enfeeble the column that the weight would bring it down and destroy a great part of the church. But after Il Mellino had given security that the work would be finished without any harm being done to the church, they gave way. Accordingly Benedetto strengthened the part of the column covered by the pulpit with bronze supports, and introduced the steps to mount into it. In proportion as he hollowed out the interior he strengthened the exterior with hard stone, as may be seen, and he completed the work to the amazement of all who saw it, for it possesses the utmost perfection in every part. It is said that when Filippo Strozzi the elder was about to build his palace he desired the opinion of Benedetto, who made him a model, in conformity with which the building was begun, although after Benedetto's death it was continued and completed by Cronaca.

After the works just mentioned, Benedetto, who had acquired enough to live upon, would not undertake anything further in

[1] 1474-6. [2] In 1474.

marble. However, he finished the St. Mary Magdalene in S. Trinità, begun by Desiderio da Settignano, made the crucifix over the high altar of S. Maria del Fiore, and did some other similar things. In architecture, though, he attempted but few things, yet those display the same judgment as his sculpture, especially three ceilings erected under his direction at a great cost in the palace of the Signoria at Florence. The first was that of the hall now called that of the Two Hundred. Over this he had to make two chambers, namely a hall and an audience-chamber. Consequently it was necessary to make a solid partition with a marble door of considerable size, which demanded all his judgment and skill. In order not to reduce the size of the hall while still dividing the floor above into two Bendetto managed as follows: On a huge beam, a braccia thick and running the entire breadth of the hall, he joined another of two pieces, so that the thickness raised it two-thirds of a braccia. At the ends these were fixed into the walls, projecting two braccia at each end. These ends were so supported that it was possible to place upon them an arch of doubled bricks, a half-braccia thick, supported at the ends by the main walls. These two beams were joined together by iron stays like teeth so that they formed practically one. This done, the beams had nothing to bear but the weight of the wall above the arch, which carried all the rest. He strengthened the arch with two iron ties which entered the beams and support the whole, and even if not sufficient of themselves, the arches being supported by the bands, and two in number, on either side of the marble door, would carry a much greater weight than that of the wall, which consists of bricks a half-braccia thick. Yet he caused the bricks to be so cut as to project into the sides supported by this foundation, thus rendering it more stable. In this way, thanks to the judgment of Benedetto, the hall of the Two Hundred retained its size, and above it he made the hall called dell' Oriuolo as well as the audience-chamber containing the Triumph of Camillus, painted by Salviati. The soffit of the ceiling was richly carved and inlaid by Marco del Tasso and by his brothers Domenico and Giuliano, who also did those of the Sala dell' Oriuolo and the audience-chamber. As the marble door was made double by Benedetto, and as he had already done the outside, he made a marble Justice seated over the arch on the inside, holding the orb in one hand and a sword in the other, with the words: "*Diligite justitiam qui judicatis terram.*" This work was executed with marvellous diligence and skill.

At the Madonna delle Grazie, a little outside Arezzo, Benedetto made a portico with steps leading up to the door, and in the portico he joined the columns by arches, surrounding the roof with an architrave, frieze and cornice, introducing as a gutter a garland of large roses of macigno projecting one and a third braccia. This added to the projection of the roof, and the lace-work and egg pattern below the gutter makes two and a half braccia, and with the half-braccia formed by the tiles gives a roof projecting three braccia, a fine, rich, useful and ingenious construction. This contrivance is worthy of the careful con-sideration of artists, as wishing the roof to project without brackets or corbels, he made the blocks on which the roses are carved so large that only one half projects, the other half being built into the wall, and being thus in counterpoise, they bear the weight and all that is above, the building having stood without accident to this day. As Benedetto did not wish his ceiling to appear to consist of pieces, as it did, he surrounded them with a cornice forming a ground for the roses and uniting them so that it looks like a single piece. In the same place he made a ceiling covered with gilt roses, which is much admired

Benedetto bought a farm about half a mile from Prato on the side of the Florentine gate, and he made a most lovely chapel on the highway to Florence, with a Madonna and Child in a niche, done in clay so well that it is as beautiful as marble, although without colour. Equally beautiful are two angels on the top, each holding a candlestick in its hand. The front of the altar contains a fine marble Pietà with Our Lady and St. John.

At his death Benedetto left many sketches in clay and marble in his house. He drew very well, as may be seen from some sheets in our book. He died at the age of fifty-four in 1498, and was honourably buried in S. Lorenzo. His will provided that after the death of certain relations his property should go to the company of the Bigallo.

While Benedetto, in his youth, was engaged upon wood and inlaid work, he had as a rival Baccio Cellini, piper of the Signoria of Florence, who did some fine inlaid work in ivory, and among others a most beautiful octagon of ivory figures outlined in black, now in the duke's wardrobe. Girolamo della Cecca, Baccio's pupil and also piper to the Signoria, did much work in joinery. Another contemporary was David Pistolese, who did a St. John the Evangelist in marquetry in S. Giovanni Evangelista at Pisa at the entrance to the choir, a work of great labour and excellent design. There was also Geri of Arezzo, who did the choir and pulpit of S. Agostino at Arezzo in inlaid work, containing figures and landscapes. This Geri was very ingenious, and made a beautiful organ of sweet tone composed of pieces of wood, which is now in the Vescovado of Arezzo over the sacristy door, as fine as ever it was, a marvellous work, entirely devised by him. But none of them approached the excellence of Benedetto, so that he deserves to be enumerated and honoured among the best artists in his professions.

ANDREA VERROCCHIO,[1] Painter, Sculptor and Architect of Florence

(1435–1488)

ANDREA DEL VERROCCHIO of Florence was in his time a goldsmith, perspectivist, sculptor, carver, painter and musician. But his style in sculpture and painting was somewhat hard and crude, as if he had acquired his skill rather by indefatigable study than by any natural gift or facility. This facility, although not so advantageous as study and diligence, would have rendered him a most excellent artist, but when either study or Nature is lacking, the highest excellence is rarely found, although study confers more than the other. However, Andrea, by his unequalled diligence, won a place among the rare and excellent artists. In his youth he studied science and especially geometry. While a goldsmith he made, besides other things, some clasps for copes which are in S. Maria del Fiore at Florence, and a cup, the body of which is surrounded by animals, leaves and other curious things, a work well known to all goldsmiths. In another he has very prettily represented some boys dancing. Having disclosed his merit by these things, Andrea was employed by the art of the merchants to make two silver bas-reliefs for the altar of S. Giovanni,[2] from which when done he acquired much glory and reputation.

Rome did not at this time possess all of those large-sized apostles usually placed upon the altar of the Pope's chapel with some other silver-work now destroyed. Accordingly Andrea was sent for, and by the special favour of Pope Sixtus he was employed to do all that was necessary here.[3] He completed his

---

[1] Andrea di Cioni. [2] In 1477.
[3] As there is no mention of Verrocchio in the papal accounts, this statement must be regarded as doubtful.

task with the utmost diligence. Seeing that the numerous ancient statues and other things at Rome were greatly esteemed, and that the bronze horse[1] was placed by the Pope in S. Giovanni Lateran, and fragments of other things found every day were also highly valued, Andrea determined to take up sculpture. Accordingly he altogether abandoned the goldsmith's craft, and began by casting some little bronze figures which were much admired, and, encouraged by this, he began to work in marble. About this time occurred the death of the wife of Francesco Tornabuoni in child-birth, and her husband, who had greatly loved her and wished to honour her as much as possible, employed Andrea to make her tomb. He carved the lady's effigy in stone upon a marble sarcophagus, representing her confinement and passing to another life, and then did three Virtues, considered very fine, this being his first work in marble. The tomb was afterwards placed in the Minerva.[2]

Returning to Florence with money, fame and honour, Andrea was set to make a David two and a half braccia high.[3] When finished it was placed in the palace at the top of the stairs where the chain was, to his great glory. Whilst engaged upon this statue he did the marble Madonna in S. Croce above the tomb of M. Leonardo Bruni[4] of Arezzo. He did this while still young for Bernardo Rossellino, architect and sculptor, who carried out the entire work in marble, as has been said. He further made a Madonna and Child, half-length, in half-relief on a marble slab, which used to be in the Casa Medici, and is now over a door in the chamber of the Duchess of Florence, as a most beautiful thing. He also did two metal heads, one of Alexander the Great, in profile, the other of Darius, a fancy head, in half-relief with different crests and armour and variety in every particular. Both were sent by Lorenzo de' Medici the elder to Matthias Corvinus, King of Hungary, with many other things, as will be said in the proper place. Having acquired a reputation as an excellent master, especially in numerous bronze works in which he greatly delighted, Andrea made the tomb of Giovanni and Piero di Cosimo de' Medici in S. Lorenzo,[5] with a sarcophagus of porphyry borne at the four corners by bronze supports with beautifully turned leaves, finished with the utmost diligence. This tomb is placed between the chapel of the Sacrament and

---

[1] The statue of Marcus Aurelius.
[2] Lucrezia Tornabuoni died in September 1477. Fragments of the tomb are preserved in the Bargello, Florence.
[3] Done about 1476.   [4] Who died 1443.   [5] In 1472.

the sacristy, and there is no better work of bronze anywhere, especially as he had at the same time demonstrated his skill in architecture by arranging the tomb in the opening of a window five braccia wide and about ten high, placed upon a pedestal and separating the chapel of the Sacrament from the old sacristy. To fill the gap between the sarcophagus and the vaulting he made a grille of bronze rope netting, diamond pattern, ornamented in places with festoons and other remarkable fancies, executed with great skill, judgment and invention.

Donatello having made the marble niche for the Magistracy of the Six of the Mercanzia, now opposite S. Michele in the oratory of Orsanmichele, and a St. Thomas feeling the wounds of Christ being required, that work was not then carried out because some wished it to be done by Donatello and others by Lorenzo Ghiberti. The dispute having endured throughout the lives of these masters, both statues were ultimately allotted to Andrea,[1] who made the models and forms, cast them, and obtained the most satisfactory results. Having afterwards cleaned and finished them, he brought them to their present state of perfection, which is unrivalled. St. Thomas displays his incredulity and a too great readiness to ascertain the fact, though he also shows love while putting his hand in Christ's side, the Lord raising His arm with great freedom and opening His garment, thus removing the doubt of the incredulous disciple with all the grace and divinity that art can impart to a figure. The excellence of the draperies of these figures shows that Andrea was as much a master of this art as Donato, Lorenzo, and his other predecessors, so that the work deserved to be placed in a niche beside Donato's and to be held then as now in the greatest repute.

As Andrea could not rise higher in that profession, and being a man who could not be contented with excellence in one department, but eager to win distinction in others, he turned his attention to painting and did some sketches for a combat of nude figures which he proposed to execute in colours on a wall. He also made the cartoons of some pictures which he proceeded to execute in colours, but whatever the cause these remained imperfect. There are some of his drawings in our book executed with the greatest patience and judgment, among them being some female heads so beautiful and with such charming hair that Leonardo da Vinci was always imitating them. It also contains two horses with the method of enlarging things in

[1] In 1478; set up in 1483.

proportion without errors. I also have a horse's head in terra cotta copied from the antique, and a rare work, while the Very Rev. Don Vincenzio Borghini has some others on paper in his book, already mentioned. Among them is a design for a tomb made by Andrea at Venice for a doge, and the Magi adoring Christ, with a most lovely woman's head, painted on paper. For Lorenzo de' Medici he made a bronze boy hugging a fish,[1] for the fountain of the Villa Careggi, which has been set up by Duke Cosimo as the fountain in the court of his palace, and is a really marvellous work.

Upon the completion of the dome of S. Maria del Fiore [2] it was determined after much discussion to place a copper ball on the top of it, as Filippo Brunelleschi had devised. The charge of this was entrusted to Andrea, who made one four braccia high, placed on a disk and so arranged that it could safely carry the cross. This done, it was installed amid universal rejoicing.[3] It was necessary to employ both genius and diligence in its construction, because it was essential to arrange an entrance into it from below and to fortify it so that the wind should do it no harm. As Andrea never rested, but was always at work on something, whether painting or sculpture, it would sometimes happen that one thing would overlap another so that he might not, like many others, become tired of always doing the same thing. However, he did not carry out the cartoons mentioned, though he also did some paintings, among them being a well-executed picture [4] for the nuns of S. Domenico at Florence in which he considered he had done very well. Accordingly, soon after he painted another in S. Salvi for the friars of Vallombroso representing St. John baptising Christ.[5] In this work he was assisted by Lionardo da Vinci, his pupil, then quite a youth, who did an angel so far excelling the rest that Andrea resolved never to touch the brush again, because Lionardo, though so young, had so far surpassed him.

Cosimo de' Medici imported from Rome many antiquities, and inside the door of the garden or court opening into the via de' Ginori he placed a beautiful white marble Marsyas bound to a tree and ready to be flayed. Lorenzo, his nephew, having obtained a torso and head of another antique Marsyas, much finer than the first and of red stone, wished to match it with the first and could not because it was very imperfect. Accordingly

[1] Done about 1469. [2] In 1467. [3] In 1471.
[4] Now in the Budapest Gallery.
[5] Now in the Uffizi, Florence.

he gave it to Andrea to restore and finish, and that artist made the legs, sides and arms that were lacking for the one in red marble so well that Lorenzo was delighted and had it set up on the opposite side of the door to the other. This antique torso of a flayed Marsyas was made with such skill and judgment that some slender white veins in the red stone came out, through skilful carving, in the proper places, appearing like small sinews, such as are seen in natural figures when flayed, and this rendered the work most life-like when it was polished for the first time.

The Venetians desiring to honour the skill of Bartolommeo da Bergamo, who had gained many victories for them, and in order to encourage the others, invited Andrea, of whose fame they had heard, to come to Venice, and instructed him to make a bronze equestrian statue of that captain for the Piazza S. Giovanni e Paolo.[1] Andrea accordingly made the model for the horse, and had begun his preparations to cast it in bronze when by means of the favour of some nobles it was proposed that Vellano da Padova should make the figure and Andrea the horse. When Andrea heard this he broke the legs and head of his model, and without a word returned in a rage to Florence. On hearing this the Signoria warned him never to venture to return to Venice on pain of losing his head, to which he wrote in reply that he would take good care not to, because it was not in their power to replace men's heads after they had removed them, and never one like his own, though he could do so in the case of the horse's head he had broken, and make it even finer. This answer did not displease the Signoria, and they subsequently induced him to return to Venice at twice the salary. Here he repaired his first model and cast it in bronze, but did not finish it, for becoming overheated during the casting he caught a chill, of which he died in a few days, leaving unfinished not only that work, although there was little to be done, and after being finished it was set up in its appointed place, but another which he was doing in Pistoia, namely the tomb of the Cardinal Forteguerra, with the three Theological Virtues and God the Father above, afterwards finished by Lorenzetto, sculptor of Florence.[2] Andrea was fifty-six at his death, which caused great grief to his friends and numerous pupils, and especially to Nanni Grosso, the sculptor, a very eccentric man both in art and in

[1] Colleoni died 1 February, 1475. The monument was commissioned in 1479 and set up in 1496.
[2] The cardinal died in 1473 and the tomb was commissioned in 1477. Verrocchio's original design, which was not followed, is preserved in the Victoria and Albert Museum.

life. It is said that he would never do any work away from his shop, and certainly not for monks or friars, unless the entrance to the vault or cellar were left open, so that he might go and drink when he pleased without being obliged to ask permission. It is also related that once, on returning cured from some sickness from S. Maria Nuova, he told the friends who visited him and inquired after his health that he was ill. "Yet you are healed," they replied; to which he retorted, "That is why I am ill, because I want a little fever to enable me to remain comfortably here in the hospital." When he came to die they brought him a rudely made wooden crucifix, and he requested them to take it away, and bring him one by Donatello, saying that if they did not he should die in despair, so much did he detest the sight of ill-made works of his art. Pietro Perugino and Leonardo da Vinci, who will be mentioned elsewhere, were also pupils of Andrea, as well as Francesco di Simone of Florence, who did a marble tomb in S. Domenico, at Bologna, with small figures, which by their style might be by Andrea.[1] It was made for M. Alessandro Tartaglia, a doctor of Imola, and another, which corresponds, in S. Brancazio, at Florence, in the sacristy, and in a chapel of the church for M. Pier Minerbetti, knight. Yet another pupil, Agnolo di Polo, was a skilful worker in clay, and has filled the city with his productions, and if he had cared to devote himself seriously to art he would have done most beautiful things. But Andrea's favourite pupil was Lorenzo di Credi, who brought his master's remains from Venice, and laid them in the church of S. Ambruogio, in the tomb of Ser Michele di Cione, above which these words are carved:

Ser Michaelis di Cionis, et suorum:

and nearby:

Hic ossa jacent Andreae Verrochii qui obiit Venetiis
MCCCCLXXXVIII.

Andrea was very fond of making plaster casts, the material being a soft stone excavated at Volterra, Siena, and many other places in Italy. This stone, baked at the fire, and made into a paste with tepid water, may then be fashioned as desired, and being afterwards dried, it becomes hard so that whole figures may be cast in it. Andrea used it to form natural objects, so that he might have them before him and imitate them, such as hands,

[1] Francesco di Simone Feruccio (1438–93); the tomb is that of Alessandro Tartagni, who died in 1477.

feet, knees, legs, arms and busts. Later on in his life men began to make at a slight cost death masks of those who died, so that a number of these life-like portraits may be seen in every house in Florence over chimney-pieces, doors, windows and cornices. This practice has been continued to our own time, and has proved of great advantage in obtaining many of the portraits introduced into the scenes in the palace of Duke Cosimo. For this a great debt is due to Andrea, who was one of the first to make use of it.

To Andrea also is due a greater perfection in votive images, not only in Florence, but in all places where there are devotions, and where persons assemble to offer such objects for some favour received, miracles as they are called. These were first made small in silver, or small painted panels, or else very rudely moulded in wax, but in Andrea's time a much better style was introduced, for being very intimate with Orsino, a worker in wax, a man of good judgment in his art, Andrea began to show him how he could attain to excellence. An opportunity presented itself at the death of Giuliano, and the wounding of his brother Lorenzo in S. Maria del Fiore.[1] It was then decreed by the friends and relations of Lorenzo that images of him should be made in several places, rendering thanks to God for his preservation. Accordingly Orsino, with the assistance and advice of Andrea, made three life-sized wax figures, the framework being of wood, as has been said elsewhere, covered with split canes, over which cloth was stretched and waxed over, so that nothing more life-like could be desired. He made the heads, hands and feet of coarser wax, hollow inside, painting the hair and other things in oils, as was necessary, in a very natural manner. All three may still be seen, one being in the church of the nuns of Chiarito in the via di S. Gallo, opposite the crucifix which works miracles. This figure is dressed exactly as Lorenzo was when wounded in the throat, and showed himself at the windows of his house, all bandaged, to be seen by the people, who wished to know whether he was alive, as they hoped, or dead, so that they might avenge him. The second figure is in a gown, a civil habit worn by the Florentines, and this is in the church of the Servites at the Nunziata, above the lesser door, beside the desk where the candles are sold. The third was sent to S. Maria degli Angeli at Assisi and placed before that Madonna.

As I have already said, Lorenzo caused the whole of the street leading from S. Maria to the gate of Assisi towards S. Francesco

[1] In the Pazzi conspiracy of 1478.

to be paved with bricks, and he restored the fountains erected there by his grandfather Cosimo. But to return to the waxen images. Those are by Orsino, which are in the said church of the Servites, and which have on the bottom a large O with an R inside and a cross above. All are of extreme beauty, and very few have equalled them. The art has been maintained until our own days, though in a somewhat declining condition, through lack of devotion, or from some other cause.

But to return to Verrocchio. Besides the works referred to he did some wooden crucifixes, and other things in clay, in which he excelled, as we see by the models of the subjects which he did for the altar of S. Giovanni, in some beautiful children, and in a head of St. Jerome, which is considered marvellous. He also did the boy on the clock in the Mercato nuovo with movable arms, which he raises to strike the hour with a hammer. This was considered a very beautiful and curious thing at the time. We have now reached the end of the Life of that distinguished sculptor Andrea Verrocchio. A contemporary of his named Benedetto Buglioni[1] learned from his wife, a member of the house of Andrea della Robbia, the secret of glazing clay, and made many works of that sort in Florence and elsewhere, notably in the church of the Servites, near the chapel of St. Barbara, where he made a Resurrection of Christ, with some angels,[2] which are of considerable merit for works of that kind. In a chapel of St. Brancazio he painted a dead Christ, and the lunette over the door of S. Pier Maggiore. The secret was transmitted by Benedetto to Santi Buglioni, the only living man who understands this sort of sculpture.

ANDREA MANTEGNA, Painter of Mantua
(1431-1506)

THOSE who work with skill, and have received a part of their reward, know what new vigour encouragement imparts to them, for when men expect honour and rewards they do not feel the toil and fatigue, while their talents become more remarkable every day. True skill does not always meet with such recognition and reward as Andrea Mantegna received. He was born of very humble stock in the territory of Mantua,[3] and though as a

[1] 1461-c. 1521.   [2] It is the work of Agostino di Duccio.
[3] He was born at Vicenza.

child he used to tend the flocks, he rose by his merits and by good fortune to the rank of knight, as I shall presently relate. When he was a little grown he was taken to the city, where he studied painting under Jacopo [1] Squarcione, a painter of Padua, who took the boy to his house, and, discovering his great talents, subsequently adopted him, as M. Girolamo Campagnuola writes in a Latin letter to M. Leonico Timeo, a Greek philosopher, where he notices some of the old painters who served the Carrara, lords of Padua. Squarcione, well aware that he was not the most skilful painter imaginable, in order that Andrea might learn more than his master knew, made him study from plaster casts of antique statues and from paintings on canvas, which he sent for from various places, but chiefly Tuscany and Rome. In these and other ways Andrea learned much in his youth. The rivalry also of Marco Zoppo of Bologna, Dario da Trevisi and Niccolo Pizzolo of Padua, pupils of his master and adoptive father, afforded him no little aid and stimulus. When no more than seventeen he did the picture of the high altar of S. Sofia at Padua, which might well be the production of a skilled veteran and not of a mere boy. After this the chapel of St. Christopher, in the church of the Eremitani friars of St. Augustine in Padua, was allotted to Squarcione, who entrusted the work to Niccolo Pizzolo and Andrea. Niccolo did God the Father seated in majesty in the midst of the Doctors of the Church, a painting reputed to be no whit inferior to those of Andrea there. Indeed, though Niccolo did but few things, they were all good, and if he had been as fond of painting as of arms he would have become excellent, and possibly might have enjoyed a longer life, but he always went armed, and having many enemies, he was attacked one day as he was returning from work and treacherously killed. He left no other works, so far as I am aware, except another God the Father in the chapel of Urbano Perfetto.[2]

Andrea, being thus left to himself, did the four Evangelists in the chapel, considered very fine. Great hopes were now conceived of Andrea, owing to this and other works, and as success brings success, he took to wife the daughter [3] of Jacopo Bellini, the Venetian painter and father of Gentile and Giovanni, and the rival of Squarcione. When Squarcione heard this, he was angry with Andrea, and they were enemies from that time. Whereas Squarcione had previously praised Andrea's works, he

[1] Francesco. [2] The urban prefect, not a proper name.
[3] Nicolosia, in 1454.

now blamed them publicly, especially those in the chapel of St. Christopher, saying they were bad because he had imitated marble antiques, from which it is impossible to learn painting properly, since stones always possess a certain harshness and never have that softness peculiar to flesh and natural objects, which fall in folds and exhibit various movements. He added that the figures would have been greatly improved if Andrea had made them of the colour of marble and not in so many hues, because his painted figures resembled ancient marble statues and other such things, and were not like living beings. These strictures wounded Andrea, but on the other hand they did him much good, because he recognised that there was a great deal of truth in them, and so he set himself to draw living persons. He made such progress in this that in the remaining scene in the chapel he showed himself quite as able to learn from Nature as from objects of art. But nevertheless Andrea always maintained that the good antique statues were more perfect and beautiful than anything in Nature. He believed that the masters of antiquity had combined in one figure the perfections which are rarely found together in one individual, and had thus produced single figures of surpassing beauty. He considered that statues displayed the muscles, veins and nerves in a more accentuated manner than is found in nature, where they are covered by the soft flesh which rounds them off, except in the case of old or emaciated people such as are usually avoided by artists. He clung tenaciously to this opinion, a fact which renders his style somewhat sharp, more closely resembling stone than living flesh. However this may be in this last scene, which gave great satisfaction, Andrea drew Squarcione as a small, fat man holding a lance and a sword. He also introduced the portraits of Noferi di M. Palla Strozzi of Florence; M. Girolamo dalla Valle, an excellent physician; M. Bonifazio Fuzimeliga, doctor of laws; Niccolo, the goldsmith of Pope Innocent VIII., and Baldassarre da Leccio, his intimate friends, all clothed in shining white armour, in a very fine style. He also drew M. Bonramino, knight and a bishop of Hungary, a very foolish man, who wandered about Rome all day and at night slept like the beasts in the stables. Another portrait is that of Marsilio Pazzo, who is the executioner cutting off the head of St. James, and he also drew himself. In short, this work, by its excellence, greatly increased his reputation.[1] While engaged upon this chapel Andrea painted a picture which was placed in S. Justina, at the altar

[1] He was at work in the chapel from 1448 to 1455.

of St. Luke,[1] and then did in fresco the arch over the door of
S. Antonio, where he wrote his name. In Verona he did a picture [2]
for the altar of S. Cristofano and of S. Antonio and some figures
at the corner of the Piazza della Paglia. He did the high-altar
picture [3] for the friars of Monte Oliveto in S. Maria in Organo,
a lovely work, and also that of S. Zeno. While at Verona [4] he
sent pictures to various places, one of which was owned by his
friend and relation the abbot of Fiesole. It represents a Madonna
from the waist upwards, with the Child, and some heads of
angels singing, done with admirable grace. This picture is now in
the library of that place, and has always been highly valued.

While in Mantua Andrea had served Ludovico Gonzaga the
marquis, a lord who always valued him and favoured his talent.
He painted for this lord a small panel in the chapel of the castle
of Mantua containing some scenes with figures of no great size,
but very beautiful. In the same place there are a number of
figures foreshortened from below, which are much admired,
because, although the drapery is crude and slight and the
manner somewhat dry, the whole is executed with great skill
and diligence.[5]

For the same marquis Andrea painted the Triumph of Cæsar [6]
in the palace of S. Sebastiano at Mantua, and this is the best
thing which he ever did. It shows in an excellent arrangement
the beauty and decoration of the chariot, a man cursing the
victor, the relations, perfumes, incense, sacrifices, priests, bulls
crowned for sacrifice, prisoners, booty taken by the soldiers,
the array of squadrons, elephants, spoils, victories, cities and
fortresses represented in various cars, with a quantity of trophies
on spears and arms for the head and back, coiffures, ornaments
and vases without number. Among the spectators is a woman
holding a child by the hand, who has run a thorn into his foot,
and he is weeping and showing it to his mother very gracefully
and naturally. Andrea, as I may have intimated elsewhere,
had the admirable idea in this work of placing the plane on which
the figures stood higher than the point of view, and while
showing the feet of those in the foreground, he concealed those
of the figures farther back, as the nature of the point of view

[1] Now in the Brera, Milan, painted 1453.
[2] A Madonna enthroned, with saints.
[3] In 1496.
[4] 1457-9.
[5] The Triptych now in the Uffizi, painted about 1464, and representing
the Adoration of the Magi, with the Circumcision on one side and the
Ascension on the other.
[6] Now at Hampton Court; painted about 1484-94.

demanded. The same method is applied to the spoils, vases and other implements and ornaments. The same idea was observed by Andrea degli Impiccati[1] in his Last Supper in the refectory of S. Maria Nuova. Thus we see that at that time men of genius were busily engaged in investigating and imitating the truths of Nature. And, in a word, the entire work could not be made more beautiful or improved, and if the marquis valued Andrea before, his affection and esteem were greatly increased. What is more, Andrea became so famous that his renown reached Pope Innocent VIII., who, having heard of his excellence in painting and his other good qualities with which he was marvellously endowed, sent for him and for several others to adorn with paintings the walls of the Belvedere, which was just finished. Arrived at Rome with much favour and honour from the marquis, who made him a knight, Andrea was kindly received by the Pope, and immediately employed to do a small chapel in the place mentioned.[2] He carried this out with great diligence and care, and so minutely that the vaulting and the walls look like an illumination rather than a painting. The largest figures there are over the altar, done in fresco like the rest, and representing St. John baptising Christ, while some others are undressing as if they would be baptised.[3] One among them, wishing to remove a stocking which clings to his leg owing to the sweat, pulls it off inside out across his other leg, while his expression clearly indicates the effort and inconvenience. This fancy excited great wonder in those who saw it at the time. It is said that the Pope, on account of his numerous engagements, did not pay Mantegna so often as the artist's needs required, and that the latter, in painting some of the Virtues in that work, introduced Equity. The Pope, going one day to see the work, asked what the figure was, and on learning that she represented Equity, he replied, "You should have associated Patience with her." The painter understood what was meant and never uttered another word. On the completion of the work, the Pope sent Andrea back to the duke richly rewarded and highly favoured.

Whilst Andrea was working at Rome he painted, besides the chapel, a small picture of Our Lady and the Child sleeping.[4] The background is a mountain with men quarrying stones, executed with great labour and patience, so that it would seem

[1] i.e. Andrea del Castagno.
[2] In 1488.
[3] Destroyed in 1780 to erect the Museo Pio-Clementino.
[4] The Madonna of the Grotto, now in the Uffizi, dated 1491.

all but impossible to do such delicate work with the brush. It is to-day in the hands of Don Francesco Medici, prince of Florence, who keeps it among his choicest possessions. In my book there is half a folio sheet with a drawing in grisaille by Andrea of Judith putting the head of Holofernes into a bag held by her Moorish slave. It is done in chiaroscuro in a style no longer in use, as he has left the lights unpainted, and so clearly marked that the hairs and other delicate things may be seen as carefully done as if they had been painted with the brush, so that this may in some sense be called a coloured work rather than a drawing.

Like Pollajuolo, Andrea delighted in copper engraving, and, among other things, reproduced his Triumphs. They were greatly valued, because better ones had not then been seen. Among his last works was a panel at S. Maria della Vittoria, a church built under his direction by the Marquis Francesco to celebrate his victory at the River Taro when he was general of the Venetians against the French.[1] It is painted in tempera, and was placed at the high altar. Our Lady with the Child is erected upon a pedestal; beneath her are St. Michael the Archangel, St. Anne and Joachim presenting the marquis, who is drawn from life most naturally, while the Madonna stretches out her hand to him. This work, which gives pleasure to everyone, so delighted the marquis that he rewarded the genius and the pains of Andrea most liberally, the painter retaining to the end his honourable rank of knight, his works being admired by princes everywhere. Lorenzo da Lendinara, a rival of Andrea, was considered an excellent painter at Padua, and did some things in clay in the church of S. Antonio, and others of no great value. He maintained a close friendship with Dario da Trevisi and Marco Zoppo of Bologna, because they had been fellow-pupils of Squarcione. Marco did a loggia for the Minorites at Padua, which serves as their chapter-house, and a picture at Pesaro, which is now in the new church of S. Giovanni Evangelista.[2] In one picture he drew the portrait of Guidobaldo da Montefeltro, when he was captain of the Florentines. Another friend of Mantegna was Stefano, painter of Ferrara, whose works were few but meritorious. The ornamentation of the arch of S. Antonio at Padua is by him, as well as the Virgin Mary, called del Pilastro.

To return to Andrea. He built and painted a most beautiful

---

[1] To celebrate the battle of Fornovo, fought in 1495, and painted in the following year; now in the Louvre.
[2] Now at Berlin; dated 1471.

house at Mantua for his own use, and lived there all his life. He
died at the age of sixty-six in 1517,[1] and was buried honourably
in S. Andrea, the following epitaph being placed upon his tomb,
over which is his portrait in bronze:

*Esse parem hunc noris, si non praeponis, Apelli, Aenea Mantineas
qui simulacra vides.*

Andrea was so gentle and amiable in all his acts that he
will always be remembered, not only in his own country, but
throughout the world. Thus he deserves the reference of Ariosto
as much for his courteous manners as for the excellence of his
painting. I refer to the passage at the beginning of Canto
XXXIII., where, in enumerating the most celebrated painters
of the time, the poet says:

Leonardo, Andrea Mantegna, Gian Bellino.

Andrea improved the foreshortening of figures as seen from
below, and this was a difficult and fine invention. He was also
fond, as I have said, of copper engraving, a very remarkable
process, by means of which the world has been able to see the
Bacchanalia, the battle of the sea-monsters, the Deposition
from the Cross, the Burial of Christ and the Resurrection, with
Longinus and St. Andrew, all works of Mantegna, as well as the
styles of all the artists who have ever lived.

FILIPPO LIPPI, Painter of Florence
(1457–1504)

ABOUT the same time there lived in Florence a painter of the
rarest genius and most charming invention, named Filippo, the
son of Frà Filippo of the Carmine. He followed in the footsteps
of his dead father, and was kept and taught while still no more
than a boy by Sandro Botticello, in spite of the fact that his
father on his death-bed had recommended him to his intimate
friend Frà Diamante, whom he regarded as a brother. Filippo's
invention was so copious, and his ornamentation so curious and
original, that he was the first among the moderns to employ
the new method of varying the costumes, and to dress his
figures in the short antique vestments. He was also the first
to bring to light the grotesques resembling antiques, executing

[1] In 1506.

them in coloured clay in friezes, with more design and grace
than his predecessors. The strange fancies which he introduced
into his paintings are truly marvellous; moreover, he never
did a single work without making use of carefully studied
Roman antiquities, such as vases, buskins, trophies, banners,
crests, ornaments of temples, head-dresses, strange fashions
for the body, armour, scimetars, swords, togas, mantles and
such like, so that a great and everlasting debt is due to him for
having enriched art with such beautiful ornaments.

In his early youth Filippo completed the Brancacci Chapel
in the Carmine at Florence,[1] begun by Masolino and not quite
finished by Masaccio at his death. Filippo put the finishing
touches, and did the remainder of a scene where Peter and Paul
are raising the emperor's nephew,[2] the child, who is nude, being
a portrait of Francesco Granacci the painter, then a boy. He also
introduced portraits of M. Tommaso Soderini, knight, Piero
Guicciardini, father of M. Francesco the historian, Piero del
Pugliese and Luigi Pulci the poet, as well as Antonio Pollajuolo and himself, young as he was. As he never drew himself
again in his life, it is not possible to obtain a portrait of him at
a riper age. He further drew Sandro Botticello, his master, and
many other friends and great men, including Il Raggio the
broker, a very clever and witty man, who made the whole of
Dante's Hell in relief in a shell, with all the circles and pits and
the well, including all the figures and smallest details so graphic-
ally described by the great poet, a work considered marvellous
in its time. In the Chapel of Francesco del Pugliese at Campora,
belonging to the monks of the abbey outside Florence, Filippo
painted in tempera the vision of St. Bernard,[3] Our Lady appearing to him with some angels as he is writing in a wood. It is a
remarkable work for the rocks, books, grass and such things
which it contains. He introduced a portrait of this Francesco so
life-like that it only lacks speech. During the siege it was removed
for safety to the sacristy of the Badia at Florence. In S. Spirito
in the same city he painted a panel [4] with Our Lady, St. Martin,
St. Nicholas and St. Catherine for Tanai de' Nerli. In the Rucellai
Chapel in S. Brancazio he did a panel, and in S. Raffaello a
crucifix and two figures on a gold ground.[5] In front of the

[1] 1484 and 1485.
[2] Vasari seems to be confusing the legends of Peter and Paul here.
[3] 1480-2, now in the Badia, Florence.
[4] In 1493-4.
[5] The former, a Madonna with St. Jerome and St. Dominic is in the
National Gallery, London; the Crucifixion is in the Berlin Gallery.

sacristy of S. Francesco outside the S. Miniato gate he did a
God the Father with a number of babes. At the Palco, a place
of the bare-footed friars outside Prato, he did a panel,[1] and in
the audience-chamber of the priors of the district he painted
another small one,[2] which has been much admired, of Our Lady,
St. Stephen and St. John the Baptist. Next the Mercatale at
Prato and opposite the nuns of S. Margherita, near some of
their houses, he painted in fresco a lovely Madonna in a tabernacle
with a choir of seraphim on a field of glory. The serpent beneath
St. Margaret in this picture is most curious and terrible, displaying its fangs, its fire and death-dealing weapons. The rest of
the work is coloured with such freshness and brilliance that it
merits the highest praise. He also did some things at Lucca,
notably a panel in a chapel of the church of S. Ponziano of the
friars of Monte Oliveto, in the middle of which is a fine St. Andrew,
standing in a niche, by that great sculptor Andrea Sansovino.

Although invited to Hungary by King Matthias, Filippo would
not go, but did two beautiful panels [3] for the king in Florence
and sent them to him, one of them being the king's portrait as
shown on his medals. He also sent some works to Genoa, and
did a St. Sebastian [4] for the left-hand side of the chapel of
the high altar of S. Domenico at Bologna which deserves every
praise. For Tanai de' Nerli he did another panel at S. Salvadore
outside Florence, and for Piero del Pugliese, a friend, a scene of
small figures, executed with such art and diligence that when
another citizen desired one like it he refused, saying that it was
not possible. After these things he did a stupendous work at
Rome for Olivieri Caraffa, cardinal of Naples, friend of Lorenzo
de' Medici the elder, at the latter's request. On the way he passed
through Spoleto, at Lorenzo's desire, to give directions for the
making of a marble tomb for Frà Filippo, his father, at the cost
of that prince, who had not been able to obtain the body from
the Spoletans for burial in Florence. So Filippo designed the
tomb, and Lorenzo caused it to be made sumptuous and beautiful,
as is related elsewhere. Arrived at Rome, Filippo decorated a
chapel in the Minerva [5] for Cardinal Caraffa, painting scenes
from the life of St. Thomas Aquinas, and some beautiful and
ingenious poetical compositions, for which he had a natural
talent and devised them entirely himself. Here we see Faith
taking captive Infidelity, all heretics and infidels. Beneath are

---

[1] Of Christ appearing to the Virgin, painted in 1495, now in the Pinakothek, Munich.
[2] In 1503.   [3] In 1488.   [4] Dated 1501.   [5] 1488-93.

Hope and Despair, with many other virtues subduing the
opposing vices. St. Thomas is seated in a chair engaged in a
discussion, defending the Church against a school of heretics.
Beneath him are the vanquished forms of Sabellius, Arius,
Averroes and others, gracefully dressed. Filippo's own design
for this scene is in my book, as well as some others, done with a
skill which is unsurpassable. Here also is the crucifix saying to
Thomas as he prays, *Bene scripsisti de me, Thoma,* with a
companion, who stands amazed at hearing the crucifix speak.
A panel contains the Annunciation, and on the walls is an
Assumption, with the twelve Apostles surrounding the tomb.
This work has always been considered excellent and highly
finished for a fresco. It contains a portrait of the Cardinal
Olivieri Caraffa, bishop of Ostia, who was buried here in 1511,[1]
and afterwards taken to Naples to the episcopal church.

When Filippo returned to Florence he undertook to do the
Chapel of Filippo Strozzi the elder in S. Maria Novella,[2] and he
began it, but after doing the ceiling he had to return to Rome,
where he made a tomb for the cardinal in stucco. He also did a
small chapel next to this in plaster, with some figures, some of
which were by Raffaellino del Garbo, his pupil. The work was
valued at 2000 gold ducats, without reckoning the cost of the
blue and of the assistants, by Maestro Lanzilago of Padua, and
by Antonio, called Antoniasso, a Roman, two of the best painters
then in Rome. After receiving this sum Filippo returned to
Florence, where he completed the Strozzi Chapel, which excites
the admiration of all who see it for its beauty and art, and for
he variety of curious things which it contains, such as armed
men, temples, vases, crests, armour, trophies, spears, banners,
habits, buskins, head-dresses, priests' vestments, and other
things deserving the greatest praise for their arrangement. It
contains the raising of Drusiana by St. John the Evangelist,
with a remarkable expression of the amazement of the bystanders
at seeing the dead raised to life by a simple sign of the cross.
The one who marvels most is a priest or philosopher clothed in
the antique style, and holding a vase in his hand. Among a
number of women here in various dresses is a boy frightened by
a red-spotted spaniel who has seized his tunic, running to hide
himself in his mother's dress, exhibiting no less fear than she
does at the resurrection of Drusiana. Near this, where St. John
is in the boiling oil, he shows the rage of the judge who is com-
manding the fire to be made hotter, while the flames fly out in

[1] He did not die until 1551.   [2] He was at work there 1484-1502.

the faces of those engaged in the task, all the figures being in varied and well-chosen attitudes. On the other wall is St. Philip in the Temple of Mars, making the serpent come from beneath the altar, whose poisonous breath kills the king's son. The hole from which the reptile issued is shown in some steps, and is so well painted that one evening one of Filippo's boys, who wished to hide something from someone who was about to enter, ran hastily to this hole to put it in, believing it to be real. Filippo also displayed such art in painting the serpent that the poison, the stench and the fire seem real and not painted. Very much admired also is his conception of the crucifixion of the saint. He imagined, following the legend, that the saint was stretched on the cross as it lay on the ground, and that it was afterwards raised by means of ropes and pulleys. These are fixed to some broken antiquities, fragments of pillars and pedestals, and pulled by the attendants. On one side the weight of the cross and of the nude body of the saint is borne by a ladder placed against it, and on the other a man holds it in position with a stake, while two others are relieving the weight so as to allow the cross to enter a hole in the ground prepared for it. In short, it is a picture which it would be impossible for any invention, design, industry or artifice to improve. It also contains many grotesques and other things in grisaille, made like marble and designed with originality and beauty. For the Scopetine friars at S. Donato, outside Florence, called Scopeto, which is now in ruins, he did a panel of the Magi offering their gifts to Christ,[1] very carefully finished, and containing the portrait of Pier Francesco de' Medici the elder, son of Lorenzo de' Bicci, as an astrologer with a quadrant in his hand, as well as others of Giovanni son of Sig. Giovanni de' Medici and another Pier Francesco, Giovanni's brother, with other noted personages. It contains Moors, Indians, and very strange dresses and a most curious cottage. For Lorenzo de' Medici he began a sacrifice in fresco in a loggia at Poggio a Caiano, which was left unfinished. For the nuns of S. Jeronimo, upon the hill of S. Giorgio in Florence, he began the picture of the high altar, which was continued with considerable success after his death by Alonso Berughetta,[2] a Spaniard, although completed by other painters on the latter going to Spain. In the palace of the Signoria he painted a panel [3] of the room where the Eight hold their sittings, and designed another large one to adorn the council chamber, but he died before he had begun to carry it out, although

[1] Dated 1496, now in the Uffizi. [2] Alonzo Berruguete.
[3] Dated 1485, now in the Uffizi.

the frame for it was carved, and is now in the possession
of Baccio Baldini, an excellent Florentine physician and an
admirer of all talent. For the church of the Badia at Florence
Filippo did a very fine St. Jerome. For the high altar of the friars
of the Nunziata he began a Deposition from the Cross,[1] but had
only half finished the figures when he was attacked by a raging
fever and by the constriction of the throat, commonly known
as quinsy, of which he died in a few days at the age of forty-five.

He had invariably shown himself courteous, affable and
gentle, and was lamented by all who had known him, especially
by the youth of his noble city, who had always made use of his
unrivalled genius in devising things for public festivals, masquerades and other spectacles. His excellence was such that he
obliterated the stain of his birth, if any there be, not only by
his eminence as an artist, although he was inferior to no one in
his day, but by his modest and courteous bearing, and, above
all, by his lovable nature, the true power of which to win the
affections of everyone can only be realised by those who have
experienced it. Filippo was buried by his children in S. Michele
Bisdomini on 13th April, 1505. While they were carrying him to
burial all the shops in the via de' Servi were closed, which is
sometimes done at the funerals of men of eminence.

His pupils were far inferior to him. Among them was Raffaellino del Garbo, who did a number of things as I shall have
occasion to say, although he did not realise the expectations
excited about him during Filippo's lifetime, when he himself
was a boy, for the fruit does not always equal the flowers which
appear in the spring. Nor did Niccolo Zoccolo, whom some call
Niccolo Cartoni, another of Filippo's pupils, achieve great success. He did the wall over the altar of S. Giovanni Decollato at
Arezzo, and a small panel of merit in S. Agnesa, as well as a
panel in the abbey of S. Fiora over a lavabo, of Christ asking
drink of the woman of Samaria, with many other works too
mediocre to deserve notice.

[1] Begun in 1503, finished by Perugino in 1505, now in the Uffizi, Florence.

BERNARDINO PINTURICCHIO,[1] Painter of Florence
(?1454–1513)

JUST as many are aided by Fortune without being endowed with great talent, so many men of talent are pursued by a hostile fortune. Thus she seems to adopt as her children those who depend upon her, without the aid of any ability, and is pleased that some should rise by her favour who would never have attracted notice by their own merits. Thus it was with Pinturicchio of Perugia, who, prolific as he was, and enjoying the assistance of others, nevertheless possessed a far higher reputation than his works warranted. At the same time, he had great skill in large works, and always employed a number of assistants.

After working in his early youth for some time with Pietro Perugino, his master, doing many things, and receiving a third of the profits, he was invited to Siena by Cardinal Francesco Piccolomini to paint the library[2] built by Pope Pius II. in the Duomo there. It is indeed true that the sketches and cartoons for all the scenes there were by Raphael of Urbino, then a youth, who had been his companion and fellow-pupil under Piero, whose style Raphael had thoroughly mastered. One of these cartoons may still be seen at Siena, and some of these sketches of Raphael are in our book. The scenes of this work were divided into ten pictures, Pinturicchio being assisted by many boys and workmen of Pietro's school. The first shows the birth of Pius II., with his parents, Silvio Piccolomini and Vittoria, in 1405, in Valdorcia, in the district of Corsignano (now called Pienza, after him, because he made it into a city), and his being called Æneas. His parents are drawn from life. In the same scene is Domenico, cardinal of Capranica, crossing the Alps in the ice and snow to attend the council at Basel. The second scene represents the missions on which Æneas was sent by the council: to Strasburg thrice, to Trent, Constance, Frankfurt and Savoy. In the third, Æneas is sent as ambassador by the anti-Pope Felix to the Emperor Frederick III., who was so much struck by his dexterity, ability, eloquence and grace that he caused him to be crowned with laurel as a poet, after which he is made protonotary, received among his friends, and appointed chief secretary. The fourth shows him being sent by Frederick to Eugenius IV.,[3] who made him Bishop of Triest, and subsequently

---

[1] Bernardino di Betto.   [2] He did this work between 1503 and 1508.
    [3] It was Nicholas V. who gave him this preferment.

Archbishop of Siena. In the fifth, the emperor, who is anxious to come to Italy to receive the imperial crown, sends Æneas to Telamone, a port of the Sienese, to meet his wife Leonora, who is coming from Portugal. In the sixth, Æneas is sent by the emperor to Calixtus IV. to persuade him to make war on the Turks; and, as Siena has been harassed by the Count of Piti-gliano and others, at the instigation of King Alfonso of Naples, the Pope is sending Æneas to treat for peace. This done, a war is planned against the Orientals, and, on returning to Rome, Æneas is created cardinal by the Pope. The seventh shows the death of Calixtus and the election of Æneas to be Pope as Pius II. In the eighth the Pope is going to the council at Mantua for the expedition against the Turks, where the Marquis Ludo-vico receives him with great pomp and extraordinary magnifi-cence. In the ninth the Pope is canonising Catherine of Siena, a nun and holy lady of the order of the Friar Preachers. In the tenth and last the Pope, while preparing a great fleet against the Turks, with the aid of all the Christian princes, dies at Ancona, and a holy hermit of Camaldoli sees his soul carried to heaven by angels at the moment of his death, as we read. The same picture shows the body brought from Ancona to Rome, accom-panied by a crowd of lords and prelates weeping for the death of such a man, and of so rare and so holy a pope. This work is full of portraits, which it would take too long to enumerate; the colouring is fine and vigorous; it is enriched with gold ornaments, while the ceiling decoration is admirably devised. Under each scene is a Latin inscription describing its nature. To this library the three Graces [1] were brought by Cardinal Francesco Piccolomini, the Pope's nephew, and placed in the middle. These are fine marble antiques, and the first which excited admiration. Before the library was finished, which contained the books left by Pius II., Cardinal Francesco was created Pope, and chose the title of Pius III. in memory of his uncle. Over the door of the library leading to the Duomo, and occupying the whole of the wall space, Pinturicchio painted the coronation of Pius III., with many portraits from life. Beneath it are these words:

Pius III. Senensis, Pii II. nepos MDIII. Septembris XXI. apertis electus suffragiis, octavo Octobris coronatus est.

Pinturicchio, having worked at Rome in the time of Pope Sixtus,[2] while he was with Pietro Perugino, had served Domenico

---

[1] Now in the Galleria.   [2] In 1481.

della Rovere, cardinal of S. Clemente. The cardinal having erected a fine palace in the Borgo Vecchio, wished Pinturicchio to decorate it and paint the arms of Pope Sixtus on the façade, supported by two infants. He did some things in the palace of S. Apostolo for Sciarra Colonna. Not long after, in 1484, the Genoese Pope Innocent VIII. employed him to decorate some rooms and loggias in the palace of the Belvedere, where, among other things, he painted a loggia full of landscapes at the Pope's desire, with views of Rome, Milan, Genoa, Florence, Venice and Naples, in the Flemish style.[1] This being unusual at the time, gave considerable satisfaction. In the same place he did a Madonna in fresco at the entrance to the principal door. In the chapel in S. Pietro containing the lance which pierced the side of Christ, he painted a Madonna of more than life-size in tempera on a panel for Innocent VIII. In the church of S. Maria del Popolo he painted two chapels,[2] one for Domenico della Rovere, cardinal of S. Clemente, where he was afterwards buried, and the other for Cardinal Innocenzio Cibo, where he also was interred, introducing the portrait of each in his respective chapel. In the Pope's palace he painted some apartments communicating with the court of S. Pietro, the ceilings and paintings of which were restored a few years ago by Pope Pius IV. In the same palace Alexander VI. employed him to paint his own apartments[3] and all the Borgia tower, where he decorated one room with representations of the liberal arts, doing the vaulting with stucco and gold. But, as the modern manner of making stucco was not then known, these ornaments are all but entirely destroyed. Over the door of a room in this palace he painted a portrait of Signora Giulia Farnese as Our Lady, with the head of Pope Alexander adoring her.

It was a habit of Bernardino to decorate his paintings with gold ornaments in relief to please some who had little knowledge of art, and to create an imposing appearance, but it is a clumsy device in a picture. After painting a story of St. Catherine in these apartments, he made the arches of Rome in relief, and painted the scene so that, the figures being in front and the buildings behind, the receding objects are more prominent than the figures in the foreground, a capital heresy in our art. In the castle of S. Angelo he painted a number[4] of rooms with grotesques, and in the garden at the base of the great tower he did scenes of Pope Alexander, with portraits of Isabella, the Catholic queen,

Niccolo Orsino, Count of Pitigliano, Gianjacomo Triulzi, with many other relations and friends of the Pope, notably Cesare Borgia, his brother, his sisters, and many prominent men of the day. In the Chapel of Paolo Tolosa at Monte Oliveto of Naples there is an Assumption [1] by Pinturicchio. He did a number of other works all over Italy, but, as they are not very excellent, though skilful, I pass them over in silence.

Pinturicchio used to say that painters could give the best relief to their works by relying on themselves without owing anything to princes or others. He worked also at Perugia, but did only a few things. At Araceli he painted [2] the chapel of St. Bernardino, and in the vaulting of the principal chapel of St. Maria del Popolo, where, as I have said, he did the two chapels, he painted the four Doctors of the Church. [3] When he had attained the age of fifty-nine he was employed to paint a Nativity of the Virgin in S. Francesco at Siena. After he had begun it, the friars gave him a room to dwell in, entirely bare, as he desired, except for a large antique trunk, which they found too heavy to move; but Pinturicchio, who was very eccentric, made such a clamour that the friars in despair determined to take it away. In removing it they broke a plank, and out came 500 gold ducats. Pinturicchio was chagrined at this, and bore such a grudge against the poor friars for their good fortune, that he could think of nothing else, and it so weighed upon his mind that it caused his death. His works were executed about 1513.

Benedetto Buonfiglio, [4] a painter of Perugia, was his companion and friend, although older than he, and painted several things in the Pope's palace at Rome with other masters. In the Chapel of the Signoria in his native Perugia he did scenes from the life of St. Ercolano, [5] bishop and protector of that city, as well as some miracles of St. Louis. In S. Domenico he painted the story of the Magi [6] in tempera on a panel, and a number of saints on another. In the church of S. Bernardino he painted a Christ in the air, with the saint and the people below. [7] In short, he enjoyed a considerable reputation in those parts before the rise of Pietro Perugino. Another friend and a fellow-worker of Pinturicchio was Gerino of Pistoia, who was considered a careful colourist and a successful imitator of the style of Pietro Perugino,

---

[1] Now in the Naples Museum.   [2] 1497–1500.   [3] In 1489.
[4] c. 1420–96.   [5] Begun in 1454.   [6] c. 1466.
[7] 1465. All these works in the Signoria Chapel. St. Domenico and St. Bernardino are now in the Perugia Gallery.

with whom he worked until his death. He did a few things in his native Pistoia. At Borgo S. Sepolcro he did a meritorious oil-painting of the Circumcision for the company of the Buon Gesù. He painted a chapel in fresco in the Pieve there, as well as another chapel for the community on the Tiber on the way to Anghiari, also in fresco. In S. Lorenzo, an abbey of the Camaldolite monks there, he did another chapel. He stayed a long while at the Borgo while engaged upon these works, so that he almost made it his home. He was quite insignificant as an artist, but a most laborious worker, so much so that it amounted to drudgery.

There was an excellent painter in the city of Fuligno at that time named Niccolo Alunno,[1] because, as oils were not in general use before Pietro Perugino, many men were considered able who did not afterwards come to the fore. Niccolo gave considerable satisfaction by his works, although tempera was his only medium, because all his heads were portraits and seemed alive. There is a Nativity of Christ by him in S. Agostino at Fuligno,[2] with a predella of small figures. At Assisi he made a processional banner, the high-altar picture in the Duomo, and another picture in S. Francesco. But his best painting was a chapel in the Duomo containing a Pietà and two angels holding torches and weeping so naturally that I do not think any painter could have done better, however excellent. He painted the facade of S. Maria degli Angeli at the same place, and did many other works which I need not mention, as I have spoken of the best. This is the end of the Life of Pinturicchio, who, among other things, pleased many princes and lords because he finished his works quickly, though perhaps less excellently than if he had gone slowly and carefully.

FRANCESCO FRANCIA,[3] Goldsmith and Painter of Bologna (1450–1517)

FRANCESCO FRANCIA, born at Bologna in 1450 of an artisan, but of quite easy circumstances, was placed with a goldsmith in his early childhood. In this art he displayed ingenuity and spirit, and he grew up so handsome, with such a pleasant

[1] Niccolò da Foligno (1430–1502). Alunno, the Latin alumnus or pupil, is a mistake by Vasari, who confounds a description with a surname.
[2] Painted in 1492. [3] Francesco Raibolini.

conversation that he was able to distract the most melancholy individuals by his talk, so that he won the affection not only of all who knew him but of many Italian princes and other lords. Whilst with the goldsmith he studied design and took such delight in it, for it aroused him to better things, that he made great progress, as may be seen by many things he did in silver at his native Bologna and especially by some excellent works in *niello*, where in a space of little more than two fingers across he would frequently introduce twenty small figures, all well proportioned and beautiful. He also enamelled many silver things which perished in the fall and flight of the Bentivogli. In a word, in every branch of that art he excelled all who had ever practised it. But the task in which he took most delight and most excelled was in making dies for medals, a work in which he was remarkable, as some examples show, namely a life-like head of Pope Julius II., equal to one by Caradosso. Besides this he made life-like medals for Sig. Giovanni Bentivoglio and for a number of princes who stayed at Bologna in passing. He made the portrait medals in wax, and on finishing the matrices sent them to the originals, thus obtaining handsome presents as well as immortal fame. During his life he was master of the mint of Bologna and made stamps for all the dies during the rule of the Bentivogli, and after their departure, and those of Pope Julius II. so long as he lived. This is made clear by the money coined by the Pope on his entry,[1] one side containing his head frome life and the other the words *Bononia per Julium a tyranno liberata*. Francia was considered so excellent that he continued to make the dies for money until the time of Pope Leo. The impressions of his dies cannot now be obtained by amateurs for any money, so highly are they valued.

Being desirous of greater glory, and having known Andrea Mantegna and many other painters who had obtained wealth and honour by their art, Francia determined to try whether he could not succeed in colouring so that he might follow in their steps, for he was already an accomplished designer. Accordingly, as an experiment, he made some portraits and other small things, entertaining members of the profession in his house for many months to teach him the methods of colouring, and his judgment being excellent he learned quickly. His first work was a somewhat small picture[2] for M. Bartolommeo Felicini, who put it in the Misericordia, a church outside Bologna. It represents a Madonna seated, with many other figures and a

[1] In 1508.   [2] Dated 1494, now in the Pinacoteca, Bologna.

portrait of M. Bartolommeo. It is done in oils carefully finished, and was executed in 1490. The people of Bologna were so delighted, that M. Giovanni Bentivoglio, being anxious to honour the chapel of St. James there with works by this new painter, employed him to do a Madonna in the air with two figures beside her and two angels below playing instruments.[1] The work was so well executed that Francia earned a handsome present from M. Giovanni besides his warm praise. Incited by this, Monsignore de' Bentivogli employed him to do a panel for the high altar of the Misericordia, which was much admired, containing the Nativity of Christ,[2] the design being excellent, and the conception and colouring admirable. He introduced a very good portrait of the donor, as those who knew him say, in the habit which he wore when he returned from Jerusalem as a pilgrim. He did an Annunciation on a panel for the church of the Nunziata outside the Mammolo gate, with two figures at the side, considered to be very well executed.

While his fame was thus increasing, Francia determined to try whether he could succeed in fresco, as working in oils had brought him such honour and profit. M. Giovanni Bentivoglio had caused his palace to be painted by various masters of Ferrara, Bologna and Mantua, but when he had seen Francia's experiments in fresco, he determined to employ him to paint a wall of the room in which he himself lived. Here Francia represented the Camp of Holofernes, with armed guards both horse and foot watching the tents. While they are attending to other things the sleepy Holofernes is taken by a woman in widow's raiment, who holds his hair with her left hand, all wet with wine and sleep, while with her right she strikes the blow to slay the enemy. An old servant, with every appearance of a faithful attendant, regards Judith steadfastly to give her courage and leans forward holding out a basket to receive the head of the somnolent lover. This was one of the best scenes ever produced by Francia, but it perished in the ruin of the building at the fall of the Bentivogli,[3] together with another scene in the same room in bronze colour of a dispute of philosophers, excellently produced and effectively conveying the artist's meaning. These works caused M. Giovanni and the members of his house to entertain a great esteem for Francia, as did all his fellow-citizens. In the chapel of St. Cecilia, next to the church of S. Jacopo, he did two scenes in fresco, in one of which he represented Our

[1] Probably about 1499.   [2] Dated 1498, now in the Gallery, Bologna.
[3] In 1507.

Lady espoused by Joseph,[1] and in the other the death of St. Cecilia, a work much admired by the Bolognese. Indeed, Francia became so skilful, and was so much encouraged by his progress towards perfection in what he undertook, that he did a great number of things which I shall not record, contenting myself with pointing out the best and most notable of his paintings for those who are interested in them. At the same time his painting did not prevent him from pursuing his work at the mint and other work on medals which he continued to do as before. It is said that he was much grieved at the departure of M. Giovanni Bentivoglio, from whom he had received so many benefits, but, like a wise man of the world, he kept to his work. After their exile he did three pictures which went to Modena, one being a Baptism of Christ by St. John, the second a fine Annunciation, and the third a Madonna in the air, with many figures,[2] which was set up in the church of the Observantine friars. The fame of this excellent master being thus spread abroad, cities competed for the possession of his works. Thus in S. Giovanni, at Parma, for the black monks, he did a dead Christ in the lap of the Virgin,[3] surrounded by many figures, considered by all to be a most beautiful work. The friars, seeing themselves so well served, employed him to make another for their house at Reggio in Lombardy, where he did a Madonna with many figures. At Cesena he did yet another picture for the church of these monks, representing the Circumcision, delightfully coloured. Not wishing to be outdone by their neighbours, the Ferrarese determined to employ Francia to decorate their Duomo, and on a panel he did a large number of figures, which they called the picture of All the Saints. He did another for S. Lorenzo in Bologna of a Madonna with a figure on either side and two babes beneath,[4] much admired. Hardly had he finished this when he had to do another in S. Jobbe of a Crucifixion, St. Job kneeling at the foot of the cross with two figures at the sides.

Francia's fame and his works were spread abroad through Lombardy, and even from Tuscany they sent for his productions, a picture of his going to Lucca, which represented St. Anne and Our Lady with many other figures, and, above, a dead Christ

---

[1] The scene represents the marriage of St. Cecilia. These works were done between 1505 and 1507.
[2] The Baptism, dated 1508, is in the Dresden Gallery; the Annunciation, dated 1502, is at Berlin, and the Madonna, which is a work of Francesco Ferrari painted in 1510, is in the Modena Gallery.
[3] Now in the Parma Gallery.
[4] Painted 1500, in the Hermitage Gallery, Leningrad.

in his Mother's lap.[1] This work is placed in the Church of S. Fridiano, and is much valued by the Lucchese. For the church of the Nunziata at Bologna he did two other panels with the utmost care, and another in the Misericordia outside the Strà Castione gate, at the request of a gentlewoman of the Manzuoli, of Our Lady with the Child, St. George, St. John the Baptist, St. Stephen and St. Augustine,[2] while an angel at the foot clasps its hands with such grace that it appears a veritable native of Paradise. In the company of S. Francesco [3] in the same city he did another panel, and yet another in the company of S. Jeronimo.[4] His intimate friend M. Paolo Zambeccaro got him to do a picture of considerable size as a keepsake, representing a Nativity[5]; and it is very celebrated among his works. On this account M. Paolo employed him to do two beautiful figures in fresco at his villa. He executed a scene very delicately in fresco in the house of M. Jeronimo Bolognino, with a great variety of beautiful figures, all these works exciting an extraordinary reverence for him in that city, where they almost considered him a god. A pair of caparisons painted by him for the Duke of Urbino increased his reputation marvellously. In these he represented a great forest which has caught fire, and out of it come all manner of birds and beasts, with some remarkable figures, agitated by fear. He has spent much time on the feathers of the birds, and the work is also remarkable for the various species of animals, the leaves and branches, and the diversity of the trees. His labours were rewarded liberally by the duke, who was delighted with the continued praise accorded to his possession. The Duke, Guido Baldo, also has a picture of Lucretia by him in his wardrobe, which he greatly values, together with many other pictures which will be mentioned in due time. After this Francia did a panel in S. Vitale ad Agricola at the altar of the Madonna, containing two beautiful angels playing the lute. I must not mention all the pictures scattered about Bologna in the houses of noblemen, and still less the countless portraits which he painted, for fear of being prolix.

While Francia was enjoying the fruits of his labours in peace Raphael of Urbino was at Rome. Thither came many foreigners and, among others, several Bolognese noblemen, to see the master's works. As men are generally ready to praise their own

[1] Now in the National Gallery, London.
[2] Now in the Pinacoteca, Bologna.
[3] This appears to be a picture now in the Berlin Gallery.
[4] Pinacoteca, Bologna.
[5] Forli Gallery; painted in 1503.

country, these men began to sing the praises of Francia to Raphael, his works, his life and his ability, and from this it came about that the two artists exchanged friendly letters. Francia, who had heard of the renown of the divine pictures of Raphael, desired to see his works, but being old and in comfortable circumstances he would not leave Bologna. It happened that Raphael was doing a panel of St. Cecilia for the Cardinal de' Pucci Santi Quattro, which was to be sent to Bologna to be placed in a chapel in S. Giovanni in Monte, containing the tomb of the Blessed Elena dall' Olio. He directed this work to Francia, desiring him, as a friend, to place it on the altar with the ornament as devised by him. Francia was delighted, for he had long desired to see the works of Raphael. Opening Raphael's letter requesting him to set up the picture, repair any scratches and, as a friend, correct any errors he might find in it, Francia drew the masterpiece out of its case into a good light. But when he had done so his amazement and wonder, and the feeling of the presumption which he had displayed, caused him so much chagrin that he died soon after. Raphael's picture was divine rather than a painting, and it may be called something rare even among the beautiful things which he painted, although all are miraculous. Francia, half-dead at the overwhelming power and beauty of the picture, which he had to compare with his own works lying around, though thoroughly discouraged, took it to S. Giovanni in Monte, to the chapel where it was to be put. Returning home he took to his bed in an agony, feeling that in art he was reduced to insignificance as contrasted with his reputation and with what he himself had believed. He died, some suppose of grief and melancholy, due to his excessive contemplation of the brilliant picture of Raphael, just as did Fivizzano [1] from regarding his beautiful Death, of whom the following epigram is written:

> Me veram pictor divinus mente recepit
> Admota est operi deinde perita manus.
> Dumque opera in facto defigit lumina pictor
> Intentus nimium, palluit et moritur
> Viva igitur sum mors, non mortua mortis imago
> Si fungor, quo mors fungitur, officio.

However, some say that his death was so sudden that it appeared by many indications to be due to poison or apoplexy. Francia

[1] The fable runs that this artist painted such a beautiful figure of Death that, in regarding it afterwards, he suddenly fell dead. No further particulars are known about him.

was a prudent man, of regular habits and robust constitution. His body was honourably buried by his children in Bologna in 1518.

PIETRO PERUGINO,[1] Painter

(1446–1523)

THE beneficial influence of poverty in impelling men to perfect their talents is well illustrated in the life of Pietro Perugino. Escaping from the dire misfortunes of Perugia, and coming to Florence, he endeavoured to make himself a name by his talents. For many months he lived with nothing to sleep in but a chest, while he studied his profession with the utmost ardour, turning night into day. Once this had become a habit, he knew no other pleasure than the continual practice of his art and to be always painting. Moreover, the fear of poverty being continually before his eyes, he did things for gain which he probably would never have looked at but for the necessity of maintaining himself, so that wealth might have prevented that progress which he was compelled to make in order that, even if he did not attain to the highest excellence, he might at least have enough to support himself. Thus he took no heed of cold, hunger, discomfort, toil or shame, to the end that he might one day enjoy ease and rest, his favourite saying being that good weather must needs follow bad, and that houses are built in fair weather so that one may have shelter when the need arises.

But in order that the progress of this artist may be better understood, I will begin at the beginning. According to the public report he was born at Perugia, of a poor man of Castello dal Pieve called Cristofano, and was christened Pietro. Brought up amid misery and want, he was sent by his father to run errands for a painter of Perugia,[2] who, though not very skilful himself, had a great veneration for art and those who excelled therein. He never tired of telling Pietro what gain and honour painting brought to those who did well in it, describing to him the rewards of the ancients and moderns, and advising him to study the art. He succeeded in kindling the boy's imagination so that he aspired, by the help of Fortune, to join the ranks of the painters. He would often ask his master in what state artists were best treated, who invariably replied in the same way, that it was in Florence more than elsewhere that men became perfect in all the arts, but especially in painting, owing to three causes: The spirit of criticism, the air making minds naturally free and not content with mediocrity, but leading them to value works for their beauty and other good qualities rather than for their authors. The second is that whoever wishes to live there must be industrious, quick and ready, constantly employing his intellect and judgment, and then he must know how to make money, Florence not having a rich and fruitful territory, so that prices cannot be so low as where there is abundance. The third, which probably exercises no less influence than the others, is a thirst of glory and honour which the air generates strongly in the men of every profession, so that no man of ability will allow others to equal him, and still less suffer himself to be distanced by other men, fashioned like himself, even though acknowledged to be masters. This desire for their own advancement frequently renders them censorious and ungrateful if they are not naturally amiable and wise. It is true that when a man has learned what is necessary, if he wishes to do more than vegetate like the brutes, and would become rich, he must leave the city and sell his works abroad, spreading the reputation of the city, as learned men do that of their university, for Florence deals with her artists like Time, who, after creating them, casts them off and gradually consumes them. Moved by this advice and the persuasions of many others, Pietro came to Florence with the determination to excel, and succeeded so well that works in his style were very highly valued.

He studied under Andrea Verrocchio, and his first figures were for the nuns outside the Prato gate in S. Martino, now destroyed by the war. In Camaldoli he did a St. Jerome on a wall, then much valued by the Florentines and greatly praised because he had made the saint old, lean and shrivelled, his eyes fixed on a crucifix. He is wasted to a skeleton, as may be seen by a copy in the possession of Bartolommeo Gondi. In a few years Pietro had won such a reputation that not only were Florence and Italy filled with his works, but France, Spain and many other countries. His paintings being so highly valued, the merchants began to traffic in them, and sent them to different countries, with considerable profit to themselves. For the nuns of S. Chiara, Pietro did a dead Christ, on a panel,[1] the colouring being so lovely and novel that artists expected marvellous results from him. These works contain some fine heads of old

[1] Dated 1495; now in the Pitti Gallery.

men, as well as some Maries weeping as they regard the body with unspeakable reverence and love. He also introduced a landscape which was then considered most beautiful, the true method of doing them not having been found at that time. It is said that Francesco del Pugliese was willing to give the nuns three times as much as they had paid Pietro to get him to do another painting for them, and that they would not consent because Pietro said that he did not believe he could equal the first. In the convent of the Jesuits outside the Pinti [1] gate there were many things by Pietro, but the church and convent being now destroyed I will take this opportunity to say a few things about them before proceeding further.

This church, designed by Antonio di Giorgio of Settignano, was forty braccia long and twenty broad. Four steps led to a platform six braccia high, upon which was the high altar with many ornaments of carved stone, and over the altar, in a rich frame, a picture of Domenico Ghirlandajo, as has been said. In the middle was a screen across the church, with a door in the middle and an altar on either side, on each being a picture by Pietro Perugino, as I shall relate, and over the door was a fine crucifix by Benedetto da Maiano, between Our Lady and St. John, in relief. Before the platform of the high altar, and attached to the screen, was a singing-gallery of walnut wood, of the Doric order, very well made, and over the principal door of the church was another singing-gallery resting upon a wooden framework. The underside formed a ceiling or soffit handsomely partitioned, while rows of balusters formed a railing for the gallery on the side facing the high altar. The gallery was very convenient for the friars of the convent at night for their hours, for their private devotions, and also for feast days. Over the principal door of the church, which possessed a beautiful stone framework, and had a porch on columns reaching as far as the door of the convent, was a lunette with St. Just the bishop between two angels, by the hand of Gherardo the illuminator, a beautiful work. This was because the church was dedicated to that saint, of whom they have an arm as a relic. At the entrance of the convent was a small cloister of about the same size as the church, that is to say forty braccia by twenty, the surrounding arches with their vaulting resting upon stone columns, forming a very spacious and convenient loggia. In the

[1] S. Giusto alla Mura; the church was demolished in 1529 when Prince Philibert of Orange was threatening to besiege Florence. The convent was suppressed in 1668.

middle of the courtyard of this cloister, which was paved throughout with squared stones, was a beautiful well with a loggia above, also resting upon stone columns and forming a rich and handsome decoration. This cloister contained the chapter-house of the friars, the side door to the church, and the steps leading to the dormitory and the other apartments and conveniences of the friars. From the cloister to the principal door of the convent was a passage as long as the chapter-house and buttery, corresponding with another larger cloister more beautiful than the first. All this way, namely the 40 braccia of the loggia of the first cloister, the passage and that of the second made an inexpressibly fine and lengthy vista, especially as there was an avenue in the garden in the same direction, 200 braccia long, and thus a remarkably fine view was obtained from the principal door of the convent. In the second cloister there was a refectory 60 braccia long and 18 broad, with the necessary apartments, and what the friars call the offices, required by such a convent. Above was a T-shaped dormitory, the right-hand side of which, 60 braccia long, was double, that is to say it had cells on either side with an oratory at the end in a space of 15 braccia. Above the altar here was a picture by Pietro Perugino, and another work in fresco by the same hand over the door. On the same floor above the chapter-house was a large room in which the friars made stained-glass windows, with the furnaces and other things necessary for that work. While Pietro lived he did the cartoons for many of their works, which were consequently excellent. The garden of the convent was the finest, the best kept and best arranged about Florence, with vines surrounding the whole. Moreover, the rooms for the customary distilling of scented waters and medicinal things possessed every imaginable convenience. In fine, the convent was among the most beautiful and the best appointed of Florence, and this is why I was anxious to leave a record of it, especially as the majority of the paintings there were by Pietro Perugino. None of those, however, which he did there has been preserved, except the panels, because the remainder were destroyed during the siege, together with the entire structure. The panels were taken to the S. Pier Gattolini gate, where the friars received a house in the church and convent of S. Giovannino.[1] The two pictures on the screen were by Pietro, one representing Christ in the Garden, with the Apostles sleeping. Here Pietro shows how sleep quiets fears and troubles,

[1] They are now in the Uffizi, Florence.

representing the Apostles as resting very comfortably. In the other he did a Pietà,[1] namely Christ on his Mother's knees, with four figures about, quite equal to his other works. He represented the dead Christ as if stiffened by the cold and the time spent on the cross, and borne with grief and lamentation by John and the Magdalene. In another panel he did a Crucifixion, with the Magdalene and St. John the Baptist, St. Jerome and the Blessed John Colombino, the founder of the order, executed with infinite diligence. These three panels have suffered considerably, having darkened, and cracked where the shadows are. The reason for this is that three coatings of paint are superimposed, and when the first coating laid upon the composition is not quite dry, the colours contract in drying and after a time the cracks appear. Pietro could not know this because oil-colouring was then in its infancy.

As Pietro's works were much praised by the Florentines, a prior of the same convent of the Jesuits, who was fond of art, employed him to do a Nativity, with the Magi, in the minute style, on a wall of the first cloister. This was executed by him with great loveliness and perfect finish. It contained a great number of different heads and not a few portraits, among them being his master, Andrea Verrocchio. In the same court he did a frieze over the arches of the columns, with very well executed life-size heads. One of these was that of the prior, done with such vigour and life that many of the most skilful artists considered it to be Pietro's best work. In the other cloister, over the door leading into the refectory, he did Pope Boniface[2] confirming the habit of the Blessed John Colombino, introducing the portraits of eight of the friars, and a lovely receding perspective which won much well-deserved praise, because Pietro paid special attention to this branch. Below, in another scene, he began the Nativity of Christ, with angels and shepherds, very freshly coloured; and over the door of the oratory he did a Madonna, a St. Jerome and the Blessed John, three half-figures in the tympanum, so finely executed that they were ranked among Pietro's best works on the wall.

I have heard it said that the prior was very skilful in making ultramarine blue, and having a great deal he wished Pietro to use it freely, but he was so miserly and mistrustful that he insisted on being present when Pietro used it. Pietro, who was a just man, and never desired what he did not earn, took this want of confidence in very ill part, and resolved to shame the

---

[1] Uffizi, Florence.　　　　[2] It should be Urban V., in 1367.

prior. Accordingly he took a basin of water whenever he did draperies or other parts which he intended to paint in blue and white, and kept applying to the prior who, in his miserly way, took the ultramarine from his bag to put in the vessel when it was tempered with water. Then Pietro set to work, and dipped his brush in the basin at every two strokes, so that more remained in the water than was on the work. The prior, on seeing his paint disappear and the work progressing but slowly, kept on exclaiming, "What a quantity of ultramarine this lime consumes!" "You see how it is for yourself," replied Pietro. When the prior had gone, Pietro took the ultramarine which had settled at the bottom of the basin, and when he thought the moment opportune presented it to the prior, saying, "Father, this is yours. Learn to trust honest men who never deceive those who put confidence in them, but who are perfectly able if they choose to deceive suspicious men like you."

Having become famous by these and many other works, Pietro was all but compelled to go to Siena, where he painted a magnificent picture in S. Francesco, and another in S. Agostino, of a Crucifixion and some saints.[1] Shortly after he did a St. Jerome in penitence in the church of S. Gallo at Florence, which is now in S. Jacopo tra' Fossi, where the friars live, near the corner of the Alberti. He was next employed to do a dead Christ, with St. John and the Madonna over the steps of the side door of S. Pier Maggiore, and succeeded so well that it has maintained its original freshness in spite of the wind and rain. Pietro was undoubtedly a skilful colourist both in fresco and in oils. Thus all skilled artists are under obligations to him, because it is to him that they owe their knowledge of lights, as seen in his works. In S. Croce, in the same city, he did a Pietà, with the dead Christ, and two marvellous figures, remarkable not so much for their excellence as for the way in which the colours painted in fresco have remained so fresh and new. He was employed by Bernardino de' Rossi, citizen of Florence, to do a St. Sebastian to be sent to France, the price being fixed at 100 gold crowns, but Bernardino sold it to the King of France for 400 gold ducats. At Vallombrosa he painted a picture for the high altar,[2] and did another for the friars in the Certosa of Pavia.[3] For the Cardinal Caraffa he painted an Assumption, with the Apostles

[1] Painted in 1506; the S. Francesco picture was destroyed by fire in 1655.
[2] Painted in 1500; now in the Uffizi, Florence.
[3] The middle portion, with a Madonna and Child with St. Raphael and Tobias and St. Michael on either side is now in the National Gallery, London.

about the tomb, at the high altar of the Piscopio; and for Abbot Simone dei Graziani he did a large picture at Borgo S. Sepolcro, painted at Florence, and taken on the shoulders of porters to S. Gilio of the Borgo, at a great cost. For the church of S. Giovanni in Monte, at Bologna, he did a panel with some upright figures, and a Madonna in the air.[1]

Pietro's fame being spread abroad throughout Italy, he was, to his great glory, invited to Rome by Pope Sixtus IV. to work in the chapel with other famous artists.[2] Here he did Christ giving the keys to St. Peter, in conjunction with Don Bartolommeo della Gatta, abbot of S. Clemente, Arezzo, and also the Nativity and Baptism of Christ, the birth of Moses, and when he is taken out of the ark by Pharoah's daughter. On the wall where the altar is he did an Assumption of the Madonna, with a portrait of Sixtus kneeling. But these works were destroyed in the time of Pope Paul III. to make the wall for the Last Judgment of the divine Michelagnolo. He did the vaulting in the Borgia tower, in the Pope's palace, with stories of Christ, and some foliage in grisaille, which had an extraordinary reputation for excellence in his day. In S. Marco at Rome he did a story of two martyrs, next to the Sacrament, one of the best works executed by him in that city. In the palace of S. Apostolo he did a loggia and other apartments for Sciarra Colonna, all of which works brought a great deal of money into his hands. Accordingly he decided to stay no longer in Rome, and left in high favour with all the court, returning to his native Perugia. Here he completed a number of easel pictures and frescoes, notably an oil-painting of the Virgin and other saints in the Chapel of the Signori in the palace.[3] At S. Francesco del Monte he painted two chapels in fresco,[4] one of the Magi offering their gifts, the other of some Franciscan friars who went to the Sultan of Babylon and were killed. In the convent of S. Francesco he painted two panels in oils, one being a Resurrection of Christ and the other St. John the Baptist and saints.[5] In the church of the Servites [6] he also did two pictures, one a Transfiguration and the other, next the sacristy, the story of the Magi; but as they

---

[1] Now in the Pinacoteca, Bologna.
[2] 1481-2.
[3] Painted in 1496; now in the Vatican Gallery.
[4] Commissioned in 1502.
[5] The Resurrection is in the Vatican Gallery, the St. John in the Pinacoteca, Perugia.
[6] i.e. S. Maria Nuova, now in the Pinacoteca, Perugia.

are not of Pietro's usual excellence it is considered certain that they are among his earliest works. In S. Lorenzo, the Duomo of that city, the Chapel of the Crucified contains a Madonna, St. John and the other Maries, St. Laurence, St. James and other saints. At the altar of the Sacrament, which contains the marriage-ring of the Virgin, he painted her marriage.[1] After that he did all the audience-chambers of the Cambio, representing in the divisions of the vaulting the seven planets drawn upon chariots by various animals, according to the ancient custom. On the wall opposite the door of entrance he did the Nativity and Resurrection of Christ, and St. John the Baptist on a panel, in the midst of other saints. On the side walls he painted in his characteristic style Fabius Maximus, Socrates, Numa Pompilius, Fulvius Camillus, Pythagoras, Trajan, L. Sicinius, Leonidas the Spartan, Horatius Cocles, Fabius, Sempronius, Pericles the Athenian, and Cincinnatus. On the other wall are the prophets Isaiah, Moses, Daniel, David, Jeremiah, Solomon and the Erethrian, Lybian, Tiburtine, Delphic and other sibyls. Under each figure he wrote an appropriate inscription. In the border he introduced a very life-like portrait of himself, with his name thus:

Petrus Perusinus egregius pictor,
Perdita si fuerat, pingendo hic retulit artem :
Si nunquam inventa esset hactenus, ipse dedit
Anno D. 1500.

This beautiful work won more praise than any which Pietro had executed in Perugia, and is highly valued to-day by the men of that city in memory of their great countryman. In the principal chapel of St. Agostino he did a large isolated panel, in a rich frame, the front representing St. John baptising Christ,[2] and the back, that is the side facing the choir, the Nativity, with the heads of some saints. The predella contains some scenes of small figures, very carefully finished. In the chapel of St. Nicholas, in the same church, he did a picture for M. Benedetto Calera. Returning afterwards to Florence he did for the monks of Cestello[3] a St. Bernard in a panel, and in the chapter-house a Crucifixion, the Virgin, St. Benedict, St. Bernard and St. John. On the right-hand side of the second chapel in S. Domenico at Fiesole is a Madonna, with three figures, one of which, a St. Sebastian, is most admirable.[4]

[1] Painted in 1495; now at Caen and attributed to Lo Spagna.
[2] Now in the Pinacoteca, Perugia.
[3] i.e. S. Maria Maddalena de' Pazzi; commissioned 1493, finished 1496.
[4] Painted 1493; now in the Uffizi.

Pietro worked so hard, and had always so much to do, that he frequently repeated himself, and his theory of art led him so far that all his figures have the same air. When Michelagnolo arose, Pietro was most anxious to see the figures which were so belauded by artists. Seeing the greatness of his own name, acquired with so much toil, in danger of eclipse, he tried hard with biting words to mortify those who were at work. For this he richly deserved Michelagnolo's publicly-uttered description of him as a blockhead in art, as well as other rough words from the artists. Pietro, unable to brook such an insult, brought his rival before the Eight, but made a sorry exhibition.

Meanwhile the Servite friars at Florence, who wished the picture of their high altar to be by some famous master, had entrusted the work to Filippino, since Lionardo da Vinci had departed for France. But when Filippino had done half of one of the two pictures which were to go there he died, so that the friars entrusted the work to Pietro, in whom they had great confidence. Filippino had finished a Deposition of Christ from the Cross, with Nicodemus handing the body down, while Pietro did the Virgin fainting and other figures.[1] The work being in two pictures, one turned to the choir of the friars and the other towards the body of the church, the Deposition was to face behind the choir and the Assumption in front. But Pietro did so moderately that they altered this arrangement, putting the Deposition in front and the Assumption behind. Both have been removed to make room for the tabernacle of the Sacrament, and have been placed upon other altars, only six sections of the work remaining, containing some saints painted by Pietro, in niches. It is said that when this work was uncovered it was severely criticised by all the new artists, chiefly because Pietro had employed figures of which he had already made use. Even his friends declared that he had not taken pains, but had abandoned the good method of working either from avarice or in order to save time. Pietro answered, "I have done the figures which you have formerly praised and which have given you great pleasure. If you are now dissatisfied and do not praise them, how can I help it?" But they attacked him bitterly with sonnets and epigrams. Accordingly, though now old, he left Florence and returned to Perugia, doing some works in fresco in S. Severo, a monastery of the Camaldolite order.[2] Here his young pupil, Raphael of Urbino, had done some figures, as will be related in his Life. Pietro also worked at Montone,

[1] In 1505; now in the Uffizi, Florence.   [2] In 1521.

La Fratta and in many other places round Perugia, especially at S. Maria degli Angeli at Assisi, where he painted a Christ on the Cross and many other figures in fresco on the wall behind the chapel of the Madonna, which communicates with the choir of the friars. In the church of S. Piero, an abbey of the black monks in Perugia, he painted a large picture of the Ascension at the high altar, with the Apostles below looking heavenwards.[1] The predella contains three scenes done with great diligence, namely the Magi, the baptism and resurrection of Christ, the whole work being replete with fine efforts so that it is Pietro's best oil-painting in Perugia. He began a work in fresco of considerable importance at Castello della Pieve, but did not finish it. As he trusted no one, he was accustomed, in going and coming between the Castello and Perugia, to carry his money with him, but some men lay in wait for him in a pass and robbed him. He begged for his life and obtained it, and afterwards, by means of his numerous friends, he recovered a great part of his money, though his grief at the loss brought him to death's door.

Pietro was not a religious man, and would never believe in the immortality of the soul, obstinately refusing to listen to all good reasons. He relied entirely upon the good gifts of fortune, and would have gone to any lengths for money. He acquired great wealth, and built and bought houses in Florence. At Perugia and Castello della Pieve he acquired much real property. He took to wife a beautiful girl, and had children by her, and he liked her to wear pretty head-dresses both out of doors and in the house, and is said to have often dressed her himself. Having attained a good old age, Pietro died at the age of seventy-eight at Castello della Pieve, where he was honourably buried in 1524.

Pietro made many masters of his style, but one greatly excelled the others, and having devoted himself entirely to the honourable study of painting, far surpassed his master. This was that wonder, Raphael Sanzio of Urbino, who worked for many years with Pietro, together with Giovanni de' Santi, his father. Pinturicchio, the Perugian painter, was another pupil, and he always retained Pietro's style, as has been said in his Life.

Another pupil was Rocco Zoppo, painter of Florence, of whom Filippo Salviati has a very beautiful Madonna, though, indeed, it was finished by Pietro. Rocco painted many Madonnas and a number of portraits of which I need not speak, except to say that in the Sistine Chapel at Rome he drew those of Girolamo

[1] Commissioned 1495.

Riaro and of F. Pietro, cardinal of S. Sisto. Another pupil of Pietro was il Montevarchi, who painted many scenes in S. Giovanni di Valdarno, and notably the story of the miracle of the Virgin's milk. He also left a number of pictures in his native Montevarchi. Gerino da Pistoia also learned of Pietro, and remained some time with him. He is mentioned in the Life of Pinturicchio, and so is Baccio Ubertino of Florence, a diligent colourist and designer, of whom Pietro made great use. There is a pen-and-ink drawing by him in our book, of Christ at the Column, a very charming thing.

Francesco, brother to this Baccio, and also a pupil of Pietro, was called il Bacchiacca, and was a diligent master of small figures, as is shown by many of his works in Florence, especially in the house of Gio. Maria Benintendi and in the house of Pier Francesco Borgherini. Il Bacchiacca was fond of making grotesques, and for Duke Cosimo he did a book of studies full of rare animals and plants taken from life, which are considered very beautiful. He also drew the cartoons for many tapestries, afterwards woven in silk by Maestro Giovanni Rosto, a Fleming, for the apartments of the palace of his excellency.

Another pupil of Pietro, Giovanni the Spaniard, called lo Spagna,[1] coloured better than any of those whom Pietro left behind him. He would have remained in Perugia after Pietro's death had not the envy of the painters there, who hated foreigners, driven him to withdraw to Spoleto, where he won a lady of good blood as his wife by his goodness and ability, and was made a citizen of the place. Here he did many works, as in all the other cities of Umbria, whilst at Assisi he painted the altarpiece in the chapel of St. Catherine in the lower church of S. Francesco[2] for the Spanish cardinal Egidio, and another in S. Damiano. In the little chapel of S. Maria degli Angeli, where St. Francis died, he painted some half-length figures of life-size, namely some of the companions of the saint and other saints, very full of life, surrounding a statue of St. Francis.

But the best of the pupils of Pietro was Andrea Luigi of Assisi, called l'Ingegno, who in his early youth competed with Raphael of Urbino himself under Pietro's instruction, the master employing him more and more on all his most important works, such as that in the audience-chamber of the Cambio at Perugia, where there are some beautiful figures by his hand; those which he did at Assisi, and, lastly, those in the Sistine Chapel at Rome. In all these works Andrea promised to far surpass his master.

[1] fl. 1500–20.   [2] In 1516.

He undoubtedly would have done so, but Fortune, which seems always to frown upon high beginnings, would not allow him to attain to perfection, for he was overtaken by a disease of the eyes and became totally blind, to the great grief of all who knew him. When Pope Sixtus heard of this lamentable misfortune, he ordained, like a true friend of talent, that his steward should grant him a yearly provision during his life. This was done until Andrea died at the age of eighty-six.

Other pupils of Pietro, Perugians like himself, were Eusebio S. Giorgio, who painted the picture of the Magi in S. Agnostino; Domenico di Paris,[1] who did many works in Perugia and the neighbourhood, followed by Orazio, his brother; Gian. Niccola [2] also, who painted Christ in the Garden in S. Francesco and the picture of All Saints in the chapel of the Baglioni in S. Domenico, while he did scenes from the life of St. John the Baptist in fresco in the Chapel of the Cambio; Bendetto Caporali or Bitti also, many of whose pictures are in his native Perugia, and he also practised architecture, producing many works. He wrote a commentary on Vitruvius, as all may see, since it is printed, and he was followed in these studies by his son Giulio, painter of Perugia. But not one of these numerous pupils ever equalled Pietro for his finish, or the grace of his colouring, or his style, which so pleased his time that many came from France, Spain, Germany and other countries to learn it. As I have said, quite a trade was done with his works before the advent of the style of Michelagnolo, who has shown the true and good methods of art, and has brought them to the perfection which will be seen in the third part, where I shall treat of the excellence and perfection of the arts, showing that artists who work and study steadily, and not capriciously, or by fits and starts, leave works which bring them fame, wealth and friends.

VITTORE SCARPACCIA [3] and the other Venetian and Lombard Painters

IT is an ascertained fact that when artists begin to work in some provinces, they are followed by many others, one after the other, and frequently there are several at the same time, for strife and emulation, and sitting at the feet of one or the

---

[1] Domenico di Paris Alfani.   [2] Gianiccolo di Paolo Manni.
                    [3] Carpaccio.

other of the first masters, induce artists to exert themselves to the utmost to surpass each other. But when many follow one master only, the moment they are separated by his death, or for some other cause, there is immediately a division in their wishes, so it is a generally received opinion that it is best for every man to be his own master and to show his own worth independently. I wish to speak here of many men who flourished at the same time and in the same province, and not being able to give every particular, I will write a few lines about them in order that I may not omit any who have endeavoured to adorn the world by their labours, now that I am coming to the end of the second part of my work. In addition to my inability to write the whole of their Lives, I have not found any portraits except that of Scarpaccia, which I have put at the beginning of this section on that account. Here, then, I must do what I can, seeing that I cannot do what I should like. There lived in the March of Treviso and in Lombardy for many years Stefano of Verona, Aldigieri da Zevio, Jacopo Davanzo of Bologna, Sebeto da Verona, Jacobello de Flore, Guariero da Padova, Giusto and Girolamo Campagnuola, Guilio his son, Vincenzo of Brescia, Vittore, Sebastiano and Lazzaro Scarpaccia, Venetians, Vincenzio Catena, Luigi Vivarini, Gio. Battista of Conegliano, Marco Basarini, Giovanetto Cordegliaghi, il Bassiti, Bartolommeo Vivarino, Giovanni Mansueti, Vittore Bellino, Bartolommeo Montagna of Vicenza, Benedetto Diana and Giovanni Buonconsigli, with many others whom I need not mention.

To begin at the beginning, Stefano of Verona,[1] of whom I gave some particulars in the Life of Agnolo Gaddi, was a painter of considerable merit in his day. When Donatello was working at Padua, as I have related in his Life, he happened on one occasion to go to Verona, and was astonished at the works of Stefano, declaring that his frescoes were superior to any yet produced in those parts. Stefano's first works were in S. Antonio at Verona on the screen at the end of the wall on the left-hand under the groin of the arch, representing a Virgin and Child, between St. James and St. Anthony. This is considered beautiful in that city to this day for the vigour displayed in the figures and especially in the graceful heads. In S. Niccolo, a church and parish of that city, he painted a magnificent St. Nicholas in fresco, and in the via di S. Paolo leading to the Porta del Vescovo, he painted on the wall of a house the Virgin with some lovely angels and a St. Christopher. In the via del Duomo, in a

[1] Stefano Zevio.

niche made in a wall of the church of S. Consolata, he did a Madonna with some birds, including a peacock, his device. In S. Eufemia, a convent of the Eremite friars of St. Augustine, he painted St. Augustine and two other saints above the side door, there being a number of friars and nuns of the order under the saint's mantle. But the best part of this work is two half-length prophets of life-size, whose heads are the finest and most vigorous that Stefano ever did. The colouring, having been manipulated with care, has remained in good condition to our own day in spite of much exposure to wind and weather. If it had been under cover it would have remained as fresh as when it left his hands, because he did not retouch it *a secco*, but was careful to do the work well in fresco; as it is it has been slightly damaged. In the chapel of the Sacrament inside the church, about the tabernacle, he made some flying angels, some playing, some singing, and others censing the Sacrament. A figure of Jesus Christ occupies the top as a finish to the tabernacle, while below some angels support it, dressed in white robes down to their feet, which seem to finish in clouds. This was Stefano's peculiar manner of representing angels, which always possessed very gracious faces and a lovely expression. On one side of this work is St. Augustine and on the other St. Jerome, both life-size figures, supporting the Church of God with their hands as if to show that they defended the Holy Church from heretics by their learning. In the same church he painted a St. Euphemia in fresco on a pilaster of the principal chapel, with a beautiful and gracious countenance, writing his name in letters of gold perhaps because he thought it one of his best efforts, as indeed it was. According to his custom, he introduced a fine peacock and two lions nearby, but the latter were not very good because he could not draw them from life as he did the peacock. In the same place he painted some half-length figures on a panel as was then usual, namely St. Nicholas of Tolentino and others, filling the predella with scenes from the life of that saint in small figures. In S. Fermo, a church of the Franciscan friars, in the same city, he did twelve half-length prophets of life-size to adorn a Deposition from the Cross opposite a side door, with Adam and Eve lying at their feet and the usual peacock with which he signed his paintings. In the church of S. Domenico, at the gate of the Martello, Stefano painted a lovely Madonna, whose head has been placed by the friars, who wanted to build there, on the screen at the chapel of St. Ursula belonging to the family of the Recuperati, which contains some frescoes by the same hand.

The church of S. Francesco contains a row of chapels on the right of the principal entrance, built by the noble family of the Ramma, the vaulting of one of them being by Stefano. Here he did the four Evangelists seated, with a background of roses on trellis-work, almond and other trees and foliage filled with birds, especially peacocks; there are also some lovely angels. On a column in the same church, on the right of the entrance, he painted a St. Mary Magdalene of life-size. In the street called Rompilanza he painted on the portal of a door in fresco a Madonna and Child with some angels kneeling before her, the background full of fruit-trees. These are the works which are found to have been done by Stefano, though, as he enjoyed a long life, he probably did many more. But I have not been able to find any others, nor have I discovered his surname, his father's name, his portrait, or any other particulars. Some assert that before he came to Florence he was a pupil of Maestro Liberale, a Veronese painter, but this is of no importance, for he learned all that was worth knowing at Florence of Agnolo Gaddi.

In the same city of Verona lived Aldigieri da Zevio, who was very intimate with the Scala family, and in addition to many other works he painted the great hall of their palace where the podesta now dwells, doing the war of Jerusalem as described by Josephus. In this Aldigieri displayed great spirit and judgment, separating the scenes from each other by an ornamental border. In the upper part of this border he did a series of medallions which are believed to contain the portraits of many distinguished men of the day, including several of the Scalas, but I can say no more because I am not sure of the facts. By this work Aldigieri proved that he possessed genius, judgment and invention, and had taken count of everything noteworthy in war. The colours are well preserved, and among many other portraits of great men that of M. Francesco Petrarca may be recognised.

Jacopo Avanzi, painter of Bologna, competed with Aldigieri in decorating this hall, and under the latter's paintings he did two fine triumphs in fresco with such art and in so excellent a style that Girolamo Campagnuola declares that Mantegna praised them as remarkable works. The same Jacopo, in conjunction with Aldigieri and Sebeto da Verona, painted the chapel of S. Giorgio beside the church of S. Antonio at Padua, in accordance with the terms of the will of the Marquises of Carrara. Jacopo did the upper part, Aldigieri did some stories of St. Lucy and a Last Supper beneath, while Sebeto painted the life of St. John. All three masters subsequently returned to Verona, when they painted two weddings in the house of the Counts Serenghi, with many portraits and costumes of the day, the share of Jacopo being considered the best. But as mention is made of him in the Life of Niccolo d'Arezzo for his works at Bologna in competition with the painters Simone, Cristofano and Galasso, I will say no more about him here.

At the same time Jacobello di Flore was highly esteemed in Venice, although he followed the Byzantine style. He did a number of works in that city, notably a panel for the nuns of the Corpus Domini, which is on the altar of St. Dominic in their church. Giromin Morzone, a rival of his, painted a goodly number of things in Venice and many cities of Lombardy, but as he followed the old style, standing his figures on the tips of their toes, I will say no more about him except that there is a picture by him at the altar of the Assumption in S. Lena, with many saints.

A far better master was Guariero,[1] painter of Padua, who, besides many other things, painted the principal chapel of the Eremitani friars of St. Augustine at Padua and a chapel in the first cloister. He did another small chapel in the house of Urban Perfetto and the hall of the Roman emperors, where the students go to dance at carnival-time.[2] He also did some scenes from the Old Testament in the Chapel of the Podestà in that city.

Giusto,[3] another Paduan painter, did some scenes from the Apocalypse of St. John the Evangelist, in addition to stories of the Old and New Testaments in the chapel of S. Giovanni Battista outside the church of the Vescovado. In the upper part he did choirs of angels in a Paradise and other decorations with many fine ideas. In the church of S. Antonio he did the chapel of St. Luke in fresco,[4] and painted in a chapel in the Eremitani the liberal arts with the virtues and vices near them, as well as those distinguished for their virtues and those plunged into wretchedness and cast into hell for their vices. At the same time Stefano, painter of Ferrara,[5] was also at work in Padua. As related elsewhere, he decorated the chapel and the shrine containing the body of St. Anthony with various paintings, and also

---

[1] i.e. Guariento.
[2] The Capitanio was destroyed in 1769. Urban Perfetto should be the Civic Prefect.
[3] Guisto di Menabuoi.
[4] The church was rebuilt in 1610. Some of the frescoes were uncovered in 1897.
[5] Stefano Falzagalloni.

painted the Madonna del Pilastro. A Brescian painter named Vincenzio [1] was also in repute at that time, as Filarete relates, and so was Girolamo Campagnuola, also a painter of Padua and a pupil of Squarcione. Giulio, Girolamo's son, painted, illuminated and engraved on copper some beautiful things in Padua as well as in other places. In the same city Niccolo Moreto did many things. He lived eighty years, practising art all the time. Besides these there were many who followed Gentile and Gio. Bellini.

But Vittore Scarpaccia [2] was really the first among them to produce works of note. His first were in the school of St. Ursula, where he painted the greater part of the story of her life and death on canvas.[3] His labours upon this task were to such good purpose that he acquired the reputation of being a very skilful and resourceful master. This is said to have induced the Milanese to employ him to do a panel with many figures in tempera in their chapel of S. Ambrogio in the Minorites.[4] In a picture of Christ's appearance to the Magdalene and the other Maries on the altar of the risen Christ in the church of S. Antonio, he did a very beautiful receding perspective of a distant landscape. In another chapel he painted the story of the Martyrs, when they were crucified,[5] introducing more than three hundred figures, great and small, many horses, several trees, and open sky, men nude and draped in various attitudes, many foreshortenings, and such a quantity of other things that the work must have cost him extraordinary pains. In the church of S. Job in Canareio, at the altar of the Madonna, he did the Presentation of Christ to Simeon.[6] The Madonna is standing, and Simeon in his cope stands between two ministers dressed as cardinals. Behind the Virgin are two women, one with two doves, and below are three children playing a lute, a storta, and a lyre or viol, the colouring being very pleasing. Indeed, Vittore was a very diligent and skilful master, and many of his pictures at Venice and portraits and other things are much valued for their time. He taught his art to his two brothers, Lazzaro and Sebastiano,[7] who imitated him. They did a Virgin seated between St. Catherine and St. Martha, with other saints and two angels playing, and a beautiful

[1] Foppa.
[2] Carpaccio, 1478-1527.
[3] Painted between 1490 and 1495; now in the Accademia, Venice.
[4] i.e. the Frari.
[5] Now in the Accademia, Venice.
[6] Dated 1510, also in the Accademia, Venice.
[7] Lazzaro Sebastiani is one person, and not a brother or pupil of Carpaccio.

perspective of houses as a background for the work at the altar of the Virgin in the church of the nuns of Corpus Domini. I have the artists' drawings for this in my book.

Another meritorious painter of that time was Vincenzio Catena,[1] who was much more employed in painting portraits than in other kinds of painting; indeed, there are some remarkable ones by his hand, among others that of a German of the Fuggers,[2] a notable man then staying at Venice in the Fondaco dei Tedeschi, painted with much vigour.

About the same time Gio. Battista of Conigliano,[3] a pupil of Gio. Bellini, did many works, among others a panel in the church of the nuns of Corpus Domini at the altar of St. Peter Martyr, representing that saint, St. Nicholas and St. Benedict, with a landscape, an angel playing a zither, and many small figures of considerable merit; if he had not died young he would probably have equalled his master.

Another man of that time deserving the name of a good master was Marco Basarini,[4] born in Venice of Greek parents, who painted a Deposition from the Cross[5] in S. Francesco della Vigna at Venice. In the church of S. Job he did Christ in the Garden, the three Apostles sleeping beneath, and St. Francis and St. Dominic, with two other saints.[6] But the most admired part of the work was a landscape with many small figures gracefully executed. In the same church he painted St. Bernardino on a rock with other saints.

Giannetto Cordegliaghi[7] made a number of chamber pictures in that city; indeed he did practically nothing else, and in truth his style in such work was very delicate and sweet and considerably better than that of the others mentioned above. In the chapel next to the principal one in S. Pantaleone he did St. Peter conversing with two other saints, who are wearing beautiful clothes and are finely executed.

Marco Basaiti enjoyed a considerable reputation at the same time, and there is a large panel by him in the church of the friars of Certosa at Venice, representing Christ between Peter and Andrew on the Sea of Tiberias and the sons of Zebedee, with an arm of the sea, a mountain and part of a city, with

[1] Vincenzo di Biagio, ?1470 – ?1531.
[2] Now in the Berlin Gallery.
[3] Generally known as Cima, 1460–1517.
[4] Basaiti, c. 1470–1527, again mentioned in the next paragraph but one.
[5] Possibly the picture now in the Pinakothek, Munich.
[6] In 1510; now in the Accademia, Venice.
[7] Andrea Previtali, 1480–1528.

many small figures.[1] I might cite many more of his works, but let this one suffice as it is the best.

Bartolommeo Vivarino of Murano [2] did some very good work as we see by his picture for the altar of St. Louis in the church of S. Giovanni e Paolo, representing the saint seated in his cope, St. Gregory, St. Sebastian, and St. Dominic, and on the other side St. Nicholas, St. Jerome and St. Roch, with a quantity of saints above, half-figures. Giovanni Mansueti [3] did his works well, being fond of imitating natural things, figures and distant landscapes, copying the style of Gentile Bellini, and he did many pictures in Venice. At the top of the audience-chamber in the Scuola of S. Marco he painted the saint preaching in the piazza, drawing the façade of the church, with Turks, Greeks and men of divers nations in curious costumes assembled to hear him. In the same place, in another scene where St. Mark is healing a sick man, he made a perspective of two staircases and many loggias. In another near this he did St. Mark converting a great multitude to Christ, with an open temple and a crucifix on the altar, with great variety in the expression, costumes and heads.[4]

Vittore Bellini followed these, working in the same place. He represented St. Mark taken and bound, with a good perspective of houses and a number of figures in which he imitated his predecessors. After these Bartolommeo Montagna of Vicenza [5] was a meritorious painter. He lived at Venice, and did many pictures there and a panel in the church of S. Maria d'Artone at Padua. Benedetto Diana [6] also was no less admired than these, as his works at Venice show, in S. Francesco della Vigna, where at the altar of St. John he painted the saint standing between two other saints, each with a book in his hand.

Giovanni Buonconsigli was also reputed a good master. At the altar of St. Thomas Aquinas in the church of S. Giovanni e Paolo he painted the saint in the midst of a throng to whom he is reading the Scriptures, and made a very excellent perspective of houses. Simon Bianco, sculptor of Florence, and Tullio Lombardo, a very skilful carver, spent almost all their lives at Venice.

In Lombardy Bartolommeo Clemente of Reggio and Agostino Busto [7] were excellent sculptors, and Jacopo Davanzio of Milan

---

[1] Painted 1510; now in the Accademia, Venice.
[2] c. 1431–99.   [3] 1470–1530.
[4] Their pictures in the Scuola were painted between 1490 and 1500.
[5] 1450–c.1523. He was a native of Brescia.
[6] ?1460–1525.   [7] Commonly known as Bambaia.

and Gasparo and Girolamo Misceroni were good engravers. In Brescia Vincenzio Verchio was skilful at fresco-work, and acquired a great reputation in his native place. So also did Girolamo Romanino, a skilful designer, as his works in and around Brescia show. Alessandro Moretto surpassed these, being a delicate colourist and of great diligence, as is proved by his works.

But to return to Verona, where excellent artists have always flourished and still continue to do so. Francesco Buonsignori and Francesco Caroto were remarkable, and so was Maestro Zeno of Verona, who did the altarpiece of S. Martino at Arimini and two others with great diligence. But the one who has made the most remarkable figures from life is il Moro of Verona, or Francesco Turbido as some call him, who has done the portrait of a gentleman of Ca Badovaro, now in the house of Monsignor de' Martini, as a shepherd, which is very life-like, and may compare with any produced in those parts. Battista d'Angelo,[1] his son-in-law, is a beautiful colourist and a skilful designer, who must be placed above il Moro rather than below him. But as I do not propose to speak of the living at present, I wish, as I said at the beginning of this Life, to make this a record of those of whom I do not know every particular, so that their talents and merits may receive what little I can do for them.

JACOPO, called L'INDACO, Painter
(1476–?1534)

JACOPO, called l'Indaco, who was a pupil of Domenico del Ghirlandajo, and who worked at Rome with Pinturicchio, was a meritorious master of his day, and although he did not produce much, the works which he did are worthy of praise. It is not remarkable that but few works came from his hands, because, being fond of amusements and pleasure, he entertained no anxious thought and never worked except when he was obliged. He used to say that to do nothing but toil without ever taking any pleasure was not fit for a Christian. He was very familiar with Michelagnolo, and when that most famous artist of all time wished to divert himself from his ceaseless exertions of body and mind, no one suited his humour better than Jacopo. The latter worked for many years at Rome, or rather he remained

[1] Giambattista del Moro.

there a long while and worked very little. There is a painting by
him at the entrance to the church of S. Agostino by the door or
the façade, on the right of the first chapel, the vaulting of which
contains the Apostles receiving the Holy Spirit, and on the wall
beneath are two stories of Christ, one where he calls Andrew and
Peter from their nets and the other the banquet of Simon and
the Magdalene, containing a very good ceiling of beams and
rafters. In the picture of the same chapel, which he painted in
oils, is a dead Christ, executed with great skill and diligence.
In the Trinità at Rome there is a Coronation of the Virgin on a
small panel. But what need to say more of him? It is enough to
say that he was a charming gossip and always detested work
and painting. As Michelagnolo was fond of chatting with him
and took delight in the pranks he was frequently playing, he
almost always had him to dine. But one day Michelagnolo
became tired of him (as generally happens in such friendships
which consist in gossiping frequently without rhyme or reason,
for I cannot call it conversation) and sent him to buy some figs
in order to get rid of him at a time when he may have had some
other fantasy, and immediately Jacopo was out of the house
he fastened the door, intending to keep it shut when he returned.
Presently Jacopo came back from the piazza, and perceiving
after knocking for a while that Michelagnolo would not open
the door, he became angry, and taking the leaves and figs, he
spread them out on the threshold and departed. It was many
months before he would speak to Michelagnolo, but at length
he was mollified and they became more friendly than ever. He
ultimately died at Rome at the age of sixty-eight.

Not unlike Jacopo was a younger brother called by his own
name of Francesco and afterwards l'Indaco also. He again was
a painter of merit. He was not dissimilar also in his distaste for
work and fondness for talking, but in this he went farther than
Jacopo, because he spoke evil of everyone and blamed the
works of every other artist. After doing some things in Montepulciano, both in painting and in clay, he painted an Annunciation [1] on a panel for the oratory of the Nunziata for the audience-
chamber, and a God the Father in heaven surrounded by angels
represented as children. In the same city, the first time that
Duke Alessandro went there, he did a splendid triumphal arch
at the gate of the palace of the Signori, with many figures in
relief. In competition with many other painters, who prepared
a quantity of things for the duke's entry, he did the scenery

[1] Commissioned in 1533.

for a comedy, which was much admired. Proceeding to Rome
when they were expecting the Emperor Charles V., he did some
clay figures and arms in fresco at the Capitol for the Roman
people, which were much admired. But his best and most
admired work was a cabinet in stucco in the palace of the
Medici for the Duchess Margaret of Austria, so fine and beautifully decorated that it would not be possible to improve it. I
do not think that it would be possible to obtain the same
results in silver. We may judge from this that if Francesco had
been fond of work, and had given his genius play, he would have
become excellent. Francesco designed fairly well, but Jacopo
was much better, as our book shows.

LUCA SIGNORELLI, Painter of Cortona
(1441-1523)

LUCA SIGNORELLI, an excellent painter, of whom we must now
speak, following the chronological order, was in his day considered
more famous in Italy and his works were more highly valued
than almost any other master's, no matter of what period, because
he showed the way to represent nude figures in painting so as
to make them appear alive, although with art and difficulty.
He was the pupil of Pietro of Borgo a S. Sepolcro, and made
great efforts in his youth to equal and even to surpass his
master. Whilst he was working at Arezzo with his master and
living with his uncle Lazzaro Vasari, as has been said, he
imitated Pietro's style so well that it was hardly possible to
perceive any difference. His first works were at S. Lorenzo at
Arezzo, where he painted the chapel of St. Barbara in fresco in
1472, and did the processional banner in oils on cloth for the
company of St. Caterina as well as that of la Trinità, which seems
rather the work of Pietro dal Borgo than his own. In S. Agostino
in that city he did the picture of St. Nicholas of Tolentino, with
beautiful small scenes executed with design and invention. In
the chapel of the Sacrament in the same place he did two angels
in fresco. In the Chapel of the Accolti in the Church of S. Francesco he did a picture of M. Francesco, doctor of laws, with
portraits of the doctor and some members of his family. In
this work is an admirable St. Michael weighing souls, showing
Luca's knowledge in the splendour of the arms, in the reflections, and indeed in the whole work. He puts in his hands a

pair of scales, the nudes in either scale, one up and the other down, being finely foreshortened. Among other ingenious things there is a nude figure finely transformed into a devil, while a lizard licks the blood flowing from his wound. Here are also a Virgin and Child, St. Stephen, St. Lawrence and St. Catherine, two angels playing, one a lute and the other a rebec, all these figures being draped and wonderfully adorned. But the predella is the most remarkable, full of small figures of the friars of St. Catherine. In Perugia Luca did many works, among others a panel in the Duomo[1] for M. Jacopo Vannucci, of Cortona, the bishop there, with Our Lady, St. Onofrio, St. Hercullan, St. John the Baptist and St. Stephen, and a beautiful angel tuning a lute. At Volterra he painted a fine Cirumcision of Christ[2] in fresco over the altar of an oratory in S. Francesco, which is considered very remarkable, although the babe having suffered from the damp was restored by Sodoma much less finely than the original. Indeed, it is sometimes better to keep the works of famous men even half-destroyed than to have them retouched by inferior hands. In S. Agostino in the same city he did a panel in tempera with a predella of small figures representing scenes from the Passion of Christ,[3] which is considered extraordinarily fine. For the lords of Monte a S. Maria he painted a dead Christ and a Nativity in S. Francesco at Città di Castello,[4] and a St. Sebastian[5] on another panel in S. Domenico. In S. Margherita in his native Cortona, a house of the bare-footed friars, he did a dead Christ,[6] one of his finest works, and in the oratory of the Gesù in the same city he did three panels, the one near the high altar being marvellous, representing Christ communicating with the Apostles and Judas putting the Host in the money-bag.[7] In the Pieve, now called the Vescovado, he painted some life-size prophets in fresco in the chapel of the Sacrament, with angels about the tabernacle opening a pavilion, while St. Jerome and St. Thomas Aquinas are at the sides. At the high altar of this church he did a fine Assumption and designed the glass for the principal rose-window, afterwards carried out by Stagio Sassoli of Arezzo. In Castiglione Aretino he did a dead Christ[8] above the chapel of the Sacrament with the Maries, and the

---

[1] Painted in 1484.
[2] Painted about 1490; now in the National Gallery, London.
[3] Possibly the picture now in the Louvre.
[4] Probably the picture now in the National Gallery, painted in 1496.
[5] Commissioned in 1498.
[6] In 1502. [7] Painted in 1512.
[8] Probably the picture in the Berlin Gallery.

doors of the presses in S. Francesco di Lucignano, in which is a coral tree with a cross at the top. He did a panel of the chapel of St. Christopher in St. Agostino at Siena, containing some saints surrounding a St. Christopher in relief.[1] From Siena he went to Florence to see the works of the masters then living and those of the dead. Here he painted some naked gods[2] on canvas for Lorenzo de Medici, which were much praised, and a picture of Our Lady with two small prophets; this is now at Castello, a villa of Duke Cosimo. He gave both works to Lorenzo, who would never allow himself to be surpassed by anyone in liberality and magnificence. He also painted a Madonna[3] in a round, which is in the audience-chamber of the captains of the Guelph party. At Chiusuri of Siena, one of the principal houses of the monks of Monte Oliveto, he painted on one side of the cloister eleven scenes of the life and acts of St. Benedict.[4] From Cortona he sent some of his works to Montepulciano, the picture which is on the high altar of the Pieve at Foiano, and others to other places of Valdichiana. In the Madonna, the principal church of Orvieto, he finished the chapel begun by Frà Giovanni da Fiesole,[5] representing all the scenes of the end of the world with curious and fanciful invention, with angels, demons, ruins, earthquakes, fires, miracles of Antichrist, and many other such things, in addition to nudes, foreshortenings, and a number of fine figures, and their terror on that great and awful day. So he paved the way for his successors, who have found the difficulties of that manner smoothed away. Accordingly I do not wonder that Luca's works were always highly praised by Michelagnolo, who in his divine Last Judgment in the chapel partly borrowed from Luca such things as angels, demons, the arrangement of the heavens, and other things in which Michelagnolo imitated Luca's treatment, as all may see. Into this work Luca introduced many portraits of friends, including his own and those of Niccolo, Paolo and Vittellozzo Vitelli, Giovan. Paolo and Orazio Baglioni, and others whose names I do not know. In S. Maria at Loreto he painted in fresco in the sanctuary[6] the four Evangelists, the four Doctors, and other saints, which are very fine, being liberally rewarded by Pope Sixtus. It is said that on a son, of whom he was very fond, of beautiful face and figure, being killed at Cortona, Luca caused him to be stripped, and with extraordinary fortitude, without shedding a

---

[1] In 1498.   [2] The "School of Pan" (Berlin, destroyed 1944).
[3] Now in the Uffizi.   [4] Commissioned in 1497.
[5] Between 1499 and 1509.   [6] About 1479.

tear, drew the body so that he might always behold in this work of his hands what Nature had given him and cruel Fortune taken away. Being summoned by Pope Sixtus to work in the chapel of the palace with other painters, he did two scenes [1] which are reckoned among the best, one being the testament of Moses to the Hebrew people after seeing the Land of Promise, and the other his death.

At length, after working for almost every prince in Italy, and being now old, Luca returned to Cortona, where he passed his last years in working more for love of it than anything else, as if after spending his life in toil he could not remain idle. He then did a panel for the nuns of S. Margherita at Arezzo,[2] and one at the oratory of S. Girolamo, part of the cost being paid for by M. Niccolo Gamurrini, doctor of laws, auditor of the Ruota, whose portrait is there, kneeling before the Madonna, to whom St. Nicholas presents him. St. Donato and St. Stephen are also there, and lower down St. Jerome naked and David singing with a psalter. Here also are two prophets who treat of the Conception, to judge by the scrolls in their hands. This work was taken from Cortona to Arezzo on the shoulders of the men of that company, and Luca, old as he was, wanted to set it up there and revisit his friends and relations. He stayed in the house of the Vasari, and as a child of eight [3] I remember the worthy old man, so gracious and refined, and when he heard from my master who taught me my letters that I did nothing but draw figures in school, he turned to my father Antonio and said, "Antonio, in order that Giorgio may not grow worse, get him to learn to draw, because even with his other studies this cannot fail to be of assistance and honour to him as it is to all worthy men." Then turning to me as I stood before him, he said, "Learn, little kinsman, learn." He said a great deal more, which I will not repeat, because I know that I have not nearly realised the expectations which he formed of me. Knowing also that I suffered severely from bleeding at the nose, which sometimes left me in a fainting condition, he very tenderly put a jasper on my neck. This memory of Luca will remain with me for ever. Having set up the picture, he returned to Cortona, accompanied for a great part of the way by citizens, friends and relations, as his great qualities merited, and he lived rather like a great lord and gentleman than as a painter.

About this time Benedetto Caporali, a painter of Perugia, had

---

[1] Between 1482 and 1484.   [2] In 1520; now in the Gallery, Arezzo.
[3] It would therefore be in 1519.

erected a palace for Silvio Passerini, cardinal of Cortona, half a mile outside the city. Benedetto, being fond of architecture, had just previously written a commentary on Vitruvius.[1] The cardinal wished the whole palace to be painted, and Benedetto set to work on it with the help of Maso Papacello of Cortona, his pupil, who had also studied under Giulio Romano, as will be said, and of Tommaso, and other pupils and boys, and painted almost the whole in fresco. But the cardinal desired to have some painting of Luca, and, old and paralytic as he was, he did in fresco the altar-wall of the chapel of the palace, representing John baptising the Saviour. He did not quite finish it, as he died while he was still at work on it, at the age of eighty-two. Luca was a man of the highest character, sincere and loving with friends, of gentle and pleasing conversation with everyone, and, above all, courteous to all who needed his skill, and a good master to his pupils. He lived magnificently, and was fond of fine clothes. For his good qualities he was always revered at home and abroad. I shall therefore finish this second part with the close of his life, which took place in 1521,[2] Luca being the one who by his ground-work of design, and especially of nudes, by his grace of invention and the grouping of his scenes, paved the way for the final perfection of art, and for most of those artists with whom we shall now have to deal, who put the finishing touches.

[1] Published in 1536. [2] 1523.

PART III

PREFACE

THOSE masters whose Lives we have written in the second part made substantial additions to the arts of architecture, painting and sculpture, improving on those of the first part in rule, order, proportion, design and style. If they were not altogether perfect, they came so near the truth, that the third category, of whom we are now to speak, profited by the light they shed, and attained the summit of perfection, producing the more valuable and renowned modern works. But in order that the nature of these improvements may be better appreciated, I will describe in a few words the five points already enumerated, and relate succinctly the source of that excellence which, by surpassing the achievements of the ancients, has rendered the modern age so glorious.

Rule in architecture is the measurement of antiques, following the plans of ancient buildings in making modern ones. Order is the differentiation of one kind from another so that every body shall have its characteristic parts, and that the Doric, Ionic, Corinthian and Tuscan shall no longer be mingled indiscrim: nately. Proportion in sculpture, as in architecture, is the making of the bodies of figures upright, the members being properly arranged, and the same in painting. Design is the imitation of the most beautiful things of nature in all figures whether painted or chiselled, and this requires a hand and genius to transfer everything which the eye sees, exactly and correctly, whether it be in drawings, on paper panel, or other surface, both in relief and sculpture. Style is improved by frequently copying the most beautiful things, and by combining the finest members, whether hands, heads, bodies or legs, to produce a perfect figure, which, being introduced in every work and in every figure, form what is known as a fine style. Giotto and the early artists did not do this, although they had discovered the principles of every difficulty and superficially treated them, as, for example, in drawing more correctly than had been done before, and in approaching nature more nearly in blending colours, in the composition of figures in scenes, and many other things, of which enough has been said.

But although the artists of the second period made great additions to the arts in all these particulars, yet they did not attain to the final stages of perfection, for they lacked a freedom which, while outside the rules, was guided by them, and which was not incompatible with order and correctness. This demanded a prolific invention and the beauty of the smallest details. In proportion they lacked good judgment which, without measuring the figures, invests them with a grace beyond measure in the dimensions chosen. They did not attain to the zenith of design, because, although they made their arms round and their legs straight, they were not skilled in the muscles, and lacked that graceful and sweet ease which is partly seen and partly felt in matters of flesh and living things, but they were crude and stunted, their eyes being difficult and their style hard. Moreover, they did not possess that lightness of touch in making all their figures slender and graceful, especially the women and infants, who should be rendered as truthfully as the men, while avoiding coarseness so that they may not be clumsy, as in nature, but refined by design and good judgment. Their draperies lacked beauty, their fancies variety, their colouring charm, their buildings diversity and their landscapes distance and variety. Although many of them, like Andrea Verrocchio, Antonio del Pollajuolo and others of more recent date endeavoured to improve the design of their figures by more study while approaching nature more closely, yet they were not quite sure of their ground. However, their work would bear comparison with the antique, as we see by Verrocchio's restoration of the marble legs and arms of the Marsyas of the Casa Medici at Florence. They also lacked finish and perfection in feet, hands, hair, beards, and did not make all the members correspond to the antique with the proper proportions. If they had possessed this finish, which is the perfection and flower of the arts, they would have also possessed a resolute boldness in their work, and would have obtained a lightness, polish and grace to which they did not attain, despite all their efforts which give the supreme results of art to fine figures, whether in relief or painted. That finish and assurance which they lacked they could not readily attain by study, which has a tendency to render the style dry when it becomes an end in itself. The others were able to attain to it after they had seen some of the finest works mentioned by Pliny dug out of the earth: the Laocoon, the Hercules, the great torso of Belvedere, the Venus, the Cleopatra, the Apollo, and endless others, which are copied in their softness and in their hardness from the best living examples, with actions which do not distort them, but give them motion and display the utmost grace. This removed a certain dryness and crudeness caused by overmuch study, observable in Piero della Francesca, Lazzaro Vasari, Alesso Baldovinetti, Andrea del Castagno, Pesello, Ercole Ferrarese, Giovan. Bellini, Cosimo Rosselli, the abbot of S. Clemente, Domenico del Ghirlandajo, Sandro Botticello, Andrea Mantegna, Filippo [1] and Luca Signorelli. All these endeavoured to attain the impossible by their labours, especially in foreshortening and unpleasant objects, but the effort of producing them was too apparent in the result. Thus, although most were well designed and flawless, vigour was invariably absent from them, and they lacked a soft blending of colour, first observable in Francia of Bologna and Pietro Perugino. The people, when they beheld the new and living beauty, ran madly to see it, thinking that it would never be possible to improve upon it. But the works of Lionardo da Vinci clearly proved how much they erred, for he began the third style, which I will call the modern, notable for boldness of design, the subtlest imitation of Nature in trifling details, good rule, better order, correct proportion, perfect design and divine grace, prolific and diving to the depths of art, endowing his figures with motion and breath. Somewhat later followed Giorgione da Castel Franco, who gave tone to his pictures and endowed his things with tremendous life by means of the well-managed depth of the shadows. No less skilful in imparting to his works force, relief, sweetness and grace was Frà Bartolommeo of S. Marco; but the most graceful of all was Raphael of Urbino, who, studying the labours of both the ancient and the modern masters, selected the best from each, and out of his garner enriched the art of painting with that absolute perfection which the figures of Apelles and Zeuxis anciently possessed, and even more, if I may say so. Nature herself was vanquished by his colours, and his invention was facile and appropriate, as anyone may judge who has seen his works, which are like writings, showing us the sites and the buildings, and the ways and habits of native and foreign peoples just as he desired. Besides the grace of his heads, whether young or old, men or women, he represented the modest

[1] i.e. Filippino Lippi.

with modesty, the bold as bold, and his infants sometimes with mischievous and sometimes with playful eyes. His draperies are neither too simple nor too involved, but simply natural. Andrea del Sarto followed him in this manner, but with a softer and less bold colouring, and it may be said that he was a rare artist because his works are faultless. It is impossible to describe the delicate vivacity which characterises the works of Antonio da Correggio. He depicted hair in a manner unknown before, for it had previously been made hard and dry, while his was soft and downy, the separate hairs polished so that they seemed of gold and more beautiful than natural ones, which were surpassed by his colouring. Francesco Mazzola Parmigiano did the like, surpassing him in many respects in grace, ornament and fine style, as many of his paintings show, the faces laughing, the eyes speaking, the very pulses seeming to beat, just as his brush pleased. An examination of the wall-paintings of Polidoro and Maturino will show how marvellous are their figures, and the beholder will wonder how they have been able to produce those stupendous works, not by speech, which is easy, but with the brush, as they have done in their skilful representations of the deeds of the Romans.

How many are there among the dead whose colours have endowed their figures with such life as is imparted by Il Rosso, Frà Sebastiano Giulo Romano, Perino del Vaga, not to speak of the many celebrated living men. But the important fact is that art has been brought to such perfection to-day, design, invention and colouring coming easily to those who possess them, that where the first masters took six years to paint one picture our masters to-day would only take one year to paint six, as I am firmly convinced both from observation and experience; and many more are now completed than the masters of former days produced.

But the man who bears the palm of all ages, transcending and eclipsing all the rest, is the divine Michelagnolo Buonarroti, who is supreme not in one art only but in all three at once. He surpasses not only all those who have, as it were, surpassed Nature, but the most famous ancients also, who undoubtedly surpassed her. He has proceeded from conquest to conquest, never finding a difficulty which he cannot easily overcome by the force of his divine genius, by his industry, design, art, judgment and grace, and this not only in painting and in colours, comprising all forms and bodies, straight and not straight, palpable and impalpable, visible and invisible, but in the extreme rotundity of his statues.

With the point of his chisel and by his fruitful labours he has spread his branches far, and filled the world with more delicious fruit than the three noble arts had produced before, in such marvellous perfection that it may well and safely be said that his statues are in every respect much finer than the ancient ones, as he knew how to select the most perfect members, arms, hands, heads, feet, form them into a perfect whole, with the most complete grace and absolute perfection, the very difficulties appearing easy in his style, so that it is impossible ever to see better. If by chance there were any works of the most renowned Greeks and Romans which might be brought forward for comparison, his sculptures would only gain in value and renown as their manifest superiority to those of the ancients became more apparent. But if we so greatly admire those who devoted their lives to their work, when induced by extraordinary rewards and great happiness, what must we say of the men who produced such precious fruit not only without reward but in miserable poverty? It is believed that if there were just rewards in our age we should become undoubtedly greater and better than the ancients ever were. But the necessity of fighting against famine rather than for fame crushes men of genius and prevents them from becoming known, which is a shame and disgrace to those who could improve their condition and will not. Let this suffice; it is now time to turn to the Lives and treat separately all those who have produced celebrated works in this third style. The first of these was Lionardo da Vinci, with whom we now begin.

LIONARDO DA VINCI, Painter and Sculptor of Florence

(1452–1519)

THE heavens often rain down the richest gifts on human beings, naturally, but sometimes with lavish abundance bestow upon a single individual beauty, grace and ability, so that, whatever he does, every action is so divine that he distances all other men, and clearly displays how his genius is the gift of God and not an acquirement of human art. Men saw this in Lionardo da Vinci, whose personal beauty could not be exaggerated, whose every movement was grace itself and whose abilities were so extraordinary that he could readily solve every difficulty. He possessed great personal strength, combined with dexterity, and a spirit and courage invariably royal and magnanimous, and the fame of his name so spread abroad that, not only was he valued in his own day, but his renown has greatly increased since his death.

This marvellous and divine Lionardo was the son of Piero da Vinci. He would have made great profit in learning had he not been so capricious and fickle, for he began to learn many things and then gave them up. Thus in arithmetic, during the few months that he studied it, he made such progress that he frequently confounded his master by continually raising doubts and difficulties. He devoted some time to music, and soon learned to play the lyre, and, being filled with a lofty and delicate spirit, he could sing and improvise divinely with it. Yet though he studied so many different things, he never neglected design and working in relief, those being the things which appealed to his fancy more than any other. When Ser Piero perceived this, and knowing the boy's soaring spirit, he one day took some of his drawings to Andrea del Verrocchio, who was his close friend, and asked his opinion whether Lionardo would do anything by studying design. Andrea was so amazed at these early efforts that he advised Ser Piero to have the boy taught. So it was decided that Lionardo should go to Andrea's workshop.[1] The boy was greatly delighted, and not only practised his profession, but all those in which design has a part. Possessed of a divine and marvellous intellect, and being an excellent geometrician, he not only worked in sculpture, doing some heads of women

[1] About 1468.

smiling, which were casts, and children's heads also, executed like a master, but also prepared many architectural plans and elevations, and he was the first, though so young, to propose to canalise the Arno from Pisa to Florence. He made designs for mills, fulling machines, and other engines to go by water, and as painting was to be his profession he studied drawing from life. He would make clay models of figures, draping them with soft rags dipped in plaster, and would then draw them patiently on thin sheets of cambric or linen, in black and white, with the point of the brush. He did these admirably, as may be seen by specimens in my book of designs. He also drew upon paper so carefully and well that no one has ever equalled him. I have a head in grisaille which is divine. The grace of God so possessed his mind, his memory and intellect formed such a mighty union, and he could so clearly express his ideas in discourse, that he was able to confound the boldest opponents. Every day he made models and designs for the removal of mountains with ease and to pierce them to pass from one place to another, and by means of levers, cranes and winches to raise and draw heavy weights; he devised a method for cleansing ports, and to raise water from great depths, schemes which his brain never ceased to evolve. Many designs for these notions are scattered about, and I have seen numbers of them. He spent much time in making a regular design of a series of knots so that the cord may be traced from one end to the other, the whole filling a round space. There is a fine engraving of this most difficult design, and in the middle are the words: *Leonardus Vinci Academia*. Among these models and designs there was one which he several times showed to many able citizens who then ruled Florence, of a method of raising the church of S. Giovanni and putting steps under it without it falling down. He argued with so much eloquence that it was not until after his departure that they recognised the impossibility of such a feat.

His charming conversation won all hearts, and although he possessed nothing and worked little, he kept servants and horses of which he was very fond, and indeed he loved all animals, and trained them with great kindness and patience. Often, when passing places where birds were sold, he would let them out of their cages and pay the vendor the price asked. Nature had favoured him so greatly that in whatever his brain or mind took up he displayed unrivalled divinity, vigour, vivacity, excellence, beauty and grace. His knowledge of art, indeed, prevented him from finishing many things which he had begun, for he felt that his hand would be unable to realise the perfect creations of his imagination, as his mind formed such difficult, subtle and marvellous conceptions that his hands, skilful as they were, could never have expressed them. His interests were so numerous that his inquiries into natural phenomena led him to study the properties of herbs and to observe the movements of the heavens, the moon's orbit and the progress of the sun.

Lionardo was placed, as I have said, with Andrea del Verrocchio in his childhood by Ser Piero, and his master happened to be painting a picture of St. John baptising Christ.[1] For this Lionardo did an angel holding some clothes, and, although quite young, he made it far better than the figures of Andrea. The latter would never afterwards touch colours, chagrined that a child should know more than he. Lionardo was next employed to draw a cartoon of the Fall for a portière in tapestry, to be made in Flanders of gold and silk, to send to the King of Portugal. Here he did a meadow in grisaille, with the lights in white lead, containing much vegetation and some animals, unsurpassable for finish and naturalness. There is a fig-tree, the leaves and branches beautifully foreshortened and executed with such care that the mind is amazed at the amount of patience displayed. There is also a palm-tree, the rotundity of the dates being executed with great and marvellous art, due to the patience and ingenuity of Lionardo. This work was not carried farther, and the cartoon is now in Florence in the fortunate house of Ottaviano de' Medici the Magnificent, to whom it was given not long ago by Lionardo's uncle.

It is said that when Ser Piero was at his country-seat he was requested by a peasant of his estate to get a round piece of wood painted for him at Florence, which he had cut from a fig-tree on his farm. Piero readily consented, as the man was very skilful in catching birds and fishing, and was very useful to him in such matters. Accordingly Piero brought the wood to Florence and asked Lionardo to paint something upon it, without telling him its history. Lionardo, on taking it up to examine it one day, found it warped, badly prepared and rude, but with the help of fire he made it straight, and giving it to a turner, had it rendered soft and smooth instead of being rough and rude. Then, after preparing the surface in his own way, he began to cast about what he should paint on it, and resolved to do the Medusa head to terrify all beholders. To a room, to which he alone had access, Lionardo took lizards, newts, maggots,

---

[1] About 1470.

snakes, butterflies, locusts, bats, and other animals of the kind, out of which he composed a horrible and terrible monster, of poisonous breath, issuing from a dark and broken rock, belching poison from its open throat, fire from its eyes, and smoke from its nostrils, of truly terrible and horrible aspect. He was so engrossed with the work that he did not notice the terrible stench of the dead animals, being absorbed in his love for art. His father and the peasant no longer asked for the work, and when it was finished Lionardo told his father to send for it when he pleased, as he had done his part. Accordingly Ser Piero went to his rooms one morning to fetch it. When he knocked at the door Lionardo opened it and told him to wait a little, and, returning to his room, put the round panel in the light on his easel, and having arranged the window to make the light dim, he called his father in. Ser Piero, taken unaware, started back, not thinking of the round piece of wood, or that the face which he saw was painted, and was beating a retreat when Lionardo detained him and said, "This work has served its purpose; take it away, then, as it has produced the effect intended." Ser Piero indeed thought it more than miraculous, and he warmly praised Lionardo's idea. He then quietly went and bought another round wheel with a heart transfixed by a dart painted upon it, and gave it to the peasant, who was grateful to Piero all his life. Piero took Lionardo's work secretly to Florence and sold it to some merchants for 100 ducats, and in a short time it came into the hands of the Duke of Milan, who bought it of them for 300 ducats.

Lionardo next did a very excellent Madonna, which afterwards belonged to Pope Clement VII. Among other things it contained a bowl of water with some marvellous flowers, the dew upon them seeming actually to be there, so that they looked more real than reality itself. For his good friend Antonio Segni he drew a Neptune on paper, with so much design and care that he seemed alive. The sea is troubled and his car is drawn by sea-horses, with the sprites, monsters, and south winds and other fine marine creatures. The drawing was given by Antonio's son Fabio to M. Giovanni Gaddi with this epigram:

Pinxit Virgilius Neptunum, pinxit Homerus;
Dum maris undisoni per vada flectit equos
Mente quidem vates illum conspexit uterque
Vincius ast oculis; jureque vincit eos.

Lionardo then had the fancy to paint a picture of the Medusa's head in oils with a garland of snakes about it, the most extraordinary idea imaginable, but as the work required time it remained unfinished, the fate of nearly all his projects.[1] This is among the treasures in the palace of Duke Cosimo, together with the head of an angel, who is raising an arm in the air, this arm being foreshortened from the shoulder to the elbow, while the other rests on its breast. So marvellous was Lionardo's mind that, desiring to throw his things into greater relief, he endeavoured to obtain greater depths of shadow, and sought the deepest blacks in order to render the lights clearer by contrast. He succeeded so well that his scenes looked rather like representations of the night, there being no bright light, than of the lightness of day, though all was done with the idea of throwing things into greater relief and to find the end and perfection of art.

Lionardo was so delighted when he saw curious heads, whether bearded or hairy, that he would follow about anyone who had thus attracted his attention for a whole day, acquiring such a clear idea of him that when he went home he would draw the head as well as if the man had been present. In this way many heads of men and women came to be drawn, and I have several such pen-and-ink drawings in my book, so often referred to. Among them is the head of Amergio Vespucci, a fine old man, drawn in carbon, and that of Scaramuccia, the gipsy captain, which afterwards belonged to M. Donato Valdambrini of Arezzo, canon of S. Lorenzo, left to him by Giambullari. He began a picture of the Adoration of the Magi,[2] containing many beautiful things, especially heads, which was in the house of Amerigo Benci, opposite the loggia of the Peruzzi, but which was left unfinished like his other things.

On the death of Giovan. Galeazzo, Duke of Milan, and the accession of Ludovico Sforza in the same year, 1493, Lionardo was invited to Milan with great ceremony by the duke to play the lyre, in which that prince greatly delighted.[3] Lionardo took his own instrument, made by himself in silver, and shaped like a horse's head, a curious and novel idea to render the harmonies more loud and sonorous, so that he surpassed all the musicians who had assembled there. Besides this he was the best reciter of improvised rhymes of his time. The duke, captivated by Lionardo's conversation and genius, conceived an extraordinary

[1] The picture answering to this in the Uffizi is a work of the later sixteenth century, painted from Vasari's description.
[2] Now in the Uffizi, supposed to be the high-altar picture for S. Donato in Scopeto which he was commissioned to paint in 1481.
[3] Lionardo was at Milan from 1483. Ludovico il Moro became duke in 1494, but he had been the real ruler of the state some time before.

affection for him. He begged him to paint an altar-picture of the Nativity, which was sent by the duke to the emperor. Lionardo then did a Last Supper for the Dominicans at S. Maria delle Grazie in Milan,[1] endowing the heads of the Apostles with such majesty and beauty that he left that of Christ unfinished, feeling that he could not give it that celestial divinity which it demanded. This work left in such a condition has always been held in the greatest veneration by the Milanese and by other foreigners, as Lionardo has seized the moment when the Apostles are anxious to discover who would betray their Master. All their faces are expressive of love, fear, wrath or grief at not being able to grasp the meaning of Christ, in contrast to the obstinacy, hatred and treason of Judas, while the whole work, down to the smallest details, displays incredible diligence, even the texture of the tablecloth being clearly visible so that actual cambric would not look more real. It is said that the prior incessantly importuned Lionardo to finish the work, thinking it strange that the artist should pass half a day at a time lost in thought. He would have desired him never to lay down the brush, as if he were digging a garden. Seeing that his importunity produced no effect, he had recourse to the duke, who felt compelled to send for Lionardo to inquire about the work, showing tactfully that he was driven to act by the importunity of the prior. Lionardo, aware of the acuteness and discretion of the duke, talked with him fully about the picture, a thing which he had never done with the prior. He spoke freely of his art, and explained how men of genius really are doing most when they work least, as they are thinking out ideas and perfecting the conceptions, which they subsequently carry out with their hands. He added that there were still two heads to be done, that of Christ, which he would not look for on the earth, and felt unable to conceive the beauty of the celestial grace that must have been incarnate in the divinity. The other head was that of Judas, which also caused him thought, as he did not think he could express the face of a man who could resolve to betray his Master, the Creator of the world, after having received so many benefits. But he was willing in this case to seek no farther, and for lack of a better he would do the head of the importunate and tactless prior. The duke was wonderfully amused, and laughingly declared that he was quite right. Then the poor prior, covered with confusion, went back to his garden and left Lionardo in peace, while the artist indeed

[1] Between 1495 and 1498.

finished his Judas, making him a veritable likeness of treason and cruelty. The head of Christ was left unfinished, as I have said. The nobility of this painting, in its composition and the care with which it was finished, induced the King of France to wish to take it home with him. Accordingly he employed architects to frame it in wood and iron, so that it might be transported in safety, without any regard for the cost, so great was his desire. But the king was thwarted by its being done on the wall, and it remained with the Milanese.

While engaged upon the Last Supper, Lionardo painted the portrait of Duke Ludovico, with Maximilian, his eldest son, at the top of this same refectory, where there is a Passion in the old style. At the other end he did the Duchess Beatrice with Francesco, her other son, both of whom afterwards became Dukes of Milan, the portraits being marvellous. While thus employed, Lionardo suggested that the duke should set up a bronze horse of colossal size with the duke upon it in memory of himself. But he began it on such a scale that it could never be done. Such is the malice of man when stirred by envy that there are some who believe that Lionardo, as with so many of his things, began this with no intention of completing it, because its size was so great that extraordinary difficulties might be foreseen in having it cast all in one piece. And it is probable that many have formed this opinion from the result, since so many of his things have been left unfinished. However, we can readily believe that his great and extraordinary talents suffered a check from being too venturesome, and that the real cause was his endeavour to go on from excellence to excellence and from perfection to perfection. "*Talche l'Opera fusse ritardata dal desio*," as our Petrarca says.[1] In truth, those who have seen Lionardo's large clay model aver that they never beheld anything finer or more superb. It was preserved until the French came to Milan with King Louis of France, and broke it all to pieces. Thus a small wax model, considered perfect, was lost, as well as a book of the anatomy of horses, done by him. He afterwards devoted even greater care to the study of the anatomy of men, aiding and being aided by M. Marcantonio della Torre, a profound philosopher, who then professed at Padua and wrote

---

[1] The full quotation runs:

"Tu sai ' esser mio
E l'amor di saper che m'ha si acceso
Che l'opra e ritardata dal desio."

(*Trionfo d'Amore, cap.* 3. ll. 7-9)

upon the subject. I have heard it said that he was one of the
first who began to illustrate the science of medicine, by the
learning of Galen, and to throw true light upon anatomy, up
to that time involved in the thick darkness of ignorance. In this
he was marvellously served by the genius, work and hands of
Lionardo, who made a book about it with red crayon drawings [1]
outlined with the pen, in which he foreshortened and portrayed
with the utmost diligence. He did the skeleton, adding all the
nerves and muscles, the first attached to the bone, the others
keeping it firm and the third moving, and in the various parts
he wrote notes in curious characters, using his left hand, and
writing from right to left, so that it cannot be read without
practice, and only at a mirror. A great part of the sheets of this
anatomy is in the hands of M. Francesco de Melzo, a nobleman
of Milan, who was a lovely child in Lionardo's time, who was
very fond of him, and being now a handsome and courteous
old man, he treasures up these drawings with a portrait of
Lionardo. Whoever succeeds in reading these notes of Lionardo
will be amazed to find how well that divine spirit has reasoned
of the arts, the muscles, the nerves and veins, with the greatest
diligence in all things. N. N., a painter of Milan, also possesses
some writings of Lionardo, written in the same way, which treat
of painting and of the methods of design and colour.[2] Not long
ago he came to Florence to see me, wishing to have the work
printed. He afterwards went to Rome to put it in hand, but I
do not know with what result.

To return to Lionardo's works. When Lionardo was at Milan
the King of France came there and desired him to do something
curious; accordingly he made a lion whose chest opened after he
had walked a few steps, discovering himself to be full of lilies.
At Milan Lionardo took Salai [3] of that city as his pupil. This was
a graceful and beautiful youth with fine curly hair, in which
Lionardo greatly delighted. He taught him many things in art,
and some works which are attributed in Milan to Salai were retouched by Lionardo. He returned to Florence, where he found
that the Servite friars had allotted to Filippino the picture of
the high altar of the Nunziata. At this Lionardo declared that he
should like to have done a similar thing. Filippino heard this, and
being very courteous, he withdrew. The friars, wishing Lionardo
to paint it, brought him to their house, paying all his expenses
and those of his household. He kept them like this for a long

---

[1] Now in the British Museum.
[2] *Trattato della Pittura*, published in 1651.   [3] Andrea Salaino.

time, but never began anything. At length he drew a cartoon of the Virgin and St. Anne with a Christ, which not only filled every artist with wonder, but, when it was finished and set up in the room, men and women, young and old, flocked to see it for two days, as if it had been a festival, and they marvelled exceedingly. The face of the Virgin displays all the simplicity and beauty which can shed grace on the Mother of God, showing the modesty and humility of a Virgin contentedly happy, in seeing the beauty of her Son, whom she tenderly holds in her lap. As she regards it the little St. John at her feet is caressing a lamb, while St. Anne smiles in her great joy at seeing her earthly progeny become divine, a conception worthy of the great intellect and genius of Lionardo. This cartoon, as will be said below, afterwards went to France. He drew Ginevra, the wife of Amerigo Benci, a beautiful portrait, and then abandoned the work of the friars, who recalled Filippino, though he was prevented from finishing it by death.

For Francesco del Giocondo Lionardo undertook the portrait of Mona Lisa, his wife, and left it incomplete after working at it for four years.[1] This work is now in the possession of Francis, King of France, at Fontainebleau. This head is an extraordinary example of how art can imitate Nature, because here we have all the details painted with great subtlety. The eyes possess that moist lustre which is constantly seen in life, and about them are those livid reds and hair which cannot be rendered without the utmost delicacy. The lids could not be more natural, for the way in which the hairs issue from the skin, here thick and there scanty, and following the pores of the skin. The nose possesses the fine delicate reddish apertures seen in life. The opening of the mouth, with its red ends, and the scarlet cheeks seem not colour but living flesh. To look closely at her throat you might imagine that the pulse was beating. Indeed, we may say that this was painted in a manner to cause the boldest artists to despair. Mona Lisa was very beautiful, and while Lionardo was drawing her portrait he engaged people to play and sing, and jesters to keep her merry, and remove that melancholy which painting usually gives to portraits. This figure of Lionardo's has such a pleasant smile that it seemed rather divine than human, and was considered marvellous, an exact copy of Nature.

The fame of this divine artist grew to such a pitch by the excellence of his works that all who delighted in the arts and the whole city wished him to leave some memorial, and they endeavoured to think of some noteworthy decorative work through which the state might be adorned and honoured by the genius, grace and judgment characteristic of his work. The great hall of the council was being rebuilt under the direction of Giuliano da S. Gallo, Simone Pollajuolo called Cronaca, Michelagnolo Buonarroti and Baccio d'Agnolo, by the judgment and advice of the gonfaloniere and leading citizens, as will be related at greater length in another place, and being finished with great speed, it was ordained by public decree that Lionardo should be employed to paint some fine work. Thus the hall was allotted to him [1] by Piero Soderini, then gonfaloniere of justice. Lionardo began by drawing a cartoon at the hall of the Pope, a place in S. Maria Novella, containing the story of Niccolo Piccinino, captain of Duke Filippo of Milan.[2] Here he designed a group of horsemen fighting for a standard, a masterly work on account of his treatment of the fight, displaying the wrath, anger and vindictiveness of men and horses; two of the latter, with their front legs involved, are waging war with their teeth no less fiercely than their riders are fighting for the standard. One soldier, putting his horse to the gallop, has turned round and, grasping the staff of the standard, is endeavouring by main force to wrench it from the hands of four others, while two are defending it, trying to cut the staff with their swords; an old soldier in a red cap has a hand on the staff, as he cries out, and holds a scimetar in the other and threatens to cut off both hands of the two, who are grinding their teeth and making every effort to defend their banner. On the ground, between the legs of the horses, are two foreshortened figures who are fighting together, while a soldier lying prone has another over him who is raising his arm as high as he can to run his dagger with his utmost strength into his adversary's throat; the latter, whose legs and arms are helpless, does what he can to escape death. The manifold designs Lionardo made for the costumes of his soldiers defy description, not to speak of the scimetars and other ornaments, and his incredible mastery of form and line in dealing with horses, which he made better than any other master, with their powerful muscles and graceful beauty. It is said that for designing the cartoon he made an ingenious scaffolding which rose higher when pressed together

[1] In 1503.
[2] The Battle of Anghiari, in which the Florentines routed the army of the Duke of Milan on 29 June, 1440.

and broadened out when lowered. Thinking that he could paint on the wall in oils, he made a composition so thick for laying on the wall that when he continued his painting it began to run and spoil what had been begun, so that in a short time he was forced to abandon it.

Lionardo had a high spirit and was most generous in every action. It is said that when he went to the bank for the monthly provision that he used to receive from Piero Soderini, the cashier wanted to give him some rolls of farthings, but he would not take them, saying that he was not a painter for farthings. Learning that Piero Soderini accused him of deceiving him and that murmurs rose against him, Lionardo with the help of his friends collected the money and took it back, but Piero would not accept it. He went to Rome with Duke Giuliano de' Medici on the election of Leo X.,[1] who studied philosophy and especially alchemy. On the way he made a paste with wax and constructed hollow animals which flew in the air when blown up, but fell when the wind ceased. On a curious lizard found by the vine-dresser of Belvedere he fastened scales taken from other lizards, dipped in quicksilver, which trembled as it moved, and after giving it eyes, a horn and a beard, he tamed it and kept it in a box. All the friends to whom he showed it ran away terrified. He would often dry and purge the guts of a wether and make them so small that they might be held in the palm of the hand. In another room he kept a pair of smith's bellows, and with these he would blow out one of the guts until it filled the room, which was a large one, forcing anyone there to take refuge in a corner. The fact that it had occupied such a little space at first only added to the wonder. He perpetrated many such follies, studied mirrors and made curious experiments to find oil for painting and varnish to preserve the work done. At this time he did a small picture for M. Baldassare Turini of Pescia, the datary of Leo, of the Virgin and Child, with infinite diligence and art. But to-day it is much spoiled either by neglect or because of his numerous fanciful mixtures and the colouring. In another picture he represented a little child, marvellously beautiful and graceful, both works being now at Pescia in the possession of M. Giulio Turini. It is said that, on being commissioned by the Pope to do a work, he straightway began to distil oil and herbs to make the varnish, which induced Pope Leo to say: "This man will never do anything, for he begins to think of the end before the beginning!"

[1] This was in 1513, but Leonardo did not go till 1515.

There was no love lost between him and Michelagnolo Buonarroti, so that the latter left Florence owing to their rivalry, Duke Giuliano excusing him by saying that he was summoned by the Pope to do the façade of S. Lorenzo. When Lionardo heard this, he left for France, where the king had heard of his works and wanted him to do the cartoon of St. Anne in colours. But Lionardo, as was his wont, gave him nothing but words for a long time. At length, having become old, he lay sick for many months, and seeing himself near death, he desired to occupy himself with the truths of the Catholic Faith and the holy Christian religion. Then, having confessed and shown his penitence with much lamentation, he devoutly took the Sacrament out of his bed, supported by his friends and servants, as he could not stand. The king arriving, for he would often pay him friendly visits, he sat up in bed from respect, and related the circumstances of his sickness, showing how greatly he had offended God and man in not having worked in his art as he ought. He was then seized with a paroxysm, the harbinger of death, so that the king rose and took his head to assist him and show him favour as well as to alleviate the pain. Lionardo's divine spirit, then recognising that he could not enjoy a greater honour, expired in the king's arms, at the age of seventy-five. The loss of Lionardo caused exceptional grief to those who had known him, because there never was a man who did so much honour to painting. By the splendour of his magnificent mien he comforted every sad soul, and his eloquence could turn men to either side of a question. His personal strength was prodigious, and with his right hand he could bend the clapper of a knocker or a horseshoe as if they had been of lead. His liberality warmed the hearts of all his friends, both rich and poor, if they possessed talent and ability. His presence adorned and honoured the most wretched and bare apartment. Thus Florence received a great gift in the birth of Lionardo, and its loss in his death was immeasurable. To the art of painting he added a type of darkness to the style of colouring in oils whereby the moderns have imparted great vigour and relief to their figures. He proved his powers in statuary in three figures in bronze over the door of S. Giovanni on the north side. They were executed by Gio. Francesco Rustici, but under Lionardo's direction, and are the finest casts for design and general perfection that have as yet been seen. To Lionardo we owe a greater perfection in the anatomy of horses and men. Thus, by his many surpassing gifts, even though he talked much more about his works than he actually achieved, his name and fame will never be extinguished. Therefore M. Gio. Battista Strozzi wrote thus in his praise:

> *Vince costui pur solo*
> *Tutti altri, e vince Fidia e vince Apelle,*
> *E tutto il lor vittorioso stuolo.*[1]

Gio. Antonio Boltraffio of Milan[2] was a pupil of Lionardo, and a very skilful and intelligent man, who in 1500 painted a panel in oils in the church of the Misericordia, outside Bologna, with the Virgin and Child, St. John the Baptist, and a nude St. Sebastian, including a portrait of the donor kneeling.[3] To this fine work he signed his name, adding that he was a pupil of Lionardo. He did other works at Milan and elsewhere, but the one I have just referred to is the best. Marco Uggioni,[4] another pupil, painted the Death of the Virgin and the Marriage of Cana in Galilee in S. Maria della Pace.

GIORGIONE DA CASTELFRANCO, Painter of Venice
(1477-1510)

WHILE Florence was acquiring so much fame by the works of Lionardo, the ability and excellence of a citizen proved of no less ornament to Venice. He far surpassed the Bellini of whom the Venetians thought so much, and all the others who had painted in that city up to that time. His name was Giorgio, born in Castelfranco in the Trevisano in 1478, under the dogeship of Giovan. Mozzenico, brother of Doge Piero. From his stature and the greatness of his mind he was afterwards known as Giorgione (great George). Though he was of very humble origin, his manners were gentle and polished all his life. Brought up in Venice, he displayed very amorous propensities, and was exceedingly fond of the lute, playing and singing so divinely that he was frequently invited to musical gatherings and meetings of noble persons. He studied design, and was so fond of it, Nature assisting him to her utmost, and he was so enamoured of the beauty of that art, that he would never introduce anything into his works which he had

---

[1] " Single-handed he overcame all others, Phidias, Apelles and their victorious band." This epigram is based on a play upon words, Vinci and the verb *vincere*, to conquer or overcome.

[2] 1467-1516.
[3] Formerly in the Brera, Milan, now in the Louvre.
[4] Marco d'Oggionno, 1470-1530.

not drawn from life. So closely did he follow Nature, and so carefully did he imitate her, that not only did he acquire the reputation of having surpassed Gentile and Giovanni Bellini, but he competed with the Tuscan masters, the authors of the modern style. Having seen and greatly admired some things of Lionardo, richly toned and exceedingly dark, as has been said, Giorgione made them his model, and imitated them carefully in painting in oils. Keenly appreciative of anything good, he used to pick and chose, adopting the finest and most varied things that he found. Nature had so richly endowed him that he succeeded wonderfully both in oils and in fresco, making certain things so soft and harmonious and his shadows so vaporous, that many artists of recognised standing admitted that he was born to infuse his figures with spirit and to counterfeit the freshness of living flesh better than any painter, not in Venice alone but everywhere.

At first he did many Madonnas at Venice, and other portraits which are vigorous and fine, three lovely heads in oils by his hand being in the study of the Very Rev. Grimani, Patriarch of Aquileia. One represents David, and is reputed to be his own portrait, the hair falling to the shoulders as was customary at that time, so vigorous and well-coloured that it is like flesh. The arms and breast are protected by armour, and he holds the severed head of Goliath in his hand.[1] The second is a larger head forming a portrait from life, holding the red cap of a commander in his hand, with a collar of skin, and underneath a vest in the antique style. It is supposed to represent a general. The third is a child of surpassing loveliness, his hair displaying the excellence of Giorgione as well as the affection which the patriarch has always cherished for his ability, valuing it most highly, and deservedly so. In the house of the sons of Giovan. Borgherini, at Florence, there is the portrait of Giovanni himself when he was a young man at Venice, with his tutor in the same picture.[2] No two heads in existence exhibit better flesh-colouring or finer shadows. In the house of Anton de' Nobili there is another head of a captain in armour, very vivacious and vigorous. It is said to be one of the captains whom Gonsalvo Ferrante [3] brought with him to Venice when he visited the Doge Agostino Barberigo. It is said that at this time Giorgione drew the great Gonsalvo

---

[1] Possibly the picture at Vienna, though it is considered a copy by some.
[2] Possibly the picture now in the Berlin Gallery.
[3] Gonsalvo of Cordova, called the " great captain " (1443–1515), who conquered the Kingdom of Naples for Spain and held it against the French.

in armour, a remarkable work, unequalled for its beauty, and that the general took it away with him. Giorgione did many other fine portraits which are scattered throughout Italy, as may be seen by that of Lionardo Loredano, done when he was doge, seen by me on exhibition one Ascension Day, so that I seemed to see that most serene prince alive. There is yet another at Faenza, in the house of Giovannni di Castel Bolognese,[1] an excellent carver of cameos and crystals, done for his father-in-law. This is indeed a divine work for the soft blending of the colours, and it seems in relief rather than painted. Giorgione was very fond of painting in fresco, and among many things did all one side of Ca Soranzo on the piazza of S. Paolo, where, in addition to many pictures, scenes and other fancies, there is one done in oils upon lime, which has preserved it from the rain, sun and wind, so that it still exists. There is a Spring, which I think one of the loveliest works in fresco, and it is a great pity that time has injured it so cruelly. Personally I know of nothing that injures fresco so much as the scirocco, especially near the sea, where it always brings some saltness with it.

In the year 1504 there was a terrible fire[2] at Venice, in the Fondaco de' Tedeschi at the Rialto bridge, which consumed all the merchandise, inflicting great loss upon the merchants. The Signoria of Venice directed that it should be rebuilt, and it was speedily finished, with more convenient dwelling-rooms, greater magnificence, decoration and beauty than before. The fame of Giorgione being now considerable, those in charge of the building decided that he should paint it in fresco, colouring it according to his fancy, in order to display his ability in producing an excellent work, the site being the finest and the best position in all the city. Accordingly Giorgione set to work,[3] but with no other purpose than to make figures at fancy to display his art, for I cannot discover what they mean, whether they represent some ancient or modern story, and no one has been able to tell me. Here is a lady and there a man, in various attitudes, one has a lion's head hard-by, another an angel in the guise of a cupid, and I cannot tell what it means. There is certainly a woman over the principal door towards the Merzeria seated, with the head of a dead giant beneath, almost like a Judith. She is raising the head with a sword and speaking to a German below. I cannot explain this in any way unless he wished her to represent Germania. However, we see his figures well grouped and that he was always improving. There are heads and parts of figures which are excellently done and brilliantly coloured. Giorgione was careful in all that he did there to copy straight from living things, and not to imitate any one style. This building is celebrated and famous in Venice no less for these paintings than for its convenience for commerce and utility to the public. He did a picture of Christ bearing the Cross and a Jew dragging him along, which, after a time, was placed in the church of S. Rocco,[1] and now works miracles, as we see, through the devotion of the multitudes who visit it. He worked at various places, such as Castelfranco in the Trevisano, and did several portraits for various Italian princes, while many of his works were sent out of Italy as things of distinction, to show that if Tuscany overflowed with artists in all ages, Heaven had not entirely forgotten or passed over the district near the mountains.

Giorgione is said to have once engaged in an argument with some sculptors at the time when Andrea Verrocchio was making his bronze horse. They maintained that sculpture was superior to painting, because it presented so many various aspects, whereas painting only showed one side of a figure. Giorgione was of opinion that a painting could show at a single glance, without it being necessary to walk about, all the aspects that a man can present in a number of gestures, while sculpture can only do so if one walks about it. He offered in a single view to show the front and back and the two sides of a figure in painting, a matter which greatly excited their curiosity. He accomplished this in the following way. He painted a nude figure turning its back; at its feet was a limpid fount of water, the reflection from which showed the front. On one side was a burnished corselet which had been taken off, and gave a side view, because the shining metal reflected everything. On the other side was a looking-glass, showing the other side of the figure, a beautiful and ingenious work to prove that painting demands more skill and pains, and shows to a single view more than sculpture does. This work was greatly admired and praised for its ingenuity and beauty. Giorgione also drew a portrait of Catherine, Queen of Cyprus, which I have seen in the hands of the most excellent M. Giovan. Cornaro. In our book there is a head coloured in oils of a German of the house of Fugger, then one of the foremost merchants of the Fondaco dei Tedeschi. This marvellous work is accompanied by other pen-and-ink sketches and designs of his.

[1] Modern critics accept this as a work of the master, but in the Life of Titian, Vasari ascribes it to that artist.

Whilst Giorgione was doing honour to his country and to himself, he went frequently into society to entertain his numerous friends with music, and fell in love with a lady, so that they became greatly enamoured of each other. However, in 1511, she caught the plague, and Giorgione, being ignorant of this, associated with her as usual, took the infection, and died soon after at the age of thirty-four, to the infinite grief of his numerous friends, who loved him for his talents, and damage to the world which lost him. They were the better able to support the loss because he left behind two excellent pupils, Sebastiano of Venice, afterwards friar of the Piombo at Rome, and Titian of Cadore, who not only equalled but far excelled his master. I shall have occasion to speak of these hereafter, and of the honour and benefit which they have conferred upon art.

ANTONIO DA CORREGGIO, Painter
(?1494–1534)

I DO not leave this country from which Mother Nature, to escape the charge of partiality, has given to the world distinguished men of the stamp of those who have adorned Tuscany for so many years. Among them was Antonio da Correggio, a most remarkable painter, who adopted the modern style perfectly, and being endowed with a rare genius, of great natural ability and well trained in art, he became in a few years a sublime and marvellous artist. He was of a very timid disposition, and, at great personal inconvenience, worked continually for the family which depended upon him. Although naturally good, he allowed himself to be unreasonably afflicted in resisting those passions which usually affect men. In art he was very melancholy, enduring its labours, but most skilful in overcoming difficulties, as we see in the great tribune of the Duomo of Parma,[1] which contains a multitude of well-finished figures in fresco, where he has marvellously foreshortened the view as seen from below. He was the first to introduce the modern style into Lombardy, so that it was thought he might have done marvels and endangered the laurels of many who were considered great in his time if he had left Lombardy and gone to Rome. But not having seen any antiques or good modern works, he was obliged to follow what he had seen, and he would necessarily have done better, with

[1] Begun in 1526; left unfinished at his death.

greater advantages, to the infinite improvement of his works, raising him to the highest excellence.

It is considered certain that there never was a better colourist, or any artist who imparted more loveliness or relief to his things, so great was the soft beauty of his flesh-tints and the grace of his finish. In the same Duomo he did two other large pictures in oils, one being a much-admired dead Christ. In S. Giovanni, in the same city, he did a picture in fresco for the tribune of the Virgin ascending into heaven amid a throng of angels and other saints.[1] The beauty of the drapery and the air of the figures are of a loveliness which one would have thought it impossible to conceive, far less to express with the hands. Some of these figures drawn by him in red chalk are in our book, with a border of beautiful children and other decorative borders, with various fancies of sacrifices in the antique style. But if Antonio had not brought his works to that perfection which we see in them, his designs, although possessing good style, charm and masterly skill, would not have won him such a reputation as his more ambitious efforts. This art has so many branches that an artist frequently cannot master them all perfectly, for some have drawn divinely and been faulty colourists, while others have been marvellous colourists and only mediocre draughtsmen. This is due to a decision and practice adopted in youth, some taking up design and some colouring. But as all is learned in order to produce perfect work at length, that is colouring with design, Correggio deserves great praise for having attained perfection in his works, both in oils and in fresco. Thus, in the church of S. Francesco[2] of the bare-footed friars in the same city he did an Annunciation in fresco so finely that, when the wall on which it was painted threatened to fall down, the friars shored it up with wood and iron supports, and, cutting the wall away piece by piece, they saved it, and transported it to another and safer place in the same convent. Over a gate of that city he painted a Madonna and Child, marvellous for its beautiful colouring in fresco, so that travellers who have not seen his other works admire it greatly. In S. Antonio in the same city he did a picture of the Virgin and St. Mary Magdalene with a laughing child near, like a little angel, holding a book in his hand.[3] It is so natural that no one who sees it can refrain from smiling, and a melancholy person is made happy. There is also a St. Jerome of such marvel-

---

[1] 1520–4.   [2] It is in S. Annunziata.
[3] Painted in 1523. Both this and the preceding picture are in the Parma Gallery.

lous and stupendous colouring that painters admire it for this character, seeing that it is not possible to paint better. He did other paintings for Lombardy, and for many lords, and, among others, two in Mantua [1] for Duke Federigo II., to be sent to the emperor, a work worthy of such a prince. When Giulio Romano saw these paintings, he said that he had never seen colouring to approach it. One was a naked Leda, and the other a Venus, the colouring so lovely and the flesh-tints so well done that it appears actual flesh and not paint. One of them contains a remarkable landscape, in which no Lombard has ever surpassed him. He also did hairs so lightly coloured and so finely polished and threaded that nothing better can be seen. Some cupids shoot arrows of gold and lead at a stone, a very skilfully executed subject. A clear and limpid stream runs between rocks, and bathes the feet of Venus, enhancing her loveliness, and it is hard to regard her delicateness and whiteness without emotion. Therefore Antonio merited every possible honour when alive and the praises of writers after his death. At Modena he painted a Madonna,[2] valued by all artists, and considered to be the best painting in that city. At Bologna, in the house of the Ercolani, Bolognese noblemen, there is a Christ in the Garden appearing to Mary Magdalene,[3] a very beautiful thing. Reggio possessed a fine and remarkable picture, which not long ago came under the notice of M. Luciano Pallavicino, who was very fond of paintings, and, without minding the cost, he bought it as if it had been a jewel and sent it to his house at Genoa. There is another picture at Reggio of a Nativity of Christ,[4] who emits a radiance which illuminates the shepherds and those who are regarding Him. Among many ideas contained in this subject there is a woman who wishes to look steadily at the Christ, but, as mortal sight could not bear the radiance of His divinity, she puts her hand before her eyes in a marvellously natural manner. Above the manger is a choir of angels singing, so well done that they seem to have rained from heaven rather than to be the mere creation of a painter. In the same city is a small picture of the size of a foot, the most remarkable and beautiful of his works. It represents Christ in the Garden, with small figures, at night-time, and the radiance of the angel appearing to Him illuminates the Christ in an extraordinarily true and striking manner. The

[1] About 1532; the Leda is in the Borghese Gallery, Rome.
[2] Probably the one at Dresden, painted in 1525 for the brotherhood of S. Sebastiano, Modena.
[3] In the Wellington Museum, London.
[4] Painted for S. Prospero, Reggio, in 1522, now in the Dresden Gallery

three Apostles lie sleeping on a plain at the foot of the mountain on which Christ is praying, the shadow of which lies across this plain and gives an extraordinary force to the figures. In the distance the dawn is coming, and from one of the sides soldiers approach with Judas. This small scene is so well conceived that it cannot be equalled in a work of its size for patience or study. I might say much more of this artist's work, but as everything by his hand is admired by our foremost artists as a divine thing, I will say nothing further. I have taken the utmost pains to obtain his portrait, and have not been able to find it, because he did not draw himself, and was never drawn by others. Indeed he was a modest man, and felt that he had not mastered his art so thoroughly as he would have desired, for he realised its difficulties. He was content with little, and lived as a good Christian should.

Antonio was anxious to save, like everyone who is burdened with a family, and he thus became excessively miserly. It is said that payment of 60 crowns being made to him at Parma in coppers, which he wished to take to Correggio for his affairs, he set out with this burden on foot. Becoming overheated by the warmth of the sun, he took some water to refresh himself, and caught a severe fever, which terminated his life in the fortieth year of his age or thereabouts. His paintings date about 1512, and he greatly enriched art by his masterly colouring, whereby he opened the eyes of Lombardy, where so many fine spirits have been seen in painting, following him in the production of fine pictures, worthy of being remembered. By his facile treatment of hair, so difficult to do, he has taught the proper methods of representing it, for which all painters owe him an eternal debt. At their instance M. Fabio Segni, a nobleman of Florence, wrote the following epigram:

Hujus cum regeret mortales spiritus artus
Pictoris, Charites supplicuere Jovi :
Non alia pingi dextra, Pater alme, rogamus,
Hunc praeter, nulli pingere nos liceat.
Annuit his votis summi regnator olympi,
Et juvenem subito sydera ad alta tulit
Ut posset melius Charitum simulacra referre,
Praesens, et nudas cerneret inde Deas.

At this same time flourished Andrea del Gobbo, painter of Milan,[1] and a charming colourist. Many of his works are to be

[1] Andrea Solari. His brother Cristofano Solari, the sculptor, was known as Il Gobbo, i.e. hunch-back. The Assumption was painted by Andrea after 1515.

found in private houses in Milan, and there is a large picture of the Assumption in the Certosa of Pavia, left unfinished owing to his death. This picture shows the extent of his excellence and his love for the labours of his art.

PIERO DI COSIMO, Painter of Florence
(1462-1521)

WHILE Giorgione and Correggio were winning praise and glory for Lombardy, Tuscany was not devoid of distinguished men. Not the least of these was Piero, son of one Lorenzo, a goldsmith, and godson of Cosimo Rosselli, and owing to these circumstances he was always known as Piero di Cosimo. Indeed, he who instructs ability and promotes well-being is as truly a father as the one who begets. Piero's father, seeing the intelligence of his son and his fondness for design, entrusted him to Cosimo, who took the charge willingly, and always loved and regarded Piero as a son among all the pupils whom he saw about him, and watched him growing in years and ability. This youth naturally possessed a very lofty spirit, and he was very abstracted, and differed in tastes from the other pupils of Cosimo. He was sometimes so absorbed in what he was doing that those who conversed with him were frequently obliged to repeat all that they had said, for his mind had wandered to other ideas. He was so fond of solitude that his one delight was to wander alone, free to build his castles in the air. His master Cosimo had reason to hope that they might be extensive, for he employed him frequently on his own works, continually entrusting him with matters of importance, knowing that Piero possessed a finer style and better judgment than himself. For this reason he took him to Rome when summoned by Pope Sixtus to decorate the chapel. In one of the scenes there[1] Piero did a beautiful landscape, as I have said in the Life of Cosimo. As he drew most excellently from life, he did a quantity of portraits of distinguished persons at Rome, notably Verginio Orsino and Ruberto Sansovino, whom he introduced into the scenes. He also drew Duke Valentino, son of Pope Alexander VI. So far as I know this picture cannot now be found, but the cartoon exists in the possession of M. Cosimo Bartoli, provost of S. Giovanni. He painted a quantity of pictures at Florence for the houses of various persons, many good

[1] The Sermon on the Mount, painted in 1482.

examples having come under my notice, and he also did various
things for many other people. In the Noviciate of S. Marco he
did a Madonna standing with the Child, coloured in oils. In the
church of S. Spirito at Florence, in the Chapel of Gino Capponi,
he did a picture of the Visitation, with St. Nicholas and a
St. Anthony reading, the latter wearing a pair of spectacles, a
vigorous figure. There is an excellent representation of an old
parchment book, and the balls of St. Nicholas are made lustrous,
reflecting each other, showing the curious fancies of Piero's
brain, and how he sought out and performed difficult things.

After his death it appeared that he had lived the life of a
brute rather than a man, as he had kept himself shut up and
would not permit anyone to see him work. He would not allow
his rooms to be swept, he ate when he felt hungry, and would
never suffer the fruit-trees of his garden to be pruned or trained,
leaving the vines to grow and trail along the ground; the fig-
trees were never pruned nor any others, for he loved to see
everything wild, saying that nature ought to be allowed to look
after itself. He would often go to see animals, herbs, or any
freaks of nature, and his contentment and satisfaction he
enjoyed by himself. He would repeat his remarks so many times
that at length they became wearisome, however good they may
have been. He stopped to examine a wall where sick persons had
used to spit, imagining that he saw there combats of horses and
the most fantastic cities and extraordinary landscapes ever
beheld. He cherished the same fancies of clouds. He practised
colouring in oils after seeing some things of Lionardo toned and
finished with the extreme diligence characteristic of that master
when he wished to display his art. This method pleased Piero
and he strove to imitate it, though he was a long way behind
Lionardo, and any other eccentric things; indeed we may say
that this spirit pervaded everything which he did. If Piero
had not been so eccentric, and had possessed more self-respect,
he would have displayed his great genius and commanded
admiration, whereas he was rather considered a fool for his
uncouthness, though he really harmed no one but himself and
greatly benefited art by his works. Thus every man of ability
and every excellent artist ought to consider the end in the light
of these examples.

In his youth Piero, possessing a capricious and extravagant
invention, was in great request for the masquerades of carnival-
time, and was a great favourite with the noble Florentine youths,
because by his inventive mind he greatly improved those amuse-

ments in ornament, grandeur and pomp. He is said to have been
one of the first to give them the character of triumphs, and at
any rate he greatly improved them with his scenes, with music
and appropriate speeches, and a grand procession of men on
horses and foot, in costumes adapted to the subject. These
proved very rich and fine, combining grandeur and ingenuity.
It was certainly a fine sight at night to see twenty-five or thirty
couples of horses, richly caparisoned, with their masters dressed
in accordance with the subject of the invention; six or eight
footmen in the same livery, in single file, carrying torches in
their hands, sometimes more than four hundred, and then the
car or triumph full of ornaments, spoils and curious fancies,
which enchanted the people and instructed their minds.

Among these things, which were fairly numerous and ingenious, I will briefly describe one of Piero's chief efforts [1] when
he was already mature. It was not, like many others, pleasant
and pretty, but curious, horrible and surprising, giving no small
pleasure to the people. For as acid things give wonderful delight
in food, so horrible things in these amusements tickle the fancy,
as, for instance, in tragedy. This particular device was the car
of Death secretly prepared by Piero in the Pope's Hall, so that
nothing transpired until it was made public to all at the same
time. It was a large car drawn by black buffaloes and painted
with white death's heads and crossbones. At the top of the car
a gigantic Death held his scythe, while round the car were many
tombs with their stones. When the car stopped, these opened,
and figures clothed in black issued out, with the complete
skeleton painted on their draperies, the white set off by the
black. From a distance there appeared some of the torches with
masks painted behind and before like skulls, including the throat,
most realistic but a horrid and terrible sight. At the raucous,
dead sound of some trumpets, they came half out of the tombs
and, sitting on them, sang the following noble canzone to a
music full of sadness:

Dolor, pianto e penitenza, etc.

In front of and following the car were a great number of dead
mounted on the leanest and boniest horses that could be found,
with black trappings marked with white crosses. Each one had
four footmen dressed as the dead, carrying black crosses and a
great black standard with crosses, skulls and cross bones. After
the triumph they dragged ten black standards, and as they

[1] For the carnival of 1511.

marched they sang the Miserere, a psalm of David, in unison, with trembling voices. This lugubrious spectacle, by its novelty and tremendous character, as I have said, at once terrified and amazed the whole city, and although it did not seem at first sight suited to the carnival, yet it pleased everyone because of its novelty and because everything was admirably arranged. Piero, the inventor, received hearty praise for his work, and this encouraged him to produce witty and ingenious devices, for the city has no rival in the conduct of such festivals. Old people who saw this spectacle preserve a lively recollection of it and are never tired of talking about this curious invention. I have heard it said by Andrea di Cosimo, who helped him with this work, and by Andrea del Sarto, his pupil, who also had a share in it, that this invention was intended to signify the return to Florence of the house of the Medici, exiles at the time and practically dead. Thus they interpret the words:

> *Morti siam, come vedete*
> *Cosi morti vedrem voi*
> *Fummo gia come voi sete*
> *Voi sarete come noi*, etc.

to indicate their return, like a resurrection of a dead man to life, and the banishment of their opponents. However this may be, it was natural that a special significance should be attributed to these words when this illustrious house returned to Florence, as men are apt to apply words and acts that happen before to events that follow after. The opinion was certainly entertained by many, and it was much discussed.

But to return to art and the achievements of Piero. He was commissioned to do a picture at the Chapel of the Tedaldi in the church of the Servite friars, where the vest and pillow of St. Philip, their founder, are preserved. Here he did a Madonna standing, raised from the ground on a dado; she is without the Child, holds a book in her hand, and raises her head to heaven while the Holy Spirit above irradiates her. The light emitted by the doves is the only thing which illuminates her and the other figures, St. Margaret and St. Catherine, who are adoring her on their knees, while St. Peter and St. John the Baptist, with St. Philip, the Servite friar, and St. Antonino, Archbishop of Florence, stand and regard her. There is a remarkable landscape of strange trees and some caves. It indeed contains some very beautiful parts, such as certain heads, displaying design and grace, with a very even colouring. Certainly Piero possessed the art of colouring in oil to perfection. He did the predella of small scenes, excellently painted, among them being St. Margaret issuing from the belly of the serpent. This animal is caricatured and so ugly that I do not consider that a better example of the kind is to be found, presenting a truly fearful aspect with its poisonous eyes, fire and death. I do not think that anyone painted such things better than Piero, nor conceived them so well, as for example a marine monster which he did and presented to M. Giuliano de' Medici, of remarkable and curious deformity, so that it appears impossible that Nature should have produced anything so fantastic. This monster is now in the wardrobe of Duke Cosimo, which also contains a book of similar curious and strange animals by Piero, carefully drawn with the pen and executed with admirable patience. The book was presented by my good friend M. Cosimo Bartoli, provost of S. Giovanni, who is a great admirer of the profession. In the house of Francesco del Pugliese, Piero did some scenes of fables in small figures about a room, the diversity of the fantastic creations in which he delighted, houses, animals, costumes, various instruments and other things defying description. After the death of Francesco and his children they were removed, and I do not know what has become of them. There is a picture of Mars and Venus and their loves, and a Vulcan represented with great art and incredible patience. For Filippo Strozzi the elder Piero painted a picture of Perseus releasing Andromeda from the monster, in small figures, containing some most beautiful things. It is now in the house of Sig. Sforza Almeni, first chamberlain of Duke Cosimo,[1] having been given to him by M. Giovanni Battista di Lorenzo Strozzi, who knew how fond he was of painting and sculpture. He values it highly, for Piero never did a more lovely or a better-finished picture; no more curious sea-monster can be seen than the one which he drew there, while the attitude of Perseus is fine as he raises his sword to strike. Andromeda's beautiful face is torn between fear and hope, as she stands bound, and before her are many people in various curious costumes, playing and singing, some laughing and rejoicing at seeing her release. The landscape is very lovely and the colouring soft, graceful, harmonious and well blended. Piero finished this work with the greatest care. He also painted a picture of a nude Venus with a nude Mars lying asleep in a meadow full of flowers, surrounded by cupids who are carrying his helmet, gauntlets and other armour.[2] It also contains

---

[1] Now in the Uffizi Gallery.
[2] Probably the picture in the Berlin Gallery.

a myrtle bush and a cupid frightened by a rabbit, with the doves of Venus and other accessories of Love. This picture is in Florence in the house of Giorgio Vasari, treasured in memory of the author whose fancies always delighted him. The master of the hospital of the Innocents was a great friend of Piero, and when he wanted a picture for the Chapel of the Pugliese on the left-hand on entering the church, he allotted it to Piero, who completed it to his satisfaction. But he drove the master to desperation, as he was not allowed to see it before it was finished. It seemed strange to him that a friend should be always thinking of the money and not allow him to see the work, and he refused to make the last payment unless he was allowed to see the work. But when Piero threatened to destroy what was done he was forced to give him the rest, with anger exceeding his former patience. The work certainly contains many good things.[1] Piero undertook to do a panel in the church of S. Pier Gattolini, representing a Madonna seated, surrounded by four figures, while two angels in the air are crowning her, a work conducted with such diligence that he won much praise and honour. It may now be seen in S. Friano,[2] as the other church is destroyed. He did a small panel of the Conception[3] on the screen of the church of S. Francesco at Fiesole, a charming little thing, the figures not being very large. He did some bacchanalian scenes about a chamber for Giovan. Vespucci, who lived opposite S. Michele in the via de' Servi, now via di Pier Salviati, introducing curious fauns, satyrs, wood-nymphs, children and bacchantes, the diversity of creatures and garments being marvellous, with various goatish faces, all done with grace and remarkable realism. In one scene Silenus is riding an ass, with a throng of children some carrying him and some giving him drink, the general joy being ingeniously depicted.

Piero's works betray a spirit of great diversity distinct from those of others, for he was endowed with a subtlety for investigating curious matters in nature, and executed them without a thought for the time or labour, but solely for his delight and pleasure in art. It could not be otherwise, for so devoted was he to art that he neglected his material comforts, and his habitual food consisted of hard-boiled eggs, which he cooked while he was boiling his glue, to save the firing. He would cook not six or eight at a time, but a good fifty, and would eat them one by

---

[1] It represents a Madonna and saints, painted about 1500.
[2] Probably the picture now in the Louvre.
[3] The Immaculate Conception now in the Uffizi.

one from a basket in which he kept them. He adhered so strictly to this manner of life that others seemed to him to be in slavery by comparison. The crying of babies irritated him, and so did the coughing of men, the sound of bells, the singing of the friars. When it rained hard he loved to see the water rushing off the roofs and splashing on to the ground. He was much afraid of lightning and was terrified of the thunder. He would wrap himself up in his mantle, shut up the windows and doors of the room and crouch into a corner until the fury of the storm had passed. His conversation was so various and diversified that some of his sayings made his hearers burst with laughter. But in his old age, when eighty years old, he became so strange and eccentric that he was unbearable. He would not allow his apprentices to be about him, so that he obtained less and less assistance by his uncouthness. He wanted to work, and not being able on account of the paralysis, he became so enraged that he would try to force his helpless hands, while he doddered about and the brush and maul-stick fell from his grasp, a pitiful sight to behold. The flies annoyed him, and he hated the dark. Thus fallen sick of old age, he was visited by a friend who begged him to make his peace with God. But he did not think he was going to die and kept putting it off. It was not that he was bad or without faith, for though his life had been uncouth he was full of zeal. He spoke sometimes of long wasting sicknesses and gradual dying, and its wretchedness. He abused physicians and apothecaries, saying that they made their patients die of hunger, in addition to tormenting them with syrups, medicines, clysters and other tortures, such as not allowing them to sleep when drowsy. He also spoke of the distress of making a will, seeing relations weep, and being in a room in the dark. He praised capital punishment, saying it was a fine thing to go to death in the open air amid a throng of people, being comforted with sweetmeats and kind words, the priest and people praying for you, and then going with the angels to Paradise, and that those were very fortunate who died suddenly. And thus he went on with these most extraordinary notions, twisting things to the strangest imaginable meanings. After such a curious life he was found dead one morning at the foot of the stairs, in 1521, and was buried in S. Pier Maggiore. He had several pupils, among them Andrea del Sarto, who counted for many. His portrait [1] is obtained from Francesco da S. Gallo, who did it when Piero was an old man, for he was a great and intimate friend. I must not omit

[1] Now in the Mauritshuis at The Hague.

to say that this Francesco has a very fine head of Cleopatra by Piero, with the serpent about her neck,[1] and two portraits, one of Giuliano, his father, the other of Giamberti, his grandfather, most life-like.

BRAMANTE DA URBINO, Architect

(1444-1514)

THE modern methods of Filippo Brunelleschi proved of great assistance to architecture, as he had copied and brought to light after long ages the excellent productions of the most learned and distinguished ancients. But Bramante has been no less useful to our own century, for he followed in the footsteps of Filippo, and paved a safe way for those who succeeded, his spirit, courage, genius and knowledge of the art being displayed not only in theory but in practice. Nature could not have formed a mind better adapted than his to put into practice the works of his art with invention and proportion and on so firm a basis. But it was necessary that she should create at the same time a Pope like Julius II., ambitious of leaving a great memory. It was most fortunate that this prince should have afforded Bramante such unrivalled opportunities of displaying his abilities and of showing the full force of his genius, for such a thing rarely happens. Bramante took full advantage of his chance, the mouldings of his cornices, the shafts of his columns, the grace of his capitals, his bases, corbels, angles, vaults, steps, projections and every other detail of architecture being marvellously modelled with the best judgment, and men of ability seem to me to be under as great a debt to him as to the ancients. Because, while the Greeks invented architecture and the Romans imitated them, Bramante not only added new inventions, but greatly increased the beauty and difficulty of the art, to an extent we may now perceive.

He was born at Castello Durante, in the state of Urbino, of a poor man of good condition. In his childhood, besides reading and writing, he was continually doing the abacus. But as it was necessary that he should learn some trade, his father, perceiving his great fondness for design, apprenticed him while still a child to the art of painting. Here he carefully studied the productions of Frà Bartolommeo, otherwise Frà Carnovale da Urbino, who

[1] A portrait of Simonetta Vespucci; now in the Musée Condé, Chantilly.

did the picture of S. Maria della Bella at Urbino. But as he always delighted in architecture and perspective, he left Castel Durante, and, passing to Lombardy, worked as best he could in one city after another, not producing things of great cost or value, because as yet he had neither fame nor credit. Determined to see at least one notable thing, he preceeded to Milan [1] to visit the Duomo, where there happened to be one Cesare Cesariano, reputed a good geometrician and architect, who had written a commentary on Vitruvius. Enraged at not having received the reward which he had expected, Cesare refused to work any more, and, becoming eccentric, he died more like a beast than a man. There also was Bernardino da Trevio,[2] a Milanese engineer and architect of the Duomo, and a great draughtsman. He was considered a rare master by Lionardo da Vinci, even though his manner in painting was crude and somewhat dry. There is a Resurrection of his [3] with some fine foreshortenings at the top of the cloister of the Grazie, and a Death of SS. Peter and Paul in fresco in a chapel of S. Francesco. He painted many other works in Milan, and did several others in the neighbourhood, which were valued, and our book contains a very meritorious woman's head in charcoal and white lead, a good example of his style.

But to return to Bramante. After an examination of the Duomo, and having met these masters, he determined to devote himself entirely to architecture. Accordingly he left Milan, and arrived at Rome before the Holy Year 1500. Here he was welcomed by some friends and natives of Lombardy and commissioned to paint in fresco the arms of Pope Alexander VI., supported by angels and figures, over the holy door of S. Giovanni Lateran, which was opened for the Jubilee. Bramante had earned money in Lombardy and at Rome, and on this he hoped to live, by dint of severe economy, and to be able to measure all the ancient buildings of Rome without it being necessary to work. He set about this task, going alone and wrapped in thought. In a little while he had measured all the buildings there and in the neighbourhood, going even as far as Naples, and wherever he knew antiquities to be. He measured what there was at Tivoli and the villa of Hadrian, and made considerable use of this, as I shall have occasion to relate. Bramante's spirit being thus disclosed, the cardinal of Naples [4] happened to observe him,

---

[1] Probably about 1472.
[2] Bernardino Zenale of Treviglio, 1436-1526.
[3] It is the work of Bernardo Butinone.
[4] Oliviero Caraffa.

and took him into favour. Thus Bramante pursued his studies, and was charged to restore in travertine the cloister of the friars of the Pace, which the cardinal wished to have done. Being anxious to make a name and to please the cardinal, Bramante displayed the utmost industry and diligence, and speedily completed the work.[1] Although it was not of perfect beauty, it brought him a great reputation, as there were not many in Rome who devoted so much love, study and activity to architecture as he.

Bramante began by serving Pope Alexander VI. as under-architect, at the fountain of Trastevere and the one on the piazza of S. Piero. His reputation increasing, he was one of the eminent artists consulted about the palace of S. Giorgio, and the church of S. Lorenzo in Damaso, near the Campo di Fiore, put in hand by Raffaello Riario, cardinal of S. Giorgio, which, though improved after, was and still is considered a convenient and magnificient abode for its size. The director of this building was one Antonio Montecavallo. Bramante was also on the council for the enlargement of S. Jacopo degli Spagnuoli at Navona, and took part in the deliberation concerning S. Maria *de Anima*, afterwards carried out by a German architect.[2] The palace of the Cardinal Adriano da Corneto in the Borgo Nuovo was also his design. It was built slowly, and was left unfinished owing to the flight of the cardinal. He also designed the enlargement of the principal chapel of S. Maria del Popolo. These works brought him such credit at Rome that he was considered the foremost architect for his resolution, rapidity and excellent invention, so that he was constantly employed by all the great men of the city upon their chief requirements. On the election of Pope Julius II. in 1503 he began to serve him. That Pope had a fancy to cover the space between the Belvedere and the palace, and that it should take the form of a square theatre, embracing a depression between the old papal palace and the building erected there for the pope's dwelling by Innocent VIII., and that there should be a passage by two corridors on either side of the depression leading from the Belvedere to the palace covered by loggias, and so from the palace to the Belvedere, the level of which should be reached from the valley by flights of steps, variously arranged. Bramante, who possessed a good judgment and a fanciful genius in such matters, divided the bottom part into two stories, first a fine Doric loggia like the Coliseum of the Savelli,[3] but instead of half-columns, he put

[1] In 1504.   [2] Begun in 1500.   [3] i.e. the theatre of Marcellus.

pilasters, building the whole of travertine. The second stage was of the Ionic order and with windows, rising to the level of the first apartments of the papal palace and of those of the Belvedere, to form subsequently a loggia more than four hundred paces on the side towards Rome and another towards the wood, with the valley between, so that it was necessary to bring all the water of the Belvedere and to erect a beautiful fountain. Of this design Bramante completed the first corridor rising from the palace and leading to the Belvedere on the Roman side, except the last loggia, which was to go above. Of the part towards the wood he laid the foundations, but could not finish it, owing to the death of Julius, followed by his own. It was considered such a fine idea that it was believed that Rome had never seen better since the time of the ancients. But, as I have said, nothing but the foundations of the other corridor were laid, and it has barely been completed even in our own day, Pius IV. putting the finishing touches. Bramante also did the antique gallery in the Belvedere for the ancient statues with the arrangement of niches. Here in his own lifetime Laocoon was put, a very rare and ancient statue, and the Apollo and Venus, and others later on by Leo X., such as the Tiber, the Nile and the Cleopatra, some others by Clement VII., and a number of important improvements were carried out at great expense in the time of Paul III. and Julius III.

But to return to Bramante, if those who supplied him were not sparing he was very expeditious and he understood the art of construction thoroughly. This building of the Belvedere was carried out with great rapidity, his own energy being equalled by the fever of the Pope, who wanted his structures not to be built but to grow up as by magic. Thus the builders carried away by night the sand and earth excavated by day in the presence of Bramante, so that he directed the laying of the foundations without taking further precautions. This careless-ness has occasioned the cracking of his works, so that they are in danger of falling. Of the corridor in question eighty braccia fell down in the time of Pope Clement VII., and it was rebuilt by Pope Paul III., who caused it to be restored and enlarged. There are many other flights of steps of Bramante in the palace, high or low, according to their situation, in the Corinthian, Ionic and Doric orders, very beautiful, and executed with the utmost grace. His model is said to have been of marvellous beauty, as we may judge by the part actually constructed. In addition to this, he made a spiral staircase on rising columns, which a horse may go up, the Doric merging into the Ionic and the Ionic into the Corinthian, all carried out with the utmost grace and art, doing him no less honour than his other works at the same place. This idea was borrowed by Bramante from Niccolo of Pisa, as has been said in the Life of Giovanni and Niccolo Pisani. It entered Bramante's fancy to make a frieze on the front of the Belvedere, with some letters like ancient hieroglyphics to show his skill, and thus to spell out the Pope's name and his own. Thus he had begun: *Julio II. Pont. Maximo*, making a head in profile of Julius Cæsar and a bridge with two arches for *Julio II. Pont.*, and an obelisk of the Circus Maximus for *Max.*, at which the Pope laughed, and told him to do it in letters a braccia long, in the ancient style, which are there to-day. Bramante said he had borrowed that folly from over a door at Viterbo, where a French architect had done a St. Francis, an arch (*arco*), a roof (*tetto*) and a tower (*torre*), to signify Maestro Francesco Architettore. The Pope was very gracious to Bramante for his great talents in architecture, and he deserved the Pope's affection and his appointment to the office of the Piombo,[1] for which he made a machine for stamping the bulls, with a fine winch.

When Bologna returned to the Church in 1504, Bramante accompanied the Pope thither, and was busy during the war of Mirandola [2] in many ingenious matters of great importance. He drew many ground-plans and elevations, which were excellently designed, some well-measured and artistically conceived ones being in our book. He instructed Raphael of Urbino in many points of architecture, and sketched for him the buildings which he afterwards drew in perspective in the Pope's chamber, representing Mount Parnassus. Here Raphael drew Bramante measuring with a sextant. The Pope resolved to employ Bramante to collect into one place in the Strada Giulia all the offices and bureaux of Rome for the benefit of those who had affairs there, and who had previously suffered much inconvenience. Accordingly Bramante began the palace at S. Biagio su'l Tevere, containing an unfinished Corinthian temple, a very rare thing, and the remainder in rustic work of great beauty. It is a pity that a work of such nobility and advantage should remain incomplete, for professional men consider it the best thing of the kind ever produced. At S. Piero a Montorio he did a round temple of travertine in the first cloister, unequalled for its proportions, order and variety, with unsurpassable grace and

---

[1] For the sealing of bulls.　　　　[2] In 1511.

finish. It would have been even better if his design had been carried out in the cloister, which is unfinished. He erected the palace for Raphael of Urbino in the Borgo, built of bricks and blocks of concrete, the columns and the bosses being of Doric and rustic-work of great beauty, and the concrete blocks a new invention. He also designed the decoration of S. Maria di Loreto, afterwards continued by Andrea Sansovino, and made endless models of palaces and temples in Rome and for the States of the Church. So tremendous was his genius that he made a very large design for restoring the Pope's palace.

Bramante's spirit being thus grown great, and seeing the Pope's wish corresponded with his own desire to pull down the church of S. Pietro and build it anew, he made a great number of designs, one being especially admirable, displaying his wonderful skill. It has two campaniles, one on either side of the façade, as we see in the coins of Julius II. and Leo X., designed by Caradosso, an excellent goldsmith, unequalled for his dies, and by the fine medal of Bramante himself. The Pope then decided to undertake the stupendous task of building S. Pietro, and caused a half to be pulled down, intending that in beauty, invention, order, size, richness and decoration it should surpass all the buildings ever erected in that city by the power of the republic and by the art and genius of so many able masters. Bramante laid the foundation with his accustomed speed, and before the Pope's death [1] the walls were raised as high as the cornice, where the arches to all four pilasters are, and he vaulted these with the utmost rapidity and great art. He also vaulted the principal chapel where the niche is, and proposed to push forward the chapel called after the King of France. He discovered, the means of making vaulting by using wooden frames, that it may be carved with friezes and foliage of stucco, and showed the way to make the arches with a hanging scaffolding, an invention followed by Antonio da San Gallo. In this part, finished by himself, the cornice running round the interior is such that it would be impossible to improve its design. The strange and beautiful olive leaves of the capitals and the beauty of the exterior Doric work show the tremendous character of Bramante's genius, so that if his strength had equalled his genius he would have accomplished unheard-of marvels. Since his death many architects have meddled with this work, so that, excepting the four outside arches bearing the tribune, there is nothing of his left. Raphael of Urbino and Giuliano da S. Gallo, who had

[1] 18 April, 1506.

charge of the work after the death of Julius II., together with Giocondo of Verona, began to change it. After their death Baldassare Peruzzio made the alterations in building the chapel of the King of France in the crossing towards the Camposanto, while, under Paul III., Antonio da S. Gallo changed everything, and finally Michelagnolo Buonarroti did away with their various ideas and useless expenditure, and brought it to a unified whole of great beauty and perfection, feeling himself, as he has frequently told me, the executor of the plan and design of Bramante, an idea which had never entered the heads of the others, who only thought of their own designs and judgment, although those who begin the construction of an edifice are its real authors. Bramante's conception of this work seemed limitless; he initiated a great building, and if he had begun this magnificent church on a lesser plan it would not have been possible for S. Gallo and the others, no, not even for Michelagnolo, to increase it, indeed they diminished the size, for Bramante conceived something larger.

It is said that Bramante was so anxious for the work to progress that he destroyed in S. Pietro many fine tombs of popes, paintings and mosaics, thus obliterating the memory of many portraits of great men scattered about the principal church in Christendom. He only retained the altar of St. Peter and the old tribune, introducing a fine Doric decoration of peperigno stone, so that when the Pope went to S. Pietro to say Mass he could stand there with all his court and the ambassadors of the Christian princes. Death prevented him from finishing it, and Baldassare of Siena completed it afterwards.

Bramante was of a happy temperament and loved to help his neighbours. He was a great friend to men of ability, and assisted them as much as possible, as in the case of the ever-celebrated painter Raphael Urbino, whom he brought to Rome. He lived in honour and splendour in the rank to which his merits had raised him, but he would have been far more lavish had he possessed more. He was very fond of poetry, and loved to hear and compose improvisations on the lyre. He composed sonnets which, if not so nice as those of to-day, were grave and faultless. He was greatly esteemed by prelates, and rewarded by the numberless lords who knew him. His reputation stood very high during his life, and became greater after his death, because the building of S. Pietro was delayed for many years. He lived seventy years, being carried to his grave by the papal court, and by all the sculptors, painters and architects. His funeral took place in S. Pietro in 1514. His death was a very great loss to architecture, as he investigated many auxiliary arts, such as forming vaults of gypsum and the making of stucco, used by the ancients, but lost until his day. Those who measure ancient monuments find no less science and design in the works of Bramante. Thus he is evidently one of the most remarkable of the men of genius who have illustrated our century. He left behind him his familiar friend Giulian Leno, who was more skilled in executing the designs of others than in framing his own, though he possessed judgment and experience.

Bramante employed in his works Ventura, a carpenter of Pistoia, very skilful and ingenious in design. This man was fond of measuring the monuments at Rome, and when he returned to Pistoia in 1509 there was a Virgin there, known as the Madonna della Umilita, which works miracles. As this brought much alms, the Signoria determined to erect a temple in its honour. As this opportunity presented itself to Ventura, he made a model with eight sides, . . . braccia broad and . . . braccia high, with a vestibule or closed porch in front, beautifully decorated within. The heads of the city being delighted with this, the building was begun under Ventura. He laid the foundations of the vestibule and church, completed the former, richly decorating it with pilasters and cornices of the Corinthian order, while fluted cornices were prepared for the vaulting, made of stone and adorned with bosses. The church was also built as far as the last cornice, the tribune remaining to be vaulted while Ventura lived. Not being very skilled in a work of such proportions, he did not consider the weight of the tribune, and in the thickness of the walls in the first and second rows of windows he had made a passage round the church, which weakened the walls, so that as the church was without buttresses it was dangerous to vault it, especially at the corner angles, where the whole weight of the vaulting would fall. Accordingly, after his death, no one had sufficient courage to vault it, and they brought beams to make a flat roof. This did not satisfy the citizens, who would not begin it, and the building remained roofless for many years, until in 1561 the wardens besought Duke Cosimo to grant that the tribune might be made. His Highness directed Giorgio Vasari to go there and devise a means of vaulting the church. He did so, and made a model, raising the edifice eight braccia above the cornice left by Ventura to make buttresses, tieing together the space between the walls of the passage and strengthening the buttresses, the angles and the parts beneath the passages made by Ventura between the windows, chaining them with great iron limbs doubled at the angles, so that the vaulting might be imposed with safety. His Excellency went to the spot, and, being pleased with everything, gave orders that the work should be carried out. Thus all the buttresses were made and the vaulting begun, as rich as the work of Ventura, but larger, more ornamental, and with better proportion. But Ventura deserves a notice, because that church is the most notable modern work in the city.

FRÀ BARTOLOMMEO OF S. MARCO, Painter of Florence
(1472-1517)

BARTOLOMMEO, called Baccio after the Tuscan usage, was born in the territory of Prato, at a place called Savignano, ten miles from Florence. In his boyhood he showed great inclination and aptitude for design, and by the influence of Benedetto da Maiano he was put with Cosimo Rosselli, lodging in the house of some relatives who lived at the gate (*porta*) of S. Piero Gattolini. Here he remained for many years, so that he became generally known as Baccio della Porta. After leaving Cosimo Rosselli, he began earnestly to study the things of Lionardo da Vinci, and in a short time made such progress in colouring that he became known as one of the best of the young artists both for colour and design. He associated with Mariotto Albertinelli,[1] who soon acquired his style. and together they did many Madonnas which are scattered about Florence, to speak of which would take too long. I may mention one excellent example, in the house of Filippo di Averardo Salviati. Another, bought not long ago, sold among some old tapestries, was acquired by Pier Maria delle Pozze, a great lover of paintings, who recognised its beauty and did not spare his money. This Madonna is executed with extraordinary diligence. Pier del Pugliese had a small marble Madonna in bas-relief by Donatello, a lovely work, to receive which he had a wooden tabernacle made with two small doors, which he gave to Baccio to paint. The artist did two scenes, one a Nativity, the other the Circumcision, executed like illuminations, in the best possible workmanship, and on the outside he painted an Annunciation in grisaille, the entire work being in oils. This work is now in the Scriptorium of Duke Cosimo,[2] where he

[1] They were partners from 1492 to 1500.   [2] Now in the Uffizi.

keeps all his small bronze antiquities, medals and other rare illuminations, and it is highly valued by him for its undoubted excellence.

Baccio was loved in Florence for his ability; was an assiduous workman, quiet, good-natured, and God-fearing. He preferred a quite life and avoided vicious pleasures, was very fond of sermons, and always sought the society of learned and staid people. It is rare when Nature creates a man of genius and a clever artist that she does not prove his worth. So it was with Baccio, who, as I shall say presently, fulfilled her desires to show the full extent of his excellence, and so spread abroad his name that Gerozzo di Monna Venna Dini employed him to do a chapel in the cemetery containing the bones of the dead from the hospital of S. Maria Nuova. He there began a Last Judgment in fresco, working with such diligence and in so good a style in the part which he completed, that he largely increased his reputation, and was much celebrated for having so well rendered the glory of Paradise and Christ, with the twelve Apostles judging the twelve tribes, the draperies being fine and the colouring charming. In the unfinished portion we see the despair of the damned and the pain and shame of eternal death, in contrast with the joy of the elect. The work was left unfinished because the artist thought more of the welfare of his soul than of painting.[1]

At this time Frà Jeronimo Savonarola, a Dominican of Ferrara and a most famous theologian, was at S. Marco, and Baccio became deeply attached to him and intimate with him from hearing his preaching, being almost always at the convent, where he made friends with the other friars. Frà Jeronimo, continuing his preaching, declared daily from the pulpit that lascivious pictures, music and amorous books often lead men astray, and that he was persuaded that it was not good to have pictures of naked men and women in houses where there are young girls. The following carnival, it being a custom of the city to make bonfires on the piazzas on Tuesday evening, accompanied by amorous dances, the men and women taking hands and dancing round them, the people, stirred up by Frà Jeronimo, brought numbers of profane paintings and sculptures, many of them the work of great masters, with books, lutes and collections of love-songs to be burned.[2] This was most unfortunate, especially

---

[1] Painted in 1499; now in the Uffizi.
[2] The burning of the Vanities under the influence of Savonarola took place on Shrove Tuesday, 1496.

in the case of paintings, for Baccio brought all his studies of the nude, his example being imitated by Lorenzo di Credi and many others who were called Piagnoni. It was not long before Baccio's affection led him to make a fine portrait of Frà Jeronimo.[1] It was taken to Ferrara, and not long since it came back to Florence to the house of Alamanno Salviati, who greatly values it for the artist's sake. One day, however, the friar's opponents rose to put him to death, because of the sedition which he had stirred up in the city. Frà Jeronimo's friends rallied to his defence, more than five hundred in number, and shut themselves up in S. Marco, Baccio being among them. But, being a timid and cowardly man, when he heard the assault on the convent and that men were being killed and wounded, he began to be seriously alarmed and vowed that if he escaped he would at once assume the habit of the order, a vow which he strictly observed. The fight ended, the friar was taken and condemned to death, as the historians have related in detail, and Baccio departed to Prato, where he entered the Dominican order, as recorded in the chronicles of the convent there, on 26 July, 1500, to the regret of all his friends, who were most sorry at having lost him, especially as they heard that he had determined to give up painting. Mariotto Albertinelli, Baccio's friend and companion, at the prayers of Gerozzo Dini, took up the mantle of Frà Bartolommeo, as the prior called him in giving him the habit, and completed his work at S. Maria Nuova, drawing a portrait of the master of the hospital there and of some friars skilful in surgery, with Gerozzo himself and his wife at the side, kneeling, while a nude figure seated is Giuliano Bugiardini, his young pupil, with a shock of hair as then worn, his hairs being so carefully done that they may be counted. He drew himself, a shock-headed man, one of those coming out of a tomb. The work also contains a portrait of Frà Giovanni of Fiesole, the painter, numbered among the blessed, whose Life we have written. The entire work, both Bartolommeo's and Mariotto's, is in fresco, and is in such an excellent state of preservation that it is much valued by artists, because it is not possible to go much farther in that branch.

After remaining for many months at Prato, Frà Bartolommeo was sent by his superiors to S. Marco, in Florence, where he was warmly welcomed by the friars on account of his ability. In the Badia of Florence, Bernardo del Bianco had about that time erected a chapel in macigno, richly carved and decorated from

[1] Now in the convent of S. Marco, Florence.

designs by Benedetto da Rovezzano, who was and still is of great
repute for ornate and varied work. Here Benedetto Buglioni
did some figures and angels in full relief,[1] in glazed terra cotta,
in niches, as a finish, covering the friezes with cherubim and
designs. Wishing to have a picture worthy of this framework,
it occurred to him that Frà Bartolommeo was the man, and he
employed every effort and the persuasion of friends to induce
him to do it. The friar was in the convent, intent only on the
divine offices and other things of his rule. The prior and his
dearest friends had continually pressed him to do some painting,
but for more than four years he had steadily refused. Being
pressed, however, by Bernardo del Bianco he at length began
the picture of St. Bernard writing, and seeing a vision of Our
Lady with the Child,[2] and many angels and cherubs, smoothly
coloured by him. The saint is wrapped in contemplation, exhibiting an indescribable celestial fervour which illuminates the
whole work, to the eyes of an attentive observer. Baccio displayed every care and diligence in doing this and an arch
in fresco above it. He also did some pictures for Cardinal Giovanni de' Medici, and painted a Madonna [3] of extraordinary
beauty for Agnolo Doni, which serves for an altar in a chapel
in his house.

At this time Raphael of Urbino, the painter, came to Florence
to learn the art, and taught the first principles of perspective
to Frà Bartolommeo, and being anxious to colour like the friar,
he associated constantly with him because he liked his manage-
ment and blending of colours. At this time Bartolommeo did
a panel with a quantity of figures in S. Marco at Florence.[4] It
is now in the possession of the King of France, to whom it was
given, and it remained on exhibition in S. Marco for many
months. He did another in that place, containing a large number
of figures, to replace the one sent to France, with some children
flying in the air, holding a canopy open, with such art, design
and relief that they seem to be coming out of the picture.[5] The
flesh-colouring is of that excellence which every talented artist
would like to give to his things, and this work is still considered
of the highest excellence. There are many very admirable figures
about a Madonna, of wonderful grace and vigour, with fine

[1] In 1504.
[2] Commissioned in 1504 and finished in 1507; now in the Accademia,
Florence.
[3] Now in the Corsini Gallery, Rome; dated 1516.
[4] "The Mystic Marriage of St. Catherine," in the Louvre, dated 1511.
[5] Now in the Pitti Gallery; painted about 1512.

expressions and full of life. The colouring is so bold that they
seem to be in relief. This was because Baccio was anxious to
show that in addition to a good design he could bring out his
figures by means of shadows. This is seen by the cherubs flying
about the canopy, which seem to be coming out of the picture.
Besides these there is a Christ-child espousing St. Catherine the
nun, and nothing more vivid than this is possible in the dark
colouring which he has chosen. A group of saints on one side,
following the curve of a large niche and diminishing as they
recede, are so well arranged that they seem alive, and there is
a like group on the other side. Indeed, in this colouring he
imitated Lionardo, especially in the shadows, using printers'
fumes and the black of burnt ivory. Owing to this black the
picture has become much darker than he painted it, the colours
being deeper and more obscure, Among the chief figures he did
a St. George in the foreground, in armour, with a standard in
his hand: a noble, vigorous, animated figure in a fine pose. There
is also a St. Bartholomew standing, deserving great praise, with
two children playing a lute and a lyre respectively. One has bent
back his leg and rests his instrument upon it, while his fingers
are on the strings to moderate them as he listens to the music;
his head is raised and the mouth slightly open, so that it is hard
to believe that his voice will not be heard. The other leans over
with an ear against the lyre to see whether it is in tune with the
lute, to which he is playing second, his eyes on the ground and
carefully following his companion. These ingenious ideas are
marvellously executed by Frà Bartolommeo, with wonderful
industry, the children being seated, in light draperies, and the
whole work immersed in deep vaporous shadow. In a little while
he did another much-admired panel opposite this, of a Madonna
and saints. He deserves great praise for his introduction of the
toning of the figures, a great gain to art, as they seem to be in
relief, and are executed with vigour and perfection.

Hearing of the great works of Michelagnolo at Rome, and of
those of the gracious Raphael, Frà Bartolommeo went to the
Eternal City by the prior's permission,[1] impelled by the desire
to see the marvels of these two divine artists, of which he heard
so much. There he was lodged by Frà Mariano Fetti, the friar
of the Piombo, at Montecavallo and S. Salvestro, his place, where
he painted two pictures of St. Peter and St. Paul. The air did not
suit him so well as Florence, as among the ancient and modern
works which he saw in such abundance he became dazed, and

[1] In 1514.

as this seriously impaired his skill and excellence he decided to return. He left to Raphael the St. Peter one of the pictures he had not completed, and after that marvellous master had retouched it, it was given to Frà Mariano.

Meanwhile Bartolommeo returned to Florence, where he was frequently taunted with being unable to do nudes. This stirred him to make proof of himself and show that he was most apt in every branch of his art. Accordingly he did a nude St. Sebastian with very good flesh-colouring, of sweet aspect and great personal beauty, so that he won great praise among artists. It is said that while this figure was on exhibition in the church the friars found out by the confessional that women had sinned in regarding it, owing to the realistic skill of Frà Bartholomeo; accordingly they removed it, and put it in the chapter-house, where it had not been long before it was bought by Gio. Battista della Pella and sent to the King of France.

Bartolommeo had fallen out with the carvers who made the frames for his pictures and who habitually covered up an eighth of the figures as they do still. He therefore determined to find some way of obviating this, and for his St. Sebastian, done on a half-circle, he made a niche in perspective, which seems in relief on the picture, and he formed a frame by painting an ornament about it. He did the same with our St. Vincent and St. Mark, as I shall presently relate. Over the arch of a door leading into the sacristy he did a St. Vincent of his order, on wood in oils, representing his preaching of the Last Judgment,[1] his forcible expression and gestures being very characteristic of preachers when they are endeavouring to redeem men from their evil ways by threats of the judgment of God, so that the figure appears a living thing and not paint, to the attentive observer. It is a great pity, seeing that it has been done with such strong relief, that it should have been spoiled and cracked owing to the fresh colours being put on wet glue, as I said of the work of Pietro Perugino in the Ingesuati.

Bartolommeo, wishing to show that he could do large figures, as some objected that his style was small, did a St. Mark the Evangelist,[2] a panel of five braccia, to be placed on the wall with the door of the choir, executed with fine design and of great beauty. A Florentine merchant, Salvador Billi, returning from Naples, hearing the fame of the friar and seeing his works, commissioned him to do a panel of Christ the Saviour, in allusion to his name, surrounded by the four Evangelists, with two

[1] Now in the Accademia, Florence.   [2] Pitti Gallery; painted in 1516.

cherubs at the feet holding the sphere of the earth, a beautiful reproduction of fresh and tender flesh, like the rest of the work. It also contains two much-admired prophets. This picture is in the Nunziata at Florence,[1] under the great organ, as Salvador desired, and is a beautiful work, finished with loving care by the friar, who had the marble frame carved by Piero Rosselli.

Bartolommeo requiring a change of air, the prior, being his friend, sent him to another monastery. While he stayed there, being led to the contemplation of death, he did a panel at S. Martino, Lucca, where at the feet of the Virgin is a small angel playing the lute, with St. Stephen and St. John in excellent design and colouring, showing his skill.[2] At S. Romano he did a picture on canvas of Our Lady of Mercy, placed on a stone dado, and some angels holding her mantle.[3] With her are figures, upon steps, some standing, some seated, some kneeling, regarding a Christ in the air who is sending lightning and thunder among them. In this painting Frà Bartolommeo displayed his power of shading the dark parts, producing a striking relief, showing his mastery of the difficulties of the art, and his colouring, design and invention, the work being of the highest perfection. On another picture on canvas he did Christ and St. Catherine the Martyr, with St. Catherine of Siena in an ecstasy, an unequalled figure in that style.[4] Returning to Florence, he devoted himself to music, and being very fond of it he would sometimes sing as a pastime. Opposite the prison at Prato he did an Assumption,[5] and in the Medici palace he painted Madonnas and other things for various persons. Such are a Madonna in the chamber of Lodovico di Lodovico Capponi, and another Madonna with the Child, with the heads of two saints, in the possession of the renowned M. Lelio Torelli, principal secretary of the illustrious Duke Cosimo, who values it very highly as a work of Frà Bartolommeo, and also because he loves and favours all artists, and, indeed, all men of genius. In the house of Pier del Pugliese, now of Matteo Botti, citizen and merchant of Florence, Bartolommeo did a St. George armed and on horseback in a recess at the top of a staircase, He is slaying the serpent, the vigorous figures being painted in oils in grisaille, of which Baccio was so fond. We see this by his cartoons, whether in ink or crayon, and in many pictures and panels which he left unfinished at his death, as well as in his drawings in grisaille, now mostly in the mon-

---

[1] Now in the Uffizi Gallery.   [2] Dated 1509.   [3] In 1515.
[4] Now in the Pinacoteca, Lucca.
[5] Painted in 1516; now in the Naples Museum.

astery of S. Caterina at Siena, on the piazza of S. Marco, in the possession of a nun who paints, of whom I shall write a notice later. There are many others still kept in memory of him in our book of designs, and M. Francesco del Garbo the physician has an excellent one.

It was a plan of Frà Bartolommeo to have the living objects before him as he worked, and in order to draw draperies, arms and such things, he had a large wooden model of life-size, with movable joints, and this he dressed in natural clothes. Thus he was able to obtain excellent results, by keeping the figure in any position he desired, until he had completed his work. This model, though very dilapidated, is in my possession, in memory of him. In the abbey of the black monks, at Arezzo, he did the head of Christ in grisaille, a lovely thing, and the altarpiece of the company of the Contemplanti,[1] which has been preserved in the house of M. Ottaviano de' Medici the Magnificent, being now placed in a chapel in the house of his son M. Alessandro, with many ornaments, valued for the sake of Frà Bartolommeo and because he was extremely fond of painting. In the chapel in the Noviciate of S. Marco is a fine picture of the Purification,[2] excellently designed and finished, and while the friar was staying for pleasure at S. Maria Maddalena, a house of his order outside Florence, he did a Christ and the Magdalene and some frescoes for the convent. In a tympanum in the guest chamber at S. Marco he painted in fresco Christ with Cleophas and Luke, with a portrait of Frà Niccolo della Magna, as a young man, who afterwards became Archbishop of Capua and finally cardinal. Frà Bartolommeo began a panel at S. Gallo, which was afterwards finished by Giuliano Bugiardini, and is now at the high altar of S. Jacopo fra' Fossi[3] at the corner of the Alberti. A picture of the rape of Dinah, in the possession of M. Cristofano Rinieri, coloured afterwards by Giuliano, is full of buildings and greatly admired ideas.[4] Piero Soderini employed him to do the picture of the Council Chamber, which he executed in grisaille, and in such a way as to win the greatest honour. It is now in S. Lorenzo in the Chapel of Ottaviano de' Medici the Magnificent, imperfect as it is, and contains all the protecting saints of Florence and those on whose festivals the city has won victories. Here is the portrait of Frà Bartolommeo himself, done with the

---

[1] Probably the picture now in the Berlin Gallery.
[2] Painted in 1516; Vienna, Kunsthistorisches Museum.
[3] Now in the Pitti Gallery.
[4] Vienna, Kunsthistorisches Museum.

aid of a mirror.[1] After beginning this painting, the friar became paralysed through working under a window with the sun on his back. Being advised by the physicians to go to the bath at S. Filippo, he spent much time there, but was very little benefited. He was very fond of fruits, although they were most harmful to him. One morning, after eating a great quantity of figs, he fell into a raging fever in addition to the malady from which he was already suffering and died in four days, at the age of forty-eight, and so, in full consciousness, rendered his soul to heaven. His friends, and especially the friars, were much grieved by his death, and they gave him honourable burial in S. Marco on 8 October, 1517. He received a dispensation from the prohibition of the friars to go into the choir during the office. The profits of his works fell to the convent after he had taken what was necessary for the colours and painting materials. He had as pupils Cecchino del Frate, Benedetto Cianfanini, Gabbriel Rustici and Frà Paolo Pistoiese, to whom he left all his things. Many pictures were done from his designs after his death, three being in S. Domenico at Pistoia and one at S. Maria del Sasso in Casentino. Frà Bartolommeo imparted such charm of colouring to his figures, and endowed them with such a modern grace, that he deserves a place among the benefactors of the art.

MARIOTTO ALBERTINELLI, Painter of Florence (1474–1515)

MARIOTTO ALBERTINELLI, the son of Biagio di Bindo Albertinelli, was a close and intimate friend of Frà Bartolommeo, and may be called his other self, not only because of their constant association, but by the similarity of their style. Until the age of twenty he was brought up as a gold-beater, and he learned the first principles of painting in the workshop of Cosimo Rosselli, where he became so intimate with Baccio della Porta that they were of one mind and body, and when Baccio left Cosimo to set up for himself Mariotto accompanied him. They both lived for some time at the gate of S. Piero Gattolini, doing many things together.[2]

Not being so well grounded in design as Baccio, Mariotto studied the antiquities then in Florence, the best and the greater

[1] Now in the Uffizi Gallery.
[2] They were partners from 1492 to 1500.

number being in the Medici palace. He frequently drew small bas-reliefs under the loggia of the garden towards S. Lorenzo, one being a fine Adonis with a dog, and another two marvellous nude figures, one seated with a dog at his feet, the other standing, with his legs crossed, leaning on a stick. There are two other pictures of the same size, one of two babes carrying the lightnings of Jove, the other a nude old man representing Chance, with wings on his shoulders and at his feet, and carrying a pair of scales. Besides these the garden was full of the torsos of men and women, forming a studio not only for Mariotto, but for all the sculptors and painters of his time. A large proportion of them is now in the wardrobe of Duke Cosimo, the remainder are in the palace, such as the two torsos of Marsyas, the busts over the windows, and those of the emperors over the doors. By studying these antiquities Mariotto benefited greatly in design, and entered the service of Madonna Alfonsina, mother of Duke Lorenzo, and, as he was endeavouring to improve himself, she gave him every assistance. He thus became quite skilful, doing now design, now colour, as we see by some pictures executed for that lady and sent by her to Rome to Carlo and Giordano Orsini, coming afterwards into the hands of Cesare Borgia. He drew a very good portrait of Madonna Alfonsina, whose favour promised to establish his fortune. But when Piero de' Medici was banished in 1494 that help and favour failed him, and he returned to the rooms of Baccio, where he devoted himself more zealously than ever to making clay models and the study of Nature, imitating Baccio, so that in a few years he became a diligent and skilful master. Encouraged by this he continued in his imitation, and so successfully that many mistook his work for that of the friar. So when Baccio took the cowl Mariotto was in despair at losing his companion. The news deprived him of the joy of life, and if he had not hated the ways of the friars so heartily, for he constantly spoke ill of them and was of the faction contrary to Frà Girolamo of Ferrara, he also would have taken the cowl in the same convent for Baccio's sake. But being asked by Gerozzo Dini to complete the Last Judgment in the cemetery, left unfinished by Baccio, in the same style, he did so, aided by the original cartoon of Baccio and other designs. The friar, being troubled in his conscience for not having finished it, also pressed Mariotto to take up this work. He completed it with such loving care and diligence that many ignorant of the facts have taken it to be the production of a single hand, and thus Mariotto won great credit in art. In the chapter-house of the Certosa of Florence he did a Crucifixion with the Madonna and the Magdalene at the foot of the cross, and some angels in the air collecting the blood of Christ, a fresco executed with diligence and tenderness as well as skill.[1] But some of Mariotto's young pupils, unknown to their master, thinking that the friars were not feeding them with the same fare as themselves, counterfeited the keys of the windows where the friars' portions were put, and which opened into their cells, and would secretly rob the food first of one and then of another. There was great consternation among the friars, for they think of their stomachs as much as other folk, but as the apprentices acted with great dexterity and were trusted, the friars attributed the fault to the hatred between some of their number, until the affair was discovered. The friars, however, in order to have the work finished, doubled the portions of Mariotto and his apprentices, and they joyfully completed their labours. For the nuns of S. Giuliano at Florence Mariotto did the high-altar picture, painting it in his rooms at Gualfonda, where he also did another for the same church of a Crucifixion and angels, with God the Father, representing the Trinity, in oils on a gold ground.[2]

Mariotto was a restless man, a follower of Venus, and a good liver. He thus came to hate the subtleties of painting and its brain weaving, and, being frequently attacked by the envious tongues of painters, as is their custom, maintained through generations, he resolved to take up a baser, less difficult and more cheerful craft. Accordingly, he kept open for many months a fine inn outside the gate of S. Gallo, and a tavern at the Dragon, at the Ponte Vecchio. He continued there for some months, saying that he had found an art which did not need muscles, foreshortening or perspectives, and, better still, without critics, while the one he had abandoned possessed all these disadvantages; the one imitated flesh and blood, but the other created them. And now everyone praised him, for he had good wine, and he was not obliged to listen to criticisms every day. But he grew tired of this also, becoming disgusted with the baseness of the trade, and returned to painting, doing pictures for private citizens in Florence, while for Giovan. Maria Bentivogli he did three small scenes. In the Casa Medici he painted Faith, Hope and Charity, in a round picture in oils, for the creation of Pope Leo X., with the pontiff's arms, which remained for some time over the door of the palace. For the company of St. Zanobi, next the canonicate of S. Maria del Fiore, he undertook to do an Annunciation, bestowing great pains upon it.[1] He arranged the light on the work as it would be when in position, so that he might increase or diminish it at will. He conceived the notion that paintings without relief, and vigour combined with sweetness, had no value, and seeing that he could not avoid flatness without shadows, that those which are too dark remain obscure, while those that are soft lack power, he hoped to employ a method which would still retain the softness, which he thought had not been adopted in art till then. As this work gave him an opportunity to put his theories into practice, he threw himself into it with extraordinary energy, as we see in a God the Father in the air, with cherubs, which are thrown into great relief by the dark background consisting of a barrel vault, the arches curving and the lines diminishing to a point, so that it seems to be in relief. There are also some angels scattering flowers very gracefully. This work was done and redone several times by Mariotto before he actually finished it, changing the colouring to make it clearer or darker, or more or less brilliant. But he was not satisfied, as it did not realise his idea, for he wanted a more brilliant white than white lead, so that he adopted a method of his own for the light. Even so he could not represent what he had in his mind, and was obliged to rest contented with what he had done. Accordingly he added no more to it, and the work won him praise and honour among artists, with the prospect of obtaining better things from patrons, but this fell through, because disputes arose between the artist and those who employed him. But Pietro Perugino, then an old man, Ridolfo Ghirlandajo and Francesco Granacci valued the picture, and fixed a price.

In S. Brancazio at Florence Mariotto did a Visitation in a half-circle, and in S. Trinità he did a panel with the Virgin, St. Jerome and St. Zanobius, with diligence, for Zanobi del Maestro.[2] For the church of the congregation of the priests of St. Martino he did a much-admired Visitation.[3] Invited to the convent of la Quercia, outside Viterbo, he began a panel, when he determined to go to Rome. There he finished for Frà Mariano Fetti, in the chapel of S. Salvestro di Montecavallo, an oil-painting of St. Dominic, St. Catherine of Siena espoused by Christ, with the Madonna, in a delicate style. He returned to la Quercia, where he had some love-affairs, and being anxious to appear to advantage, he wished, while at Rome, to show his powers in jousting, and he exerted himself beyond his strength. As he was neither

---

[1] Painted in 1510; now in the Accademia.
[2] Now in the Louvre.   [3] In the Uffizi, dated 1503.

young nor skilful in such matters, he was forced to take to his bed, and as the air of the place did not suit him he was carried to Florence; but no remedies availed and he died of his disease in a few days at the age of forty-five, and was buried in S. Piero Maggiore there.

There are designs in grisaille by him in our book, some of them very good, especially a spiral staircase, drawn in perspective, the difficulties of which he thoroughly understood. He had several pupils, among them being Giuliano Bugiardini, Franciabigio, both Florentines, and Innocenzio da Imola, of whom I shall speak. Visino, painter of Florence, was another, superior to the first in design, colouring and diligence, and possessing a better style, as shown by his works. A few of them are still in Florence, in the house of Gio. Battista di Agnol Doni, where there is an oil-painting of a sphere coloured like a miniature, on which are Adam and Eve, naked, eating the apple, a very careful work, and a Deposition from the Cross, with the thieves, the ladders being very cleverly mixed up. Some are helping to lower the Christ, some are carrying a thief to burial on their shoulders, in curious and varied attitudes adapted to the subject, showing the artist's ability.

Some Florentine merchants took him to Hungary, and there he did many works, being in considerable repute. But this poor man came near falling into serious trouble, because, being naturally outspoken and independent, he could not bear the contempt of some Hungarians who annoyed him every day by praising their country, as if there was no happiness apart from their ovens, eating and drinking, and no greatness and nobility which was better than dirt compared with their king and court. Believing, as he did, that Italy provided a different kind of excellence, suavity and beauty, Visino broke in upon their extravagances one day when he may have been slightly intoxicated, making bold to say that a flask of Trebian and a Tuscan cake were worth more than all the kings and queens who ever ruled there. If the matter had not fallen into the hands of a worthy bishop, a man of the world and, more important still, discreet, who turned the dispute into a jest, it would have gone ill with him, for the brutish Hungarians, not understanding him, and thinking he had uttered something serious, as if he wished to kill them all and depose their king, would have torn him to pieces in their fury. But the bishop rescued him, knowing the value of his ability and, looking at the light side of the matter, restored him to the king's favour, who allowed himself to be mollified.

After this adventure, Visino's talent was honoured and valued in that country. But his visit did not last long, as he could not support the stoves or the cold air of the country, and so he brought it to an end, although his fame and favour survived among those who had known him, and were kept alive by those who had known him and by those who saw his pictures. His works were executed about 1515.

RAFFAELLINO DEL GARBO, Painter of Florence (1466–1524)

RAFFAELLO DEL GARBO, whom his elders called Raffaellino when he was a little child, so that he kept the name ever afterwards, gave such promise in his early years that from the first he was enumerated among the most excellent, the experience of very few; but he disappointed these well-grounded hopes, his end being very weak, a still rarer circumstance, for generally artists progress from small beginnings to ever-greater attainments, until they reach the goal of perfection. But in art, as in nature, matters do not always follow the accustomed order, and this should give the censorious pause. However this may be, Raffaellino began with extraordinary brilliance, the middle of his career was extremely mediocre, and his end wretched. In his youth he drew as well as any painter who has ever prospered, and we may still see a large number of drawings which were circulated at a very small price by a son of his. They are partly done with the stylo, partly in pen and ink and partly water-colours, but all on tinted sheets, the lights in white lead and executed with extraordinary boldness and skill, many very excellent ones being in our book. Besides this, he learned to colour so well in fresco and tempera that his first works are executed with marvellous patience and diligence, as has been said. The vault above the tomb of Cardinal Caraffa in the Minerva is of such delicate workmanship that it resembles an illumination, so that it was highly esteemed by the artists of the day, and his master, Filippo, considered him much better than himself in some things; indeed, Raffaello had so far acquired his master's style that it was difficult to distinguish the one from the other. After leaving his master, Raffaello softened his style in the draperies, making the hair and the carriage of the heads more lovely; and artists expected so much of him that while he worked in this manner he was considered the finest painter of his years. Thus he was employed to do a picture for the family of the Capponi, who had built a chapel called il Paradiso, under S. Bartolommeo at Monte Oliveto, outside the S. Friano gate, in which he painted a Resurrection in oils, with some soldiers lying like the dead about the tomb, of great vigour and beauty, with the most graceful heads, a young man there being an admirable portrait of Niccolo Capponi, and a figure crying out from under the stone covering of the tomb, which has fallen on him, has a very fine and curious head.[1] The Capponi, seeing the excellence of this work, employed Raffaello to make a carved framework, with stone columns, richly overlaid with gold. Not many years afterwards lightning struck the campanile there, cleft the vaulting and broke it near this picture, which suffered no harm, being done in oils, but consumed the gold entirely, leaving the ground only. I have spoken thus of oil-painting because it shows how important it is to know how to protect oneself from such injury, for this is by no means a solitary example.

Raffaello did a small tabernacle in fresco on the corner of a house, now Matteo Botti's, between the corner of the Ponte alla Carraia and that of the Cuculia, containing a Virgin and Child, St. Catherine and St. Barbara, both kneeling, a very graceful and carefully executed work. In the villa of Marignolle de' Girolami, he did two fine panels of the Virgin, St. Zanobius and other saints, the predella being full of small figures in stories of those saints, carefully finished. For the nuns of S. Giorgio, on a wall at the door of the church, he did a Pietà with the Maries, and below this another arch with the Madonna, in 1504, a work worthy of great praise. In the church of S. Spirito at Florence, in a picture above that of the Nerli by Filippo, his master, he painted a Pietà,[2] a work considered admirable, but his St. Bernard in another panel is less perfect. Under the door of the sacristy he did two panels, one of the Mass of St. Gregory, where Christ appears bearing the cross on His shoulder and shedding His blood, while the deacon and sub-deacon serve Him, in their vestments, and two angels cense the body of Christ. Below, in another chapel, he did a panel of Our Lady, St. Jerome and St. Bartholomew, expending great pains on these two works. But he grew worse every day, and I cannot find any cause for this failure, because he did not spare study, care or labour, though they availed him little. Thus he found it necessary to make the most of what he earned, and, not

[1] Now in the Uffizi, Florence.
[2] Probably the picture now in the Munich Gallery.

being a man of much spirit, he undertook work of small value, continually becoming worse, though his things always contained some good points. In the refectory of the monks of Cestello he did a large scene in fresco on the wall, representing the Feeding of the Five Thousand. For the abbot of the Panichi he did the high-altar picture of the church of S. Salvi, outside the S. Croce gate, with the Virgin, St. John Gualbert, St. Salvi, St. Bernard degli Uberti, the cardinal, St. Benedict, the abbot, with St. Sebastian and St. Fidele in armour in two niches on either side.[1] The picture had a rich framework, and the predella contains several scenes in small figures from the life of St. John Gualbert. Raffaello did well in these, because the abbot had taken pity on him in his misery, so that he introduced the abbot's portrait into the predella with that of the general of the order at that time. In S. Piero Maggiore Raffaello painted a panel on the right side on entering the church, and in the Murate he did St. Sigismund the king. In S. Brancazio he did a Trinity for Girolamo Federighi, who was buried there, with portraits of Girolamo and his wife kneeling. In this he began to return to the minute manner. He also did two figures in tempera at Castello, namely St. Roch and St. Ignatius, for the chapel of St. Sebastian. In a chapel at the end of the Ponte Rubaconte, towards the mills, he did the Virgin, St. Laurence and another saint. At last he was reduced to take any mechanical work. For some nuns and others he made designs for embroidery for their churches, in grisaille, with borders of saints and scenes, for a very small price, for, much as he had deteriorated, the most beautiful designs and ideas still came from his hands, as many sheets prove which have come to light after the death of the embroiderers, and have been sold in various places. Many of them are in the book of the master of the hospital, and show Raffaello's skill in drawing. In this way many ornaments and borders were made for the churches of Florence and her territory, as well as for cardinals and bishops at Rome, which are considered very beautiful. This method of embroidery, as practised by Pagolo da Verona, Galieno Fiorentino and others, is now all but lost, another and easier method having been found, but it is not so beautiful and careful, and lasts considerably less time than the other. For this Raffaello deserves glory and honour, although his life was pinched by poverty.

His manners were coarse, because he associated with poor and base people, as if he was ashamed of himself in his poverty, after the high expectations formed in his youth, and owing to the

[1] Now in the Louvre.

great falling away from his first excellence. He had declined so far that in his old age his productions did not look like works of the same hand, and he grew worse daily, and would paint anything, so that everything turned out ill for him, especially his large family of children. Overcome by infirmity and poverty, he died in want, at the age of fifty-eight. He was buried by the company of the Misericordia in S. Simone in Florence in 1524. He left many skilled artists behind him. In his childhood Bronzino, the Florentine painter, went to learn the principles of art from Raffaello, and afterwards distinguished himself under the care of Jacopo da Pontormo, painter of Florence, winning a reputation equal to his master's. The portrait of Raffaello has been taken from a drawing which Bastiano da Montecarlo had, who also was a pupil and a skilful master, although he could not draw.

TORRIGIANO, Sculptor of Florence
(1472–1528)

WRATH has especially great power over those who wish to be thought excellent in a profession, in their haughtiness and pride, when some genius in the same art rises unexpectedly to equal and in time to surpass them. There is no iron that they would not gnaw, no evil which they would not inflict, as it is too dreadful for them to see the rise of mere babes to equal them. They do not consider that there is no limit to the progress of youth when assisted by constant study, whereas the old, if impelled by fear, pride and ambition, become clumsy and deteriorate, going backwards when they believe themselves to be progressing. Thus the envious never give the young credit for their excellencies, however clearly they may perceive them, owing to their obstinacy, for we see that when they exert themselves to the utmost to show their powers they often merely succeed in rendering themselves ridiculous and a byword. Indeed, when artists have reached the term when their eye is not firm or their hand steady, they can, if they have made any progress themselves, give their advice to younger men. The arts of painting and sculpture demand a spirit at once alert and vigorous, as it is at the time when the blood runs hot, when one is full of ardent desires and the mortal enemy of the pleasures of the world. But let the intemperate avoid the study of any art or science, because such pleasures and close study are irreconcilable. And the toll demanded by these virtues is so great that but few arrive at the highest excellence. Those who set out with enthusiasm are therefore more numerous than those who win the prize in the race, for their merits. Thus we perceive more pride than art in Torrigiano, sculptor of Florence, though he by no means lacked ability. He was maintained in his youth by Lorenzo de' Medici the elder, in the garden of that magnificent citizen on the piazza of S. Marco in Florence, full of ancient and modern sculptures, so that the loggia, the paths and all the rooms were adorned with good ancient figures of marble, with paintings and other masterpieces of the greatest artists in Italy and elsewhere. All those things, besides adding grace and beauty to the garden, formed a school and academy for young painters and sculptors and all others who studied design, especially young nobles. For it was a tenet of Lorenzo the Magnificent that all who are nobly born can generally attain perfection in everything, more easily and quickly than men of low extraction, because the latter do not usually exhibit that quickness of perception and genius so often seen in men of good blood, and, in addition to their lack of nobility, they usually have to fight against poverty and want. Being thus compelled to take up the mechanical arts, they are unable to use their genius or arrive at the highest excellence. Well said the learned Alciato, in speaking of fine spirits born poor who are unable to rise, being confined by poverty, though raised on the pinions of genius:

Ut me pluma levat; sic grave mergit onus.

Thus Lorenzo the Magnificent favoured all men of genius, but chiefly the nobles, who were inclined to the arts; so that we need not wonder that his school has produced men who have amazed the world, and he further gave a provision of money and clothes to those whose poverty would have hindered them from pursuing the study of design, munificently rewarding those who did better than the others. Thus the young students competed among themselves and became very excellent. Their warden and head at that time was Bertoldo, an old Florentine sculptor and skilled master, who had been a pupil of Donato. He was at once their teacher, and had charge of the garden and of numerous drawings, cartoons and models of Donato, Pippo,[1] Masaccio, Paolo Uccello, Frà Giovanni, Frà Filippo and other masters, native and foreign. Indeed, these arts cannot be learned except

[1] i.e. Brunelleschi.

by long study and the steady imitation of good things. Those who are deprived of such an advantage can only attain perfection later, however great their genius.

But to return to the antiquities of the garden. They were all sold by auction in 1494, when Piero, Lorenzo's son, was banished from Florence,. However, most of them were restored to Giuliano the Magnificent in 1512, when he and the other Medici returned to their native place, and they are now mostly preserved in the wardrobe of Duke Cosimo. May this noble example of Lorenzo be ever imitated by princes and other distinguished men. It will bring them eternal honour and praise, for whoever assists lofty and soaring genius in their vast designs, from whom the world receives so much beauty, honour, convenience and benefit, deserves an immortal name in men's minds.

Among those who successfully studied design in this garden were Michelagnolo di Ludovico Buonarroti, Gio. Francesco Rustici, Torrigiano Torrigiani, Francesco Granacci, Niccolo di Domenico Soggi, Lorenzo di Credi, Giuliano Bugiardini, and among foreigners Baccio da Monte Lupo, Andrea Contucci dal Monte Sansovino, and others who will be noticed in due course.

This Torrigiano, then, whose Life I am now writing, studied in the garden with the others, and was of so proud and choleric a temper, and so violent and overbearing, that he was continually attacking his fellows, both in deeds and in words. His chief profession was sculpture, but he worked very skilfully in clay, his style being good and beautiful. But not being able to suffer anyone to surpass him, he set himself to ruin the works of those which he could not hope to equal, and if they resented it he usually went farther than words. He cherished a special dislike for Michelagnolo, simply because he studied so hard and would secretly work at home in the night and on feast days, so that he succeeded far better than the others in the garden, and was in consequence made much of by Lorenzo the Magnificent. Full of envy, Torrigiano never lost an opportunity of injuring him by word or deed, and one day he gave Michelagnolo such a blow on the nose that he broke it, and the artist was disfigured for life. When the Magnificent heard of this he was so enraged that if Torrigiano had not run away from Florence he would have been severely punished. He went to Rome, where Alexander VI. was erecting the Borgia tower,[1] and did many things in stucco there in conjunction with other masters. Duke Valentino, who was making war on the Romagna,[2] gave him money, and,

[1] In 1493 and 1494.   [2] 1493-1500.

influenced by some Florentine youths, he became a soldier and bore himself courageously in battle. He showed himself equally brave with Paolo Vitelli in the war of Pisa [1] and with Piero de' Medici, being present at the affair on the Garigliano,[2] where he won a decoration and the reputation of being a valiant standard-bearer. Recognising at length that he would never obtain the rank of captain, although he deserved it, and that he had profited nothing in war, though he had wasted much time, he returned to sculpture. He did some small works in marble and bronze in small figures for some Florentine merchants for private houses in Florence, and having designed many things, boldly and in good style, as some sheets in our book show, done in competition with Michelagnolo, he was taken by the merchants to England. Here he did a number of works in marble, bronze and wood for the king in competition with the masters of the country.[3] He surpassed them all, and won such rich rewards that if he had not been proud, thoughtless and ungoverned he would have lived in peace and come to an honoured end. The contrary was the case. Leaving England for Spain, he there did many works, which are scattered in various places and are much valued. Among them is a crucifix in clay, the most wonderful thing in all Spain. In a monastery of the friars of St. Jerome, outside Seville, he did another crucifix, and a St. Jerome in penitence,[4] with his lion, the saint being a portrait of an old steward of the Botti, Florentine merchants in Spain, and a Madonna and Child, so beautiful that he had to do another for the Duke of Arcos, who made such liberal promises to Torrigiano that he thought his fortune was assured. When the work was finished the duke gave him so many of the coins called maravedis, worth little or nothing, that Torrigiano was confirmed in his belief that he was a rich man, for two people were required to carry it to the house. But after he had counted it and got a friend to tell him the value in Italian money, he found it was no more than thirty ducats. Greatly enraged at what he considered a trick, he went to where the figure was which he had made for the duke and completely destroyed it. The Spaniard, resenting the insult, accused Tortigiano of heresy, for which he was imprisoned and examined every day, being sent from one inquisition to another. At length he was judged worthy of a very heavy punishment. But it was never carried out, because Torrigiano fell into such a state of

[1] 1498.   [2] 1503.
[3] The tomb of Henry VII. in Westminster Abbey was completed in 1519.
[4] Now in the Seville Museum.

melancholy that he remained several days without food, and becoming gradually weaker he died. He thus escaped a shameful end, because it was believed that he had been condemned to death. His works were executed about 1515, and he died in 1522.

GIULIANO and ANTONIO DA S. GALLO, Architects of Florence (1445–1516; 1455–1534)

FRANCESCO DI PAOLO GIAMBERTI, who was a meritorious architect in the time of Cosimo de' Medici, and much employed by
him, had two sons, Giuliano and Antonio, who practised the
art of wood-carving. He put them with Francione, a clever
joiner, who practised both wood-carving and perspective, and
with whom he was very friendly, as they had done many works
together in carving and architecture for Lorenzo de' Medici.
One of the two boys, Giuliano, learned very well what Francione
taught him, and carved the most beautiful perspectives for the
choir of the Duomo of Pisa, where they are considered marvellous
even among new works. While Giuliano was studying design, in
all the flush of youth, the army of the Duke of Calabria, who
hated Lorenzo de' Medici, encamped at la Castellina to occupy
the territory of Florence, intending, in case of success, to push
the attack. Lorenzo being thus obliged to send an engineer to
Castellina to make bastions and to direct the artillery, a thing
then understood by few, dispatched Giuliano as being the best
fitted and the most dexterous and quick, knowing him, as the
son of Francesco, to be a devoted servant of the Medici house.
When Giuliano reached Castellina,[1] he fortified it within and
without with good walls, bastions and other necessary things
for defensive works. Perceiving the men to be slow and timid in
manœuvring the artillery, he turned his attention to this, and
from that time no more accidents occurred, whereas many had
previously lost their lives through ignorance of their duties.
Giuliano then undertook the care of the artillery, and his prudence
in firing and making use of it was so great, and he so terrified the
duke's camp, that his highness at length came to terms and
departed. From this Giuliano won no small praise from Lorenzo
at Florence, where he was ever afterwards in great favour.

Meanwhile, having devoted himself to architecture, Giuliano

---

[1] Castellina was taken in 1478.

began the first cloister of Cestello,[1] where he did the part in the Ionic style, setting the capitals on the columns, with the volutes descending in a curve to the collarine where the shaft terminates. Below the egg and anchor ornament he made the frieze one-third of the diameter of the column. He copied this capital from a very ancient marble one found at Fiesole by M. Lionardo Salutati, the bishop there, who at one time preserved this and other antiquities in his house and garden in the via di S. Gallo, opposite S. Agata. This capital is now in the possession of M. Gio. Battista de' Ricasoli, bishop of Pistoia, and is valued for its beauty and uniqueness, no other ancient capital having been found to match it. But the cloister was left unfinished because the monks could not bear the great cost. Giuliano's reputation with Lorenzo being thus increased, and the latter desirous to build at Poggio a Caiano between Florence and Pistoia, for which he obtained several models from Francione and others, employed Giuliano to make a model of what he wanted. He produced one so unique and so different from those of the others, and so exactly in harmony with Lorenzo's ideas, that he caused the work to be begun immediately. Giuliano from this time received a provision. Afterwards, when Lorenzo wished to make a vault, such as we now call a barrel vault, for the great hall of the palace, he feared that the distance between the walls was too great. But Giuliano, who was building his own house in Florence, vaulted his hall in this fashion to hearten Lorenzo, so that he was allowed to successfully undertake that of Poggio. His fame being thus increased, he made a model for a palace for Naples by the commission of Lorenzo at the request of the Duke of Calabria, spending much time over it.

Meanwhile Rovere, the castellan of Ostia and a bishop, afterwards Pope Julius II., wished to put the fortress in good repair, and hearing of the fame of Giuliano, sent to Florence for him. Giving him a good provision, he kept him for two years in producing useful and convenient works by his art. In order that the Duke of Calabria's model should not suffer, Giuliano left it to his brother Antonio to finish it after his design. This was done with great diligence, for Antonio was not inferior to his brother. Giuliano was advised by Lorenzo to present the model himself in order to show the difficulties which he had overcome. Accordingly he set out for Naples, presented the work, and was received with honour, the surprise and wonder being equally great that Lorenzo should behave so handsomely and that the workmanship

[1] i.e. S. Maria Maddalena de' Pazzi, begun in 1492.

of the model should be so remarkable. It gave so much satisfaction that the work was soon put in hand near the Castelnuovo. After remaining a while at Naples, Giuliano requested permission to return, and was presented by the king with horses, raiment, and a silver cup containing some hundreds of ducats. These Giuliano would not accept, saying that he represented his master, who needed neither gold nor silver, but if the king wished to make him a present as a memento, he should like to be allowed to choose among his antiquities. The king freely granted this out of his friendship to Lorenzo the Magnificent and his esteem for Giuliano's ability. The latter chose a head of the Emperor Hadrian, now over the door of the garden of the Casa Medici, wonderfully natural, a nude woman, more than life-size, and a marble Cupid asleep. Giuliano sent these as a present to Lorenzo, who was overjoyed and never tired of praising this act of the liberal artist, who refused gold and silver, a thing that few would have done. The Cupid is now in the wardrobe of Duke Cosimo. When Giuliano returned to Florence he was warmly welcomed by Lorenzo. This prince determined to gratify Friar Mariano da Ghinazzano, a learned man of the Eremitani of St. Augustine, by building for him outside the S. Gallo gate a convent for one hundred friars.[1] Many artists prepared models, but that of Giuliano was finally chosen, and from this circumstance Lorenzo called him Giuliano da S. Gallo. Hearing everyone call him by this name, he one day said jestingly to Lorenzo: " It is your fault in calling me 'da S. Gallo' that I have lost my ancient family name, and so while I have been flattering myself at my progress due to my ancient stock I am going backwards." Lorenzo retorted that he ought rather to desire to be the founder of a new house through his own abilities than be dependent on others, and so Giuliano was satisfied.

The work of S. Gallo being followed by many other undertakings of Lorenzo, none of them were finished owing to the death of that prince, and very little of the structure remained standing, because it was pulled down in 1530 with the rest of the quarter, owing to the siege of Florence, and thus the whole piazza, formerly full of very beautiful structures, now shows no trace of house, church, or convent.

At this time the King of Naples died,[2] and Giuliano Gondi, a wealthy Florentine merchant, returned to Florence and employed Giuliano to build a palace of rustic-work opposite S. Firenze, above where the lions stand, as he had become

---

[1] Rebuilt about 1488.   [2] Ferdinand I. died 25 January, 1494.

intimate with the artist during his stay at Naples. This palace was to form the corner and face the Mercatanzia Vecchia, but the death of Giuliano Gondi put a stop to it. Among other things it contained a chimney-piece with rich carvings unlike anything seen before, beautifully composed, and with a great quantity of figures. Giuliano also built a palace for a Venetian outside the Pinti gate in Camerata, and many houses for private citizens which I need not mention.

Lorenzo the Magnificent, wishing to fortify Poggio Imperiale above Poggibonsi, on the road to Rome, to found a city there, as a public benefit and an ornament to the state, and to leave a memorial of himself in addition to his countless other projects, would do nothing without the counsel of Giuliano. Accordingly he began that renowned structure,[1] with its fortifications and its beauties as we see them to-day. This brought him such renown that, by the influence of Lorenzo, he went to Milan to make the model of a palace for the duke there. Here he was no less honoured by the duke than he had been at Naples by the king. When he presented his model in the name of Lorenzo, the duke was filled with wonder and admiration at seeing the arrangement and distribution of so many fine ornaments, each artistically adapted to its place. Accordingly he lost no time in procuring the necessary materials and beginning the work. Giuliano and Lionardo da Vinci were both working for the duke in the same city, the latter being full of the bronze horse which he was making, producing many studies; but this was broken in pieces by the French, and so the horse was not finished, and it was not possible to complete the palace either.

When Giuliano returned to Florence he found that his brother Antonio, who helped him with his models, had become so excellent that no one at that time could surpass him in carving, especially large crucifixes of wood, as we see by one on the high altar of the Nunziata at Florence, and one in the possession of the friars of S. Gallo in S. Jacopo tra Fossi, and yet another in the company of the Scalzo, all considered excellent. But Giuliano took him from this and got him to devote his attention to architecture, as he was full of work, both private and public.

As is usually the case, Fortune, which is hostile to ability, removed that prop of men of genius, Lorenzo de' Medici, causing great harm to the foremost artists, to his country, and to all Italy. Thus Giuliano was left disconsolate, as well as the other master spirits of the time, and withdrew to Prato, near Florence,

_____
[1] In 1488.

to build a church to the Madonna delle Carceri,[1] because all the structures in Florence, both public and private, were at a standstill. He remained at Prato for three years, supporting the expense, discomfort and trouble as best he could.

At that time it had become necessary to roof in the church of the Madonna at Loreto, and to vault the cupola begun by Giuliano da Maiano, but those in charge of the work feared that the piers would be too weak to bear the weight. Accordingly they wrote to Giuliano, asking if he would come and see the work; so he went, and, being a man of courage and spirit, showed them that the vaulting could easily be done, that all they needed was confidence, and so heartened them that they entrusted the work to him.[2] With this new task he hurried on the work at Prato, and brought his masters, builders and stone-cutters at Loreto. To strengthen the stonework and bind it together, he sent to Rome for *pozzolana*, which he mixed with all his mortar. Thus, in the space of three years, the building was perfectly finished.

Proceeding to Rome, he restored the falling roof of S. Maria Maggiore for Pope Alexander VI., constructing the present ceiling. In serving the court, the Bishop Rovere, created cardinal of S. Pietro ad Vincola, Giuliano's friend from the time when he was castellan at Ostia, employed him to make the model of the palace of S. Pietro ad Vincola. Soon after he further wished another palace to be created at his native Savona, under Giuliano's direction, but this was difficult, because the ceiling was not finished, and Pope Alexander would not allow him to go. Accordingly he caused it to be finished by his brother Antonio, who possessed a rich and versatile mind, and who, in serving the court, won the favour of the Pope. Alexander employed him to restore and strengthen the mole of Adrian,[3] now the castle of St. Angelo, in the form of a fortress. Great towers were constructed beneath, ditches, and the other fortications were made as we now see them, the work bringing Antonio into great favour with the Pope and his son Duke Valentino, and leading to his employment to make the fortress at Città Castellana. During the Pope's life he was in continual employment, being highly rewarded and esteemed by him.

At Savona Giuliano had the work well advanced when the cardinal returned to Rome on his affairs, leaving several wardens to finish the structure in accordance with Giuliano's plan. The

---

[1] Commissioned 1485 and finished 1491.
[2] Completed 1500.   [3] In 1495.

cardinal took the artist with him to Rome, and he went very willingly, for he wished to see his brother Antonio and his works, and he remained there several months. But at that time the cardinal fell into disgrace with the Pope, and left Rome to escape imprisonment, Giuliano following him. Arrived at Savona, they employed more builders and other workmen, but as the Pope's wrath seemed increasing, the cardinal thought it prudent to withdraw to Avignon, and presented to the king the model of a palace made for him by Giuliano, a very richly decorated work, with spacious apartments capable of accommodating all the court. The king's court was at Lyons when Giuliano presented his model, and the king was so delighted that he rewarded the architect liberally, praising him loudly, and heartily thanking the cardinal, who was at Avignon. Receiving the news that the palace at Savona was nearly finished, the cardinal sent Giuliano there to see the work, and soon after his arrival it was completed. Desiring to return to Florence, which he had not seen for a long time, Giuliano went thither with some of the builders, and, as the King of France had at that time set Pisa free, and war reigned between Florence and Pisa, Giuliano obtained a safe conduct at Lucca, as he mistrusted the Pisan soldiers. Nevertheless, in passing near Altopascio, they were taken prisoners by the Pisans,[1] who paid no attention to the safe conduct, and they were detained six months at Pisa, nor did they return to Florence until they had paid a ransom of 300 ducats. Antonio had heard of this at Rome, and, as he wished to see his brother and his native place again, he obtained licence to leave the city, and on his way back designed the fortress of Montefiascone for Duke Valentino. He reached Florence in 1503, being received joyfully by his friends. Then occurred the death of Alexander VI., and, after a short pontificate of Pius III., the cardinal of S. Pietro ad Vincola was elected Pope as Julius II. This was welcome news to Giuliano, who had long served the cardinal, and he determined to go and kiss his feet. On reaching Rome he was received with great favour, and was at once appointed to direct the constructions before the arrival of Bramante.

Antonio remained at Florence, where Piero Soderini was gonfaloniere, and, as Giuliano was away, he continued the building of Poggio Imperiale, at which all the Pisan prisoners were sent to work in order that it might be finished more quickly. The old fortress being ruined in the troubles of Arezzo,[2] Antonio

---

[1] In 1497. [2] In 1502.

made the model for a new one, with the consent of Giuliano, who came from Rome for the purpose and returned immediately. This work led to the appointment of Antonio as architect of Florence for all the fortifications.

When Giuliano returned to Rome, the question arose as to whether the divine Michelagnolo Buonarroti should make the tomb of Julius. Giuliano strongly advised the Pope to have it done, adding that, in his opinion, a chapel ought to be built expressly to hold it, and that it ought not to be placed in old S. Pietro, for there was no room, and a chapel would render the work more perfect. After many architects had prepared plans, the matter gradually grew until, instead of a chapel, they began the great structure of the new S. Pietro. In those days Bramante da Castel Durante, the architect, had arrived in Rome, having returned from Lombardy, and he contrived, by means of his extraordinary fancies and by the favour of Baldassare Peruzzi, Raphael of Urbino, and other architects, to throw the whole work into confusion, much time being lost in argument. At length the work was given to Bramante, who knew how to manage things, as possessing the best judgment and finest invention. Giuliano was angered, considering himself slighted by the Pope, whom he had so well served when he was less important, the structure having been promised to him. Though he had been appointed the colleague of Bramante for other buildings being erected in Rome, he left and returned to Florence, laden with many gifts from the Pope. This gave great satisfaction to Piero Soderini, who immediately gave him employment. Ere six months had passed, M. Bartolommeo della Rovere, the Pope's nephew and Giuliano's friend, wrote to him in the name of His Holiness that it would be to his advantage to return to Rome. But he could not prevail upon Giuliano to come, because he thought himself slighted. At length they wrote to Piero Soderini to use every means to send Giuliano to Rome, because the Pope wished to finish the strengthening of the large round tower begun by Nicholas V., the Borgo, the Belvedere, and other things. Giuliano at length allowed himself to be persuaded, and went to Rome, where the Pope welcomed him and gave him many gifts.

After this the Pope went to Bologna, the Bentivogli were driven out, and, by the advice of Giuliano, Julius determined to get Michelagnolo to make him a bronze statue. This was done, as I shall relate in the Life of Michelagnolo. Giuliano also accompanied the Pope to Mirandola, and, as he had borne many discomforts and labours, he returned to Rome with the Court on its capitulation.

As the Pope's passion to drive the French out of Italy had not entirely left his head, he attempted to deprive Piero Soderini of the government of Florence, as he was no small obstacle in the way of this project. The Pope being in this way diverted from his building to war, Giuliano was left unemployed, and asked for his *congé*, seeing that the building of S. Pietro alone received any attention, and even that not much. The Pope wrathfully asked him, "Do you think there are no other Giulianos da S. Gallo?" To which he replied that he would find none with a loyalty and devotion equal to his, but that he would find princes who kept their promises better than the Pope had kept his to him. However, he did not obtain his *congé*, the Pope saying that he would talk of it at another time.

Raphael of Urbino had meanwhile been brought to Rome by Bramante, who set him to paint the papal apartments. Giuliano, seeing that the Pope was delighted with pictures, and that he wished to have the vaulting of the chapel of his uncle Sixtus painted, suggested Michelagnolo to him, saying that he had already done the bronze statue at Bologna. The idea pleased the Pope, who sent for Michelagnolo, and on his arrival the vaulting was allotted to him. Soon after Giuliano renewed his application for his *congé*, and the Pope, seeing him so persistent, agreed that he should return to Florence with his good favour. After giving him his blessing, he handed him a red satin purse containing 500 crowns, saying that he ought to return home to rest, and that he would always be his friend. Giuliano having kissed the holy foot, returned to Florence at the very time that Pisa was surrounded and besieged by the Florentine army. No sooner had he arrived and been welcomed by Piero Soderini than he was sent to the camp to the commissaries, who could not prevent the besieged from revictualling Pisa by the Arno. Giuliano, after designing a bridge of boats to be built at a better season, returned to Florence. When spring came he took Antonio, his brother, and they went to Pisa, where he super-intended the construction of this very ingenious bridge. As it rose and fell it was safe against floods, and being well chained together it enabled the commissaries to besiege Pisa on the sea-side of the Arno as they wished, so that the garrison, seeing themselves deprived of succour, were forced to come to terms with the Florentines. Not long after Piero Soderini sent

Giuliano to Pisa[1] with a great number of builders to erect with great speed the fortress at the S. Marco gate, which is in the Doric style. While Giuliano was engaged upon this until 1512, Antonio went through all the territory surveying and repairing fortresses and other public structures.

When the Medici were restored in Florence by the favour of Pope Julius, after having been driven out on the coming of Charles VIII., King of France, to Italy, Piero Soderini being turned out of the palace, the services rendered by Giuliano and Antonio to the Medici in the past were recognised by that house. When, not long after the death of Julius II., Giovanni de' Medici, the cardinal, was made Pope, Giuliano was compelled to go to Rome once more, and as Bramante died soon after, it was proposed to entrust the building of S. Pietro to him. But as he was worn out by toil, enfeebled by old age, and suffering from the stone, he obtained permission from His Holiness to return to Florence, and the work was entrusted to Raphael of Urbino.

After suffering for two years, Giuliano died in 1517, aged seventy-four, leaving his name to the world, his body to the earth, and his soul to God. He was lamented by his brother Antonio, who loved him dearly, and by a son called Francesco, who studied sculpture, although of somewhat tender age. This Francesco has reverently preserved all the works of his ancestors, and among his own works in sculpture and architecture is the marble group of the Virgin and Child in the lap of St. Anne in Orsanmichele. This group, made of a single block, the figures in full relief, is considered a fine work. He has also done the tomb of Piero de' Medici, erected by Pope Clement at Monte Cassino, and other works, many of which are not mentioned because he is still alive.

Antonio lingered on after Giuliano's death, and made two large crucifixes of wood, one being sent to Spain and the other taken to France by Domenico Buoninsegni by order of the Cardinal Giulio de' Medici, the vice-chancellor. Then Antonio was sent to Livorno by the Cardinal de' Medici to make a design for the fortress there. This he did, although the work was not undertaken thoroughly and his plan was not followed. After this the men of Montepulciano proposed to erect a costly temple for an image of the Madonna which worked miracles.[2] Antonio made the model and directed the work, visiting the building twice a year. It may now be seen completed with its beautiful

[1] In 1509. [2] S. Biagio, building 1518-37.

grouping and variety, executed with the utmost grace by Antonio's genius. All the stones are of a whitish tint like travertine. This work is outside the S. Biagio gate, on the right-hand, half-way up the hill. At this same time he began the palace of Antonio di Monte, cardinal of S. Prassede, in the castle of Monte S. Savino, and did another for the same at Montepulciano, beautifully made and finished. He built a side wing for the houses of the Servite friars on their piazza,[1] following the arrangement of the loggia of the Innocenti. At Arezzo he made the models of the aisles of the Madonna delle Lagrime. But this was badly designed, because it does not match the rest of the structure, and the arches at the top are not properly turned. He also made a model of the Madonna in Cortona, but I do not think that it was carried out. During the siege he was employed to make fortifications and bastions in the city, being assisted by his nephew Francesco. After Michelagnolo's colossal statue for the piazza was put in hand, in the time of Giuliano, Antonio's brother, and another by Baccio Bandinelli was to be taken to its site, Antonio was charged with this. Obtaining the assistance of Baccio d'Agnolo, he brought it with very strong engines and set it safely upon the pedestal appointed for it.[2] In his extreme old age he cared for nothing but agriculture, of which he knew a great deal. When he could no longer support the cares of the world, he rendered his soul to God, in 1534, and was laid to rest with his brother Giuliano in the tomb of the Giamberti in S. Maria Novella.

The marvellous works of these two brothers testify to the world of their wonderful genius, as their life and conduct constitute a good example. They left the art of architecture in the Tuscan style inheritor of a better form than before, the Doric order being endowed with better measure and proportion than can be found in the rules and theories of Vitruvius. They collected in their house at Florence a great quantity of beautiful marble antiquities, which adorned the city as they adorned art. Giuliano brought from Rome the method of casting vaulting of materials which came out already carved, as we see in a room in his house and in the vaulting of the great hall at Poggio a Caiano. What a debt, then, do we owe them, for they fortified the Florentine territory and adorned the city, and wherever they worked they increased the reputation of Florence and of

[1] At Florence, in 1517.
[2] The David in 1504, and Bandinelli's in 1534.

the Tuscans, so that these lines have been written in their
honour:

Cedite Romani structores, cedite, Graii
Artis, Vitruvi, tu quoque cede parens.
Etruscos celebrare viros testudinis areus,
Urna, tholus, statuae, templa, domusque potunt.

RAPHAEL OF URBINO, Painter and Architect
(1483–1520)

THE liberality with which Heaven now and again unites in one
person the inexhaustible riches of its treasures and all those
graces and rare gifts which are usually shared among many
over a long period is seen in Raphael Sanzio of Urbino, who was
as excellent as gracious, and endowed with a natural modesty
and goodness sometimes seen in those who possess to an unusual
degree a humane and gentle nature adorned with affability
and good-fellowship, and he always showed himself sweet and
pleasant with persons of every degree and in all circumstances.
Thus Nature created Michelagnolo Buonarroti to excel and
conquer in art, but Raphael to excel in art and in manners also.
Most artists have hitherto displayed something of folly and
savagery, which, in addition to rendering them eccentric and
fantastical, has also displayed itself in the darkness of vice
and not in the splendour of those virtues which render men
immortal. In Raphael, on the other hand, the rarest gifts were
combined with such grace, diligence, beauty, modesty and good
character that they would have sufficed to cover the ugliest
vice and the worst blemishes. We may indeed say that those
who possess such gifts as Raphael are not mere men, but rather
mortal gods, and that those who by their works leave an
honoured name among us on the roll of fame may hope
to receive a fitting reward in heaven for their labours and
their merits.

Raphael was born at Urbino, a most important city of Italy,
in 1483, on Good Friday, at three in the morning, of Giovanni
de' Santi, a painter of no great merit, but of good intelligence
and well able to show his son the right way, a favour which
bad fortune had not granted to himself in his youth. Giovanni,
knowing how important it was for the child, whom he called
Raphael as a good augury, being his only son, to have his

mother's milk and not that of a nurse, wished her to suckle it, so that the child might see the ways of his equals in his tender years rather than the rough manners of clowns and people of low condition. When the boy was grown, Giovanni began to teach him painting, finding him much inclined to that art and of great intelligence. Thus Raphael, before many years and while still a child, greatly assisted his father in the numerous works which he did in the state of Urbino. At last this good and loving father perceived that his son could learn little more from him, and determined to put him with Pietro Perugino, who, as I have already said, occupied the first place among the painters of the time. Accordingly Giovanni went to Perugia, and not finding Pietro there he waited for him, occupying the time in doing some things in S. Francesco. When Pietro returned from Rome,[1] Giovanni being courteous and well bred, made his acquaintance, and at a fitting opportunity told him what he wished in the most tactful manner. Pietro, who was also courteous and a friend of young men of promise, agreed to take Raphael. Accordingly Giovanni returned joyfully to Urbino, and took the boy with him to Perugia, his mother, who loved him tenderly, weeping bitterly at the separation.[2] When Pietro had seen Raphael's method of drawing and his fine manners and behaviour, he formed an opinion of him that was amply justified by time. It is well known that while Raphael was studying Pietro's style he imitated him so exactly in everything that his portraits cannot be distinguished from those of his master, nor indeed can other things, as we see in some figures done in oils on a panel in S. Francesco at Perugia for Madonna Maddalena degli Oddi.[3] It represents an Assumption, Jesus Christ crowning the Virgin in heaven, while the twelve Apostles about the tomb are contemplating the celestial glory. The predella contains three scenes: the Annunciation, the Magi adoring Christ, and the Presentation in the Temple. This work is most carefully finished, and anyone not skilled in style would take it to be by the hand of Pietro, though there is no doubt that it is by Raphael. After this Pietro returned on some business to Florence, and Raphael left Perugia, going with some friends to Città di Castello. Here he did a panel in S. Agostino in that style, and a Crucifixion in S. Domenico, which, if not

[1] Perugino was in Perugia in 1490 and again in 1499.
[2] Raphael's mother died in 1491 when he was only eight years old. His father remarried and himself died in 1494.
[3] Painted 1502; now in the Vatican Gallery.

signed with Raphael's name, would be taken by everyone to be a work of Perugino. In S. Francesco in the same city he also did a Marriage of the Virgin,[1] which shows that Raphael was progressing in skill, refining upon the style of Pietro and surpassing it. This work contains a temple drawn in perspective, so charmingly that it is a wonder to see how he confronted the difficulties of this task. Raphael had thus acquired a great reputation in this style when the library of the Duomo at Siena was allotted by Pope Pius II. to Pinturicchio.[2] As he was a friend of Raphael, and knew him to be an admirable draughtsman, he brought him to Siena, where Raphael drew some of the cartoons for that work. He did not finish it because his love for art drew him to Florence,[3] for he heard great things from some painters of Siena of a cartoon done by Lionardo da Vinci in the Pope's Hall at Florence of a fine group of horses, to be put in the hall of the palace, and also of some nudes of even greater excellence done by Michelagnolo in competition with Lionardo. This excited so strong a desire in Raphael that he put aside his work and all thought of his personal advantage, for excellence in art always attracted him.

Arrived in Florence, he was no less delighted with the city than with the works of art there, which he thought divine, and he determined to live there for some time. Having struck up a friendship with Ridolfo Ghirlandajo, Aristotele S. Gallo, and other young painters, he was well received, especially by Taddeo Taddei, who was always inviting him to his house and table, being one who loved the society of men of ability. Raphael, who was courtesy itself, in order not to be surpassed in kindness, did two pictures for him in a transitional style between the early manner of Pietro and of the other which he learned afterwards, and which was much better, as I shall relate. These pictures are still in the house of the heirs of Taddeo.[4] Raphael was also very friendly with Lorenzo Nasi, and as Lorenzo had newly taken a wife, he painted him a picture of a babe between the knees of the Virgin, to whom a little St. John is offering a bird, to the delight of both. Their attitude displays childish simplicity and affection, while the picture is well coloured and carefully finished, so that they appear to be

---

[1] The Sposalizio of the Brera, Milan, painted in 1504.
[2] In 1502, but by the nephew of Pius II., Francesco Piccolomini, who afterwards became Pope as Pius III.
[3] In 1504.
[4] The Madonna del Giardino in the Vienna Gallery is one, the other is possibly that of Bridgewater House

actual living flesh.[1] The Madonna possesses an air full of grace and divinity, the plain, the landscape and all the rest of the work being of great beauty. This picture was greatly valued by Lorenzo Nasi in memory of his close friend and for its excellent workmanship. But it was severely damaged on 17 November, 1548, when the house of Lorenzo was crushed, together with the beautiful houses of the heirs of Marco del Nero and many others, by a landslip from Monte S. Giorgio. However, the pieces were found among the débris, and were carefully put together by Battista, Lorenzo's son, who was very fond of the arts. After these works Raphael was forced to leave Florence and go to Urbino, because, owing to the death of his father and mother, all his things were in disorder. While staying there he did two small but very beautiful Madonnas in his second manner for Guidobaldo da Montefeltro, then captain of the Florentines.[2] These are now the property of the illustrious Guidobaldo, Duke of Urbino. For the same captain he did a small picture of Christ praying in the Garden, the three Apostles sleeping in the distance. This painting is as delicately finished as a miniature. After remaining for a long time in the possession of Francesco Maria, Duke of Urbino, it was given by his illustrious consort, Leonora, to Don Paolo Giustiniano and Don Pietro Quirini, Venetians, hermits of the Camaldoli. They placed it in a principal chamber of the hermitage, as a thing of rare virtue, a work of Raphael, and the gift of so great a lady, and there it is held in the esteem which it merits.

After settling his affairs, Raphael returned to Perugia, where he painted for the Ansidei Chapel, in the church of the Servites, a picture of Our Lady, St. John the Baptist and St. Nicholas.[3] In the Lady Chapel of S. Severo, in the same city, a small Camaldo-lite monastery, he painted in fresco a Christ in Glory, God the Father surrounded by angels, with six saints seated, three on either side, St. Benedict, St. Romuald, St. Laurence, St. Jerome, St. Maur and St. Placidus.[4] To this fine fresco he put his name in large letters, easily seen. The nuns of S. Antonio da Padova, in the same city, employed him to paint a Madonna with a clothed Christ, as they desired, with St. Peter, St. Paul, St. Cecilia and St. Catherine, the heads of the two holy virgins being the sweetest and purest imaginable, with their varied attire, a rare

---

[1] Now in the Uffizi, known as the Madonna del Cardellino.
[2] Captain from 1495 to 1498.
[3] Painted 1506; now in the National Gallery.
[4] In 1505.

thing in those days. Above this he painted a fine God the Father in a lunette, and three scenes of small figures in the predella of Christ praying in the Garden, bearing the cross, the soldiers driving Him being very vigorous, and dead in the lap of His Mother.[1] This is a marvellous work, greatly valued by the nuns and much admired by all artists. It is well known that after his stay in Florence Raphael greatly altered and improved his style, through having seen the works of the foremost masters, and he never reverted to his former manner, which looks like the work of a different and inferior hand.

Before Raphael left Perugia, Madonna Atalanta Baglioni begged him to do a panel for her chapel in the church of S. Francesco. But not being able to do so then, he promised that he would not fail her when he returned from Florence, where he had affairs. At Florence he devoted infinite pains to the study of his art, and did the cartoon for this chapel, intending to carry it out as soon as he had the opportunity, as he did. Agnolo Doni was then in Florence, and though sparing in other things, spent willingly upon paintings and sculpture, of which he was very fond, though he saved as much as he could. He had portraits of himself and his wife done,[2] which may be seen in the house of his son Gio. Battista, built by Agnolo, a fine structure and most convenient in the Corso de' Tintori, near the corner of the Alberti in Florence. For Domenico Canigiani Raphael did a Madonna with the Child Jesus playing with a St. John held to him by St. Elizabeth, who is regarding St. Joseph, leaning with both hands on a staff and bending his head towards Elizabeth, as if marvelling and praising the greatness of God that so old a woman should have a little child.[3] All of them seem to be marvelling at the attitude of the children as they play, one reverencing the other, the colouring of the heads, hands and feet being faultless, and the work of a master. This noble picture is now the property of the heirs of Domenico Canigiani, who value it as a work of Raphael deserves.

This excellent artist studied the old paintings of Masaccio at Florence, and the works of Lionardo and Michelagnolo which he saw induced him to study hard, and brought about an extraordinary improvement in his art and style. While at Florence Raphael became very friendly with Frà Bartolommeo of S. Marco, whose colouring pleased him greatly, and this he tried to imitate. On his part he taught the good father the

---

[1] Now in the Naples Museum. [2] Now in the Pitti Gallery.
[3] Now at Munich.

methods of perspective, which he had previously neglected. In the midst of this intimacy Raphael was recalled to Perugia, where he began by finishing the work for Atalanta Baglioni, for which he had prepared the cartoon at Florence, as I have said. This divine picture represents Christ carried to burial, so finely done that it seems freshly executed.[1] In composing this work Raphael imagined the grief of loving relations in carrying to burial the body of their dearest, the one on whom all the welfare, honour and advantage of the entire family depended. Our Lady is fainting, and the heads of the figures in weeping are most graceful, especially that of St. John, who hangs his head and clasps his hands in a manner that would move the hardest to pity. Those who consider the diligence, tenderness, art and grace of this painting may well marvel, for it excites astonishment by the expressions of the figures, the beauty of the draperies, and the extreme excellence of every particular.

On returning to Florence after completing this work, Raphael was commissioned by the Dei, citizens there, to paint a picture for the chapel of their altar in S. Spirito.[2] He began this and made good progress with the outline. Meanwhile he did a picture[3] to send to Siena, which at his departure he left to Ridolfo del Ghirlandajo to finish some blue drapery in it. This was because Bramante, who was in the service of Julius II., wrote to him on account of a slight relationship, and because they were of the same country, saying that he had induced the Pope to have certain apartments done, and that Raphael might have a chance of showing his powers there. This pleased Raphael so that he left his works at Florence and the picture of the Dei unfinished (but so far complete that M. Baldassarre da Pescia had it put in the Pieve of his native place after Raphael's death), and went to Rome.[4] Arrived there, Raphael found a great part of the chambers of the palace already painted, and the whole being done by several masters. Thus Pietro della Francesca had finished one scene, Luca da Cortona had completed a wall, while Don Pietro della Gatta, abbot of S. Clemente, Arezzo, had begun some things. Bramantino da Milano also had painted several figures, mostly portraits, and considered very fine. Raphael received a hearty welcome from Pope Julius, and in the chamber of the Segnatura he painted the theologians recon-

---

[1] Borghese Gallery, Rome; painted 1507.
[2] The Madonna del Baldacchino, now in the Pitti Gallery.
[3] Either La Belle Jardiniere of the Louvre or the Colonna Madonna of Berlin.
[4] In 1508.

ciling Philosophy and Astrology with Theology, including portraits of all the wise men of the world in disputation.[1] Some
astrologers there have drawn figures of their science and various
characters on tablets, carried by angels to the Evangelists, who
explain them. Among these is Diogenes with a pensive air,
lying on the steps, a figure admirable for its beauty and the
disordered drapery. There also are Aristotle and Plato, with
the Ethics and Timæus respectively, and a group of philosophers in a ring about them. Indescribably fine are those
astrologers and geometricians drawing figures and characters
with their sextants. Among them is a youth of remarakble
beauty with his arms spread in astonishment and head bent.
This is a portrait of Federigo II., Duke of Mantua, who was
then in Rome. Another figure bends towards the ground, holding a pair of compasses in his hand and turning them on a
board. This is said to be a life-like portrait of Bramante the
architect. The next figure, with his back turned and a globe
in his hand, is a portrait of Zoroaster. Beside him is Raphael
himself, drawn with the help of a mirror. He is a very modest-
looking young man, of graceful and pleasant mien, wearing
a black cap on his head. The beauty and excellence of
the heads of the Evangelists are inexpressible, as he has given
them an air of attention and carefulness which is most
natural, especially in those who are writing. Behind St. Matthew,
as he is copying the characters from tablets, held by an
angel, is an old man with paper on his knees copying what
Matthew dictates. As he stands in that uncomfortable position,
he seems to move his lips and head to follow the pen. The
minor considerations, which are numerous, are well thought
out, and the composition of the entire scene, which is admirably
portioned out, show Raphael's determination to hold the field,
without a rival, against all who wielded the brush. He further
adorned this work with a perspective and many figures, so
delicately and finely finished that Pope Julius caused all the
other works of the other masters, both old and new, to be
destroyed, that Raphael alone might have the glory of replacing
what had been done. Although the work of Gio. Antonio
Sodoma of Vercelli, which was above the scene of Raphael's,
was to have been destroyed by the Pope's order, Raphael
decided to make use of its arrangement and of the grotesques.
In each of the four circles he made an allegorical figure to point

[1] In the following description Vasari has confused in the most astonishing
manner the "Disputà" and the "School of Athens."

the significance of the scene beneath, towards which it turns. For the first, where he had painted Philosophy, Astrology, Geometry and Poetry agreeing with Theology, is a woman representing Knowledge, seated in a chair supported on either side by a goddess Cybele, with the numerous breasts ascribed by the ancients to Diana Polymastes. Her garment is of four colours, representing the four elements, her head being the colour of fire, her bust that of air, her thighs that of earth, and her legs that of water. Some beautiful children are with her. In another circle towards the window looking towards the Belvedere is Poetry in the person of Polyhymnia, crowned with laurel, holding an ancient instrument in one hand and a book in the other. Her legs are crossed, the face having an expression of immortal beauty, the eyes being raised to heaven. By her are two children, full of life and movement, harmonising well with her and the others. On this side Raphael afterwards did the Mount Parnassus[1] above the window already mentioned. In the circle over the scene where the holy doctors are ordering Mass is Theology with books and other things about her, and children of no less beauty than the others. Over the window looking into the court, in another circle, he did Justice with her scales and naked sword, with similar children of the utmost beauty, because on the wall underneath he had represented civil and canon law, as I shall relate. On the same vaulting, at the corners, he did four scenes, designed and coloured with great diligence, though the figures are not large. In one of them, next the Theology, he did the sin of Adam in eating the apple, in a graceful style. In the one where Astrology is, he represented that science putting the fixed and moving stars in their appointed places. In the one of Mount Parnassus he did Marsyas flayed at a tree by Apollo; and next the scene of the giving of the Decretals is a Judgment of Solomon. These four scenes are full of feeling and expression, executed with great diligence in beautiful and graceful colouring.

I must now relate what was done on the walls below. On the wall towards the Belvedere, containing the Mount Parnassus and Fountain of Helicon, he made a shady laurel grove about the mount, so that the trembling of the leaves in the soft air can almost be seen, while a number of naked cupids, with lovely faces, are floating above, holding laurel branches, of which they make garlands and scatter them over the mount. The beauty of the figures and the nobility of the painting

[1] Finished in 1511.

breathe a truly divine afflatus, and cause those who examine them to marvel that they should be the work of a human mind, through the imperfect medium of colours, and that the excellence of the design should make them appear alive. The poets scattered about the mountain are remarkable in this respect, some standing and some writing, others talking, and others singing or conversing in groups of four or six according to the disposition. Here are portraits of all the most famous poets, both ancient and modern, taken partly from statues, partly from medals, and many from old pictures, while others were living. Here we see Ovid, Virgil, Ennius, Tibullus, Catullus, Propertius and Homer, holding up his blind head and singing verses, while at his feet is one writing. Here in a group are the nine Muses, with Apollo, breathing realities of wonderful beauty and grace. Here are the learned Sappho, the divine Dante, the delicate Petrarca, the amorous Boccacio, all full of life; Tibaldeo is there also, and numerous other moderns, the whole scene being done with exquisite grace and finished with care. On another wall he did Heaven, with Christ and the Virgin, St. John the Baptist, the Apostles, Evangelists, martyrs in the clouds, with God the Father above sending out the Holy Spirit over a number of saints who subscribe to the Mass and argue upon the Host which is on the altar. Among them are the four Doctors of the Church, surrounded by saints, including Dominic, Francis, Thomas Aquinas, Bonaventura, Scotus, Nicholas of Lyra, Dante, Frà Girolamo Savonarola of Ferrara, and all the Christian theologians, including a number of portraits. In the air are four children holding open the Gospels, and it would be impossible for any painter to produce figures of more grace and perfection than these. The saints in a group in the air seem alive, and are remarkable for the foreshortening and relief. Their draperies also are varied and very beautiful, and the heads rather celestial than human, especially that of Christ, displaying all the clemency and pity which divine painting can demonstrate to mortal man. Indeed, Raphael had the gift of rendering his heads sweet and gracious, as we see in a Madonna with her hands to her breast contemplating the Child, who looks incapable of refusing a favour. Raphael appropriately rendered his patriarchs venerable, his apostles simple, and his martyrs full of faith. But he showed much more art and genius in the holy Christian doctors, disputing in groups of six, three and two. Their faces show curiosity and their effort to establish the certainty of which they are in doubt, using their hands in arguing and certain gestures of the body, attentive ears, knit brows, and many different kinds of astonishment, various and appropriate. On the other hand, the four Doctors of the Church, illuminated by the Holy Spirit, solve, by means of the Holy Scriptures, all the questions of the Gospels, which are held by children flying in the air. On the other wall, containing the other window, he did Justinian giving laws to the doctors, who correct them; above are Temperance, Fortitude and Prudence. On the other side the Pope being a portrait of Julius II., while Giovanni de' Medici the cardinal, afterwards Pope Leo, Cardinal Antonio di Monte, and Cardinal Alessandro Farnese, afterwards Pope Paul III., are also present, with other portraits. The Pope was greatly delighted with this work, and in order to have woodwork of equal value to the paintings, he sent for Frà Giovanni of Verona from Monte Oliveto of Chiusuri, in the Siena territory, then a great master in marquetry. He not only did the wainscoting, but the fine doors and seats with perspectives, which won him favour, rewards and honours from the Pope. Certainly no one was ever more skilful in design and workmanship in that profession than Giovanni, as we see by the admirable perspectives in wood in the sacristy of S. Maria in Organo in his native Verona, the choir of Monte Oliveto di Chiusuri and that of S. Benedetto at Siena, as well as the sacristy of Monte Oliveto of Naples, and the choir in the chapel of Paolo di Tolosa there. Thus he deserves to be held in honour by his order, in which he died at the age of sixty-eight in 1537. I have mentioned him as a man of true excellence, because I think his ability deserves it, for he induced other masters to make many rare works subsequently, as I shall say elsewhere.

But to return to Raphael. His style improved so greatly that the Pope entrusted to him the second chamber towards the great hall. His reputation had now become very great, and at this time he painted a portrait of Pope Julius in oils so wonderfully life-like and true that it inspired fear as if it were alive. This work is now in S. Maria del Popolo,[1] with a fine painting of Our Lady done at the same time, and containing a Nativity of Christ, the Virgin covering the Child with a veil. This is of great beauty, the air of the head and of the whole body showing the Child to be the veritable Son of God. The head and face of the Madonna are of equal beauty, and also display her joy and pity. Joseph leans with both hands on a staff in pensive contemplation of the King and Queen of Heaven, in the wonder of

[1] Now in the Uffizi Gallery.

a most holy old man. Both these pictures are shown on solemn festivals.

At this time Raphael had acquired great renown at Rome. But although his graceful style commanded the admiration of all, and he continually studied the numerous antiquities in the city, he had not as yet endowed his figures with the grandeur and majesty which he imparted to them henceforward.

It happened at this time that Michelagnolo caused the Pope so much upset and alarm in the chapel, of which I shall speak in his Life, whereby he was forced to fly to Florence. Bramante had the keys of the chapel, and, being friendly with Raphael, he showed him Michelagnolo's methods so that he might understand them. This at once led Raphael to do over again the Prophet Isaiah in S. Agostino above the St. Anne of Andrea Sansovino, which he had just finished. Aided by what he had seen of Michelagnolo, he greatly improved and enlarged the figure, endowing it with more majesty. When Michelagnolo saw it afterwards he concluded that Bramante had played him this bad turn to benefit Raphael. Not long after, Agostino Chisi, a wealthy merchant of Siena and patron of men of genius, allotted to Raphael a chapel, because shortly before he had painted in the sweetest manner, in a loggia of the merchant's palace, now called i Chisi in Trastevere, a Galatea in the sea on a car drawn by two dolphins, surrounded by tritons and many sea gods.[1] After making a cartoon for this chapel, which is on the right-hand on entering the principal door of the church of S. Maria della Pace, Raphael carried it out in fresco in a new style, considerably finer and more magnificent than his first. Here he did some prophets and sibyls, before the chapel of Michelagnolo was opened publicly, though he had seen it, which are considered the best of his works and the most beautiful among so many others, because the women and children are represented with great vivacity and perfect colouring. This work established his renown for ever, as being the most excellent that he produced in his life. At the prayers of a chamberlain of Julius [2] he painted the picture of the high altar of Araceli, representing Our Lady in the air, a beautiful landscape, St. John, St. Francis and St. Jerome as a cardinal. Our Lady shows the humility and modesty proper to the Mother of Christ, the Child is very prettily playing with his Mother's cloak. St. John shows the effect of fasting, his

---

[1] In the Farnesina; painted in 1514.

[2] Sigismondo de' Conti. This picture, known as the Madonna di Foligno, is now in the Vatican Gallery.

head expressive of great sincerity and absolute certainty, like those who are far removed from the world, who speak the truth and hate falsehood. St. Jerome raises his head and eyes to Our Lady in contemplation, indicative of the learning and wisdom displayed in his writings; with both hands he is presenting the chamberlain, who is very life-like. Raphael was equally successful with his St. Francis, who kneels on the ground with one arm stretched out, and with his head raised he regards the Virgin, burning with love and emotion, his features and the colouring showing his consuming love and the comfort and life which he derives from regarding her beauty and that of the Child. Raphael did a boy standing in the middle of the picture under the Virgin, looking up to her and holding a tablet. For his beautiful face and well-proportioned limbs he cannot be surpassed. Besides this there is a landscape of remarkable perfection and beauty. Continuing the rooms in the palace, Raphael did the miracle of the Sacrament of the Corporale of Orvieto, or Bolsena, as it is called.[1] We see the priest blushing with shame in saying Mass at seeing the Host melted into blood on the Corporale owing to his incredulity. Fear is in his eyes, and he seems beside himself in the presence of his auditors, as he stands irresolute. His hands tremble, and he shows other signs of terror natural on such an occasion. About him are many varied figures, some serving the Mass, some kneeling on the steps in beautiful attitudes, astonished at the event, showing the many various effects of the same emotion, both in the men and women. There is one woman seated on the ground in the lower part of the scene, holding a child in her arms. She turns in wonder at hearing someone speak of what has happened to the priest with a very charming and vivacious feminine grace.

On the other side Raphael represented Pope Julius hearing the Mass, introducing the portrait of the cardinal of S. Giorgio and many others. In the part interrupted by the window he introduced a flight of steps, shown entire, so that the story is uninterrupted, and it seems that if this gap had not been there the scene would have suffered. Thus we see that in inventing and composing scenes no one ever excelled Raphael in arrangement and skill. This appears opposite in the same place where St. Peter is represented guarded in prison by armed men, by Herod's order.[2] Here his architecture and his discretion in treating the prison are such that beside him the work of others seem more confused than his are beautiful, for he always

[1] In 1512.   [2] Painted in 1514.

endeavoured to follow the narrative in his scenes and introduce beautiful things. Thus, for example, in the horrible prison we see the aged Peter chained between two armed men, the heavy sleep of the guards, the shining splendour of the angel in the darkness of the night, showing all the details of the cell and making the armour glisten so that it appears to be burnished and not a painted representation. No less art and genius is displayed in the scene where Peter leaves the prison, freed from his chains, accompanied by the angel, the Apostle's face showing that he believes himself to be dreaming. The other armed guards outside the prison are terror-stricken as they hear the sound of the iron door. A sentinel holds a torch in his right hand, the light of which is reflected in all the armour, and where this does not fall there is moonlight. Raphael did this above the window, and thus makes the wall darker. But in looking at the picture, the painted light and the various lights of the night seem due to Nature, so that we fancy we see the smoke of the torch, the splendour of the angel, and the deep darkness of the night, so natural and true that it is hard to believe they are only painted, where every difficult thing that he has imagined is so finely presented. Here in the darkness we see the outlines of the armour, the shading, the reflections, the effects of the heat of the lights, showing Raphael to be the master of the other painters. No better representation of the night has ever been made, this being considered the divinest and most remarkable of all. On one of the bare walls Raphael further did the Divine worship, the ark of the Hebrews and the candlestick, and Pope Julius driving Avarice from the church, scenes of beauty and excellence like the night just mentioned. They contain portraits of the bearers then living, who are carrying the Pope in a chair, for whom some men and women make way to allow him to pass.[1] An armed man on horseback, accompanied by two on foot, is fiercely striking the proud Heliodorus, who, by the command of Antiochus, intended to despoil the Temple of all the deposits of widows and orphans. We see the property and treasures being taken away, but all thrown to the ground and scattered at the fall of Heliodorus, beaten to the earth by the three, whom he alone sees, those engaged in carrying them being seized with sudden terror like all the other followers of Heliodorus. Apart from these kneels the High Priest Onias in his pontificals, his eyes and hands turned to heaven in fervent prayer, filled with compassion for the poor who are losing their possessions, and

[1] Painted in 1512.

with joy at the succour sent by Heaven. By a happy idea of Raphael the plinths of the pedestals are filled with many who have climbed up by the columns, and are looking on in their uneasy postures, while the astonished multitude, in various atittudes, is awaiting the event. This work[1] is so marvellous in every particular that even the cartoons for it are greatly prized. Some parts of them belong to M. Francesco Masini, a nobleman of Cesena, who, without the help of any master, but guided from his childhood by an extraordinary natural instinct, has himself studied painting and produced pictures which are much admired by connoisseurs. These cartoons are among his designs with some ancient reliefs in marble, and are valued by him as they deserve. I must add that M. Niccolo Masini, who has supplied me with these particulars, is a genuine admirer of our arts as he is distinguished in every other particular.

But to return to Raphael. In the vaulting of this chamber he did four scenes: the appearance of God to Abraham, promising the multiplication of his seed, the sacrifice of Isaac, Jacob's ladder, and the burning bush of Moses, displaying no less art, invention, design and grace than in his other works. While he was engaged in producing these marvels, envious Fortune deprived Julius II. of his life, removing that patron of talent and admirer of every good thing. On Leo X. succeeding[2] he wished the work to be continued. Raphael's abilities ascended to the heavens, and he was much gratified at meeting so great a prince, who inherited the love of his family for the arts. Accordingly he was heartened to continue the work, and on the other wall did the coming of Attila to Rome, and his meeting with Leo III. at the foot of Monte Mario, and being driven away with a simple benediction. In the air are St. Peter and St. Paul with drawn swords coming to defend the Church. Although the history of Leo III. does not relate this, the artist no doubt wished it to be so, just as the poets often introduce some fresh matter to their work as an ornament, and yet do not depart from the main idea. The Apostles show a valour and celestial ardour that the divine judgment often puts into the faces of its servants to defend the most holy religion. Attila, mounted on a black horse of the utmost beauty with a white star on his forehead, betrays great fear in his face as he takes to flight. There are other very fine horses, notably a dappled Spanish jennet, ridden by a man whose bare parts are covered with scales like a fish. He is copied from Trajan's Column, where the men are

[1] Finished in 1514.   [2] 13 February, 1513.

armed in this way, and it is supposed to be made of crocodile skin. Monte Mario is burning, showing that on the departure of soldiers their quarters are always left in flames. Raphael also drew some mace-bearers accompanying the Pope, who are very life-like, and the horses they ride, with the court of the cardinals and other bearers, holding the hackney, upon which the man in pontificals is mounted, who is a portrait of Leo X., as fine as the others, and many courtiers. This is a truly charming thing, thus adapted to such a work, and most useful to our art, especially for those who delight in such things. At the same time Raphael did a panel for Naples which was placed in S. Domenico in the chapel containing the crucifix which spoke to St. Thomas Aquinas. It represents the Virgin, St. Jerome dressed as a cardinal, and the Angel Raphael accompanying Tobias.[1] He did a picture for Leonello da Carpi, lord of Meldola, who is still alive, though over ninety. This was a marvel of colouring and of singular beauty, being executed with vigour and of such delicate loveliness that I do not think it can be improved upon. The face of the Madonna expresses divinity and her attitude modesty. With joined hands she adores her Child, who sits on her knees and is caressing a little St. John, who adores him, as do St. Elizabeth and Joseph. This picture belonged to the Cardinal di Carpi, son of Leonello, a distinguished patron of the arts, and it must now be in the possession of his heirs. When Lorenzo Pucci, cardinal of Sante Quattro, was appointed chief penancer, Raphael obtained a commission from him to do a picture for S. Giovanni in Monte at Bologna. It is now placed in the chapel containing the body of the Blessed Elena dall' Olio.[2] In this work we see the full power of the delicate grace of Raphael joined to art. St. Cecilia listens entranced to a choir of angels in heaven, absorbed by the music. Her face is abstracted like one in an ecstasy, on the ground musical instruments are scattered, which look real and not painted, as do her veil and vestments of cloth of gold and silk, with a marvellous haircloth beneath. St. Paul rests his right arm on a naked sword and his head on his hand, showing his knowledge and his fiery nature turned to gravity. He is bare-footed and dressed like an apostle in a simple red mantle, with a green tunic beneath. St. Mary Magdalene lightly holds a vase of precious stone in her hand, and turns her head in joy at her conversion; these are of unsurpassable beauty, and so are the heads of St. Augustine and St.

[1] Madonna del Pesce, now in the Prado, Madrid.
[2] Now in the Bologna Academy; painted 1513.

John the Evangelist. While we may term other works paintings, those of Raphael are living things; the flesh palpitates, the breath comes and goes, every organ lives, life pulsates everywhere, and so this picture added considerably to his reputation. Thus many verses were written in his honour in the vulgar and Latin tongues. I will quote the following only, not to make my story too long:

> *Pingant sola alii referantque coloribus ora*
> *Cæciliae os Raphael atque animum explicuit.*

After this Raphael did a small picture of little figures, also at Bologna, in the house of Count Vincenzio Ercolani, containing Christ, as Jove, in heaven, surrounded by the four Evangelists as described by Ezekiel, one like a man, one as a lion, one as an eagle and one as an ox, with a landscape beneath,[1] no less beautiful for its scale than the large works. To the counts of Canossa at Verona he sent a large picture of equal excellence of a Nativity, with a much-admired Dawn, and a St. Anne. Indeed, the whole work is fine, and to say that it is by Raphael is to bestow the highest praise, and it is greatly prized by the counts. Though offered great sums by many princes they have refused to part with it. For Bindo Altoviti Raphael did his portrait as a young man,[2] considered most wonderful. He also did a picture of the Virgin, which he sent to Florence.[3] This is now in the palace of Duke Cosimo in the chapel of the new apartments built and painted by myself, where it serves as the altarpiece. It represents an aged St. Anne seated, offering the Christ-child to the Virgin, the baby being a beautiful nude figure with a lovely face that gladdens all beholders by its smile. Raphael in painting this Madonna shows with what beauty art can endow the aspect of a Virgin, with her modest eyes, her noble forehead, her graceful nose and her virtuous mouth, while her dress displays the utmost simplicity and virtue. Indeed, I do not think a better can be seen. There is a nude St. John, seated, and a very beautiful female saint. The background is a house with a window lighting the room in which the figures are. At Rome Raphael did a picture with the portraits of Pope Leo, Cardinal Giulio de' Medici and and the Cardinal de' Rossi.[4] The figures seem to stand out in relief; the velvet shows its texture, the damask on the Pope is shining and lustrous, the fur lining soft and real, and the gold

---

[1] Pitti Gallery.
[2] Pinakothek, Munich, ascription doubtful.
[3] Madonna dell' Impannata, Pitti Gallery.
[4] Pitti Gallery; painted in 1518.

and silk look like the actual materials and not colours. There is an illuminated parchment book, of remarkable realism, and a bell of chased silver of indescribable beauty. Among other things is the burnished gold ball of the seat, reflecting, such is its clearness, the lights of the windows, the Pope's back, and the furniture of the room like a mirror, so wonderfully done that it would seem that no master can improve upon it. For this work the Pope largely rewarded him, and the picture is still in Florence in the duke's wardrobe. He also painted Duke Lorenzo and Duke Giuliano as finely as these, with equal grace in the colouring. These are in the possession of the heirs of Ottaviano de' Medici in Florence. Thus the glory and the rewards of Raphael increased together. To leave a memory of himself he built a palace in the Borgo Nuovo at Rome, decorated with stucco by Bramante.

By these and other works the fame of Raphael spread to France and Flanders. Albert Dürer, a remarkable German painter and author of some fine copper engravings, paid him the tribute of his homage and sent him his own portrait, painted in water-colours, on cambric, so fine that it was transparent, without the use of white paint, the white material forming the lights of the picture. This appeared marvellous to Raphael, who sent back many drawings of his own which were greatly valued by Albert. This head was among the things of Giulio Romano, Raphael's heir, in Mantua.

Having seen the engravings of Albert Dürer, Raphael was anxious to show what he could do in that art, and caused Marco Antonio of Bologna to study the method. He succeeded so well that he had his first things engraved: the Innocents, a Last Supper, a Neptune, the St. Cecilia [1] boiled in oil. Marco Antonio then did a number of prints which Raphael afterwards gave to Il Baviera, his boy, who had the charge of one of his mistresses whom Raphael loved until his death He made a beautiful life-like portrait of her which is now in Florence in the possession of the most noble Botti, a Florentine merchant, the friend and intimate of all distinguished men, especially painters He keeps it as a reminder of his love for art and especially of Raphael. His brother Simone Botti is not behind him in his love of art, and besides his reputation among artists as one of the best patrons of their profession, he is especially esteemed by me as the best friend I have ever had, while he possesses a good artistic judgment.

But to return to engravings. The favour of Raphael to Il

[1] It should be St. Felicita.

Baviera quickened the hand of Marco da Ravenna so that copper engravings from being scarce became as plentiful as we now see them. Then Ugo da Carpi, a man whose head was full of ingenious ideas and fancies, discovered wood engraving, so that by three impressions he obtained the light and the shade of chiaroscuro sketches, a very beautiful and ingenious invention. Quantities of these prints may now be seen, as I shall relate more in detail, in the Life of Marco Antonio of Bologna. For the monastery of Palermo, called S. Maria dello Spasmo, of the friars of Monte Oliveto, Raphael did Christ bearing the Cross, which is considered marvellous, seeing the cruelty of the executioners leading Him to death on Mount Calvary with fierce rage.[1] The Christ in his grief and pain at the approach of death has fallen through the weight of the cross, and, bathed in sweat and blood, turns towards the Maries, who are weeping bitterly. Here Veronica is stretching out her hand and offering the handkerchief with an expression of deep love. The work is full of armed men on horse and foot, who issue from the gate of Jerusalem with the standards of justice in their hands, in varied and fine attitudes. When this picture was finished, but not set up in its place, it was nearly lost, because on its way by sea to Palermo a terrible storm overtook the ship, which was broken on a rock, and the men and merchandise all perished, except this picture, which was washed up at Genoa in its case. When it was fished out and landed it was found to be a divine work, and proved to be uninjured, for even the fury of the winds and waves respected such painting. When the news had spread, the monks hastened to claim it, and no sooner was it restored to them through the influence of the Pope than they handsomely rewarded those who had saved it. It was again sent by ship, and was set up in Palermo, where it is more famous than the mountain of Vulcan. While Raphael was at work on these things, which he had to do, since it was for great and distinguished persons, and he could not decline them in his own interest, he nevertheless continued his work in the Pope's chambers and halls, where he kept men constantly employed in carrying on the work from his designs, while he supervised the whole, giving assistance as he well knew how. It was not long before he uncovered the chamber of the Borgia tower. On every wall he painted a scene, two above the windows and two others on the sides. During a fire in the Borgo Vecchio at Rome,

[1] The "Spasimo di Sicilia," now at Madrid; Vasari is wrong about Veronica.

which could not be put out, St. Leo IV. had gone to the loggia of the palace and extinguished it with a benediction. This scene [1] represents various perils. In one part we see women whose hair and clothes are blown about by the fury of the wind, as they carry water to extinguish the fire in vessels in their hands and on their heads. Others endeavouring to cast water are blinded by the smoke. On the other side is a sick old man, beside himself with infirmity and the conflagration, borne as Virgil describes Anchises to have been borne by Æneas, the youth showing his spirit and putting out his strength to carry his burden. A lean, bare-footed old woman follows them, fleeing from the fire, with a naked child before them. From the top of some ruins is a naked, dishevelled woman, who throws her child to one who has escaped from the flames and stands on tip-toe in the street, with arms stretched out to receive the little one in its swaddling-clothes. The desire of the woman to save the child and her own fear of the approaching fire are well depicted, while the one receiving the child is disturbed by fear for his own safety while anxious to save his charge. Equally remarkable is a mother, dishevelled and ragged, with some clothes in her hand, who beats her children to make them run faster from the fire. Some women kneeling before the Pope seem to be begging him to cause the fire to cease.

The other scene is also of St. Leo IV., where he has represented the port of Ostia, occupied by the Turks, who came to make him prisoner. We see the Christians fighting the fleet at sea, a number of prisoners already taken to the port, coming out of a boat, led by soldiers by the beard, the attitudes being very fine. In their varying costumes they are led by galley-slaves before St. Leo, who is a portrait of Leo X., the Pope standing in his pontificals between Bernardo Divizio of Bibbiena, the Cardinal S. Maria in Portico, and Cardinal Giulio de' Medici, afterwards Pope Clement. I cannot relate at length the numerous fine devices employed by the artist in representing the prisoners, and how, without speech, he represents grief, fear and death. There are two other scenes, one [2] of Leo X. consecrating the Most Christian King Francis I. of France, singing the Mass in his pontificals and blessing the anointing oil, with a number of cardinals and bishops in pontificals assisting, including the portraits of several ambassadors and others, some dressed in the French fashion of the time. The other scene is the coronation

---

[1] Begun in 1514.
[2] Dated 1517, the scene represents the coronation of Charlemagne.

of the king, the Pope and Francis being portraits, the one in armour and the other in pontificals. All the cardinals, bishops, chamberlains, squires, grooms of the chamber, are in their robes, and seated according to rank, after the custom of the chapel, and are portraits, including Giannozzo Pandolfini, bishop of Troyes, a great friend of Raphael, and many other noted men of the time. Near the king is a boy kneeling and holding the royal crown. This is a portrait of Ippolito de' Medici, who afterwards became cardinal and vice-chancellor, and a great friend of the arts and other talents. To his memory I acknow-ledge my indebtedness, for it is to him that I owe my start on my career, such as it has been. I cannot enter into every minute detail concerning the productions of this artist whose very silence is like speech. Beneath these scenes are figures of the defenders and benefactors of the Church each surrounded by a different border and everything carried out with spirit, ex-pression and good ideas, with a harmony of colours that cannot be described. As the vaulting of this room was painted by Pietro Perugino, his master, Raphael would not efface it, from respect for the memory of him who had taught him the first elements of his art.

Such was the greatness of this man that he kept draughtsmen in all Italy, at Pozzuolo, and as far as Greece, to procure every-thing of value to assist his art. Continuing his series, he did a room with some figures on the ground-level of apostles and saints in tabernacles, and employed Giovanni da Udine, his pupil, unique in drawing animals, to do all the animals of Pope Leo: a chameleon, the civet cats, apes, parrots, lions, elephants, and other curious creatures. He further decorated the palace with grotesques and varied pavements, designing the papal stair-cases and other loggia begun by Bramante the architect, but left unfinished at his death. Raphael followed a new design of his own, and made a wooden model on a larger scale and more ornate than Bramante's. As Pope Leo wished to display his magnificence and generosity, Raphael prepared the designs for the stucco ornaments and the scenes painted there, as well as of the borders. He appointed Giovanni da Udine head of the stucco and grotesque work, and Giuliano da Romano of the figures, though he did little work on them. Gio. Francesco,[1] also Il Bologna, Perino del Vaga, Pellegrino da Modana, Vin-cenzio da S. Gimignano, and Polidoro da Caravaggio, with many other painters, did scenes and figures and other things for that

[1] Giovanni Francesco Penni.

work, which Raphael finished with such perfection that he sent to Florence for a pavement by Luca della Robbia. Certainly no finer work can be conceived, with its paintings, stucco, disposition and inventions. It led to Raphael's appointment as superintendent of all works of painting and architecture done in the palace. It is said that his courtesy was so great that the builders, to allow him to accommodate his friends, did not make the walls solid, but left openings above the old rooms in the basement, where they might store casks, pipes and firewood. These openings enfeebled the base of the structure, so that it became necessary to fill them up owing to the cracks which began to show. For the gracefully finished inlaid work of the doors and wainscoting of these rooms Raphael employed Gian Barile, a clever wood-carver. He prepared architectural designs for the Pope's villa, and for several houses in the Borgo, notably the palace of M. Gio. Battista dall' Aquila, which was very beautiful. He did another for the bishop of Troyes in the via di S. Gallo in Florence. For the black monks of S. Sisto at Piacenza he did the high-altar picture representing the Madonna, with St. Sixtus and St. Barbara, a rare and unique work.[1] He did many pictures for France, notably a St. Michael fighting the devil,[2] for the king, considered marvellous. He represented the centre of the earth by a half-burned rock, from the fissures of which issue flames of fire and sulphur. Lucifer, whose burned members are coloured several tints, exhibits his rage and his poisoned and inflated pride against Him who has cast him down, and his realisation of his doom of eternal punishment. Michael, on the other hand, is of celestial aspect, in armour of iron and gold, courageous and strong, having already overthrown Lucifer, at whom he aims his spear. In fine, this work deserved a rich reward from the king. He drew portraits of Beatrice of Ferrara and other ladies, including his own mistress.

Raphael was very amorous, and fond of women, and was always swift to serve them. Possibly his friends showed him too much complaisance in the matter. Thus, when Agostino Chigi, his close friend, employed him to paint the first loggia in his palace, Raphael neglected the work for one of his mistresses. Agostino, in despair, had the lady brought to his house to live in the part where Raphael was at work, contriving this with difficulty by the help of others. That is why the work was completed. Raphael did all the cartoons of this work, and coloured

[1] The Sistine Madonna, now at Dresden.
[2] Now in the Louvre; dated, 1518.

many figures in fresco with his own hand. In the vaulting he did the council of the gods in heaven, introducing forms and costumes borrowed from the antique, with refined grace and design. Thus he did the espousal of Psyche, with the ministers who serve Jove, and the Graces scattering flowers. In the lower part of the vaulting he did many scenes, including Mercury with the flute, who seems to be cleaving the sky in his flight. In another, Jove, with celestial dignity, is kissing Ganymede. Beneath is the chariot of Venus and Mercury, and the Graces taking Psyche to heaven, with many other poetical scenes. In the arched space between the corbels he did a number of cherubs, beautifully foreshortened, carrying the implements of the gods in their flight: the thunderbolts and arrows of Jove, the helmet, sword and target of Mars, the hammers of Vulcan, the club and lion's skin of Hercules, the wand of Mercury, the pipe of Pan, the agricultural rakes of Vertumnus, all with animals appropriate to their nature, a truly beautiful painting and poem. As a border to these scenes he caused Giovanni da Udine to make flowers, leaves and fruits in festoons, which could not be better. He designed the architecture of the stables of the Ghigi, and Agostino's chapel in the church of S. Maria del Popolo, where, besides the painting, he designed a marvellous tomb, directing Lorenzetto, a sculptor of Florence, to make two figures, which are still in his house in the Macello de' Corbi at Rome; but the death of Raphael, followed by that of Agostino, led to the work being given to Sebastiano Viniziano.

Raphael had become so great that Leo X. ordained that he should begin the large upper hall, containing the Victories of Constantine, which he began. The Pope also desired to have rich tapestry hangings of gold and silk. For these Raphael made large coloured cartoons of the proper size, all with his own hand, which were sent to weavers in Flanders,[1] and, when finished, the tapestries came to Rome. The work is so marvellously executed that it excites the wonder of those who see it that such things as hair and beards and delicate flesh-colouring can be woven work. It is certainly a miracle rather than a production of human art, containing, as it does, water, animals, buildings, all so well done that they seem the work of the brush and not of the loom. It cost 70,000 crowns, and is still preserved in the papal chapel. For the Cardinal Colonna Raphael did a

[1] The cartoons were done in 1515 or 1516. They were bought by Charles I. in 1630 and are now in the Victoria and Albert Museum.

St. John[1] on canvas, greatly prized by its owner, who, falling sick, gave it to the physician who healed him, M. Jacopo da Carpi, feeling under a great obligation, and it is now in Florence in the hands of Francesco Benintendi. For Cardinal Giulio de' Medici, the vice-chancellor, he painted the Transfiguration, to be sent to France. He worked steadily at this with his own hands, bringing it to its final completion. It represents Christ transfigured on Mount Tabor with the eleven disciples at the foot, awaiting their Master. A boy possessed by a devil is brought so that Christ when he has come down from the mount may release him. The sufferings of this boy through the malignity of the spirit are apparent in his flesh, veins and pulse, as he thrusts himself forward in a contorted attitude, shouting and turning up his eyes, while his pallor renders the gesture unnatural and alarming. An old man is embracing and supporting him, his eyes shining, his brows raised, and his forehead knit, showing at once his resolution and fear. He steadily regards the Apostles, as if to derive courage from them. A woman there, the principal figure of the picture, kneels in front of the Apostles, and is turning her head towards them, while she points out the misery of the boy possessed. The Apostles, standing, sitting and kneeling, show their great compassion for this great misfortune. Indeed, the figures and heads are of extraordinary beauty, and so new and varied that artists have commonly reputed this work the most renowned, the most beautiful and the most divine. Whoever wishes to imagine and realise the transfiguration of Christ should examine this work, where the Lord is in the shining air, with Moses and Elias illuminated by His splendour. Prostrate on the ground lie Peter, James and John in varied and beautiful attitudes. One has his head on the ground, one shades his eyes with his hands from the rays of light of the splendour of Christ, who, clothed in snow white, opens His arms and lifts His head, showing the Divine Essence of the three persons of the Trinity thus displayed in the perfection of Raphael's art. The artist seems to have gathered all his force to worthily present the face of Christ, which was the last thing he did, as death overtook him before he again took up the brush.

Having hitherto described the works of this great man, I will make some observations on his style for the benefit of our artists, before I come to the other particulars of his life and death. In his childhood Raphael imitated the style of Pietro Perugino, his master, improving it greatly in design, colouring

[1] Uffizi Gallery.

and invention. But in riper years he perceived that this was too far from the truth. For he saw the works of Lionardo da Vinci, who had no equal for the fashion of the heads of women and children, and in rendering his figures graceful, while in movement he surpassed all other artists; these filled Raphael with wonder and amazement. As this style pleased him more than any he had ever seen, he set to work to study it, and gradually and painfully abandoning the manner of Pietro, he sought as far as possible to imitate Lionardo. But in spite of all his diligence and study he could never surpass Lionardo, and though some consider him superior in sweetness, and in a certain natural facility, yet he never excelled that wonderful groundwork of ideas, and that grandeur of art, in which few have equalled Lionardo. Raphael, however, approached him more closely than any other painter, especially in grace of colouring.

But to return to Raphael himself. The style which he learnt of Pietro when young became a great disadvantage to him. He had learned it readily because it was slight, dry and defective in design, but his not being able to throw it off rendered it very difficult for him to learn the beauty of nudes, and the method of difficult foreshortening of the cartoon of Michelagnolo Buonarroti for the Hall of the Council at Florence. Another man would have lost heart at having wasted so much time, but not so Raphael, who purged himself of the style of Pietro, and used it as a stepping-stone to reach that of Michelagnolo, full as it was of difficulties in every part. The master having thus become a pupil again, applied himself to do as a man in a few months the work of several years, at an age when one learns quickly. Indeed, he who does not learn good principles and the style which he means to follow at an early age, acquiring facility by experience, seeking to understand the parts and put them in practice, will hardly ever become perfect, and can only do so with great pains, and after long study. When Raphael began to change and improve his style, he had never studied the nude as it should be studied, but had only done portraits as he had seen his master Pietro do them, assisted by his own natural grace. Accordingly he studied the nude, comparing the muscles of dead men with those of the living, which do not seem so marked when covered with skin as they do when the skin is removed. He afterwards saw how the soft and fleshy parts are made, and graceful turnings and twists, the effects of swelling, lowering and raising a member or the whole body, the system of bones, nerves and veins, becoming excellent in all the parts as a great master should. But seeing that he could not in this respect attain to the perfection of Michelagnolo, and being a man of good judgment, he reflected that painting does not consist of representing nude figures alone, but that it has a large field, and among the excellent painters there were many who could express their ideas with ease, felicity and good judgment, composing scenes not overcrowded or poor, and with few figures, but with good invention and order, and who deserved the name of skilled and judicious artists. It was possible, he reflected, to enrich his works with variety of perspective, buildings and landscapes, a light and delicate treatment of the draperies, sometimes causing the figure to be lost in the darkness, and sometimes coming into the clear light, making living and beautiful heads of women, children, youths and old men, endowing them with suitable movement and vigour. He also reflected upon the importance of the flight of horses in battle, the courage of the soldiers, the knowledge of all sorts of animals, and, above all, the method of drawing portraits of men to make them appear life-like and easily recognised, with a number of other things, such as draperies, shoes, helmets, armour, women's head-dresses, hair, beards, vases, trees, caves, rain, lightning, fine weather, night, moonlight, bright sun, and other necessities of present-day painting. Reflecting upon these things, Raphael determined that, if he could not equal Michelagnolo in some respects, he would do so in the other particulars, and perhaps surpass him. Accordingly he did not imitate him, not wishing to lose time, but studied to make himself the best master in the particulars mentioned. If other artists had done this instead of studying and imitating Michelagnolo only, though they could not attain to such perfection, they would not have striven in vain, attaining a very hard manner, full of difficulty, without beauty or colouring, and poor in invention, when by seeking to be universal, and imitating other parts, they might have benefited themselves and the world. Having made this resolution, and knowing that Frà Bartolommeo of S. Marco had a very good method of painting, solid design and pleasant colouring, although he sometimes used the shadows too freely to obtain greater relief, Raphael borrowed from him what he thought would be of service, namely a medium style in design and colouring, combining it with particulars selected from the best things of other masters. He thus formed a single style out of many, which was always

considered his own, and was, and will always be, most highly
esteemed by artists. This is seen to perfection in the sibyls
and prophets done in the Pace, as has been said, for which
he derived so much assistance from having seen the work of
Michelagnolo in the Pope's chapel. If Raphael had stopped
here, without seeking to aggrandise and vary his style, to show
that he understood nudes as well as Michelagnolo, he would
not have partly obscured the good name he had earned, for his
nudes in the chamber of the Borgia tower in the Burning of
the Borgo Nuovo, though good, are not flawless. Equally un-
satisfactory are those done by him on the vaulting of the palace
of Agostino Ghigi in Trastevere, because they lack his characteristic grace and sweetness. This was caused in great measure
by his having employed others to colour from his designs.
Recognising this mistake, he did the Transfiguration of S. Pietro
a Montorio by himself unaided, so that it combines all the
requisites of a good painting. If he had not employed printers'
lampblack, through some caprice, which darkens with time, as
has been said, and spoils the other colours with which it is
mixed, I think the work would now be as fresh as when he did
it, whereas it has now become rather faded.

I have entered upon these questions at the end of this Life
to show how great were the labours, studies and diligence of
this famous artist, and chiefly for the benefit of other painters,
so that they may rise superior to disadvantages as Raphael
did by his prudence and skill. Let me also add that everyone
should be contented with doing the things for which he has a
natural bent, and ought not to endeavour out of emulation to
do what does not come to him naturally, in order that he may
not labour in vain, frequently with shame and loss. Besides
this, he should rest contented and not endeavour to surpass
those who have worked miracles in art through great natural
ability and the especial favour of God. For a man without natural
ability, try how he may, will never succeed like one who successfully progresses with the aid of Nature. Among the ancients
Paolo Uccello is an example of this, for he steadily deteriorated
through his efforts to do more than he was able. The same
remark applies in our own day to Jacopo da Pontormo, and
may be seen in many others, as I have related and shall relate
again. Perhaps this is because when Heaven has distributed
favours it wishes men to rest content with their share.

Having spoken upon these questions of art, possibly at
greater length than was necessary, I will now return to Raphael.

A great friend of his, Bernardo Divizio, cardinal of Bibbiena, had for many years urged him to take a wife. Raphael had not definitely refused, but had temporised, saying he would wait for three or four years. At the end of this time, when he did not expect it, the cardinal reminded him of his promise. Feeling obliged to keep his word, Raphael accepted a niece of the cardinal [1] for wife. But being very ill-content with this arrangement, he kept putting things off, so that many months passed without the marriage taking place. This was not done without a purpose, because he had served the court so many years, and Leo was his debtor for a good sum, so that he had received an intimation that, on completing the room which he was doing, the Pope would give him the red hat for his labours and ability, as it was proposed to create a good number of cardinals, some of less merit than Raphael.

Meanwhile Raphael continued his secret pleasures beyond all measure. After an unusually wild debauch he returned home with a severe fever, and the doctors believed him to have caught a chill. As he did not confess the cause of his disorder, the doctors imprudently let blood, thus enfeebling him when he needed restoratives. Accordingly he made his will, first sending his mistress out of the house, like a Christian, leaving her the means to live honestly. He then divided his things among his pupils, Giulio Romano, of whom he was always very fond, Gio. Francesco of Florence, called "il Fattore," and some priest of Urbino, a relation. He ordained and left a provision that one of the antique tabernacles in S. Maria Rotonda should be restored with new stones, and an altar erected with a marble statue of the Madonna. This was chosen for his tomb after his death. He left all his possessions to Giulio and Gio. Francesco, making M. Baldassare da Pescia, then the Pope's datary, his executor. Having confessed and shown penitence, he finished the course of his life on the day of his birth, Good Friday, aged thirty-seven. We may believe that his soul adorns heaven as his talent has embellished the earth. At the head of the dead man, in the room where he worked, they put the Transfiguration, which he had done for the Cardinal de' Medici. The sight of the dead and of this living work filled all who saw them with poignant sorrow. The picture was placed by the cardinal in S. Pietro a Montorio, at the high altar, and was always prized for its execution.[2] The body received honoured

---

[1] Maria Bibbiena; but she seems to have died before the artist.
[2] Now in the Vatican Gallery.

burial, as befitted so noble a spirit, for there was not an artist who did not grieve or who failed to accompany it to the tomb. His death caused great grief to the papal court, as he held office there as groom of the chamber, and afterwards the Pope became so fond of him that his death made him weep bitterly. O happy spirit, for all are proud to speak of thee and celebrate thy deeds, admiring every design! With the death of this admirable artist painting might well have died also, for when he closed his eyes she was left all but blind. We who remain can imitate the good and perfect examples left by him, and keep his memory green for his genius and the debt which we owe to him. It is, indeed, due to him that the arts, colouring and invention have all been brought to such perfection that further progress can hardly be expected, and it is unlikely that anyone will ever surpass him. Besides these services rendered to art, as a friend he was courteous alike to the upper, the middle and the lower classes. One of his numerous qualities fills me with amazement: that Heaven endowed him with the power of showing a disposition quite contrary to that of most painters. For the artists who worked with Raphael, not only the poor ones, but those who aspired to be great—and there are many such in our profession—lived united and in harmony, all their evil humours disappearing when they saw him, and every vile and base thought deserting their mind. Such a thing was never seen at any other time, and it arose because they were conquered by his courtesy and tact, and still more by his good nature, so full of gentleness and love that even animals loved him, not to speak of men. It is said that he would leave his own work to oblige any painter who had known him, and even those who did not. He always kept a great number employed, assisting and teaching them with as much affection as if they had been his own sons. He never went to court without having fifty painters at his heels, all good and skilful, who accompanied him to do him honour. In short, he did not live like a painter, but as a prince. For this cause, O Art of Painting, thou mayest consider thyself fortunate in having possessed an artist who, by his genius and character, has raised thee above the heavens. Blessed indeed art thou to have seen thy disciples brought together by the instruction of such a man, uniting the arts and virtues, which in Raphael compelled the greatness of Julius II. and the generosity of Leo, men occupying the highest dignity, to treat him with familiarity, and practise every kind of liberality, so that by means of their favour, and the wealth they gave him, he was able to do great

honour to himself and to his art. Happy also were those who
served under him, because all who imitated him were on a safe
roaɑ, and so those who imitate his labours in art will be rewarded by the world, as those who copy his virtuous life
will be rewarded in heaven. Bembo wrote the following epitaph
for Raphael:

D. O. M.

RAPHAELI SANCTO IOAN. F. VRBINATI
PICTORI EMINENTISS. VETERVMQ. AEMVLO
CVIVS SPIRANTEIS PROPE IMAGINEIS
SI CONTEMPLERE
NATVRAE ATQVE ARTIS FOEDVS
FACIELE INSPEXERIS.
IVLII II. ET LEONIS X. PONT. MAX.
PICTVRAE ET ARCHITECT. OPERIBVS
GLORIAM AVXIT
VIXIT AN XXXVII. INTEGER INTEGROS
QVO DIE NATVS EST EO ESSE DESIIT
VII. ID APRIL MDXX.

" ILLE HIC EST RAPHAEL TIMUIT QUO SOSPITE VINCI
RERUM MAGNA PARENS QUO MORIENTE MORI."

The Count Baldassare Castiglione wrote of his death as
follows:

Quod lacerum corpus medica sanaverit arte
Hippolytum Stygiis et revocarit aquis
Ad Stygias ipse est raptus Epidaurius undas.
Sic precium vitae mors fuit artifici
Tu quoque dum toto laniatam corpore Romam
Componis miro, Raphael, ingenio,
Atque urbis lacerum ferro, igni, annisque cadaver
Ad vitam, antiquum jam revocasque decus
Movisti superum invidiam, indignataque mors est,
Te dudum extinctis reddere posse animam ;
Et quod longa dies paullatim aboleverat, hoc te
Mortali spreta lege parare iterum.
Sic miser heu ! prima cadis intercepte juventa,
Deberi et morti nostraque nosque mones.

GUGLIELMO DA MARCILLA, French Painter and Master of Stained-Glass Windows
(1467 – 1537)

AT this same time, so blessed by God with the greatest happiness that our arts can enjoy, lived Guglielmo da Marcilla, a Frenchman, who may be said to have made Arezzo his native place from his affection for it and his long stay there; indeed, he was universally reputed and called an Aretine. This is one of the advantages of ability that a man of any strange, distant, barbarous or unknown country, if only he possesses talent and is skilful with his hands, may establish himself in any city through which he passes and displays his powers, so that in a short while he makes a name and his qualities are greatly prized and honoured. Very frequently those who travel far from their homes, and live among nations friendly to ability and to foreigners, find themselves so warmly welcomed and recognised that they abandon their old home and choose a new one for their last rest. It was thus that Guglielmo chose Arezzo. In his youth he studied design in France, and did windows in stained glass, making pictures as harmonious and beautiful as oil-paintings. Owing to the entreaties of some friends he was present at the death of an enemy of theirs, and was forced to take the habit of St. Dominic in France to escape trial and justice. Although in religion, he did not abandon the study of art, but by steady progress he attained the highest perfection.

By the order of Pope Julius II. Bramante was commissioned to introduce a number of stained-glass windows into the palace. On making inquiries as to who were the best in this work, he was informed that France possessed several excellent masters. The French ambassador at the papal court had a window in a frame in his study done in one piece of white glass with a number of colours burned into the glass. With Bramante's authority a letter was written to France, inviting an artist to come to Rome, offering him good payment. Maestro Claudio, a Frenchman and the head of the art, knowing the excellence of Guglielmo, succeeded by means of promises in getting him away from the friars without difficulty, because on account of the malice and envy rampant among them he was more willing to go than Claudio was to take him away. Accordingly he went to Rome,[1]

[1] About 1508.

exchanging the habit of St. Dominic for that of St. Peter. Bramante had just done two windows of travertine in the Pope's palace, in the hall before the chapel, now embellished with vaulting by Antonio da S. Gallo and with marvellous stucco by Perino del Vaga of Florence. These windows were made by Maestro Claudio and Guglielmo in a truly marvellous manner, but they were broken during the sack, the lead being taken for bullets. Besides these they did a great number for the papal chambers, which suffered the same fate as the others, but one may still be seen in the room with Raphael's fire, in the Borgia tower, containing angels supporting the arms of Leo X. In S. Maria del Popolo they did two admirable windows in the chapel behind the Madonna, with scenes from her life. These brought them fame and renown and the comforts of life. But Maestro Claudio was very intemperate in eating and drinking, a common failing among his countrymen, and falling sick of a severe fever in the pestilent air of Rome, he died in six days.

Being thus left by himself, and feeling lost without his companion, Guglielmo painted a window in S. Maria de Anima, the German church in Rome. This led to Selvio,[1] cardinal of Cortona, engaging him to do some windows and other works in Cortona. Accordingly he went to Cortona to live, and the first thing he did there was the front of the cardinal's house, facing the piazza, painting in grisaille Croton and the other founders of the city. The cardinal, perceiving Guglielmo to be a worthy man and skilful at his art, got him to do the window of the principal chapel in the Pieve at Cortona, representing a Nativity and the Magi adoring. Guglielmo did his work with spirit, intelligence and great skill, especially in distributing the colours, making the principal figures the lightest, and gradually darkening the others as they receded, displaying great excellence in this respect. In painting them he showed the greatest judgment, so contriving that his figures should gradually recede without becoming confounded with the buildings or landscape, and they seemed painted on a panel, or rather in relief. His composition of scenes displays invention and variety, and he made them rich and well arranged, simplifying the method of uniting pieces of glass, though it seems most difficult to those who are not skilled in the mysteries. He designed his pictures for the windows so well that the lead and iron framework was dissimulated in the shadows or folds of the draperies and strengthened the outlines, imparting as much grace as the brush, and converting a difficulty into an

[1] Selvio Passerini. He went to Cortona in 1517.

embellishment. He only employed two colours for shading the glass, which was to be baked: one was iron filings and the other copper filings. The iron shaded in black draperies, hair, buildings, and the copper, being tawny, the crimson. He also made considerable use of a hard stone coming from Flanders and France, now called *lapis amotica*,[1] which is of a rich colour and is useful for burnishing gold. It is first ground in a bronze mortar, and after being mixed with gum by an iron pestle upon a plate of copper or brass, it produces an entrancing effect on the glass.

When he arrived in Rome, Guglielmo was not a good designer, though he was skilled in other things. However, in the course of years, he studied design and gradually improved himself, as we see by his windows in the cardinal's palace at Cortona, in the others outside, and in a rose-window in the Pieve on the front, on the right-hand on entering the church, containing the arms of Leo X., as well as in two small windows in the company of Jesus, one of a Christ and the other of St. Onofrio. These works are a great advance upon his first efforts.

During Guglielmo's stay at Cortona, Fabiano di Stagio Sassoli, an Aretine, died in Arezzo. He had been a very good workman of large windows, so that the warders of the Vescovado had employed his son Fabiano and Domenico Pecori, a painter, to do three windows in the principal chapel, of twenty braccia each. When this was finished and set up the Aretines were not very pleased, although they were quite good and rather meritorious than otherwise. M. Lodovico Bellichini, a distinguished physician and one of the principal rulers of the city, happening to go to Cortona to treat the cardinal's mother, became friendly with Guglielmo, often conversing with him when he had time. Guglielmo also became fond of the physician. He was then known as the prior, having been recently appointed to a priory. The physician one day asked him if he could obtain permission from the cardinal to go to Arezzo and do some windows. He promised to do so, obtaining the cardinal's consent, and proceeded thither. Stagio, who has been mentioned above, having dissolved his partnership with Domenico, received Guglielmo into his house. His first work was a window in St. Lucia, a chapel of the Albergotti in the Vescovado of Arezzo, representing St. Lucy and St. Silvester so well that the figures are life-like, and do not seem to be transparent coloured glass. At least they resemble a marvellous painting, for, besides his mastery of the flesh-tints, the colours melt into one another as red into yellow, and white and

[1] Lapis amatita, or hematite.

green into blue, a difficult and marvellous achievement. The
true and prime colour appears entirely on one of the sides, as
for instance red, blue or green, and the other, as thick as the
blade of a knife or rather more, remains white. Many being
afraid of breaking the glass, not being very skilful in managing
it, do not employ iron to cut it, but use a copper wheel with an
iron point, and do it gradually with emery, leaving the skin of
white glass, which is thus very clear. When this white glass is
to be coloured yellow it is put into the fire with a little calcined
silver, coloured like bole and laid on somewhat thickly. When
in the fire this eats into the substance of the glass and makes
it a fine yellow. No one knew better how to do this than Prior
Guglielmo. The difficulty consists in those matters, because
painting in colours, in oils, or otherwise, is little or nothing, and
rendering them transparent is not of much moment, but the
baking in the fire to render them everlasting and impervious to
water is a labour worthy of praise. Therefore this excellent
master merits great praise, because he has never been equalled
in this profession in invention of colouring, design and excellence.
He afterwards did the large rose-window of that church, representing the Coming of the Holy Spirit, and also the Baptism of
Christ by St. John, the Christ standing in Jordan awaiting John,
who has taken a cup of water to baptise him. A nude old man is
putting on his clothes, and some angels are making ready the
raiment of Christ. Above is the Father sending the Holy Spirit
on His Son. The window is over the font in the Duomo. Here
also Guglielmo did a window of the Resurrection of Lazarus.
It is a remarkable presentation in so small a space of so many
figures, descriptive of the fear and amazement of the people
and the stench of the body, the two sisters weeping and rejoicing
at the resurrection. Here the colours melt beautifully into each
other, and every detail is most vivid in its kind. Those who wish
to see the capabilities of the prior should examine his marvellous
treatment of the scene of Christ calling Matthew from his bench
to follow him, and opening His arms to receive the Apostle, who
abandons his accumulated treasures and riches. An Apostle
asleep at the bottom of some steps is awakened by another, with
great realism. Similarly we see St. Peter speaking to St. John, both
of them so beautiful that they seem divine. The same window
contains a temple in perspective, with steps and figures, appropriately composed, and a beautiful landscape, so that it seems
impossible they can be glass, but rather objects rained down
from heaven for the delight of man. In the same place he made

the windows of St. Anthony and St. Nicholas and two others, one of Christ driving the money-changers from the Temple, and the other of the adulteress, all excellent and marvellous works.[1]

The labours and skill of the prior were considered so admirable by the Aretines, who loaded him with favours and rewards, and he was so pleased at this, that he resolved to make the city his home, becoming an Aretine instead of a Frenchman. But feeling that work in glass was very liable to destruction, he desired to study painting, and undertook to do three large vaults in fresco in the Vescovado, for the wardens there, hoping thus to leave a memorial of himself. In recompense the Aretines gave him a farm of the fraternity of S. Maria della Misericordia near the territory, with good buildings, to hold for life. On completion the work was to be judged by a competent artist, and the wardens were to give him the price fixed. He determined to prove his capacity, and in imitation of the things of the chapel of Michelagnolo he made the figures very large. His desire to achieve excellence in the art, although he was fifty, enabled him to improve steadily, so that he showed that his knowledge of the beautiful was not inferior to his delight in representing it. He represented the beginning of the New Testament, as he had done that of the Old in the three large vaults.[2] This leads me to believe that any clever man who wishes to attain perfection may do so if only he will take pains. At the beginning the prior was fearful of the greatness of the task because he lacked experience. This induced him to send to Rome for Maestro Giovanni Franzese, an illuminator, who came to Arezzo and painted a Christ in fresco in an arch, above St. Anthony, and for the company he did the processional banner, which was given him by the prior to do, and which he executed with great diligence. At the same time he did the rose-window on the façade of the church of S. Francesco, a great work, representing the Pope in the consistory and residence of the cardinals, while St. Francis brings them roses in January, and goes to Rome to obtain the confirmation of his rule. In this work Guglielmo showed his knowledge of composition, so that it may be said to have been born in him. It seems impossible for any artist to equal him here in beauty, grace and the quantity of figures. There are a great number of windows of extraordinary beauty in the city, and the large rose-window in the Madonna delle Lagrime, with the Assumption of the Virgin, and the Apostles, and a fine Annunciation, a rose-window with the Marriage, and another of St. Jerome for the armourers.

[1] 1520-4. [2] Finished 1524.

He also did three other windows for the church, and a beautiful rose-window of the Nativity in the church of S. Girolamo, with another in S. Rocco. Some, moreover, were sent to various places, as to Castiglione del Lago and to Florence, one to Ludovico Capponi for S. Felicita, containing the painting of Jacopo da Pontormo, a most excellent work in oils and fresco, the walls and picture too. This window came into the hands of the Jesuit friars, who were working at that trade in Florence, and they took it to pieces to discover the methods employed. Thus they removed several pieces, replacing them by new ones, and finally entirely changed it from its original state.

Guglielmo also wished to colour in oils, and in the chapel of the Conception in S. Francesco at Arezzo he did a picture containing some vestments, very well done, and many heads full of life and beauty, which brought him great honour, this being his first work in oils. The prior was a man of honour, fond of order and system. Thus he bought a fine house and made many improvements. As became a man of religion, he behaved irreproachably, though his conscience troubled him for his abandonment of the friars. Therefore he did a window for S. Domenico at Arezzo, a convent of his order, for the chapel of the high altar, representing a vine issuing from the saint's body, and he did a great number of holy friars forming the tree of the religion. At the top are the Virgin and Christ espousing St. Catherine of Siena, a much-admired work, displaying great mastery. He would accept no payment for it, for he felt under a great obligation to the order. For S. Lorenzo at Perugia he produced a very fine window, and sent many others to various places about Arezzo. Having fine ideas in architecture, he did several designs for buildings and decorations for the city, the two stone gates of S. Rocco and the macigno framework round the picture of Maestro Luca in S. Girolamo. He did one in the abbey at Cipriano d'Anghiari, and another ornament in the company of the Trinità in the Chapel of the Crucifix. In the sacristy he did a fine basin, the saints being exquisitely carved. He took such delight in work, continuing at the wall both winter and summer, a labour that makes sound men ill, that he became dropsical, and after being tapped by the physicians, in a few days he rendered his soul to his Maker, when he had taken the sacraments like a good Christian and made his will. He had a special devotion for the Camaldoli hermits, who have a house on the slope of the Apennines, twenty miles from Arezzo, and he left his property to them as well as his body. He left his glass, tools and designs to his apprentice Pastorino da Siena, who had been with him many years. One design, the drowning of Pharaoh in the Red Sea, is in our book.

Pastorino afterwards practised many branches of art, and made stained-glass windows, though in this he did little. He was followed some time later by Maso Porro of Cortona, who was more skilful in joining and baking the glass than in colouring it. Guglielmo had for pupils Battista Borro of Arezzo, who imitated him closely in windows, Benedetto Spadari and Giorgio Vasari. The prior lived sixty-two years and died in 1537. He deserves great praise, for he brought stained-glass work in Tuscany to the highest pitch of mastery and refinement. As he conferred such benefits, we ought to accord to him honour and eternal praise, continually exalting his life and works.

CRONACA,[1] Architect of Florence
(1457–1508)

MANY geniuses capable of producing rare work come to nought if they do not fall in with persons who know good things and are anxious to have them carried out. But it frequently happens that those who have the power lack the knowledge or the will, and even if they possess the will to erect a fine structure they do not take pains to seek out an architect of rare genius and lofty spirit. They entrust their honour and renown to timid minds, who thus wrong their memory. In order to favour a dependant, such is the power of ambition, they often choose the worst out of good designs offered to them, leaving a clumsy memorial of themselves, though they think themselves judicious and the artist also. On the other hand, a patron, even if he possess little knowledge, who falls in with men of skill and judgment, wins no less fame from their buildings, after death, than he acquired by his rule during life. Cronaca, however, was very fortunate, for he never lacked a patron and one ready to carry out great and magnificent works.

It is related that while Antonio Pollajuolo was at Rome doing the bronze tombs in S. Pietro, he took into his house a young relation called Simone, who had fled from Florence because of some quarrels. Being much inclined to architecture, having been with a master carpenter, Simone began to observe

---

[1] His true name was Simone Pollaiuolo.

the fine antiquities of the city, measuring them with great diligence. He soon showed signs of having made great progress by work which he did. Accordingly he left Rome and returned to his native Florence. Having some skill in narration, he related the marvels of Rome and other places so vividly that they called him Il Cronaca (the chronicler) ever afterwards. He had so far succeeded that he was considered the best architect of Florence, having judgment in discerning places and proving himself of a loftier spirit than his rivals, showing himself a skilful imitator of the antique, and carefully observing the rules of Vitruvius and the works of Filippo di Ser Brunellesco. At that time there lived in Florence Filippo Strozzi, now called the elder to distinguish him from his son, who, being very rich, wished to leave a fine palace to his children and native city, as a memorial of himself. Accordingly Benedetto da Maiano was called in by him and made a model, standing alone, which was afterwards carried out, though not entirely, as will be said below, because some neighbours would not oblige him with their houses. Benedetto therefore had to begin [1] the palace as best he could, the front shell being nearly completed before Filippo's death. It is in the rustic order, and graduated, as may be seen. The blocks of the first floor, from the first windows downwards, and the door are large rustic-work, the second floor is lesser rustic-work. At the very moment when Benedetto left Florence, Cronaca returned from Rome. Obtaining an introduction to Filippo, he pleased him so much by his model of the court and the great cornice round the outside of the palace, that Filippo entrusted the entire work to him and continued to employ him ever afterwards. In addition to the beautiful exterior in the Tuscan order, Cronaca made a magnificent Corinthian cornice round the exterior at the end of the roof, half of which may now be seen, finished with such singular grace that it would be impossible to add to it or to desire better. This cornice was borrowed by Cronaca from an antique measured by him at Rome at Spogliacristo, which is ranked among the finest in the city. It is true that Cronaca increased it in proportion to his palace, and added the roof. Thus his genius appropriated the works of others, transforming them into his own, a thing in which few succeed. The difficulty is not only to borrow beautiful designs, but to know how to adapt them to the purpose they are to serve, with grace, measure, proportion and convenience. But though this cornice was and will always

[1] In 1489.

be highly praised, great blame was incurred by another in the same city made by Baccio d'Agnolo for the palace of Bartolini, who, in imitation of Cronaca, placed upon a small and graceful façade a great antique cornice measured from one at Monte-cavallo; but it is a complete failure because Baccio had not the judgment to adapt it, and so it could hardly be worse, looking like a great cap on a child's head. It is of no purpose to make excuses, as many artists do, saying they are carefully measured from antiques and are copied from good masters, for a good judgment and an exact eye are of more value than compasses.

Cronaca executed his cornice about the palace with great art, using the label and egg ornament, and finished two sides, balancing the stones and binding them together so that it would be hard to find a building executed with greater diligence and perfection. Indeed, all the stones of the palace are so joined that they seem of one piece. That everything might correspond, he caused the ironwork throughout to be done well, the lanterns at the corners all being carried out by Niccolo Grosso Caparra, a Florentine smith, with great diligence. These remarkable lanterns, with cornices, columns, capitals, bases, are the best modern ironwork produced, and exhibit great knowledge and skill.

Niccolo Grosso was an eccentric and obstinate man, reasonable in his own way, but never trusting others. He never allowed credit to anyone for his works, but always required money on account. Because of this Lorenzo de' Medici called him Il Caparra (earnest money), and as such he was known to many. The sign of his shop was Burning Books, and when anyone asked for time to pay, he said, "I cannot, because my books are burning, and I am not able to write down any more debtors." The lords captains of the Guelph party employed him to make a pair of andirons. When he finished them they were frequently sent for, but he would always say, "I sweat and toil over my furnace, and I want my money brought to me." They then sent for the work, saying that if he went for the money he should at once be paid. But he obstinately insisted upon the money being brought to him. At this the provveditore became angry, because the captains wished to see the andirons, and he sent saying that Caparra had received half the money, and if he sent the andirons he should have the remainder. Upon this Caparra gave the page one of the andirons, telling him to take it, and if they would bring him the rest they should have the other, but it was his until then. When the officials had seen his admirable workmanship they sent the money to the shop, and he sent them the other andiron. It is further related that Lorenzo de' Medici wished to have ironwork to send away so that the excellence of Caparra might be made known. Accordingly he went in person to his shop, and happened to find him at work on some things for poor people, for which he had received money on account. When Lorenzo made his request, Caparra would not promise to serve him before he had served the others, saying that they had come to the shop before him, and that their money was worth as much as Lorenzo's. Some young citizens brought him a design to make an iron to unbar and break other irons with a vice, but he would not oblige them, crying after them that he would not on any account do it, because these were the instruments of robbers, to rob or to disgrace young girls, that they did not appear to him to be the things for respectable men. Seeing that Caparra would not oblige them, they asked if there was anyone in Florence who would do it, at which he flew into a rage, and with an execration drove them away. He would never work for Jews, saying that their money was venomous and putrid. He was a good and religious man, but eccentric and obstinate, and in spite of many offers he would never leave Florence, where he lived and died. I have written this notice of him because he was unique in his profession, and he has never been equalled, and never will be, as his beautiful ironwork and lanterns for the Strozzi palace prove.

The palace was completed by Cronaca, and adorned with a very rich court, in the Corinthian and Doric orders, with an ornament of columns, capitals, cornices, windows and doors of great beauty. If the interior does not seem to correspond to the exterior, this is not the fault of Cronaca, as he was forced to adapt the interior to arrangements begun by others, in large part following their dispositions. Thus it was no small task for him to bring it to its present state of beauty. The same answer applies to those who say that the steps are not easy, or in just measure, but too steep and sudden, as well as to those who say that the chambers and other apartments do not correspond to the magnificence of the exterior. But, nevertheless, this palace will always be considered truly magnificent, and equal to any private building erected in Italy in our day, so that Cronaca deserves the highest praise for it. He also did the sacristy of S. Spirito at Florence,[1] an octagonal temple, with good proportion,

[1] In 1496.

and well finished. Among other things it contains some capitals by the happy hand of Andrea del Monte Sansovino, executed with the utmost perfection. Cronaca also did the ante-room of the sacristy, which is considered most beautiful, although the divisions over the columns are not well spaced, as will be said. He further did the church of S. Francesco of the Observantines, on the hill of S. Miniato, outside Florence, and the entire convent of the Servite friars, which is much admired. At the same time it was proposed to make the great hall of the Signoria at Florence for the council of Frà Girolamo Savonarola, the famous preacher. Upon this a consultation was held with Lionardo da Vinci, Michelagnolo Buonarroti, then a youth, Giuliano da S. Gallo, Baccio d'Agnolo and Simone del Pollajuolo, called Cronaca, who was a devoted friend and adherent of Savanorola. After many discussions it was agreed that the hall should be made as it has always stood, until its restoration in our own day, which will be referred to afterwards. The charge of the entire work was given to Cronaca, as an able artist and the friend of Savonarola. He carried it out with diligence and expedition, showing great ingenuity in making the roof, as the building is very large in every dimension.[1] He then made the framework of the roof, which is thirty-eight braccia from wall to wall, of several beams dovetailed together, because it was not possible to find beams of the requisite size. Whereas there is usually a single king post to each pair of principals, these have three each, a large one in the middle and two queen posts at the sides. The rafters are long in proportion, and so are the braces and struts, and the struts of the queen posts thrust against the rafters, on the side of the wall, and against the king post in the centre. I will describe how this framework is constructed, because it is very well managed, and I have seen drawings made to be sent to various places. The principals were placed six braccia apart, and the roof being very soon put on, the ceiling was constructed of wood divided into compartments, eight braccia square, framed with a cornice and a few members, a plane surface being formed of the size of the beams to bear the intersections and corners of the ceiling. The two ends of the hall were eight braccia out of the square, and as Cronaca did not wish to increase the thickness of the walls, as he might have done, to bring it to the square, he followed the walls up to the roof, making three large windows at each end. When completed, the hall was found to be too dark owing to its extraordinary

[1] It was done in 1495.

size, being as broad as it is long, and somewhat dwarfed in height; indeed, entirely out of proportion. They endeavoured, without much success, to improve this by adding two windows in the middle of the east side and four on the west. As a finishing touch, executed with great speed at the request of the citizens, they made on the level of the brickwork a wooden gallery round the walls of that breadth and three braccia high, with seats and balustrading in front, upon which all the magistrates of the city were to sit. In the middle of the east front is a more elevated seat for the gonfaloniere of justice and the governors, with two doors on either side, one leading to the Segreto, and the other to the Specchio.[1] Opposite, on the west side, was an altar for Mass, with a picture by Frà Bartolommeo, as has been said, and beside it the pulpit for prayer. The middle of the floor was occupied by rows of benches for the citizens, and in the middle of the surrounding platform were six steps leading up, for the use of the ushers to collect votes. The errors of this hall, then much admired for the speed with which it was made, and for many good ideas, have come to light in the course of time, such as its lowness, darkness, dulness, and being out of the square. But Cronaca and the others ought to be excused, because the work was done so quickly, the citizens wishing to adorn the place with paintings and a gilded ceiling, while no greater hall had till then been made in Italy, although that of the palace of S. Marco at Rome, that of the Vatican built by Pius II. and Innocent VIII., that of the castle of Naples, those of the palaces of Milan, Urbino, Venice and Padua, are very large. After this Cronaca made a large staircase, six braccia broad, doubling on itself twice, to ascend to the hall, decorated with macigno, pilasters, Corinthian capitals and double cornices, with arches of the same stone, barrel vaulting, mixed columns in the windows and capitals of carved marble. Although this work was much admired, it would have been more so if the staircase had not turned out badly, being too steep, for it could have been made easier, as it was in the time of Duke Cosimo, in the same space, by Giorgio Vasari, opposite the one of Cronaca. Here the ascent is easy, almost like going on a level. This work, like all carried out under Duke Cosimo, and like his rule, has proved ingenious and of great judgment, no expense being spared, all the fortifications, and public and private structures corresponding with the greatness of his mind, being at once useful and beautiful. Con-

[1] Segreto, where the votes were counted; Specchio, where the register of debtors to the commune was kept.

sidering that the body of this hall is the largest, most magnificent
and beautiful in Europe, it was decided to repair its defects,
making it the most ornate building in Italy from the designs of
Giorgio Vasari of Arezzo. Accordingly, it was raised to a height
of twelve braccia above the old walls, the distance from floor
to ceiling being thirty-two braccia; the corbels bearing the roof,
made by Cronaca, were restored and replaced in a new arrangement, the old ceiling was repaired, being ordinary and simple,
quite unworthy of the hall, with rich cornices full of carving
and all gilt, with thirty-nine pictures in squares, circles and
octagons, the majority being of nine braccia each, and some
more. They contain oil-paintings of figures, the largest of seven
or eight braccia, representing the honours, victories and notable
achievements of the city and lordship of Florence from the
beginning, notably the war of Pisa and Siena, with a quantity
of other things which it would take too long to relate. A space
of sixty braccia on each of the side walls has been left for the
insertion of three scenes in each, corresponding to the floor,
allowing room for seven pictures on each side, treating of the
wars of Pisa and Siena. These divisions are so large that no
greater ones have ever been allowed for paintings, whether
ancient or modern. They are adorned with large stones joined
to the roof, and on the north side the duke has made a construction of columns, pilasters and niches full of marble statues, begun
and completed by Baccio Bandinelli. This apartment serves as
a public audience-chamber, as will be related hereafter. Opposite
there is to be another similar façade with a fountain throwing
up water, and a rich ornamentation of columns and marble and
bronze statues, to be carried out by Ammanato, the sculptor
and architect. The raising of the roof has made the hall roomy
and given it sufficient light, through the heightening of the old
windows and the addition of three large ones at each end, looking
out on the corridor, forming a loggia inside the hall and on the
side above the work of Bandinelli, having a fine outlook over
the piazza. But a more lengthy description of the hall and other
improvements in the palace will be given in another place. I will
now say that if Cronaca and the other clever artists who designed
it could return to life, I do not think they would recognise the
palace, the hall, or anything there. The hall, where it is rect-
angular, is ninety braccia by thirty-eight, without the work of
Bandinelli and Ammanato.

But to return to Cronaca. In the last years of his life he
became so infatuated over Frà Girolamo Savonarola that he

would speak of nothing else. At length, at the age of fifty-five, he died of a rather protracted disease, and was honourably buried in the church of S. Ambruogio at Florence in 1509. Not long after the following epitaph was written by M. Gio. Battista Strozzi:

> *Vivo e mille anni e mille ancora,*
> *Merce de' vivi miei palazzi e tempi*
> *Bella Roma, vivra l'alma mia Flora.*

Cronaca had a brother called Matteo, who studied sculpture and was with Antonio Rossellino the sculptor. Possessing a good intelligence, he designed well and was skilful in working marble, but left no finished work because death removed him at the age of nineteen, so that he could not fulfil his early promise.

DOMENICO PULIGO, Painter of Florence
(1492 – 1527)

IT is remarkable that many, by dint of continual practice in colouring, aided by natural instinct or by the habit of a good style adopted without deliberate purpose or design, produce works that frequently approach excellence, and although such artists are in no respect great, yet they compel admiration and praise. There are many instances of this among our painters, and those produce the most vivacious and perfect results who naturally possess a good style and who study incessantly. This gift of Nature is so powerful that, however much it may be obscured and overlaid by study, it is evident at the first glance at the work, all the parts being excellent and striking, such as we are accustomed to see in the minutest details of the productions of those who are reputed the greatest. Experience has proved the truth of this in our own day in the work of Domenico Puligo, painter of Florence, in whose works instances of what has been said may be clearly discerned. While Ridolfo di Domenico Ghirlandajo was producing several paintings in Florence, as will be said, he kept a number of youths in his workshop engaged in painting, following his father's practice. This led to a competition which produced several excellent masters, some in portraits, some in working in fresco, some in tempera and in the ready painting of cloth. Ridolfo gave them pictures, panels, canvases to do, sending a great quantity to England, Germany and Spain, to his great advantage. His pupils, Baccio Gotti and Toto del Nunziata, went, one to King Francis of France and the other to the King of England, who asked for them, having previously seen their works. Two other pupils remained for many years with Ridolfo, as, although they had many demands from merchants and others in Spain and Hungary, they would never leave the delights of their native land, despite promises and money, and indeed they had more work there than they could deal with.

One of them was Antonio del Ceraiuolo of Florence, who had been for many years with Lorenzo di Credi, and had there learned to imitate Nature so well that he did portraits with the greatest facility, although he had not much design. I have seen some of his heads, for example, with crooked noses, one lip small and the other large, and other deformities, yet they are good likenesses, because he seized the expression. On the other hand, many excellent masters have made portraits artistically perfect, but not at all resembling those they are supposed to represent. To speak the truth, those who make portraits ought to endeavour to catch the likeness without caring whether the figure is perfect. When they are like and beautiful also, then the works may be styled remarkable and the artists excellent. This Antonio, besides several portraits, painted many panels in Florence, but for the sake of brevity I will only mention two. One is in S. Jacopo tra' Fossi at the corner of the Alberti, representing a Crucifixion with St. Mary Magdalene and St. Francis[1]; the other is a St. Michael weighing souls, in the Nunziata. The other of the two was Domenico Puligo, the best of them all in design and a more charming and graceful colourist. He rendered his painting soft without dyeing his works or making them crude, causing the distances to recede gradually as if veiled by a mist, thus endowing his productions with relief and grace. Although the outlines of his figures gradually vanish so that they cannot be exactly determined, yet the expression of his heads and his colouring give pleasure, and he always adopted the same style, causing his works to be valued while he lived. Passing by the pictures and portraits which he did while in Ridolfo's workshop, some of which were sent abroad, while some remained in the city, I will only speak of those which he did when he was rather the friend and competitor of Ridolfo than his pupil, and of those done when he was the friend of Andrea del Sarto, who was never so happy as when Domenico was in his workshop learning of him, as he showed him his

[1] Now in the corridor between the Uffizi and Pitti Galleries.

things and instructed him how to avoid the faults and errors committed by those who never take others into their confidence. For these, by trusting too much to their own judgment, incur the blame of all on the completion of their works rather than correct them by the advice of their friends.

One of Domenico's first works was a very beautiful picture of Our Lady for M. Agnolo della Stufa, who has it at his abbey of Capalona in the territory of Arezzo, and who greatly values it for the excellence of its workmanship and the beauty of its colouring. Domenico painted a Madonna of no less beauty for M. Agnolo Niccolini, now Archbishop of Pisa and cardinal. It is in his house in Florence at the corner of the Pazzi. He did yet another of equal size and beauty, which is now in the possession of Filippo dell' Antella in Florence. In another of about three braccia Domenico did a full-length Madonna with the Child on her knees, a little St. John and another head. This is considered one of his best works, the colouring being very sweet. It is now in the possession of M. Filippo Spini, treasurer of the illustrious Prince of Florence, a magnificent nobleman, who is very fond of painting. Among the numerous portraits by Domenico, all beautiful and good likenesses, the finest is that of Monsignore M. Piero Carnesecchi, then a handsome youth, for whom he did other pictures, all beautiful and executed with great care. He also drew a portrait of Barbara of Florence, a notorious and beautiful courtezan of the time, beloved of many for her beauty and good manners, and because she was a good musician and sang divinely. But Domenico's best work was a large picture of life-size representing the Virgin with angels and children, and St. Bernard writing. It is now in the possession of Gio. Gualberto del Giocondo and M. Niccolo, his brother, canon of S. Lorenzo in Florence. Domenico did many other pictures for private houses, notably some of Cleopatra causing an asp to bite her breast and Lucretia killing herself with a dagger. Some of his portraits and many beautiful paintings are at the Pinti gate in the house of Giulio Scali, an excellent judge in artistic matters and in all the other principal professions. Domenico did a panel for Francesco del Giocondo for his chapel in the principal tribune of the church of the Servites at Florence, representing St. Francis receiving the stigmata. The colouring is very soft and beautiful, the work being very carefully finished. About the tabernacle of the Sacrament in the church of Cestello he did two angels in fresco,[1] and for the picture of a chapel in

---

[1] These are by Domenico Ghirlandaio.

the same church he did a Madonna and Child, St. John the Baptist, St. Bernard and other saints.[1] The monks of the place, being very pleased with these works, employed him to paint the vision of Count Hugh,[2] who built the seven abbeys, in a cloister of their abbey of Settimo, outside Florence. Not long after Il Puligo painted a Madonna and Child espousing St. Catherine and St. Peter Martyr, in a tabernacle at the corner of the via Mozza. In an oratory near Anghiari he did a Deposition from the Cross, which may be numbered among his best works. But he was more accustomed to doing Madonnas, portraits and other heads than large works, spending almost all his time on the former. If he had studied art laboriously, and not been led away by the pleasures of the world, he would doubtless have made much profit in painting, especially as his close friend Andrea del Sarto helped him in design and with advice, so that many of his works are well drawn and beautifully coloured. But Domenico would not take pains, and he worked rather for gain than glory, so that he made no further progress. He loved to frequent the society of frivolous people, musicians and women, and frequently indulged in amours. He died in 1527 at the age of fifty-two, having taken the plague in the house of one of his mistresses. His colours are so good and so harmoniously laid on that this constitutes his chief title to praise. Among his pupils was Domenico Beceri of Florence,[3] who, by the finish of his colouring, produced good works.

ANDREA DA FIESOLE, Sculptor, and other Fiesolans
(1465 – 1526)

IT being as necessary for sculptors to be skilful with the chisel as it is for painters to manipulate colours, it frequently happens that many who work excellently in clay cannot produce any perfect work in marble, though, on the contrary, many do good work in marble without any better design than some idea of

[1] Done about 1525.

[2] Hugh, Marquis of Brandenburg, accompanied his master, the Emperor Otto III., to Italy. He was appointed the Emperor's vicar in Tuscany. One day, when hunting, he lost himself in a forest, and came upon some black, misshapen men tormenting others. These they told him were lost souls and he would suffer a like fate if he did not repent. In great fear he returned to Florence, sold all his property and founded seven abbeys—the Badia of Florence, Bon Solazzo, Arezzo, Poggibonsi, Verrucha di Pisa, Città di Castello, and Settimo.—*Villani*, bk. iv. chap. 2.

[3] Possibly Domenico di Jacopo, called Beco.

good style. They imitate things which please their judgment, and when they know them thoroughly they reproduce them. It is all but marvellous to see some sculptors, who can hardly draw at all, complete good works, as was the case with Andrea di Piero di Marco Ferrucci, sculptor of Fiesole. In his early childhood he learned the principles of sculpture from Francesco di Simone Ferrucci, sculptor of Fiesole, and although he only learned to carve foliage at first, he gradually acquired such skill that before long he began to do figures. Having a resolute and quick hand, he worked in marble with a natural judgment and skill, as if he had known design. However, he studied art more seriously later on under Michele Maini, another sculptor of Fiesole.

This Michele did the marble St. Sebastian in the Minerva at Rome, then so much admired. Being taken to work at Imola, Andrea did a chapel in macigno in the Innocenti, which was much praised. After this he went to Naples, being summoned thither by Antonio di Giorgio da Settignano, the illustrious engineer and architect of King Ferrante. Antonio was in such credit with this monarch that he not only directed all the structures of the kingdom, but all the most important affairs of that state. When Antonio reached Naples he did many things in the castle of S. Martino and other places in the city for the king. When he died, his obsequies were not those of an architect, but a king, twenty pairs of mutes accompanying him to the tomb. Andrea left Naples, recognising that the country was not made for him, and returned to Rome, where he remained for some time, working and studying art. Returning to Tuscany, he did the marble chapel in the church of S. Jacopo at Pistoia, containing the font, which he executed with great diligence, including all its decorations. On the wall of the chapel he did two life-size figures in half-relief of St. John baptising Christ, beautifully executed in good style. At the same time he did other small works which I need not mention. Although these works show more skill than art, yet they exhibit remarkable resolution and good taste. Indeed, if such artists added a thorough knowledge of design to their skill and judgment, they would surpass the excellent designers who scratch their marble and painfully maltreat it through want of knowing how to use their tools with the requisite skill. In the church of the Vescovado of Fiesole Andrea next did a marble bas-relief, placed between the two flights leading to the upper choir, with certain scenes and three figures in relief. In S. Girolamo at Fiesole he did a marble bas-relief built into the middle of the church. Becoming known by the fame of these works, Andrea was employed by the wardens of S. Maria del Fiore, at the time when Cardinal Giulio de' Medici governed Florence, to make the statue of an Apostle, four braccia high, for that church, four others like it being allotted to Benedetto da Maiano, Jacopo Sansovino, Baccio Bandinelli and Michelagnolo Buonarroti respectively. The statues were to be twelve in number, to occupy the place of the twelve Apostles painted by Lorenzo di Bicci.[1] Andrea executed his [2] with better skill and judgment than design, and if he did not win as much praise as the others, he earned the name of a master of considerable merit and skill. From this time, therefore, he was continually employed on that church, and did the head of Marsilio Ficino,[3] which may be seen inside the door leading to the Canonicate. He also did a marble fountain,[4] which was sent to the King of Hungary, and brought him great honour. He did a marble tomb, sent to Gran in Hungary, containing a finely executed Madonna, with other figures. The Cardinal of Gran [5] was afterwards buried in it. Andrea sent two marble angels in relief to Volterra; and for Marco del Nero of Florence he made a wooden crucifix of life-size, which is now in the church of S. Felicita in Florence. He did a smaller one for the company of the Assumption in Florence. Andrea was also fond of architecture, and was the master of Mangone, stone-cutter and architect, who afterwards built a number of palaces and other structures of considerable merit at Rome. In his old age Andrea only attacked minor works, rather because he enjoyed a quiet life than for any other cause. He was commissioned by Madonna Antonia Vespucci to do the tomb of M. Antonio Strozzi, her husband, but not being able to work much by himself, Andrea assigned two angels to his pupil Maso Boscoli of Fiesole, who afterwards did many works in Rome and elsewhere. The Madonna is by Silvio Cosini of Fiesole, but it was not set up at once when finished, in 1522, because of Andrea's death, who was buried by the company of the Scalzo in the Servites.

On the setting up of the Madonna and the completion of the Strozzi tomb, Silvio followed the art of sculpture with remarkable ardour, doing many graceful works in a good style. He has surpassed many, especially in curious grotesques, as we

[1] They were by his son, Bicci di Lorenzo.
[2] A St. Andrew, done in 1512.
[3] In 1521. [4] In 1517.
[5] Thomas Bakocz, who died in 1521.

may see in the sacristy of Michelagnolo Buonarroti in the marble capitals of some pilasters of the tombs, containing beautifully perforated masks. In the same place he did some fine friezes of laughing masks. Buonarroti, perceiving Silvio's genius and skill, made him begin some trophies for the completion of the tomb, but they were left unfinished, with other things, owing to the siege of Florence. Silvio did a tomb of the utmost possible beauty for the Minerbetti in their chapel in the screen of the church of S. Maria Novella; the sarcophagus is carved with targes, scimitars and other curious things, the design being admirable. When Silvio was at Pisa in 1528, he did an angel fainting upon a column at the high altar of the Duomo, to match that of Tribolo, so like it that they might be by the same hand. In the church of Montenero, near Livorno, he did a marble bas-relief of two figures for the Jesuit friars, and at Volterra he did the tomb of M. Raffaello of Volterra, a very learned man, introducing his portrait on the marble sarcophagus, with other ornaments and figures.

During the siege of Florence Niccolo Capponi, a famous citizen, died at Castelnuovo della Garfagnana, on his return from Genoa, where he had been ambassador for the republic to the emperor.[1] They sent in great haste to Silvio to make a death mask, to be copied in marble, and he did a very fine one in wax. At this time Silvio was living at Pisa with all his family, and was a member of the company of the Misericordia, who there accompany condemned men on their way to execution, and being sacristan, a most strange idea occurred to him. One night he took the body of a man who had been hanged the preceding day out of its grave, and after dissecting it in the interests of art, being fanciful and perhaps believing in charms and such follies, he flayed the body and made himself a leather jerkin of the skin, supposing it to possess some great virtue, and wore it for some time over his shirt without anyone knowing of the matter. But one day he confessed all to a good father, and following the priest's injunctions, he took off the jerkin and put it back in the grave. I might relate many similar stories of him, but I do not because they do not concern our history. His first wife dying at Pisa, he went away to Carrara, and while busy there over some things he took another wife. Not long after he took her to Genoa, and in the service of Prince Doria made a fine coat-of-arms over the door of his palace, and many stucco ornaments about the palace, from designs by Perino del Vaga,

[1] 18 October, 1529.

the painter. He also made a fine marble bust of the Emperor Charles V. But it was not his custom to remain long in one place, for he was a restless man. Becoming tired of Genoa, he set out for France. But he turned back before reaching Monsanese and stopped at Milan, doing some scenes, figures and many ornaments in the Duomo, to his great praise. At length he died there at the age of forty-five. He had a fine fanciful genius, and was dexterous in everything, knowing how to complete with diligence whatever he began to do. He was fond of composing sonnets and of improvising, while in his early youth he adopted the profession of arms. If only he had confined himself to sculpture and design he would have had no equal, and as he surpassed his master, Andrea Ferruzzi, he might have surpassed many others reputed excellent.

Another sculptor named Il Cicilia, also of Fiesole, flourished at the same time, and was a man of great skill. The church of S. Jacopo in Campo Corbolini, Florence, has a tomb by him for M. Luigi Tornabuoni, knight,[1] which is much admired, chiefly because he made the escutcheon upon the horse's head as if to show, as the ancients relate, that the shape of the shield was derived from the horse's head.

At the same period Antonio da Carrara, a most rare sculptor, did three statues at Palermo for the Duke of Montelione of the Pignatella house, a Neapolitan, and Viceroy of Sicily, namely three women in various postures, which were placed upon three altars of the Duomo of Montelione in Calabria. He did some marble bas-reliefs in Palermo for the same. He left a son, who is now a sculptor, not less excellent than his father.

VINCENZIO DA S. GIMIGNANO and TIMOTEO DA URBINO,[2] Painters.

(1492 – 1529; 1469 – 1523)

AFTER Andrea da Fiesole I must write the Life of two excellent painters, Vincenzio da S. Gimignano of Tuscany and Timoteo da Urbino. Vincenzio, whose portrait is given above, lived about the same time as Timoteo, and both were pupils and friends of Raphael. Vincenzio worked with many others for Raphael at the papal loggia, and did so well that he won great praise from his master and the others. Being on this account sent to work

---

[1] Done in 1515.   [2] Vincenzo Tamagni and Timoteo Viti.

in the Borgo, opposite the palace of M. Gio. Battista dall' Aquila, he did a frieze on the front representing the nine Muses, with Apollo in the midst and some lions above, the Pope's device, which are considered very beautiful. Vincenzio was a man of great diligence, and his colouring was soft, his figures of pleasing aspect; indeed, he always endeavoured to imitate the style of Raphael. We see this in the same Borgo, opposite the palace of the cardinal of Ancona, on the wall of a house built by M. Gio. Antonio Battiferro of Urbino, who, being a great friend of Raphael, obtained from him the design for this wall, and in the court procured many advantages and great revenues by this means. In this design, carried out later by Vincenzio, Raphael represented the Cyclops forging the thunderbolts of Jove, and in another part Vulcan forging the arrows of Cupid, with some fine nudes, and other beautiful stories and statues, an allusion to the patron's name. On a façade on the piazza of S. Luigi de' Francesi at Rome Vincenzio did the Death of Cæsar, a Triumph of Justice, and a cavalry battle on a frieze, executed with great vigour and diligence. Between the windows and near the roof he did some excellent Virtues. On the façade of the Epifani, behind the court of Pompey, and near the Campo di Fiore, he did the Magi following the Star, and many other things for the city, the air and situation of which do much to incite men to produce great works, for experience shows that the same man does not exhibit equal excellence in every place, but some do better and some worse according to the nature of the place. While Vincenzio was in such repute at Rome, the ruin and sack of the unhappy city, once mistress of the nations, took place in the year 1527. In great grief he returned to his native S. Gimignano. His misfortunes and the change of air worked such havoc that I cannot mention the works he did there, because I cannot praise them as I did those produced in Rome, but we see the injurious effects of his change of abode, which may also be remarked in Schizzone, a companion of his, who did some much-admired things in the Borgo, in the Campo Santo at Rome, and in S. Stefano degli Indiani. But by the wickedness of the soldiers he was obliged to renounce the arts, and shortly afterwards lost his life. Vincenzio died in his native S. Gimignano, having enjoyed little happiness since his departure from Rome.

Timoteo, painter of Urbino, was the son of Bartolommeo della Vite, a citizen of decent standing, and of Calliope, daughter of Maestro Antonio Alberto of Ferrara, a meritorious painter

in his day, as his works in Urbino and elsewhere show. While
Timoteo was still a child he lost his father, and was left to the
care of his mother, a good omen, Calliope being one of the nine
Muses, patrons of painting and poetry. Being carefully brought
up by his prudent mother and introduced by her to the study of
the arts and design, the youth entered the world while Raphael
was flourishing. He first studied the goldsmith's art,[1] and was
called by M. Pier Antonio, his elder brother, then studying at
Bologna, to that most noble city, that he might study under
some good master that art for which he seemed adapted by
Nature. He lived some time in Bologna, in great honour, receiving
every courtesy from the noble M. Francesco Gombruti, and
associating with the choicest spirits. Becoming known in a few
months as a youth of judgment, and being more drawn to painting than the goldsmith's craft, for he had proved his skill in
making excellent portraits of his friends and others, his brother,
acting on the advice of friends and his own judgment, took the
boy away from his file and chisel and let him devote himself to
design. Greatly rejoiced at this, Timoteo studied hard, copying
all the best works of the city, and maintaining close relations
with the painters. He thus made marvellous progress daily,
learning every difficulty, without the instruction of any particular
master. Becoming devoted to his work, he learned many secrets
merely by watching painters mix their colours and wield their
brush. Guided by himself and by the hand of Nature, he began
boldly to colour, adopting a charming style very like that of the
new Apelles, his compatriot, although he had only seen a few
things by him at Bologna. Guided by his intelligence and good
judgment, he painted on panels and walls, and feeling that he
had succeeded well in comparison with other painters, he took
heart to continue his studies, so that in process of time he
established his footing and aroused great expectations. Returning
home [2] at the age of twenty-six, he stayed there for some months,
giving proofs of his skill. He did the first picture of the Madonna
in the Duomo, containing, besides the Virgin, St. Crescentius and
St. Vitalis at the altar of S. Croce, and a small angel seated on
the ground playing the viola with a truly angelic grace and
childish simplicity, executed with art and judgment.[3] He then
did another for the high altar of the Trinità with St. Appolonia,
on the left of the altar. By these works and others his fame
spread abroad, and being urgently summoned to Rome by

[1] He studied under Francia 1490-5.　　　[2] In 1495.
[3] Now in the Brera, Milan.

Raphael, he went thither very willingly, being received with a graciousness that was as characteristic of Raphael as his excellence in art. In rather more than a year Timoteo profited greatly by working with Raphael, not only in art but in pocket, putting by a considerable sum of money. He helped the master with the sibyls in the church of la Pace, in the lunettes on the right, a work so highly valued by all painters. Some say they remember having seen him work there, and this is borne out by the cartoons still in the possession of his successors. He also did the catafalque and bier in the Scuola of St. Catherine of Siena, which are so much admired, though some over-patriotic Sienese attribute them to others.[1] But they are clearly his from the grace and softness of the colouring observable in his other works in that noble school of excellent painters. Although Timoteo occupied such a good position at Rome he could not, like many others, bear to be so far from home, and being called back by reports from his friends and the prayers of his aged mother, he returned to Urbino, to the sorrow of Raphael, who loved him for his good qualities.

Not long after Timoteo took a wife, and, finding himself honoured in his country, he resolved never to leave it again, notwithstanding letters of Raphael recalling him to Rome, especially as he began to have children. This did not prevent him from doing many works in Urbino and the neighbourhood. At Forli he painted a chapel in conjunction with Girolamo Genga, his friend and compatriot. He then did a panel by himself, which was sent to Città di Castello, another going to the Cagliesi. He did some things in fresco at Castel Durante which are really admirable, like all his other works, which show him to be an artist possessing a light touch in figures, landscapes and every branch of painting. At Urbino he did the chapel of St. Martin in the Duomo at the instance of Bishop Arrivabene of Mantua,[2] in conjunction with Genga; the altar-picture and the middle part of the chapel are entirely by his hand. In the same church he painted a Magdalene dressed in a short cloak, her hair falling to the ground, so true to life that the wind seems to be moving it, while her divine face reveals the love she bore to her Master.[3] S. Agata contains another panel by him with meritorious figures, and in S. Bernardino, outside the city, he did that much-admired Annunciation[4] on the right of the altar of the Bonaventuri, nobles of Urbino.

---

[1] To Pacchiarotto or Peruzzi.   [2] Bishop of Urbino, who died 1504.
[3] Now in the Bologna Gallery.   [4] Brera, Milan.

The Virgin is standing, full of beauty and grace, her hands joined and her eyes raised to heaven. In the air in a circle of glory stands a Child, one foot resting on the Holy Spirit in the form of a dove, and holding in his left hand an orb, symbolic of the government of the world, the other hand being raised in benediction. On the right of the Child is an angel, pointing him out to the Madonna. On the right of the Virgin stands the Baptist is his camel's skin, which is cut away to show the nude, and on the left a St. Sebastian bound to a tree, beautifully executed and in fine relief. In the court of the princes of Urbino, in a secret chamber, there are a beautiful Apollo and two Muses, half-length figures, by his hand. He did a number of pictures for those lords, and many beautiful chamber decorations. In conjunction with Genga he afterwards painted some horse armour, which was sent to the King of France, representing animals which seemed actually possessed of life and motion. He also did triumphal arches, resembling those of the ancients, for the wedding of the Duchess Leonora to the Duke Francesco Maria,[1] which gave great satisfaction, so that he became a member of the duke's household for many years, receiving a respectable salary. Timoteo was a powerful designer, but excelled in his soft and lovely colouring. He possessed a happy, joyous and festive disposition, was active in body, and keen and witty in speech. Fond of all manner of instruments, he preferred to play the lyre, improvising with extraordinary grace. He died in 1524, in his fifty-fourth year, leaving his country enriched by his name and ability, but in sorrow for his death. He left some incompleted works at Urbino, which were finished by others, who only served to make his ability appear the greater by comparison. Some of his designs are in my book; I obtained them from M. Giovanni Maria, his son, and they are certainly beautiful and worthy of praise. They comprise a pen-and-ink sketch of Giuliano de' Medici the Magnificent, done while he was visiting the court of Urbino in that most famous academy, a *Noli me tangere*, and a St. John the Evangelist sleeping, while Christ is praying in the Garden, all very beautiful.

[1] In 1509.

ANDREA DAL MONTE S. SAVINO, Sculptor and Architect
(1460 – 1529)

ALTHOUGH Andrea di Domenico Contucci dal Monte S. Savino
was the son of a poor labourer, and brought up to watch cattle,
yet his ideas were so lofty, his genius so rare, and his spirit so
ready in dealing with the difficulties of architecture and perspective, that there was no better or more subtle intellect than
his at that time, rendering all doubtful questions plain, so that
he may be considered unique in his age. He is said to have been
born in 1460, and kept cattle like Giotto, drawing in the sand
and on the ground the beasts which he was watching. One
day, as he was thus engaged, a Florentine citizen passed by,
said to have been Simone Vespucci, then podestà of the Monte,
and seeing the child intent on drawing and modelling clay,
called him, and, perceiving his natural talent, asked permission
of his father to take him away, promising to put the boy to
study design, in order to see if his natural inclination could
not be assisted by education. Domenico consented, and Simone
on returning to Florence put the boy with Antonio del Pollajuolo, so that in a few years Andrea became an excellent master.
There is still a cartoon done by him there, in Simone's house on
the Ponte Vecchio, of Christ at the Column, very carefully
finished. There are also terra-cotta heads of the Emperors Galba
and Nero, wonderfully copied from ancient medals. They served
to decorate a chimney-piece, but the Galba is now in Giorgio
Vasari's house at Arezzo. While still in Florence Andrea did a
terra-cotta panel of St. Laurence, and other saints and small
scenes, for the church of S. Agata of Monte Sansovino, of
wonderful workmanship. Not long after he did a similar one of
the Assumption with St. Agatha, St. Lucy and St. Romuald; it
was subsequently glazed by the della Robbia. Turning to sculpture, he did two capitals of pilasters in his youth for il Cronaca,
for the sacristy of S. Spirito,[1] which brought him great fame,
and led to his being employed to make the anteroom between
the sacristy and the church. The place being narrow, Andrea
had to display his resources. He constructed two rows of six
round columns in macigno of the Corinthian order, laying the
architraves, friezes and cornices upon them, and making a
barrel vault of the same stone with richly and variously carved
compartments, a much-admired novelty. It is true that the

[1] In 1490.

work would be better if the compartments forming the divisions of the squares and circles had been in a line with the columns, a thing which it would have been easy to do. Some of his old friends, however, have informed me that he defended this, saying that he had copied the Rotonda at Rome, where the ribs from the circular opening in the centre form the compartments, and then gradually diminish, and that the ribs there are not in a line with the columns. He added that if the builder of the Rotonda, which is the best designed and proportioned fane in existence, did not take these things into account in a vault of greater size and importance, it was of even less importance on a smaller scale. However, many artists, and Michelagnolo among them, are of opinion that the Rotonda was built by three architects, the first carrying it up to the cornice above the columns, the second doing from the cornice upwards, containing the more slender windows, because this second portion differs from the lower part, the vaulting not corresponding with the lines of the divisions. The third is believed to have done the beautiful portico. Thus modern masters ought not to excuse themselves like Andrea. After this he was commissioned to do the chapel of the Sacrament in the same church by the Corbinelli family. He carried this out with great diligence, imitating Donato and other excellent artists in the bas-reliefs, not sparing any pains to win honour. For two niches on either side of a fine tabernacle he did statues of St. James and St. Matthew, rather more than a braccia high, so vigorous and good that they are flawless. So also are two angels in relief for the base of this work, the draperies being remarkably fine, as they are flying. In the middle is a little nude Christ of great charm. In the predella and above the tabernacle are some scenes of small figures, almost as delicate as if they had been painted with the brush. But the most remarkable thing is that the whole work is so well executed and joined that it seems to be of one piece. Much admired also is a large marble Pietà in half-relief on the front of the altar, with the Virgin and St. John weeping. The bronze grille of the chapel is of indescribable beauty, containing deer, the arms of the Corbinelli, which also decorate the bronze candelabra. The whole work is done without sparing any pains and with every conceivable consideration.

Andrea's name being spread abroad by these and other works, the King of Portugal asked for him from Lorenzo de' Medici the Magnificent, the elder, in whose garden he studied design, as I have said. Accordingly, Lorenzo sent him, and he did many works in sculpture and architecture for the king, notably a fine palace with four towers. A part of this building was painted from Andrea's designs and cartoons, for he drew beautifully, as his crayon-drawings and clever architectural sketches in our book prove. He also made an altar of carved wood for the king, with some prophets. He made a clay model for a marble representation of a victory of the king over the Moors.[1] Nothing of his is more striking than this, with the various postures and movements of the horses, the slaughter of the dead, and the fury of the soldiers in fighting. He also did a remarkable figure of St. Mark in marble. While with the king Andrea studied some curious and difficult questions of architecture in the style of the country to please the king. I have seen a book of these in the possession of his heirs at Monte Sansovino. They say that these are now in the hands of Andrea's pupil, Maestro Girolamo Lombardo, who was left to finish some things begun by his master. After spending nine years in Portugal, Andrea became tired of the service, and desiring to see Tuscany, his relations and friends, he determined to demand his *congé* from the king, for he had amassed a considerable sum of money. He obtained leave, though with difficulty, and returned to Florence, leaving someone to complete his unfinished works. Reaching Florence he began in 1500 a St. John baptising Christ, in marble, to be put over the door of S. Giovanni, facing the Misericordia; but he did not finish it, being all but compelled to go to Genoa. There he did two admirable figures in marble, a Christ and a Madonna or St. John.[2] The things left unfinished at Florence are still in the Opera of S. Giovanni.[3] Invited to Rome by Pope Julius II., he was commissioned to do two marble tombs in S. Maria del Popolo, one for Cardinal Ascanio Sforza and the other for Cardinal di Recanati, a near relation of the Pope.[4] He finished them with admirable beauty and polish, observing the rules and proportions of art. Here also is a Temperance holding an hour-glass in her hand, considered divine, indeed it is more like an antique than a modern work, and though there are others like it, yet it is superior to them in attitude and grace. A veil surrounding the figure is a miracle of lightness and beauty. For S. Agostino at Rome he did a marble St. Anne, holding the Virgin and a Christ, nearly of life-size, on a pilaster

---

[1] The capture of Ar-Zila in 1471. The representation is now in the convent of St. Mark near Coimbra.
[2] In 1503, now in S. Lorenzo.   [3] Completed by Vincenzo Danti.
[4] 1505-07.

in the middle of the church.[1] This occupies a very high place among modern works for the joy and natural behaviour of St. Anne and the divine beauty of the Virgin and Christ, unequalled for their delicacy and lightness, and they have inspired many sonnets and various compositions, affixed to the group. The friars have a book full of them, which I have seen with no little wonder. The praise is well deserved because the work cannot be too highly admired.

Andrea's fame having thus increased, Leo X. resolved to employ him to complete the carved marble decoration of the chamber of Our Lady in S. Maria at Loreto, begun by Bramante.[2] It consisted of four double projections at the corners, adorned with pilasters, with carved bases and capitals, resting upon a richly carved base, two and a half braccia high. Between the two pilasters was a large niche to hold seated figures, and a smaller niche above each of them. These, extending to the collarino of the capitals of the pilasters, formed a frieze of that height. Above these were placed the architrave, the frieze and the cornice, richly carved, surrounding the whole wall and jutting out above the four corners, forming two empty spaces in the middle front, the length of the room being greater than the breadth, so there was the same projection in the middle as at the corners, and there was a space of five braccia on either side of the larger and smaller niches. In this space there were two doors, one on either side, leading into the chapel, and a space of five braccia for a marble subject between the niches. The façade was similiar without the niches, and the height from the basement formed an altar in line with the corners of the pilasters and the corner niches. In the middle of this front was a space of the same breadth and height as those above and below. Above the altar there was a bronze grille opposite the altar inside, for hearing Mass, and to see the inside of the chamber and the altar of the Virgin. There were seven spaces in all, one over the grille, two on each side, and two above on either side of the altar of the Virgin, and eight large and eight small niches in addition, with smaller spaces for the arms of the Pope and the church.

Finding the work at this stage, Andrea filled the lower spaces with stories of the Virgin. He began at the side with her Nativity, and half finished it, the work being completed by Baccio Bandinelli. On the other side he began her Marriage, but it was also left unfinished, being completed as it is now after

[1] 1512. [2] He went to Loreto in 1513.

his death by Raffaello da Monte Lupo. On the front he did two small squares on either side of the grille, one of a Visitation and the other of the Virgin and Joseph going to be enrolled. These scenes were afterwards executed by Francesco da S. Gallo, then a youth. In the largest space Andrea did an Annunciation,[1] which was in the chamber, containing these marbles, of indescribable grace, the Virgin being intent on the salutation, and the angel kneeling seems not marble but truly celestial, as the *Ave Maria* issues from its lips. Two other angels in relief are in the company of Gabriel, one accompanying him and the other flying. Two more advance from behind a building, and seem alive, and resting on a marble cloud, almost completely perforated, are cherubs, sustaining God the Father, who is sending the Holy Spirit by a marble ray, which looks most natural. So also is the dove representing the Holy Spirit. A vase full of flowers in this work is of indescribable beauty and delicate carving, and indeed Andrea's achievement cannot be sufficiently praised in the angels' plumage, hair, graceful faces and draperies, and, in fact, everything. The holy place, which was a suitable abode for the Mother of the Son of God, could not receive a richer decoration in this world than that of the architecture of Bramante and the sculpture of Andrea Sansovino, and it would not be nearly so precious even if it consisted of the most costly oriental gems. Andrea spent an incredible amount of time upon this work, so that he could not finish other things begun by him. He had started on one of the sides a Nativity, with the shepherds and four angels singing, finishing them so well that they seem alive. But the story of the Magi above was finished by his pupil, Girolamo Lombardo, and others. At the back-end he directed that two large scenes should be made, one above the other, of the death of the Virgin, the Apostles carrying her to burial, four angels in the air, and many Jews endeavouring to steal the holy body. This was finished after the life of Andrea by Bologna, a sculptor.[2] Below this he arranged for a representation of the miracle of Loreto, of the way in which the chapel, which was Our Lady's chamber where she was born, was raised and saluted by the angels, and where she nursed her Son until he was twelve, remaining there after his death. It was first transported to Sclavonia, next to a wood in the territory of Ricanati, and lastly to its present site, where it is so highly reverenced and visited continually by all the Christian peoples. This story was carried out by Tribolo, a

[1] In 1523.   [2] Domenico Aimo, called Il Varignana of Bologna.

Florentine sculptor,[1] as will be related. Andrea also sketched the prophets for the niches, but only completed one, the others being finished by Girolamo Lombardo, and other sculptors, as will be related in the following Lives. But Andrea's own labours are the finest works in sculpture up to that time. The palace of the canons of that church was also continued by Andrea in accordance with the design of Bramante, commissioned by Pope Leo, but as Andrea left it unfinished the building was continued under Clement VII. by Antonio da S. Gallo and then by Giovanni Boccalino, architect, under the Very Rev. Cardinal di Carpi, until 1563.

While Andrea was engaged upon the chapel of the Virgin, the fortifications of Loreto and other things were made which received the warm commendation of the invincible Giovanni de' Medici, with whom Andrea was very intimate, having previously known him at Rome. Andrea, having four months of vacations in the year, while he was at Loreto, spent the time in agriculture at his native Monte, enjoying the quiet with his relations and friends. While spending the summer at Monte he built a convenient house for himself and bought much property. For the friars of St. Augustine there he built a cloister which, though small, is very well arranged. It is not square, because the friars wanted him to build on the old walls. However, Andrea made it a half-square, increasing the pilasters at the corners, which were out of proportion, to a proper measurement. For an oratory in the cloister called S. Antonio he designed a fine Doric door as well as the screen and pulpit of the church of S. Agostino. He also designed a small chapel for the friars on the way up to the spring towards the old Pieve, although they did not want it. At Arezzo he designed a house for M. Pietro, a skilful astrologer, and made a large and remarkable figure of King Porsenna for Montepulciano. But I have never seen it since the first time, and so I fear it has suffered some harm. For a German priest, a friend, he did a St. Roch of life-size, in terra cotta, and very beautiful. This priest had it placed in the church of Battifolle in the territory of Arezzo. It was Andrea's last sculpture. He also designed the staircase for the Vescovado at Arezzo, and for the Madonna delle Lagrime in that city, where he designed a lovely marble decoration with four figures each of four braccia, but this work was stopped by his death.[2] This took place at the age of sixty-eight, for he never could be idle, and in helping to remove some stakes he caught a chill, and the fever

[1] In 1523.   [2] The former work in 1524 and the latter in 1528.

augmenting daily, he died in 1529. The death of Andrea was a great grief to his country because of the honour which he did it, and because of the love he bore to his three sons and his daughters. Not long ago Muzio Cammillo, one of the three sons, followed him to the grave, to the grief of his friends and loss of his house, as he was a brilliant student of *belles lettres*.

Besides his skill in art, Andrea was a really distinguished man, who could converse excellently upon anything. His actions were wise and prudent; he was a friend of learned men and a philosopher. He devoted considerable study to cosmography, leaving drawings and notes on distances and measurements. He was of rather small stature, but well formed and strong. His hair was long and silky, his eyes clear, nose aquiline, skin white and ruddy, while he had a slight impediment in his speech. His pupils were Girolamo Lombardo, Simone Cioli of Florence already mentioned, Domenico dal Monte Sansavino, who died shortly after him, Lionardo del Tasso of Florence, who made a wooden St. Sebastian over his tomb in S. Ambruogio in Florence and the marble slab of the nuns of S. Chiara, and Jacopo Sansovino of Florence, called after his master, of whom I shall speak at length. Architecture and sculpture are under a great debt to Andrea, who devised many rules for measurement and methods for moving weights, while he displayed a diligence previously unknown, and his sculptures were executed with marvellous judgment, finish and skill.

BENEDETTO DA ROVEZZANO, Sculptor
(1474 – after 1552)

GREAT must be the suffering of those who, after producing some noteworthy thing, hope to enjoy it in their old age, and see it proved by other minds so that its perfections may appear, and who find themselves deprived of sight by bad fortune or some other cause, so that they are unable to see the faults or perfection of those whom they know to be practising their profession. It must be even more sad for them to listen to the praises of new men, not from feelings of envy, but because they themselves can no longer judge whether the fame is deserved or not. Such was the fate of Benedetto, whose Life I am now writing to show the world his skill and ability and his care in carving marble. One of his earliest works in Florence was a chimneypiece of macigno, in the house of Pier Francesco Borgherini, on which he carved capitals, friezes, and many other ornaments, diligently perforated. There is another chimney by him in the house of M. Bindo Altoviti and a water conduit of macigno with other things very delicately worked, the architectural part being designed by Jacopo Sansovino, then a youth. In 1512 Benedetto was employed to do a marble tomb with rich ornamentation in the principal chapel of the Carmine at Florence for Piero Soderini, sometime gonfaloniere of the city. He executed this with incredible diligence, the foliage, the dead man, and other figures. A pavilion of schist made like black cloth is wonderfully graceful, and looks like a beautiful smooth cloth rather than stone. In fine, all Benedetto's work here cannot be overpraised. As he practised architecture also, he repaired the house of M. Oddo Altoviti, patron and prior of S. Apostolo in Florence, making the principal door in marble, and above it the Altoviti arms in macigno, containing the lean wolf, so much in relief that it seems separated from the body of the arms, the flying creatures and other things about it looking like paper, not stone. Over the two chapels of M. Bindo Altoviti in the same church, where Giorgio Vasari of Arezzo painted a Conception in oils, he made the marble tomb for M. Oddo, surrounded by admirable foliage, the sarcophagus being equally fine. In competition with Jacopo Sansovino and Baccio Bandinelli he did one of the Apostles, four and a half braccia high, for S. Maria del Fiore, as already related.[1] This was St. John the Evangelist, a meritorious figure, executed with design and skill, and preserved in the Opera with the others. In the following year, 1515, the chiefs of the order of Vallombrosa proposed to translate the body of St. John Gualbert from the abbey of Passignano to the church of S. Trinità in Florence, an abbey of their order. They obtained a design for a chapel and tomb from Benedetto, which he began to execute, with a large number of life-size figures skilfully disposed in niches between pilasters full of delicately carved friezes and grotesques. Below these was to be a pedestal one and a half braccia high, with scenes from the saint's life and a number of other ornaments. He worked at this for ten years continuously, assisted by many sculptors, at a great cost to the congregation, completing it in the house of Il Guarlondo, a place near S. Salvi, outside the Croce gate, where the general of the order lived. When complete this work astonished Florence. But as marbles and other excellent works of men are the sport of

[1] Allotted in 1512.

fortune, discords arose among the monks on a change of governor, and the work was left unfinished until 1530, when the results of so much labour were so terribly mutilated by the soldiers during the war round Florence that the remains were sold by the monks for very little. Those who wish to see specimens should go to the Opera of S. Maria del Fiore, for which some pieces were bought by the wardens, as broken marble, not many years ago.[1] In truth, where concord and peace reign in monasteries and elsewhere, things may be successfully completed, but where ambition and discord are supreme, nothing can ever be accomplished, for the labours of the good and wise, which have taken one hundred years to produce, may be ruined in a day by the ignorant and foolish. Fate seems to will that the ignorant and those who delight in nothing of worth shall usually be in power and destroy everything, as Ariosto has very truthfully remarked of secular princes at the beginning of Canto XVII.[2]

To return to Benedetto. It was a sin that his labours and the money of the order should have been so unhappily wasted. He was the architect and director of the door and vestibule of the Badia of Florence and also of some chapels, among them that of St. Stephen, for the Pandolfini family. Benedetto was ultimately invited to England to serve the king, for whom he did many works in marble and bronze, notably his tomb.[3] Through the king's liberality he was enabled to pass the remainder of his life in ease. On returning to Florence, after he had finished a few small things, a dazzling of the eyes which had begun to trouble him in England came upon him again, caused, it is said, by standing too much over the fire in founding metals, or by other causes, which in a short time rendered him blind. Accordingly he gave up work in 1550, and only lived a few years after. He bore his affliction with Christian patience, thanking God for having first made provision for him so that he could live honourably on the proceeds of his labours. He was a courteous and accomplished man, fond of the society of men of ability. His portrait has been copied from one done when he was a young man by Agnolo di Donino. The original is in our book of designs, which contains some very well-drawn sheets of Benedetto, who deserves a place among eminent artists.

[1] The fragments are now in the Bargello, Florence.
[2] *Orlando Furioso*, Canto XVII. stanza 1.
[3] He began in 1524 the monument that Cardinal Wolsey had set up in Windsor. It was destroyed by order of Parliament in 1646, but the sarcophagus now holds the remains of Nelson, in the crypt of St. Paul's Cathedral.

BACCIO DA MONTELUPO, Sculptor, and RAFFAELLO, his Son
(1469 –?1535; c. 1505 – 1566)

How seldom people expect the idle to succeed in what they
undertake, yet, contrary to the opinion of many, Baccio da
Montelupo succeeded in learning the art of sculpture. In his
youth he cared for nothing but pleasure, thinking little of art,
in spite of the reproaches of his friends. But on arriving at years
of discretion, he suddenly recognised what a mistake he had
made. Shamed by those who surpassed him, he determined to
study carefully what he had hitherto avoided. This resolution
produced unexpected fruits, for by devoting all his energy to
art he became excellent, showing his skill in a hard stone chiselled
for the corner of the garden next the Pucci palace with the arms
of Leo X. supported by two children, executed in good style.
He did a Hercules for Pier Francesco de' Medici, and the art
of Porta S. Maria employed him to make a St. John the Evangelist in bronze. He obtained this in spite of considerable
opposition, as several masters did models in competition. His
figure was set up at the corner of S. Michele in Orto, opposite
the office, and it was very carefully finished.[1] It is said that
those who saw the framework and modelling of his sketch in
clay considered it a very beautiful work and recognised the
skill he had shown. The facility of his founding earned him a
reputation in that branch, and he became known as an excellent
master, while this figure is now in higher repute than ever among
artists. He carved in wood a life-size crucifix, doing countless
others for all Italy, among them one for the friars of S. Marco
at Florence over the choir door. They are all exceedingly graceful, though some are better than others, such as that of the
Murate at Florence, and a not inferior one in S. Pietro Maggiore.
He did a similar one for the monks of S. Fiora e Lucilla, who put
it over the high altar in their abbey at Arezzo; it is considered
the finest of all.

When Leo X. came to Florence, Baccio constructed a handsome triumphal arch of wood and clay between the Podestà
palace and the Badia, and he did several small things for private
houses, which are now lost. Becoming tired of Florence, he went
to Lucca, where he did some works in sculpture, but more in
architecture, notably the fine and well-composed church of
S. Paulino, the patron of the Lucchese, containing much decora-

[1] In 1515.

tion. He remained in the city until the eighty-eighth year of his age, and there died, being buried honourably in S. Paulino.

He had a contemporary named Agostino Milanese,[1] a sculptor and carver of considerable repute. He began the tomb of Gaston de Foix in S. Marta at Milan, still unfinished, containing several large completed figures and some only in the rough, with half-reliefs, not placed in position, and much foliage and trophies. He also completed another tomb in S. Francesco for the Biraghi, with six large figures and bas-reliefs at the bottom and other fine ornaments to bear witness to his skill.

Baccio left behind him a son Raffaello, among others, who practised sculpture, far surpassing his father. In his youth he began by working in clay, wax and bronze, acquiring a name for himself. Being taken, with many others, by Antonio da S. Gallo to Loreto, to finish the decoration of the rooms left by Andrea Sansovino, Raffaello completed the Marriage of the Virgin, begun by Andrea, in a good style, partly from Andrea's sketches and partly from his own fantasy, earning a place among the best artists then engaged there. On the completion of this, Michelagnolo undertook, by the order of Clement VII., to finish the new sacristy and library of S. Lorenzo at Florence. Knowing Raffaello's skill, he employed him in that work, getting him to do a marble St. Damian, designed by himself, now in the said sacristy, a beautiful work, much admired by everyone. After Clement's death Raffaello served Duke Alessandro de' Medici, who was then building the citadel of Prato, making for him the arms of the Emperor Charles V. in grey stone on a principal part of the bulwarks outside, supported by two nude Victories of life-size and much admired.[2] On another bulwark towards the city on the south, he did the duke's arms in the same stone, with two figures. Not long afterwards he made a large wooden crucifix for the nuns of S. Apollonia, and on the wedding of the daughter of Alessandro Antinori, a noble and wealthy Florentine merchant of the time, he made a rich trophy with statues, scenes and other fine ornaments. Proceeding to Rome, he was employed by Buonarroti to make two marble figures[3] of five braccia for the tomb of Julius II. at S. Pietro ad Vincola, built and finished by that great artist. But as Raffaello fell sick while engaged upon the work, he could not devote his customary care and diligence to it, so that he lost in reputation and Michelagnolo was dissatisfied.

[1] Agostino Busti, il Zarabaia, generally known, incorrectly, as Bambaia.
[2] In 1527. [3] A prophet and a sibyl.

When Charles V. came to Rome, Paul III. erected a trophy for that invincible prince, carried out by Raffaello on the Ponte S. Angelo in clay and stucco, with fourteen fine statues, considered the best there. He finished them so quickly that he had time to make two rivers in clay at Florence, where the emperor was also expected, in no more than five days, for the approach to the S. Trinità bridge: the Rhine for Germany and the Danube for Hungary. Proceeding to Orvieto, he did a marble Adoration of the Magi in a chapel where Il Mosca, an excellent sculptor, had previously done many fine ornaments in half-relief, a successful work for the variety of its numerous figures and the merits of its style. Returning to Rome, he was appointed architect of the Mole of Hadrian by Tiberio Crispo, then castellan there, and accordingly he decorated several apartments with carved stones, for the chimneypieces, windows and doors. He also made a marble statue, five braccia high, of the angel of the castle for the top of the tower where the standard is, like the one which appeared to St. Gregory, sheathing his sword, on the Pope's prayer that a fearful plague might cease.[1] On Crispo becoming a cardinal, he frequently sent Raffaello to Bolsena, where he built a palace. Soon after Cardinal Salviati and M. Baldassarre Turrini of Pescia employed Raffaello to make a statue of Pope Leo, now above his tomb in the Minerva at Rome, taking him away from serving Cardinal Crispo in the castle. That done, Raffaello made M. Baldassarre's tomb for the church of Pescia, where he had built a marble chapel. At la Consolazione at Rome he did three marble figures in half-relief, in a chapel. But preferring the life of a philosopher to that of a sculptor, and loving quiet, he went to Orvieto, where he took charge of the fabric of S. Maria, spending many years in decorating it, growing old before his time. I believe that if Raffaello had undertaken great works he would have produced better and more numerous things. But he was too amiable and cautious; carefully avoiding vexation and resting content with what fell to his lot, he let slip many opportunities of doing remarkable works. He drew very skilfully, understanding art far better than his father Baccio. There are designs of both in our book, those of the son being much the more graceful and artistic. In architecture Raffaello followed the style of Michelagnolo, as we see by his chimneypieces, doors and windows in the castle of S. Angelo, and some chapels of his at Orvieto, in a rare and beautiful style.

[1] Now replaced by a bronze statue of the eighteenth century.

But to return to Baccio. His death caused considerable sorrow to the Lucchese, who knew him to be a just and good man, courteous to all. His works were executed about 1533. His intimate friend Zaccaria da Volterra profited much from his instruction. He did several works in terra cotta at Bologna, some of them being in the church of S. Giuseppe.

LORENZO DI CREDI, Painter of Florence
(1459 – 1537)

WHILE Maestro Credi, an excellent goldsmith of his day, was working with credit in Florence, Andrea Sciarpelloni sent to him his son Lorenzo, an intelligent and well-mannered youth, to learn that trade. The master was skilful and fond of teaching, so that the pupil quickly learned what was shown to him, and before long became a diligent designer and such a clever goldsmith that no youth of the time could equal him, and this was so much to Credi's credit that the boy was always called Lorenzo di Credi and not Lorenzo Sciarpelloni from that day. His ambition rising, Lorenzo went to Andrea del Verrocchio, whose whim was then painting. Under that master he had as friends and companions, although rivals, Pietro Perugino and Lionardo da Vinci, all diligently studying painting. Lionardo's style greatly delighted Lorenzo, who succeeded better than any others in imitating his polish and finish, as is seen by many pen-and-ink drawings and water-colours in our book, including some copies of clay models draped in waxed cloth, finished with incredible patience and diligence. For these causes Andrea became so fond of his pupil that, when he went to Venice to make the bronze horse and statue of Bartolommeo da Bergamo, he left to Lorenzo the administration of his affairs and all his designs, reliefs, statues and materials of art. Lorenzo, on his side, loved his master so dearly that besides carefully managing his affairs in Florence, he went more than once to Venice to see him and render account of his administration, greatly to the delight of Andrea, who would have made him his heir if Lorenzo had consented. When Andrea died, Lorenzo brought his body to Florence, handing over his master's possessions to the heirs, except the designs, paintings, sculptures and other objects of art.

Lorenzo's first work was a round painting of a Madonna, sent to the King of Spain, the design being taken from one of

Andrea's. He then did a far better picture, copied from one by Lionardo da Vinci, and also sent to Spain. It was indistinguishable from the original. He did a fine Madonna on a panel in a corner of the great church of S. Jacopo at Pistoia,[1] and another in the hospital of the Ceppo, one of the best paintings in that city. He painted many portraits, including one of himself as a young man, now owned by his pupil Gianiacopo, a painter in Florence, who has several of his master's works, including portraits of Pietro Perugino and Andrea del Verrocchio. Lorenzo also drew Girolamo Benivieni, a learned man and his great friend. In the company of St. Bastiano, behind the church of the Servites at Florence, he did a panel of the Virgin, St. Sebastian and other saints, and a figure of St. Joseph at his altar in S. Maria del Fiore. To Montepulciano he sent a panel, now in S. Agostino, of a crucifix, the Virgin and St. John, done with great diligence. But his best work, to which he devoted all his energy in order to surpass himself, was in a chapel at Cestello, on a panel representing the Virgin, St. Julian and St. Nicholas,[2] its fine finish being an excellent example of what is necessary in an oil-painting for the preservation of the picture. While still young he painted a St. Bartholomew on a pilaster in Orsanmichele, and for the nuns of S. Chiara in Florence he did a Nativity,[3] with some shepherds and angels, showing great diligence in representing certain plants, which look real. In the same place he did a Magdalene in penitence, and in another, near the house of M. Ottaviano de' Medici, he did a Madonna in a circle. He did a picture at S. Friano, some figures in S. Matteo of the hospital of Lelmo and another picture of the Archangel Michael for S. Reparata,[4] while for the company of the Scalzo he painted a panel,[5] very carefully finished. Besides these he did several Madonnas and other paintings for private houses in Florence.

Having accumulated a few savings through these labours and preferring quiet to money, Lorenzo entered S. Maria Nuova in Florence,[6] where he lived in comfortable quarters until his death. He was much drawn towards the sect of Frà Girolamo of Ferrara, always living an upright life and showing courtesy upon every occasion. At length, having reached the age of seventy-eight, he died of old age, and was buried in S. Piero Maggiore in 1530.[7]

---

[1] 1510. [2] Painted 1494; now in the Louvre.
[3] Now in the Uffizi, Florence.
[4] Painted in 1523.
[5] A Baptism, now in S. Domenico, Fiesole.
[6] On 1 April, 1531, agreeing to pay thirty-six florins a year.
[7] He died 12 January, 1537, new style.

His works are so delicately finished and polished that all other paintings look like rough, dirty sketches by comparison.

He left many pupils, among others Giovanni Antonio Sogliani and Tommaso di Stefano. Of the former I shall speak elsewhere. Tommaso closely imitated his master's polish, and did many works in Florence and elsewhere, and a finely finished panel of a Nativity at Arcetri for Marco del Nero. But his principal occupation was in painting hangings, in which he was pre-eminent. His father Stefano had been an illuminator, and had done some things in architecture, and, following in his steps, Tommaso built the bridge at Sieve, ten miles from Florence, which had been destroyed by a flood, and that of S. Piero a Ponte on the River Bisenzio, a fine work, erected after his father's death. After doing several buildings for monasteries and other places, he became architect of the art of wool, and made the model for the new houses erected by the art behind the Nunziata. He died in 1564 at the age of seventy, and was buried in S. Marco, his obsequies being attended by the Academy of Design.

To return to Lorenzo. He left many unfinished works at his death, notably a beautiful Passion of Christ, which came into the hands of Antonio da Ricasoli, and a fine panel of M. Francesco da Castiglione, canon of S. Maria del Fiore, who sent it to Castiglioni. Lorenzo did not wish to make many great works as they cost him so much labour, and chiefly because his colours were too finely ground. He purged the oil of foreign matter, and made a great many mixtures of colours on his palettes from the lightest to the darkest tint. He carried this to actual excess, for he would have from twenty-five to thirty at one time, keeping a separate brush for each. While he was working he would not allow any movement that might raise dust, his great care being hardly better than extreme negligence, for there is a mean in all things, and extremes are usually vicious.

LORENZETTO,[1] Sculptor and Architect of Florence, and BOCCACCINO, Painter of Cremona

(1490 – 1541; 1467 – ?1525)

SOMETIMES when Fortune has suppressed talent for a while through poverty, she changes her mood, and suddenly heaps benefits upon those to whom she was previously hostile, making

[1] Lorenzetto Lotti.

good in one year the troubles of many. Lorenzo di Ludovico, a bell-founder of Florence, is an instance in point. He was an architect as well as a sculptor, and intimate with Raphael of Urbino, who helped him a great deal, and gave him to wife a sister of his pupil Giulio Romano. Lorenzetto, as he was always called, when quite young, finished the tomb of Cardinal Forteguerri in S. Jacopo at Pistoia, begun by Andrea del Verrocchio, containing a very meritorious Charity by him. Soon after he made a figure for the garden of Giovanni Bartolini, and that done he went to Rome. There he did many things which I need not mention. By Raphael's influence Agostino Ghigi [1] gave him his tomb to do in S. Maria del Popolo, where he had built a chapel. Upon this work Lorenzo bestowed the utmost diligence and pains, in order to win praise and please Raphael, from whom he might hope for much favour and assistance, and to earn a rich reward from the liberality of the wealthy Agostino. His labours were well bestowed, for with Raphael's assistance he made a nude Jonah issuing from the fish's belly, a type of the Resurrection, and a graceful and life-like Elijah under the juniper-tree, with his vessel of water and bread. These statues were finished by Lorenzo and made extremely beautiful, for he exerted all his powers, but he did not obtain the reward he so richly deserved, and which the necessities of his family required, because death closed the eyes of Agostino and Raphael almost at the same time, and the figures remained in his workshop for many years owing to the indifference of Agostino's heirs. However, they have to-day been put in S. Maria del Popolo.

Lorenzo lost hope when he discovered that he had thrown away his time and labour. But soon, in execution of Raphael's will, he was employed to make a marble statue of the Virgin of four braccia for that artist's tomb in S. Maria Rotonda, the tabernacle being restored under his direction. For a merchant of the Perini he made a tomb at the Trinità in Rome, with two children in half-relief. He also designed several houses, notably that of M. Bernardino Caffarelli, and the inside wall of la Valle, as well as the stables and garden for Andrea Cardinal della Valle, introducing antique columns, bases and capitals, and as a base he distributed ancient sarcophagi containing bas-reliefs. Higher up he did a frieze of ancient fragments, placing some marble statues above in niches, and although they lacked heads or arms or legs, he managed all excellently, causing the missing parts to be replaced by good sculptors. This induced other great

[1] Chigi; the tomb was restored by Bernini in 1652.

men to do the like, such as the Cardinals Cesis, Ferrara, Farnese, and, in a word, all Rome. Antiquities thus restored certainly possess more grace than imperfect specimens. But to return to the garden. Over the niches he made a frieze of stories of the ancients in half-relief, of rare beauty, much to his advantage, for the misfortunes of Pope Clement being past, he obtained employment.

The Pope had observed that during the fighting at the Castle of St. Angelo two marble chapels at the end of the bridge had proved harmful, because they had been occupied by arquequsiers, who from their vantage ground killed all who exposed themselves on the walls. He resolved to remove the chapels and set up two marble statues on the site on two pedestals. One was a St. Paul, by Paolo Romano, spoken of elsewhere, the other a St. Peter, was given to Lorenzo, who acquitted himself well but did not surpass his rival. On the death of Clement, his tomb and that of Leo X. were allotted to Baccio Bandinelli, Lorenzo being retained to do the marble bas-reliefs, a work to which he devoted some time.

At the time of the election of Pope Paul, Lorenzo found himself in great straits, for he only had the house which he had built by himself at the Macello de' Corbi, and was burdened with five children and other charges. At this point his fortune turned. Pope Paul determined to pursue the construction of S. Pietro, and as Baldassarre of Siena and the others employed upon it were dead, Antonio da S. Gallo made Lorenzo the architect, the building being estimated at so much the canna. Thus, in a few years, with little labour, Lorenzo gained more than all his previous efforts had brought him, and had he lived longer he would have better repaired the ravages of his early misfortunes. But after attaining to the age of forty-seven, he died of a fever in 1541. His death grieved his numerous friends, who knew his amiability and modesty. His life having been well ordered, the deputies of S. Pietro granted him honourable burial, setting up this epitaph:

SCVLPTORI LAVRENTIO FLORENTINO
ROMA MIHI TRIBVIT TVMVLVM, FLORENTIA
VITAM;
NEMO ALIO VELLET NASCI ET OBIRE LOCO
MDXLI.
VIX. ANN. XLVII. MEN. II. D.XV.

Boccaccino of Cremona, who flourished about the same time, having acquired a reputation as an excellent painter in Lombardy, came to Rome to see the renowned works of Michelagnolo. No sooner had he seen them than he did his utmost to depreciate them, expecting to exalt himself by thus blaming so great a master. Being allotted the chapel of S. Maria Traspontina, he roused great expectations when he uncovered it, but when the painters of Rome came to see the Coronation of the Virgin which he had done there with some flying children, their wonder was changed into derision. Thus we see that when men cry up those who are more excellent by repute than in fact, it is hard to overcome them in argument, until the productions themselves discover the real position of those who have been so much vaunted. No greater harm can be done than by premature praise of those engaged in work, for the praise excites expectations which are not always realised by the work, and thus men become discouraged. The wise, then, should fear praise more than blame, for the former deceives by flattery, while the latter teaches by disclosing the truth.

Driven from Rome by general derision, Boccaccino returned to Cremona, and there continued to paint as best he could. Over the middle arches of the Duomo he did the life of the Virgin, which is still much valued in the city. He did yet other works in the city and elsewhere which I need not mention.

He taught art to his son Camillo, who, by means of much study, endeavoured to succeed where his father's boasting had failed. There are some works by him in S. Gismondo, a mile from Cremona, considered by the Cremonese to be the best paintings they have. He also did the front of a house on the piazza, all the vaulting of S. Agata, some panels and the façade of S. Antonio, with other things which show his skill. If death had not removed him before his time, he would have attained honourable success, as he was on the right road; but even the works which he has left deserve a mention.

But to return to Boccaccino. Without having introduced any improvements into art, he died at the age of fifty-eight. In his day there flourished in Milan a skilful illuminator called Girolamo, numerous works by his hand existing there and in all Lombardy.

Another Milanese of the same period, Bernardino del Lupino,[1] was a very refined and graceful painter, as we see by his numerous works in that city and at Sarone,[2] twelve miles out, comprising a Marriage of the Virgin, and other scenes in the church of S. Maria, perfectly executed in fresco. He also worked smoothly

[1] i.e. Luini.   [2] Saronno.

in oils, being an amiable man, liberal in all his actions. Thus he deserves the praise accorded to artists who, by their gentleness, embellish life as much as they enrich the world by their art.

BALDASSARRE PERUZZI, Painter and Architect of Siena
(1481 – 1537)

AMONG all the gifts bestowed by Heaven on mortals, none can be considered greater than ability and peace and quiet of mind, the former rendering men immortal and the latter happy. Men thus endowed, besides owing a great debt to God, shine like a light in darkness, as Baldassarre Peruzzi has in our own day, whose modesty and goodness sprang from innate tranquillity of mind, and whose works are the noble fruits of the talents implanted in him by Heaven. I have called him a Sienese because he was always known as such, but just as seven cities dispute the right of calling Homer a fellow-citizen, so three noble cites of Tuscany, Florence, Volterra and Siena, claim Baldassarre as their own. As a matter of fact, each one had a share, for, during the civil wars of Florence, Antonio Peruzzi, a noble citizen, took refuge at Volterra. After some time he married a wife there in 1482, and in a few years had two children, a son called Baldassarre and a daughter named Virginia; but the war rolling in that direction, Volterra soon after suffered sack,[1] so that Antonio was forced to fly to Siena, having lost nearly all he possessed. Meanwhile Baldassarre was growing up and associating with men of genius, especially designers and goldsmiths. He began to take pleasure in the arts and devoted himself to design. His father dying not long after, he studied painting with such ardour that he soon made marvellous progress, imitating natural objects in addition to the works of the best masters. As he earned something, he was able to help himself, his mother and sister, while pursuing his studies. His first works, without counting some insignificant things at Siena, were in a small chapel at Volterra, near the Florentine gate, the figures of which were executed with such grace that they earned him the friendship of a Volterran painter named Piero, who spent most of his time at Rome, doing some things in the palace for Alexander VI., and thither Baldassarre accompanied him. But Alexander having died, and Piero's work being interrupted, Baldassarre

[1] But this was in 1472 before Baldassarre was born.

entered the shop of the father of Maturino, not a great painter, who, in those days of mediocre workmanship, always had a great deal to do. He put a prepared panel before the youth, and, without giving him any cartoon or other design, told him to make a Madonna. Baldassarre took a crayon, and, in a few strokes, skilfully drew what he intended to paint. When he coloured it after a few days he produced such a beautiful figure as amazed his master and several painters who saw it. This led to his employment to do the high-altar chapel in the church of S. Onofrio,[1] which he executed in fresco in a graceful and beautiful style. In the church of S. Rocco at Ripa he did two other small chapels in fresco. Becoming known, he was invited to Ostia, where he painted some fine scenes in grisaille in rooms in the fortress, notably a hand-to-hand conflict, such as the ancient Romans fought, and, nearby, a squadron of soldiers attacking a fortress, the men showing great bravery, as, covered by their shields, they plant ladders against the walls, while the defenders repulse them manfully. He introduced several implements of ancient warfare and various arms. He did many other scenes in another hall, considered some of his best work, though, indeed, he had the assistance of Cesare of Milan.[2]

Returning to Rome, Baldassarre contracted a close friendship with Agostino Ghigi of Siena, for he was naturally drawn to men of genius, and so he became a Sienese. Aided by his friend, Baldassarre studied the treasures of Rome, especially in architecture, in which he made marvellous progress, thanks to the rivalry with Bramante, and this was afterwards of great advantage to him, as I shall relate. He also studied perspective, making such progress that few in our day have equalled him, as his works clearly show. For a corridor and aviary near the roof, erected in the palace by Julius II., Baldassarre painted the Months in grisaille, and the characteristic employments of each, comprising in this work countless buildings, theatres, palaces and other structures, with good invention. He then did some apartments in the palace of S. Giorgio for Cardinal Raffaello Riario, bishop of Ostia, in conjunction with other painters, and did a wall of M. Ulisse da Fano with scenes of Ulysses, which brought him a great reputation, and painted another opposite. But he won even more fame by his model of the palace [3] of Agostino Ghigi, executed with such grace that it seemed a creation, and not the work of men's hands. He adorned the

---

[1] About 1517. [2] Cesare da Sesto.
[3] The Farnesina, built 1509-11.

exterior with beautiful scenes in clay made by himself. The hall is decorated with columns in perspective, which make it appear larger than it really is. But the most remarkable part is a loggia facing the garden, decorated by him with scenes of the Medusa turning men into stone, of indescribable beauty, with Perseus cutting off her head, and many other scenes in the sections of the vaulting. The decoration in perspective, formed of stucco and colours, is so excellent that even to artists it seems in relief. I remember that, when I took the great painter Titian to see it, he could not be persuaded that it was a painting, but on being convinced he was amazed. The same place contains some things of Frà Sebastiano of Venice, in his first manner, and a Galatea carried off by the Sea Gods by the divine Raphael, as has been said. Beyond the Campo di Fiore, on the way to the Piazza Giudea, Baldassarre did a wonderful façade in perspective of clay, made for a chamberlain of the pope, and now owned by Jacopo Strozzi of Florence. In the Pace he did a chapel for M. Ferrando Ponzetti, afterwards cardinal,[1] on the left on entering the church, with small scenes from the Old Testament, and some figures of considerable size, very carefully finished for a work in fresco. But he displayed the extent of his powers in painting and perspective much more fully in the high altar, where he did the Virgin mounting the steps of the Temple, for M. Filippo da Siena, clerk of the chamber, with many admirable figures, such as a gentleman in antique costume dismounting from his horse and giving alms to a naked and wretched beggar, who is eagerly asking for charity. It also contains various buildings and beautiful decoration in imitation of stucco, looking as if the work was fixed to the wall with clamps like an oil-painting. For the great feast of the Capitol, celebrated by the Romans, when the baton of the Holy Church was conferred upon the Duke Giuliano de' Medici,[2] Baldassarre did one of the six pictures, six canne by three and a half broad, of Tarpeia betraying the Romans, which was considered the best of all. But the greatest admiration was caused by a perspective or scenery for a comedy of the utmost beauty in the variety and style of the buildings, the various loggias, the curious doors and windows, and other architectural details, so well imagined and with such wealth of invention that I cannot describe a thousandth part. For the house of M. Francesco da Norcia on the Piazza de' Farnesi he made a graceful Doric door, and did a beautiful façade near the Piazza degli Altieri for M. Francesco

[1] In 1517. [2] In 1515.

Buzio, introducing portraits of all the Roman cardinals then living into the frieze. He represented the presentation to Cæsar of tribute from the whole world, and, above this, the twelve emperors, standing on pedestals foreshortened from below with great art, a work for which he won much praise. In Banchi he did the arms of Pope Leo in fresco, with three children of beautiful flesh-colouring, and at Montecavallo, for the garden of Frà Mariano Fetti, friar of the Piombo, he made a fine clay St. Bernard. For the company of St. Caterina of Siena in Strada Giulia he made a bier, besides many other admirable things. At Siena he designed the organ of the Carmine, and did other works there, but not of great importance. Invited to Bologna [1] by the wardens of S. Petronio to make a model for the façade, he made two large plans and two sections, one in the modern and the other in the German style. They are still preserved in the sacristy as remarkable works, the perspective being so managed that the edifice appears in relief. For this same church he made several designs in the house of Count Giovanni Battista Bentivogli, of wonderful beauty for his contrivance to retain the old work and unite it to the new. For this count he designed a Nativity with the Magi in grisaille,[2] remarkable for the horses, chariots, the suite of the three kings, most gracefully executed, as are some temple walls and houses about the cottage. The count subsequently had this work coloured by Girolamo Trevigi, who did it very successfully. Baldassarre also designed the door of the church of S. Michele in Bosco, a beautiful monastery of the monks of Monte Oliveto, outside Bologna, and made a model for the Duomo of Carpi, of great beauty, erected according to the rules of Vitruvius. In the same place he began a church of S. Niccola, which was not then completed, because he was practically compelled to return to Siena to design the fortifications there, which were afterwards carried out as he arranged. Returning to Rome, where he did the house opposite the Farnese and some others, he was much employed by Leo X. As the Pope wished to finish S. Pietro, begun by Julius II. from Bramante's design, and thought the building too large and badly composed, Baldassarre made a new model of great ingenuity and magnificence, parts of which have been subsequently adopted by other architects. Indeed, the judgment and diligence displayed by this artist were such that he has never had a peer in architecture, because he combined his skill with a beautiful style in painting.

[1] In 1522.
[2] The cartoon, done in 1522, is now in the National Gallery, London.

He designed the tomb of Adrian VI.,[1] and the painting about it is by his hand, while Michelagnolo, sculptor of Siena, executed the marble work with his assistance.

When the comedy of *La Calandra*, by Cardinal Bibbiena, was performed for Pope Leo, Baldassarre designed the scenery, which was not inferior to the other scenery already mentioned. He deserved the more praise because comedies had fallen into disuse, and the scenery was consequently neglected. Before the performance of *La Calandra*, which was one of the earliest comedies in the vernacular to be presented, Baldassarre did two marvellous scenes in the time of Leo X. which prepared the way for those done afterwards in our own day. It is wonderful how, in the narrow space, he depicted his streets, palaces and curious temples, loggias and cornices, all made to make them appear to be what they represent. He also arranged the lights inside for the perspective, and all the other necessary things. These comedies, in my opinion, when performed with all their accessories, surpass all other spectacular displays in magnificence.

On the election of Pope Clement VII. in 1524, Baldassarre made the apparatus for the coronation, and finished the façade of the principal chapel of S. Pietro, begun by Bramante, in peperigno stone. In the niches behind the altar in the chapel containing the bronze tomb of Pope Sixtus he painted the Apostles in grisaille, and designed the graceful tabernacle of the Sacrament. During the sack of Rome in 1527 poor Baldassarre was made prisoner by the Spaniards, and not only lost all that he possessed but endured much suffering and anxiety. As he was grave and noble of aspect, they thought him some great prelate in disguise or some other great person able to pay a heavy ransom. But on finding that he was a painter, one of these barbarians, a friend of Bourbon, forced him to make a portrait of that infamous captain, the enemy of God and man, either by showing him the dead body or in some other way by sketches or description. After this Baldassarre left them and went towards Porto Ercole, for Siena, but on the way he was attacked and robbed of everything, reaching Siena in his shirt. However, his friends received him with honour and clothed him, and soon after the State decreed him a pension if he would see to the fortifications of the city. While there he had two children. Besides his work for the State he did many designs for his fellow-citizens. For the church of the

[1] In S. Maria de Anima, finished in 1529.

Carmine he designed the decoration of the organ, which is very beautiful.

When the imperial and papal army was besieging Florence,[1] His Holiness sent Baldassarre to the camp to Baccio Valori, the commissary, to employ his genius in the siege. But Baldassarre refused to do anything of moment, preferring the liberty of his former home to the favours of the Pope, whose indignation he did not fear, though Clement was much incensed against him when he heard of this. On the conclusion of the war, however, when Baldassarre wished to return to Rome, he was restored to favour and to his former employment through the influence of the Cardinals Salviati, Trivulzi and Cesarino, all of whom he had served. Soon after returning to Rome he designed two beautiful palaces for the Orsini, erected on the road to Viterbo, and some other buildings for La Paglia. Meanwhile he studied astrology and mathematics, of which he was very fond, began a book on the antiquities of Rome, and a commentary on Vitruvius, which he illustrated, some of his designs for this being still in the possession of Francesco da Siena, his pupil, containing drawings of antiquities and modern methods of building. While at Rome he also designed the house of the Massimi,[2] giving it an oval form, a novel and beautiful idea, the façade comprising a porch with Doric columns, the court being well devised and the stairs convenient, but he was prevented by death from finishing the work. The great abilities and labours of this noble artist benefited him but little, but assisted others, for though he was employed by popes, cardinals, and other great and wealthy men, not one of them ever rewarded him richly, though this was due more to his own retiring nature than to any want of liberality in his patrons. Though it is proper to be discreet with magnanimous and generous princes, it is necessary to importune the miserly, ungrateful and discourteous, for importunity, which is a vice in the first case, becomes a virtue in the second, just as discretion is a vice when dealing with the miserly. Thus Baldassarre found himself in his last years old, poor and burdened with a family. After having lived a well-regulated life he fell grievously sick. When Paul III. heard this, he sent 100 crowns to him by Jacopo Melighi, accountant of S. Pietro tardily recognising the loss which would be caused by the death of such a man. But Baldassarre grew worse, or else was poisoned by some rival who desired his place, which brought him 250 crowns, a thing discovered too late by

[1] In 1529. [2] Palazzo Massimi alle Colonne in the Corso.

the physicians. He died regretting life rather on account of his poor family than of himself, for he left them badly provided for. He was much lamented by his children and friends, and was buried in the Rotonda near Raphael, being followed to his grave by all the painters, sculptors and architects of Rome. The following epitaph was set up:

Balthasari Perutio Senensi, viro et pictura et architectura aliisque ingeniorum artibus adeo excellenti, ut si priscorum occubuisset temporibus, nostra illum felicius legerent. Vix. Ann. LV. Mens. XI. Dies XX.

Lucretia et Io. Salustius optimo conjugi et parenti, none sine lachrymis Simonis, Honorii, Æmiliæ ac Sulpitiæ minorum filiorum dolentes posuerunt Die IIII. Januarii MDXXXVI.

The name and fame of Baldassarre increased after his death, and his abilities were the more missed because Paul III. determined to finish S. Pietro. He would have been of great assistance to Antonio da S. Gallo, because, though Antonio did his work well, he would have better overcome some of the difficulties if Baldassarre had been at his side.

Sebastiano Serlio of Bologna inherited many of Baldassarre's things, and he did the third book of architecture and the fourth book of the survey of the antiquities of Rome, being greatly aided by the studies of Baldassarre, some of which were put in the margin. The writings of Baldassarre were mostly left to Jacopo Melighino of Ferrara, who was appointed architect to Pope Paul. Another heir was his pupil, Francesco of Siena, who did the much-admired arms of the Cardinal di Traini at Navona and some other works. He has given me a portrait of his master and information about many things which I did not know when this book was first published.

Another pupil of Baldassarre was Virgilio of Rome, who in his native city did a façade with captives in grafito in Borgo Nuovo, and many other beautiful works. From the same master Antonio del Rozzo learned the first principles of architecture. He was a Sienese and an excellent engineer. Riccio, a Sienese painter, also imitated him, although he afterwards followed the style of Giovanni Antonio Soddoma of Vercelli. Another pupil, Giovanni Battista Peloro, architect of Siena, studied mathematics and cosmography, making quadrants, compasses, and many such instruments. He also made plans for several fortifications, most of which are in the possession of his friend Giuliano, goldsmith of Siena. For Duke Cosimo de' Medici he made a beautiful plan in relief of the city and environs of

Siena at a radius of one and a half miles, with the walls, streets, forts; but being fickle he departed, although he had a good provision from the prince, and went to France, expecting to do better. But after long following the court without any success, he ultimately died at Avignon. Although a clever and skilful architect, no building exists by him, for he did not stay long enough in one place, and spent all his time in designs, fancies, measurements and models. However, he has deserved mention as a professor of the fine arts.

Baldassarre designed excellently in every way, with great judgment and finish, mostly with the pen, in water-colours and chiaroscuro. This we see in many of his designs in the possession of artists, and particularly by some sheets in our book. One of these is a fancy sketch of a piazza full of arches, coliseums, theatres, obelisks, pyramids, various temples, porticos, and other things in the ancient style. On a pedestal stands Mercury, surrounded by all manner of alchemists, with bellows, retorts, crucibles and other instruments for distilling, all directed to assist in purging him, a very amusing and whimsical idea. Among the friends of Baldassarre, who was always courteous, modest and gentle with all, were Domenico Beccafumi of Siena, an excellent painter, and Il Capanna, who, besides several other things, painted the façade of the Turchi on the piazza at Siena as well as another there.

GIOVANNI FRANCESCO, called IL FATTORE, of Florence, and PELLEGRINO DA MODENA, Painters

(?1488 – ?1528; 1483 – 1523)

GIOVANNI FRANCESCO PENNI, called Il Fattore, owed much to his natural goodness, for his qualities, his inclination to painting and his other virtues led Raphael to take him into his house to bring him up with Giulio Romano like his own son. He showed his love for them in leaving them both his heirs, of his talents as well as his property. From the time when he first went as quite a boy to Raphael, Giovanni Francesco was called Il Fattore, a name he always retained. He imitated Raphael's manner in his designs, as shown by some in our book. He was fonder of drawing than of colouring, and so it is not surprising that many designs of his are extant. His first works were done in the papal loggias at Rome in conjunction with Giovanni da Udine, Perino del Vaga, and other masters, and display much grace and a masterly attention to finish. He was versatile and very fond of doing landscapes and buildings. He coloured well in oils, fresco and tempera, and was an excellent portrait-painter, being naturally gifted without needing to study much. Thus he proved of great assistance to Raphael in painting the majority of the cartoons for the hangings of the Pope's chapel and the consistory, especially the borders. He also did several things from Raphael's cartoons, such as the vaulting of Agostino Chigi in Trastevere,[1] and many pictures and various works, so well executed that Raphael became more and more fond of him. In Monte Giordano at Rome he did a façade in grisaille, and a fine St. Christopher, eight braccia high, at the side door leading to la Pace in S. Maria de Anima. It contains a hermit in a cave holding a lantern, well and harmoniously designed. On coming to Florence, Giovanni Francesco did a much-admired tabernacle with a Virgin at Montughi, outside the S. Gallo gate, for Ludovico Capponi. On Raphael's death he and Giulio Romano remained together for some time finishing the incompleted works of their master, especially those begun in the Pope's villa and in the hall of the palace. There they did stories of Constantine with great beauty and style, the ideas and sketches being partly due to Raphael. While they were thus engaged, Perino del Vaga, a very excellent painter, married a sister of Giovanni Francesco, and the two did many works together. Being joined by Giulio, they did a panel in two pieces of an Annunciation, sent to Monteluci, near Perugia, and other works for various places. Receiving a commission from Pope Clement to do a panel like Raphael's in S. Piero a Montorio,[2] to be sent to France, where Raphael had meant it to go, they set to work. After the division of Raphael's property, designs and other things left them by Raphael, Giulio went to Mantua, where he did countless works for the marquis. Soon after Giulio's affection cooled, so that when Giovanni Francesco went to see him he had so frigid a reception, that he left immediately, and, passing through Lombardy, reached Rome, where he took a galley to Naples to visit the Marquis del Vasto, taking his finished panel, which was placed in S. Piero a Montorio, and other things, which were placed in Ischia, an island of the marquisate. Afterwards the panel was put in its present position in the church of S. Spirito degli Incurabili at Naples.

[1] Of the Farnesina.   [2] i.e. the Transfiguration.

While at Naples Giovanni Francesco drew and painted, being much favoured by Tommaso Cambi, a Florentine merchant, who managed the affairs of the marquis. But he did not stay there long, for, being of weak constitution, he fell sick and died, to the sorrow of the marquis and of all his acquaintance.

He had a brother named Luca, also a painter, who worked with Perino, his kinsman, at Genoa, at Lucca, and many other places in Italy. Ultimately he went to England, and after doing some things for the king and some merchants he took to making designs for the Flemish copper engravers, doing many things which may be identified by his name as well as his style. Among them is a sheet of some women bathing, the original of which is in our book.

Lionardo, called Il Pistoia, after his native place, was a pupil of Gian. Francesco. He did some things at Lucca, and in Rome painted many portraits; while in Naples, for Diomede Caraffa, bishop of Ariano, now cardinal, he did a Stoning of St. Stephen in his chapel. At Monte Oliveto he did another panel, placed at the high altar, but since removed to make room for a similar conception by Giorgio Vasari of Arezzo. Lionardo made considerable wealth out of the Neapolitan lords, but profited little by it, as he lost it in gaming. He died at Naples, leaving the reputation of having been a good colourist without much design. He lived forty years, and his works were produced about 1528.

A friend of Giovanni Francesco, and also a pupil of Raphael, was Pellegrino da Modena, who, after acquiring a reputation at home, on hearing of the wonders of Raphael, determined to go to Rome, in order that he might realise the hopes formed of him. Arrived there he joined Raphael, who never refused a man of ability. At that time Rome contained numbers of young painters who vied with each other in their endeavours to win the favour of Raphael and a reputation among the people. By continual study Pellegrino became a skilful master and designer, and when Leo X. employed Raphael to paint the loggia, Pellegrino worked there with the other youths, doing so well that Raphael afterwards employed him in many other things. At an altar at the entrance of S. Eustachio at Rome, Pellegrino did three figures in fresco, and decorated the chapel of the high altar in the Portuguese church at la Scrofa. Cardinal Alborense having erected a chapel decorated with many marbles in S. Jacopo of the Spaniards, with a St. James four and a half braccia high by Jacopo Sansovino, Pellegrino painted the life of the Apostle there in fresco, imitating Raphael in the gentle air of his figures, the composition showing him to be a skilful and ingenious painter. He afterwards did many other works in Rome by himself and with others. On the death of Raphael he returned to Modena, where he did many works, among others a St. John baptising Christ, in oils, for a confraternity of Flagellants, and in the church of the Servites he did SS. Cosmo and Damian, with other figures, on a panel. He took a wife and had a son, who caused his death; for, during a dispute with some young companions of Modena, the son killed one. Pellegrino ran out to rescue his son from justice, but on the way he met the kinsmen of the murdered youth seeking the murderer. Furious at meeting Pellegrino, because they had not caught his son, they inflicted so many wounds on him that he died. This chance greatly grieved the Modenese, for in him they felt they had lost a rare spirit.

Gaudenzio of Milan [1] was a companion of his, and an excellent, skilful and rapid painter. He did many works in fresco at Milan, notably a beautiful Last Supper for the friars of la Passione, left unfinished at his death. He also worked excellently in oils, there being a goodly number of fine works by his hand at Vercelli and Veralla. [2]

ANDREA DEL SARTO, Painter of Florence
(1486 – 1531)

AFTER these numerous Lives of artists, some excellent in colouring, some in design and some in invention, I have now come to Andrea del Sarto, whom Nature endowed with her rarest gifts in all three branches, so that, had his spirit been as bold as his judgment was profound, he would doubtless have been unequalled. But a timidity of spirit and a yielding simple nature prevented him from exhibiting a burning ardour and dash that, joined to his other qualities, would have made him divine. This defect deprived his work of the ornament, magnificence and wealth of style seen in many other painters. None the less his figures are simple and pure, well conceived, flawless and perfect in every particular. The heads of his women and children have a natural and graceful expression, and his young and old men possess a marvellous vivacity and vigour; his draperies

[1] Gaudenzio Ferrari, 1484-1549.   [2] Varallo.

are remarkable and his nudes show thorough knowledge, and though his design is simple his colouring is truly divine.

Andrea was born in Florence in 1478, and was called del Sarto (tailor) from his father's profession. At the age of seven he was taken from school and put with a goldsmith, but he was naturally more fond of designing than of using his tools on the silver or gold. Gian. Barile, a Florentine painter, though a coarse and plebeian man, noticed the child's good method of designing, and took him away from the goldsmith to learn painting. Andrea at once took delight in the art for which Nature had formed him, and in a short space of time he astonished Gian. Barile and the other artists of the city by his work in colours. After three years of continuous study, Gian. Barile perceived that the child would become remarkable, and accordingly he spoke to Piero di Cosimo, then considered one of the best painters in Florence, who took Andrea, who was anxious to learn, and continued zealous in his studies. Nature had endowed him with as much skill in using colours as if he had worked for fifty years, so that Piero became very fond of him, and was delighted to hear that when the boy had a little time, especially on feast days, he would devote the whole day with other youths drawing in the Pope's Hall, containing the cartoons of Michelagnolo and Lionardo. Although so young Andrea surpassed all the other designers, whether native or foreign, who gathered there. Among these Andrea derived most pleasure from the character and conversation of Francia Bigio, the painter, who returned his friendship.

Andrea one day told Francia that he could no longer stand the eccentricity of Piero, now an old man, and that he wished to have a room of his own. Francia, who was forced to do the same, because his master, Mariotto Albertinelli, had given up painting, agreed to come and live with Andrea. Accordingly they took a room on the Piazza del Grano, where they did many works together. One of these was the curtains for the picture of the high altar of the Servites,[1] given them by the sacristan, a near relation of Francia. On the side towards the choir they painted an Annunciation, and on the other a Deposition from the Cross, like the panel there by Filippo and Pietro Perugino. The men of the company of the Scalzo, dedicated to St. John the Baptist, and built in that time by several Florentine artists, used then to meet above the house of Ottaviano de' Medici the Magnificent, at the top of the via Largo, opposite the

[1] They were painted by Andrea di Cosimo, 1510-11.

garden of S. Marco. Among other things, they had built a court
with a gallery resting on small columns. Some of them, noticing
Andrea's advance as a painter, proposed that he should do
twelve scenes in grisaille there from the life of St. John the
Baptist, for they had more spirit than money. Accordingly he
set to work,[1] beginning with the Baptism of Christ, done so
well that it brought him great credit and renown, so that many
wished to employ him, believing that such a beginning promised
remarkable fruit. Among other things in his first style is a
picture now in the house of Filippo Spini, held in great veneration in memory of such an artist. Not long after he did a panel
of Christ appearing to St. Mary Magdalene in the garden, for
a chapel in S. Gallo, a church of the Eremitani friars of St. Augustine, outside the S. Gallo gate. The colouring, tone, harmony
and sweetness of this work led to his employment to do two
other pictures in the same church not long after, as I shall
relate presently. All three are now at the corner of the Alberti
in S. Jacopo tra' Fossi.[2]

After this Andrea and Francia left the Piazza del Grano
and took new rooms near the convent of the Nunziata, in the
Sapienza. This led to a friendship between Andrea and the
young Jacopo Sansovino, who was doing sculpture there under
Andrea Contucci, so close that they were never separated day
or night. They usually discussed the difficulties of art, so that
it is small wonder that both became excellent.

At that time there was a sacristan with the Servites at the
candle bench called Frà Mariano dal Canto alla Macine. Hearing
the praise of Andrea on every hand, and his marvellous progress
in painting, it occurred to him to gratify a wish at a small
expense. Approaching Andrea, who was good-natured and easy-
going, he represented that he wished to help him to win honour
and profit, and to make him known, so that he would never
be poor again. Many years before Alesso Baldovinetti had done
a Nativity on the wall joining the Nunziata in the first court
of the Servites; and on the other side Cosimo Rosselli had
begun a representation of St. Philip, the founder of the order,
taking the habit, but had not finished it at the time of his
death. The friar being anxious for its completion, thought he
could profit by the emulation between Andrea and Francia,
by getting each of them to do a part, and this would induce

[1] In 1515.
[2] The *Noli me tangere* is in the Uffizi, Florence, the other two are in the
Pitti Gallery.

them to work harder while the cost would be less. Accordingly he discovered his plan to Andrea, and persuaded him to undertake the work, showing that in a place so frequented his work would become known to foreigners as well as to Florentines, so that he ought not to think of the price, but to beg for the task. If he could not do it, there was Francia, who had offered, leaving the price to the priest. These considerations induced Andrea to undertake the task, especially as he had little spirit; but the last remark about Francia made him resolve to obtain a bond that no one else should be employed. The friar having pledged him and given him money, he began on the life of St. Philip,[1] receiving only ten ducats for each scene, for they said he was doing it more for his own ends than for the benefit of the convent. Continuing the work with the utmost diligence, as if he thought more of honour than of the profit, he soon completed and unveiled three scenes, where St. Philip as a friar clothes a naked man; where he is preaching against some gamblers who are blaspheming God, and as they are deriding his warnings a flash of lightning kills two and terrifies the others, some, putting their hands to their heads, throw themselves forward, others flee screaming, while a woman fleeing from fear of the thunder is most life-like, and a horse rears up at the sound, showing the terror caused by the unexpected, the entire scene proving that Andrea had thought out the various accidents that would occur. In the third scene St. Philip casts out a spirit from a woman, with every imaginable circumstance to illustrate the story, so that the three works brought Andrea the greatest glory. Encouraged by this, he did two more in the same court. In one St. Philip lies dead, and the friars are weeping about him, while a dead child on touching the bier is restored to life. He is seen first dead and then raised, in a very natural manner. On the last on that side the friars are putting St. Philip's clothes on the heads of some children. Here he did the portrait of Andrea della Robbia, the sculptor, as an old man dressed in red, bent down, with a staff in his hands, and one of Luca, his son. In the death scene of Philip he introduced a portrait of Andrea's son Girolamo, his great friend, and a sculptor, who died in France not long since. On completing this series, he determined to abandon the rest, as the price was too small for its quality. The friar complained bitterly and would not release Andrea from his bond unless he promised to do two more scenes at his leisure and for a larger sum, and this was arranged.

[1] St. Philip Benizzi, begun in 1509.

Having thus made a name, Andrea was commissioned to do many important works. Among these the general of the monks of Vallombrosa employed him to paint a Last Supper for an arch in the vaulting of the refectory in the monastery of S. Salvi, outside the S. Croce gate.[1] Here he did in medallions figures of St. Benedict, St. John Gualbert, St. Salvi the bishop, and St. Bernard degli Uberti of Florence, friar and cardinal; in the middle he did a circle with three faces, which are the same, representing the Trinity. The work was excellently done in fresco, and showed Andrea's worth as a painter. Thus he was employed by Baccio d' Agnolo to do an Annunciation in the minute style, still seen in a recess by Orsanmichele leading to the Mercato Nuovo, which was not much admired, probably because he made too great efforts, whereas he was able to do well without forcing Nature. Among the numerous pictures which he did for Florence, and which it would take too long to recount, one of the most remarkable is the one now in the chamber of Baccio Barbadori, representing the Virgin and Child, St. Anne and St. Joseph, beautifully executed and much valued by Baccio. He did a very good one now owned by Lorenzo di Domenico Borghini, and another for Lionardo del Giocondo, of the Virgin, now owned by Piero, his son. For Carlo Ginori he did two small ones, afterwards bought by Ottaviano de' Medici the Magnificent, one of them at present being in his beautiful villa of Campi, and the other, in company with numerous paintings by excellent modern masters, in the chamber of Sig. Bernardetto, the worthy son of his father, who values the works of famous artists, and is a magnificent and generous signor.

Meanwhile the Servites had allotted one of the scenes in their court to Francia Bigio. He had not completed his preparation of the surface when Andrea, whose jealousy was aroused, for he believed Francia to be more skilful and quick in fresco painting than himself, did cartoons for the two scenes as if in competition, to be executed in the corner between the side door of S. Bastiano and the lesser door leading from the court into the Nunziata. On finishing the cartoons he began to execute them in fresco,[2] beginning with the Birth of the Virgin, a beautiful composition of figures gracefully arranged in a chamber, where some women have come on a visit, dressed in the costumes of the day. Some of lesser estate stand about the fire and wash the new-born babe, while some are making the swathes and performing similar services. Among them are a

[1] In 1519. [2] In 1511, completed 1514.

child warming himself at the fire and an old man resting on a bed, both of them most life-like. Some women are bringing food to St. Anne, also in a very natural manner, all the figures being well managed in their expressions, draperies and everything else, including some infants throwing flowers, while the colouring is such that the flesh-tints and other things look real, and not painted. In the other scene Andrea did the Magi, guided by the star, who come to adore the Infant Christ. They are represented dismounted, and as near their destination, because there were only two doors between this and the Nativity of Alesso Baldovinetti. In this scene Andrea made the court of the kings with their chariots, followers and equipments, comprising three portraits, dressed as Florentines; Jacopo Sansovino looking out of the picture, full length, Andrea himself next, with an arm foreshortened and pointing, and, behind Jacopo, Aiolle the musician, half-face. There are also some children climbing the wall to see the procession and the extraordinary beasts in the train of the kings, the scene being of equal excellence to the other. In both these scenes Andrea surpassed himself not to speak of Francia, who also completed his work there. At the same time Andrea did a panel for the abbey of S. Godenzo, a benefice of the same friars, considered an excellent work. For the friars of S. Gallo he did an Annunciation [1] on a panel, with a most pleasing harmony of colours, the heads of some angels accompanying Gabriel being softly toned and possessing lovely expressions. Jacopo da Pontormo, Andrea's pupil, did the predella for this, showing promise thus early of the beautiful works which he afterwards produced in Florence, before he became another, so to speak, as will be related in his Life. After this Andrea did a picture of medium figures for Zanobi Girolami, representing the history of Joseph, finished with unremitting diligence, and therefore considered a fine painting. Not long after he undertook a panel for the men of the company of St. Maria delle Neve, behind the nuns of S. Ambrogio, with three figures, the Virgin, St. John the Baptist and St. Ambrose, placed on the altar of the company. Meanwhile Andrea's ability had made him intimate with Giovanni Gaddi, afterwards clerk of the chamber, who, being very fond of art and design, kept Jacopo Sansovino constantly employed. As Andrea's style pleased him, he gave him a Madonna to do. This was considered the best work of the artist up to that time, as he used models and bestowed great pains upon it, He then did another Madonna for Giovanni

[1] Pitti Gallery.

di Paolo, a mercer, the beauty of which delights all who see it; and for Andrea Sertini he did a Madonna, with Christ, St. John and St. Joseph, executed with such finish that it was always greatly valued in Florence.

All these works won Andrea such a great name in the city among the numerous painters there, young and old, that he was considered the best of them all. Although he only obtained small remuneration for his labours, he was able to live in honour and partly assist his family against the trials of poverty. But falling in love with a young woman who soon after became a widow he married her, and had much more trouble for the rest of his life, being obliged to work far harder than before, because, in addition to the usual labour and trials of such a condition, he suffered from additional ones, being tormented by jealousy and other things.

But to return to his works, which are as numerous as they are remarkable. His next was a Madonna [1] raised upon an octagonal pedestal, at the sides of which are angels kneeling to adore her, as she tenderly presses the Child to her with one arm and holds a book in the other, regarding two naked children, which form an additional ornament. This was done for a Franciscan friar of S. Croce, then governor of the nuns of S. Francesco in via Pentolini, and very fond of painting. At the right of the Virgin is a fine St. Francis, his head expressive of the goodness and simplicity of that holy man. The feet and draperies are very fine, because Andrea arranged the folds about the figures so that the outlines of the body are seen. On the right is St. John the Evangelist, a young man writing his Gospel, in beautiful style. Above the building are clouds, and the figures seen are endowed with motion, the whole forming a painting of remarkable beauty. For Nizza the joiner he did a Madonna, not considered less beautiful than his other works. The art of the merchants proposing to make some wooden triumphal cars like those of the ancient Romans, to go in procession on the morning of St. John, instead of cloth mantles and wax candles which the city and county offer as tribute, passing before the duke and principal magistrates, Andrea painted some of ten which were then made in oils, in grisaille, with some scenes, which were much admired. Although this should have been done every year, every city and district having its own, forming a magnificent show, the practice was abandoned in 1527.

While Andrea was adorning the city with these and other

---

[1] Madonna delle Arpie, painted 1517, now in the Uffizi.

works, his reputation increasing daily, the men of the company of the Scalzo determined that he should finish their courtyard, where he had already painted a Baptism of Christ. He took up the work willingly,[1] and did two scenes and Charity and Justice to decorate the entrance door. One of the scenes represents St. John preaching to the multitudes in a vigorous and life-like attitude, his head displaying much spirit. The variety and vivacity of the auditors is no less remarkable, some standing in wonder and all astonished at the new sayings and at such rare and novel teaching. But Andrea displayed far more genius in his John baptising the multitudes, some undressing, some receiving baptism, and some waiting their turn, already undressed, the expression of all being intense in their anxiety to be cleansed of sin, while all the figures are so excellently done that they resemble a marble group. While Andrea was thus employed, some copper engravings of Albert Dürer issued from the press, from which he borrowed figures, adapting them to his style, which has led some to think, not that it is bad to use the good things of others, but that Andrea was weak in invention. Baecio Bandinelli, a celebrated designer of the day, fancied he would like to colour in oils, and knowing no better man than Andrea in that art at Florence, got him to make his portrait, which was a good likeness, and may still be seen. Observing his methods of colouring, he gave up his idea and returned to sculpture, either owing to the difficulty or because he did not care for painting. For Alessandro Corsini Andrea did a Virgin seated on the ground with the Child, surrounded by cherubs, executed with great art and in pleasant colouring.[2] For a mercer, a friend of his who kept a shop in Rome, he did a lovely head. Giovanni Battista Puccini of Florence, being charmed with Andrea's style, employed him to do a Madonna to send to France, but it was so beautiful that he kept it for himself. However, as he was doing business in France, and commissioned to obtain works from great painters, he got Andrea to do a dead Christ supported by angels, who sorrowfully regard their Maker in such misery for the sins of men.[3] This work gave such universal delight that Andrea was persuaded to have it engraved at Rome by Agostino Viniziano, but as it did not succeed very well he never suffered anything to be printed again. The picture caused as much delight in France as at Florence, so that the king sent orders to Andrea

[1] He resumed the work in 1522, and finished it in 1526.
[2] Possibly the Holy Family in the Pinakothek, Munich.
[3] Vienna Gallery.

for others, and Andrea, by the advice of his friends, decided soon after to go to France.

Meanwhile, in the year 1515, the Floentines, learning that Pope Leo X. intended to favour them with a visit, prepared a great reception, with arches, façades, temples, colossal statues, and other ornaments, more sumptuous than had ever been seen before, as the city was richer then in men of genius than it had ever been. At the S. Pier Gattolini gate Jacopo di Sandro made an arch full of scenes, assisted by Baccio da Montelupo. At S. Felice, in Piazza, Giuliano del Tasso made another, and at S. Trinità he did some statues, a half-length Romulus and a Trajan column in the Mercato Nuovo. On the Piazza de' Signori, Antonio, brother of Giuliano da S. Gallo, made an octagonal temple, and Baccio Bandinelli did a giant for the loggia. Between the Badia and the Podestà palace an arch was set up by Granaccio and Aristotele da S. Gallo; at the corner of the Bischeri, Il Rosso made another, beautifully designed with a variety of figures. But the best of all was a wooden façade to S. Maria del Fiore decorated by Andrea, with scenes in grisaille. The architecture of this and of some bas-reliefs and sculptures was by Jacopo Sansovino, so that the Pope considered it as fine as if it had been of marble. It was the invention of Lorenzo de' Medici, the Pope's father. On the piazza of S. Maria Novella, Jacopo made a horse like that at Rome, of great beauty. Countless ornaments also were made for the Pope's Hall in the via della Scala, the street being half full of beautiful bas-reliefs by many artists, but most designed by Baccio Bandinelli. Thus when Leo entered Florence on 3rd September that same year the decorations were considered the finest and the most extensive ever seen.

But to return to Andrea. He soon completed another picture for the King of France, at his request, being a lovely Madonna, which was immediately sent, the merchants receiving four times as much as they had paid for it. About that time Pier Francesco Borgherini had employed Baccio d'Agnolo to make wooden arm-chairs, chests, seats and beds to furnish a room. In order to have pictures of corresponding excellence, he employed Andrea to do some medium figures of the history of Joseph,[1] to compete with some beautiful ones by Granaccio and Jacopo da Pontormo. By extraordinary efforts Andrea endeavoured to surpass these, and succeeded admirably, showing his ability in the variety of the circumstances which occur in the scenes. During the siege of Florence Giovanni Battista della Palla

[1] Pitti Gallery.

proposed to have them packed up to be sent to the King of France, but they were so firmly fixed that they could not be removed without destruction, and consequently they remain in the same place, with an admirable Madonna. Andrea next did a head of Christ, now kept by the Servite friars on the altar of the Nunziata. I do not think that the human intellect can imagine anything finer of its kind. In the chapel of the church outside the S. Gallo gate there were two other panels of Andrea, and many inferior to his. The friars, wishing to have another, induced the superior of the chapel to give it to Andrea. Beginning at once, he made four figures standing, discussing the Trinity.[1] St. Augustine, of African appearance, dressed as a bishop, turns vehemently towards St. Peter Martyr, who is holding an open book, his mien and gesture most formidable, the head and figure being much admired. Next to him is St. Francis, holding a book in one hand, striking the other on his breast, his fervour apparently making utterance difficult. St. Laurence, as a young man, gives place to the authority of the others. Kneeling beneath are two figures, one a Magdalene with beautiful draperies. This is a portrait of his wife, for he never painted a woman without using her as his model, and owing to this habit all the women's heads which he did are alike. The last of the four figures was St. Sebastian, nude, and turning his back, a life-like figure. Artists consider this his best work in oils, as the measurements of the figures are carefully observed, the expressions are suitable, the heads of the youths being soft and those of the old hard, with a medium state for those of middle age; in fact the picture is most beautiful in every detail. It is now in S. Jacopo tra' Fossi, at the Alberti corner, with others by the same hand. While Andrea was just maintaining himself in Florence with these works, without improving his condition, the two pictures he sent to King Francis in France were considered much the best out of all that came from Rome, Venice and Lombardy. The king praised them greatly, and he was told that Andrea would readily come to France to serve him. Accordingly, being paid the expenses of his journey, Andrea set out joyfully for France,[2] taking with him his pupil Andrea Sguazzella. Arrived at the court, they were graciously welcomed by the king, and before he had been a day there Andrea experienced the liberality and courtesy of that magnanimous king, receiving rich vestments and money. He then began to work, and was so highly favoured by the king and court that he seemed to have ex-

[1] Pitti Gallery.   [2] At the end of May 1518.

changed a very wretched condition for a most happy one. He drew, among his first things, a portrait of the Dauphin,[1] then only a few months old, and took it to the king, receiving for it 300 gold crowns. Continuing, he did a Charity[2] for the king, which was much admired and valued, as it deserved. The king gave him a large pension, and did everything to retain him, promising him that he should lack nothing, for he was pleased with Andrea's quickness and his satisfaction with everything. Besides this, Andrea pleased the court, doing many works for them. If he had considered his origin and the position to which Fortune had raised him, no doubt he could have attained an honourable rank, not to speak of riches. But one day, as he was doing a St. Jerome in penitence for the king's mother, some letters arrived from his wife at Florence, and he began, for some cause or another, to think of returning. He asked the king's permission to go, saying that he would return when he had arranged some affairs, and that he would bring back his wife, to enable him to live there more comfortably, and that he would bring with him valuable paintings and sculptures. The king trusted him, and gave him money, while Andrea swore on the Gospels to return in a few months. Arrived in Florence,[3] he enjoyed his wife, his friends and the city for several months. When the time for his return to France had passed, he found that in building[4] and pleasures, without working, he had spent all his money and the king's also. But though he wished to return, the tears and entreaties of his wife prevailed more than his own needs and his promise to the king. Francis became so angry at his faithlessness that he for a long time looked askance at Florentine painters, and he swore that if Andrea ever fell into his hands he would have more pain than pleasure, in spite of all his ability. Thus Andrea remained in Florence, fallen very low from his high station, and maintaining himself as best he could.

When Andrea left for France the men of the Scalzo, believing he would never return, had given the remainder of their cloister to Francia Bigio, who had already done two scenes there. When Andrea returned they induced him to take up the work, and he did four scenes in a row. The first is St. John before Herod; the second the banquet and the dancing of Herodias,[5] with excellent

---

[1] Afterwards Henry II., born 28 February, 1518.
[2] Now in the Louvre. [3] October 1519.
[4] He built a house for himself at Florence.
[5] Her daughter rather.

figures; the third is the beheading of John, the half-naked executioner being finely drawn, as are all the others; in the fourth Herodias is presenting the head, and some of the figures are in amazement. These scenes were for some time the school of many youths, now excellent artists. At a vaulted corner leading to the Ingesuati outside the Pinti gate Andrea did a Virgin seated in a tabernacle with the Child and a little St. John laughing, so perfectly done that its beauty and vivacity are highly valued. The head of the Virgin is a portrait of his wife. This tabernacle for its remarkable beauty was left standing when in 1530 the convent of the Jesuits and other beautiful buildings were destroyed during the siege of Florence.

At this time Francia Bartolommeo Panciatichi the elder was engaged in business in France, and wishing to leave a memorial of himself at Lyons, he instructed Baccio d'Agnolo to get Andrea to do a panel of the Assumption[1] with the Apostles standing about. Andrea almost completed it, but as the wood split several times it was not entirely finished at his death. It was afterwards set up in the house of Bartolommeo Panciatichi the younger as a work truly admirable for the figures of the Apostles, as well as the Virgin, standing and surrounded by a choir of cherubs, some of whom are gracefully supporting her. At the bottom of the picture Andrea has made a striking likeness of himself among the Apostles. This is now in the villa of the Baroncelli, a little outside Florence, in a small church built to receive it by Piero Salviati near his villa. In two corners at the bottom of the garden of the Servites, Andrea did two scenes of the Parable of the Vineyard,[2] the planting and laying out, and the husbandman asking for labourers among those standing idle, one of whom is seated and rubs his hands, debating whether he shall go with the other workmen, like the loafers who have no relish for work. Much finer is the husbandman paying them, while they murmur and complain. Among them is an excellent figure of a man counting the money. These scenes are in grisaille, skilfully done in fresco. At the top of a staircase in the noviciate of the same convent Andrea did a Pietà in a niche, coloured in fresco, of great beauty. He did another small Pietà and a Nativity in the chamber of Angelo Aretino, the general of the convent. For Zanobi Bracci, who greatly desired to have works of his, he did for a chamber a Virgin kneeling against a rock and regarding Christ, who rests on some clothes and looks up smiling; St. John standing by points out to her the true Son of God. Behind them is Joseph, his head in his hands, which rest on a rock, his spirit irradiated at seeing the human race made divine by this birth.[1]

When Cardinal Giulio de' Medici was commissioned by Pope Leo [2] to have the vaulting of the Medici palace at Poggio a Cajano, between Pistoia and Florence, decorated with stucco and painting, the charge of the works and payments was entrusted to Ottaviano de' Medici the Magnificent, as one who understood such matters, and a patron of art like his predecessors, more fond than others of having his houses adorned with the works of the best artists. He entrusted a third to Francia Bigio, a third to Andrea, and the rest to Jacopo da Pontormo. But in spite of Ottaviano's entreaties and offers of money he could not prevail upon them to finish the work. Andrea alone completed with great diligence a scene on a wall of Cæsar receiving tribute of all the animals. The design for this is in our book, with many others by his hand, and it is the most finished painting in grisaille that Andrea ever did. In order to surpass Francia and Jacopo, Andrea took exceptional pains, making a magnificent perspective and some very difficult steps up to Cæsar's seat. He adorned this with appropriate statues, not satisfied with the variety of figures who are bringing the various animals. There is an Indian in a yellow tunic with a cage on his shoulders containing parrots, rarely drawn in perspective. Here also some are bringing Indian boars, lions, giraffes, leopards, wolves, apes and Moors, most divinely produced in fresco. On the steps he made a dwarf seated, holding a chameleon in a box, the deformed figure being indescribably done in beautiful proportion. But the work was left unfinished owing to the death of Pope Leo. Although Duke Alessandro de' Medici wanted Jacopo da Pontormo to finish it, he could not prevail upon him to take it up. It is a pity that it is imperfect, as it is the finest hall in any villa in the world. Returning to Florence, Andrea did a half-length nude St. John the Baptist, of great beauty, for Giovan. Maria Benintendi, who afterwards gave it to Duke Cosimo.

Whilst these things were going on Andrea would sigh when he thought of France, and if he had expected pardon no doubt he would have gone back. He determined to bring his talents to help his fortune. Accordingly he did a half-naked St. John the Baptist to send to the grand master of France,[3] in order that he might restore him to the king's favour. For some reason he did not send it, but sold it to Ottaviano de' Medici the

[1] Pitti Gallery.   [2] In 1521.   [3] Anne de Montmorency.

Magnificent, who always valued him highly. He also did two Madonnas for him in the same style, which remain in his house to this day. Not long after Zanobi Bracci got him to do a picture for Monsignore di S. Biause,[1] upon which he devoted great pains, anxious to regain the favour of King Francis, whose service he hoped to re-enter. He also did a picture for Lorenzo Jacopi, much larger than usual, of a Madonna seated with the Child and two other figures sitting on steps, similar to his other works in design and colouring.[2] He further did a lovely Madonna for Giovanni d'Agostino Dini, now much valued for its beauty, and drew a most life-like portrait of Cosimo Lapi.

On the outbreak of the plague in Florence and some of the country districts in 1523, Andrea, to escape it and do some work, went to Mugello to do a panel for the Camaldolite nuns of S. Piero a Luco, taking his wife, his little daughter, his wife's sister, and a pupil. Here he worked quietly, and as the nuns did many courtesies to his wife and to him and the others, he bestowed great pains on his task. He represented a dead Christ lamented by the Virgin, St. John the Evangelist and a Magdalene,[3] the figures actually appearing alive. St. John displays his tender love, the Magdalene weeps, the face and posture of the Virgin show her extreme grief at seeing the Christ, who seems in relief, while St. Peter and St. Paul stand dazed with sorrow and compassion at seeing the Saviour dead in His Mother's lap, all proving what great delight Andrea took in the perfection of art. In truth this panel has brought more renown to the convent than all the other building and outlay made there, great and magnificent as they were. On the completion of the work, Andrea remained in the convent some weeks as the plague was still raging, and he received every attention. To occupy his time he did a Visitation, which is in the church over the Presepio, as the pediment for an ancient picture. He also did a lovely head of Christ, of no great size, like the one over the altar of the Nunziata, but did not finish it. The head may be counted among his best works, and it is now in the monastery of the Angeli at Florence, in the possession of Padre Don Antonio of Pisa, the patron not only of artists but of all men of ability. Some copies have been made, as it was entrusted by Don Silvano Razzi to Zanobi Poggoni, the painter, to make a copy for Bartolommeo Gondi, who asked for one, and others were done which

---

[1] Jacques de Beaune de Semblancay.
[2] Sold to the Duke of Mantua in 1605.
[3] Pitti Gallery; painted 1524.

are much valued in Florence. In this way Andrea avoided the dangers of the plague, while the nuns profited by his talents, obtaining a work which may stand comparison with any by the best artists. Thus it is no wonder that Ramazotto, a captain at Scaricalasino, made several attempts to get it during the siege of Florence, intending to send it to his chapel in S. Michele in Bosco at Bologna.

On returning to Florence, Andrea did a panel for his friend the glassworker, Becuccio da Gambassi, of a Virgin and Child in the air, and four figures below, St. John the Baptist, St. Mary Magdalene, St. Sebastian and St. Roch, with portraits of Becuccio and his wife in the predella. The panel is now at Gambassi, in the Valdelsa, between Volterra and Florence.[1] For a chapel of Zanobi Bracci at Rovezzano he did a lovely Madonna suckling the Child, and a Joseph, with such skill that they issue from the picture; this is now in the house of M. Antonio Bracci, Zanobi's son. At the same time Andrea did two more scenes in the courtyard of the Scalzo, one of Zacharias sacrificing and rendered dumb by the angel, the other a marvellously beautiful Visitation.

Federico II., Duke of Mantua, in passing through Florence on his way to visit Clement VII., saw over a door of the Casa Medici that portrait of Pope Leo between Cardinal Giulio de' Medici and Cardinal de' Rossi done by Raphael. It pleased him so much that he determined to get possession of it, and when at Rome he asked the Pope for it, Clement willingly granting his request. Accordingly Ottaviano de' Medici, then the guardian of Ippolito and Alessandro at Florence, was directed to pack it and send it to Mantua. The thing greatly displeased Ottaviano, who did not want to deprive Florence of such a painting, and he wondered at the Pope's action. However, he sent word that he would serve the duke, but as the frame was bad it was necessary to make a new one, and when it had been gilt he would send it to Mantua. Then he sent secretly for Andrea and explained the matter to him, saying there was nothing for it but to make a copy and to send it to the duke, keeping back Raphael's picture. Andrea promised to do his best, and set to work secretly in Ottavanio's house. He succeeded so well that Ottaviano, connoisseur as he was, could not tell the copy from the original, for Andrea had even copied the grease spots. They then sent it framed to Mantua, the duke being delighted, and the work was much admired by Giulio Romano the painter, Raphael's pupil, who did not suspect the truth. He would have

[1] Now in the Pitti Gallery.

always believed it to be Raphael's, but Giorgio Vasari, being at
Mantua, disclosed the facts to him, for when a child and the
protégé of M. Ottaviano he had seen Andrea doing it. Giulio
had displayed great courtesy to Vasari, and was showing him
many antiquities and paintings, when he finally came to this
picture as being the best of all. Giorgio said, "It is a fine work,
but not Raphael's." "What!" exclaimed Giulio, "I know that
it is, for I recognise my own handiwork in it." "You are mis-
taken," said Giorgio, "it is by Andrea del Sarto, and was done
in Florence; here is the proof," and he showed him. Giulio
turned the picture, and seeing the signature, shrugged his
shoulders and said, "I value it even more than if it was by
Raphael, for it is extraordinary that one great master should
so exactly imitate the style of another." This shows the ability
of Andrea when acting in co-operation as well as independently.
Thus the duke was satisfied and Florence retained a valuable
picture, thanks to the device of M. Ottaviano, who had the picture
given to him by Duke Alessandro and kept it for many years.
Finally he gave it to Duke Cosimo, who keeps it in his wardrobe
among many other famous pictures.[1]

While engaged upon this portrait, Andrea did for M. Ottaviano
the head of Cardinal Giulio de' Medici, afterwards Pope Clement,
alone, like Raphael's and of great beauty. It was subsequently
given by M. Ottaviano to the old Bishop de' Marzi. Not long after
M. Baldo Magini of Prato wished to have a beautiful picture
for the Madonna della Carcere on his estate, where he had
previously made a fine marble ornament. Andrea was suggested
to him, among others, and although not knowing much of the
matter, M. Baldo had almost made up his mind to employ him
when one Niccolo Soggi, of Sansovino, who had friends in Prato,
was recommended to M. Baldo and obtained the work, as they
said no better master could be had. Andrea, being sent for, went
to Prato with Domenico Puligo and other painters, feeling
certain that the work would be his. On arriving, however, he
found Niccolo in possession, and so confident that he offered
to wager any sum of money before M. Baldo that he would paint
the better picture. Although a poor-spirited man, Andrea, who
knew Niccolo's powers, replied, "My boy here does not know
much art, but if you wish to wager I will put my money on him,
but for myself I have nothing to gain in such a contest, and it
would be shameful to lose." Then telling M. Baldo to give the
work to Niccolo, for he would please the marketers, Andrea

[1] The original is in the Pitti Gallery, the copy (painted in 1524) at Naples.

returned to Florence. There he was allotted a panel for Pisa, divided into five pictures, afterwards set up in the Madonna of S. Agnesa, on the wall between the old citadel and the Duomo. In each scene he did one figure, putting St. John the Baptist and St. Peter on one side of the miracle-working Madonna and St. Catherine the Martyr, St. Agnes and St. Margaret on the other, all figures of marvellous beauty, and considered the most delicate and lovely women that he ever did. M. Jacopo, a Servite friar, had absolved a woman from a vow on condition that she would have a Madonna made to be placed over the side door of the Nunziata leading into the outside cloister. Finding Andrea, he told him that he had but little money to expend, and he thought that, as Andrea had made such a reputation at the house, he would do right to execute the work. Andrea being a mild man readily agreed, urged by the friar's arguments and by his desire for profit and glory. He soon after produced a lovely Virgin in fresco, seated with the Child in her arms, and St. Joseph leaning against a sack, his eyes fixed on an open book. This picture, in design, grace, excellence of colouring, vivacity and relief, proved him far superior to all his predecessors; indeed, the work as it stands praises itself.

Only one scene was lacking to complete the series in the court of the Scalzo. Andrea, having aggrandised his style after seeing the figures begun and almost finished by Michelagnolo in the sacristy of S. Lorenzo, put his hand to this, and giving a final proof of his progress, he painted the birth of St. John the Baptist in fine figures, much better executed and in higher relief than those previously done by him there. Among other things there is a woman carrying the new-born child to the bed where St. Elizabeth is lying, who is also a fine figure. Zacharias is writing on a sheet resting on one knee, holding it with one hand and writing the child's name with the other, the figure only lacking breath. Very fine also is an old woman on a stool, laughing at the child-bearing of the aged Elizabeth in the most natural manner. On completing this work, which is very admirable, Andrea did a panel for the general of Vallombrosa of four fine figures, St. John the Baptist, St. John Gualbert, founder of the order, St. Michael and St. Bernard, cardinal and monk of the order, with some very pretty and life-like children in the middle.[1] It is at Vallombrosa, at the top of a rock tenanted by monks separated from the others, in some rooms called the cells, where they live like hermits. For Giuliano Scala, Andrea then made a panel to send

[1] Uffizi, Florence; painted 1528.

to Serrazzana of the Virgin seated with the Child, and St. Celsus and St. Julia, from the knees up, with St. Onofrio, St. Catherine, St. Benedict, St. Anthony of Padua, St. Peter and St. Mark, a work valued as highly as his others.[1] He did an Annunciation for the same Giuliano as a pediment to the other in a lunette, which is in the Servites' church in a chapel of the choir in the principal tribune.[2]

The monks of S. Salvi remained many years without thinking of having anything done to their Last Supper, which they had given to Andrea, when he did four figures in the arch. At last one worthy abbot determined to have it finished. Andrea, having previously bound himself to do this, made no objection, and taking up the work he finished it in a few months,[3] doing a piece at a time, at his leisure, and it is considered the most facile work in the brightest colouring and best design that he ever did or that could be done. He endowed the figures with infinite grandeur, majesty and grace, so that I cannot do justice to its merits, everyone who sees it being amazed. Thus it is no wonder that it was allowed to stand during the siege of Florence in 1529, when the soldiers were directed to destroy everything in the quarters outside the city, monasteries, hospitals and buildings of every kind. They had destroyed the church and campanile of S. Salvi, and were beginning to attack the convent, but on coming to the refectory where the Last Supper is, and having perhaps heard of the marvellous painting, they stayed their hands, resolving not to touch it unless absolutely obliged.

For the company of S. Jacopo, called il Nicchio, Andrea next did a processional banner of St. James touching the chin of a boy dressed as a flagellant, and another with a book in his hand, very fine and natural. He made the portrait of a steward of the monks of Vallombrosa, who lived in the country for their affairs; this was placed under a vine arranged with various fancies, where it was exposed to wind and weather, as the steward, who was a friend of Andrea, desired. On the completion of the work Andrea called his wife Lucrezia and said, "Come here; I have some colours over and I will paint your portrait to show how well preserved you are and yet how different from your first portraits." But as she would not keep still, possibly having something else in her mind, Andrea, as if divining that he was near his end, took a mirror and painted himself, making a fine portrait.[4] This is owned by his wife, who is still alive. He also

---

[1] Berlin Gallery, also belongs to 1528. [2] Now in the Pitti Gallery.
[3] In 1519. [4] Uffizi.

drew a friend, a Pisan canon, this fine likeness being now at Pisa. For the Signoria he began the cartoons for the painting of the balustrades of the Ringhiera in the piazza, with many ingenious ideas illustrating the quarters of the city, as well as the banners of the principal arts held by boys, and also figures of the Virtues, and the famous mountains and rivers in the Florentine territory. It was left incomplete at his death, and so was a panel done for the monks of Vallombrosa for the abbey of Poppi in Casentino, though it was nearly finished. It represents an Assumption[1] with cherubs, St. John Gualbert, St. Bernard, the cardinal and monk, St. Catherine and St. Fidele, and is now in the said abbey. It was the same with a panel which should have gone to Pisa. But he completed a fine picture now in the house of Filippo Salviati, and some others.

About the same time Giovanni Battista della Palla, having bought as many notable paintings and sculptures as he could, and having the rest copied, had thus despoiled Florence of a quantity of choice things to furnish a suite of rooms for the King of France, which was to be as rich as possible in such decoration. He wished Andrea to return to the king's service and favour, and got him to do two pictures. One represented Abraham sacrificing Isaac,[2] judged his best work until then, the patriarch showing his lively faith and constancy in not fearing to slay his own son. He turns his head towards a beautiful angel, who seems to have told him to hold his hand. I say no more of the attitude, costume and other things of the patriarch, since it is impossible to say enough, but Isaac is a beautiful boy, trembling with fear and almost dead before the blow. His neck is sunburnt, but the parts covered by his clothes are white. The ram among the thorns looks alive, and the clothes of Isaac on the ground are very natural. Two naked servants are watching a grazing ass, and the landscape is of the utmost beauty. After the death of Andrea and the arrest of Battista the picture was bought by Filippo Strozzi, who gave it to Sig. Alfonso Davalos, Marquis of il Vasto, and he had it taken to the island of Ischia, near Naples, and placed in some rooms with other fine paintings. In the other picture Andrea did a lovely Charity with three infants. It was bought after Andrea's death from his widow by Domenico Conti, the painter. He sold it to Niccolo Antinori, who values it as a rare work.

Ottaviano de' Medici, seeing the improvement in Andrea's

[1] Pitti Gallery; painted 1529-31. [2] Dresden Gallery.

*L 785

style, wished to have a picture by him. Andrea being anxious to serve a lord who had always favoured men of talent, and to whom he was much indebted, made him a Virgin seated on the ground with a Child astride on her knees, turning His head to St. John held by an old St. Elizabeth, who seems alive, the whole work being produced with incredible art, design and finish.[1] On completing the picture Andrea took it to M. Ottaviano, but as Florence was then being besieged, he had other preoccupations, and told Andrea to give it to anyone he liked, excusing himself and thanking him. But Andrea replied that he had laboured for Ottaviano and his it should be. "Sell it," said M. Ottaviano, "and use the money, because I know what I am saying." Andrea accordingly went home, but would never give it to anyone. At the end of the siege, when the Medici returned to Florence, Andrea brought the picture to M. Ottaviano, who thanked him warmly and paid him double the price. It is now in the chamber of Madonna Francesca, his wife, sister of the Very Rev. Salviati, who values the pictures left by her husband just as she retains his friends. Andrea did another picture, like his Charity referred to, for Gio. Borgherini, of a Madonna and a little St. John offering the Christ a ball representing the world, and a fine St. Joseph. Povolo da Terrarossa, as the friend of all painters, having seen Andrea's sketch of Abraham, wished to have something by his hands, and asked for the figure of Abraham, which Andrea did for him readily, the small copy being no whit inferior to the large original. Pavolo, being greatly delighted, asked the price, thinking it would be high, but Andrea named a wretchedly small sum, and Pavolo, half ashamed, shrugged his shoulders and paid him. The picture was afterwards sent by him to Naples, where it is the finest to be seen. During the siege of Florence some captains of the city made off with the pay of the men. Andrea was asked to paint these and other fugitives and rebel citizens in the Podestà palace, and agreed to do so. Not wishing to earn the nickname degl' Impiccati, like Andrea del Castagno, he let it be understood that he had handed over the work to an apprentice of his called Bernardo del Buda.[2] But constructing a large shed by which he went in and out at night, he painted the figures himself and made them seem alive. The soldiers, painted on the wall of the old Mercatanzia, near la Condotta, facing the piazza, have been whitewashed over for many years, and the citizens finished by him in the palace were obliterated.

[1] Pitti Gallery; finished 1529.   [2] Bernardo de' Rosselli.

In his last years Andrea became intimate with the governors of the company of St. Bastiano, behind the Servites, and he made them a fine half-length St. Sebastian, which appears to have been his last work. At the end of the siege Andrea expected better things, though he had little hope that his design of returning to France would succeed, as Giovanni Battista della Palla was taken, Florence being full of soldiers and stores. Among the soldiers were some landsknechts infected with the plague, which they communicated to the city. Andrea, whether through fear or through having eaten too freely after the privations of the siege, fell grievously sick. He took to his bea and was much neglected, his wife fearing infection and keeping away, and he died, they say, with no one by, being buried by the men of the Scalzo with little ceremony in the church of the Servites, near his house, where the members of that company are laid.

Andrea's death was a great loss to the city and to art, because he improved steadily until his forty-second and last year, and would have continued so to do, because more certain progress is won thus gradually than by a spurt. There is no doubt that if Andrea had stayed at Rome, when he went there to see the works of Raphael and Michelagnolo and the statues and monuments, he would have greatly enriched his style of composition and endowed his figures with more refinement and force, things only attained by those who stay some time in Rome to study and examine in detail. Naturally his design was sweet and graceful, his colouring facile and very brilliant, and it is thought that had he remained in Rome he must have surpassed all the artists of his day. But some believe that he was deterred by the copious works of the city and by the sight of the numerous pupils of Raphael, with their bold designs and their unceasing toil, and, being timid, he had not the heart to continue, and concluded it would be better for him to return to Florence, where, by turning over gradually what he had seen, he made so much profit that his works are greatly valued and admired: indeed they have been more imitated since his death than when he was alive. Those who prized them and have since sold them have gained three times as much as they paid him, as he always put a low value on his things, being of a timid nature, and because the joiners, who did the best things for private houses, would never give him any work except when they knew him to be in great need and ready to accept any sum. Nevertheless, his works are most rare and deservedly valued, as he was one of the greatest masters who have lived hitherto.

Many of his designs are in our book, and all are good, especially the scene done at Poggio, where the tribute of all the oriental animals is presented to Cæsar. It is in grisaille and better finished than any other of his designs, as when he drew from Nature for his works he made rough sketches as an indication, and did not make them perfect except in the finished work, so that his designs served rather as an aid to the memory than as things to copy. His pupils were countless, but they did not all follow the same course of study under him, some stopping a little while and some longer, not through Andrea's fault, but his wife's, who tyrannously ordered them all about and rendered their lives a burden.

Among Andrea's pupils were Jacopo da Pontormo, Andrea Sguazzella, who did a palace outside Paris [1] in his style, which is much praised, Il Solosmeo, Pier Francesco di Jacopo di Sandro, who did three panels in S. Spirito, Francesco Salviati and Giorgio Vasari of Arezzo, Salviati's companion, although he was but little with Andrea, Jacopo del Conte of Florence, and Nannoccio, now in France with the cardinal of Tournon, in great credit. Jacopo, called Jacone, was another pupil and a great friend, closely imitating his style. During Andrea's life Jacone availed himself greatly of his master's help, as we see in all his works, chiefly on the façade of the house of the knight Buondelmonti on the piazza of S. Trinità. Domenico Conti was left the heir of Andrea's designs and other artistic things, but made little profit in painting, and it is believed some artists stole them one night, and it was never known what had become of them. Domenico Conti, not ungrateful for the benefits received from his master, and desirous to do him honour, induced Raffaello da Montelupo to make a marble slab set on a pilaster in the church of the Servites, with this epitaph by the learned M. Pier Vettori, then a youth:

ANDREAE SARTIO
ADMIRABILIS INGENII PICTORI
AC VETERIBUS ILLIS
OMNIUM JUDICIO COMPARANDO
DOMINICUS CONTES DISCIPULUS
PRO LABORIBUS IN SE INSTITUENDO SUSCEPTIS
GRATO ANIMO POSUIT
VIXIT ANN. XLII. OB A. MDXXX.

---

[1] Semblancay, painted 1516-24.

Not long after some wardens of the church, through ignorance rather than hostility, annoyed that the slab should have been put in that place without their licence, succeeded in having it removed, nor has it yet been set up elsewhere. Thus we see that Fortune not only influences the fate of men when alive, but also their memory. However, in despite of all, the works and name of Andrea will long survive, and I hope these writings of mine will preserve their memory for many centuries. Let us conclude then that, if Andrea in life was mean-spirited and contented with little, in art his spirit was lofty, and he was quick and skilful in work, so that he greatly assisted art by his style in design and colouring. He committed fewer errors than any other Florentine painter, for he understood light and shade and the vanishing into darkness, and painted with a very vivid sweetness, while in fresco he displayed perfect harmony and did not retouch much *a secco*, so that his works seem to have been done in a single day. Thus he should serve as an example to Tuscan artists and bear an honoured palm among their most famous men.

MADONNA PROPERZIA DE' ROSSI, Sculptress of Bologna
(c. 1490 – 1530)

IT is remarkable that women have always succeeded and become famous in all the exercises to which they have devoted themselves, as might be proved by countless examples. Everyone knows their worth in domestic matters, and in war there were Camilla, Harpalice, Valasca, Thomyris, Penthesilea, Malpadia, Orithyia, Antiope, Hippolyta, Semiramis, Zenobia and Fulvia, who is said to have frequently taken arms to defend her husband Mark Antony and herself. They have also distinguished themselves in poetry, as Pausanias relates; Corinna was a celebrated versifier, and Eustathius in Homer's catalogue of ships mentions the renowned Sappho, as does Eusebius in his Chronicle, a woman who surpassed the foremost writers of her day, if she really was a woman. Varro bestows extravagant but merited praise upon Erinna, whose three hundred verses may compare with the fame of the foremost light of Greece, her little volume called *Elicate* counterpoising the lengthy *Iliad* of Homer. Aristophanes celebrates Carissenna, a learned and excellent poetess, and also Theano, Merone, Polla, Elpis, Corni-

ficia and Telesilla, to whom a beautiful statue was erected in
the temple of Venus in recognition of her merits. Passing by
the poets, do we not read that Areta taught the learned Aristip-
pus the difficulties of philosophy? Lasthenia and Assiotea were
pupils of the divine Plato. In oratory Sempronia and Hortensia,
Roman women, were most famous. In grammar Agalla (as
Athenæus says) was most rare, and in predicting future things
or in astrology and magic I need only say that Themis, Cas-
sandra and Manto were very celebrated in their day. In agriculture we have Isis and Ceres, and in all the sciences Thespis.
But in no age is this so well illustrated as in our own, in which
women have won the greatest fame in letters, as Signora Vittoria
del Vasto, Signora Veronica Gambara, Signora Caterina Angui-
sola, la Schioppa, la Nugarola, Madonna Laura Battiferra, and
a hundred others learned in Greek and Latin, as well as in the
vulgar tongue and in every other science. They have not feared
either to turn their delicate white hands to mechanical arts,
seeking fame from rough marble and hard iron, as Properzia
de' Rossi has done in our days. She was a talented maiden both
in household duties and in other things, so skilled in sciences
that all men might envy her. She was beautiful in person, and
could sing and play better than any woman in the city of her
day. Being of an ingenious spirit, she began to carve peach-
stones, and did them so well and patiently that they were
marvellous, not only for the delicacy of the work, but for the
slender figures and her clever disposition of them. She thus did
a marvellous Passion of Christ, beautifully carved with numerous
figures besides the crucifiers and the Apostles. This gave her
courage to ask the wardens through her husband for a share
in decorating the three doors of the façade of S. Petronio with
marble figures. They agreed, provided that she should show
them some work in marble. Accordingly she at once made a
portrait for Count Alessandro de' Pepoli of his father Count
Guido which gave great delight not only to him but to all the
city, and the wardens allotted a part of the work to her. She
finished a delicate bas-relief which caused all Bologna to marvel.
Being at the time enamoured of a handsome youth who cared
little for her, the poor lady did Potiphar's wife divesting herself
in despair before Joseph with marvellous feminine grace. This
beautiful work gave her great satisfaction as a relief to her
ardent passion. She would do nothing else for the building,
though everyone asked her, except Maestro Amico,[1] who,

[1] Amico Aspertini.

through envy, always spoke ill of her to the wardens, and owing to his malignity her work was very badly paid. She also did two angels in high relief and finely proportioned, now placed in the church, though against her wish. Finally she took up copper engraving with great success. Indeed, she succeeded in everything except her unhappy love. Her fame spread through Italy and at last reached the ears of Pope Clement VII., who directly after the coronation of the emperor at Bologna asked for her, and learned that she had died that same week, being buried in the hospital of la Morte in accordance with the terms of her will. The Pope, who greatly wished to see her, was very sorry, but far greater was the grief of her fellow-citizens, who considered her the greatest miracle of modern times. Our book has some pen sketches by her and very good copies of things by Raphael. Her portrait is from some painters, friends of hers.

But there have been other women to equal her success in design and as clever in painting as she was in sculpture. The first is Sister Plautilla, a nun, now prioress of the convent of St. Caterina da Siena at Florence, on the Piazza di S. Marco, who, by imitating the works of eminent masters, has done some things so well as to excite the wonder of artists. There are two panels by her in the church of her nunnery, one much admired of an Adoration of the Magi. In the choir of St. Lucia at Pistoia is a large panel of the Madonna and Child, St. Thomas, St. Augustine, St. Mary Magdalene, St. Catherine of Siena, St. Agnes, St. Catherine the Martyr and St. Lucy, and the master of the hospital of Lelmo sent away another large panel of hers. In the refectory of her nunnery is a large Last Supper, and another panel by her is in the work-room. For private houses in Florence she did works too numerous to mention. The wife of Sig. Mondragone, a Spaniard, has a large Annunciation, and Madonna Marietta de' Fedini has another like it. A small Madonna is in S. Giovannino at Florence, and she did a predella for the altar of S. Maria del Fiore containing scenes from the life of St. Zanobius. She also illuminated before she took up works of importance, and there are many very charming examples of such work which I need not mention. But she borrowed her best things from others, thus showing that she would have become excellent, had she, like men, studied design and drawn from Nature. We see this in a Nativity, copied from one done by Bronzino for Filippo Salviati. Her women's faces also, which she could see when she liked, are much better done than her men. In her works she made the portrait of Madonna Gostanzà de' Doni, a lady of remarkable beauty and virtue of the time, with the greatest skill for a lady, after making deduction for the reasons already given.

Madonna Lucrezia, daughter of M. Alfonso Quistelli della Mirandola, now the wife of Count Clemente Pietra, also studied design and painting with great success, having learned from Alessandro Allori, pupil of Bronzino, as we see by her numerous pictures and portraits, worthy of all praise. But Sofonisba of Cremona, daughter of M. Amilcaro Angusciuola, has done more in design and more gracefully than any other lady of our day, for not only has she designed, coloured and drawn from life, and copied the works of others most excellently, but she has produced rare and beautiful paintings of her own. Thus King Philip of Spain, having heard of her merits from the Duke of Alva, sent for her to Spain, where she is in the queen's suite, with a large provision, while the court wonders at her excellence. Not long ago M. Tommaso Cavalieri, a Roman nobleman, sent to Duke Cosimo, together with a Cleopatra by Michelagnolo, a drawing by Sofonisba representing a little girl laughing at a boy crying, because his finger has been pinched by a crab in a basket, which she has offered to him, the design being most graceful and life-like. As she lives in Spain, so that few of her works are in Italy, I have put this in my book of designs, in memory of her ability. We may therefore say with the divine Ariosto that:

> *Le donne son venute in eccellenza*
> *Di ciascun' arte ov'hanno posto cura.*[1]

This is the end of the Life of Properzia, sculptress of Bologna.

ALFONSO LOMBARDI of Ferrara, MICHELAGNOLO of Siena, and GIROLAMO SANTACROCE of Naples, Sculptors; and DOSSO and BATTISTA, Painters of Ferrara.

(1497–1537; ?–?; 1502–1532; 1479–1541; ?–1548)

ALFONSO of Ferrara worked in his early youth in stucco and wax, making a quantity of portraits in small medallions for gentlemen and noblemen of his country, and some, which may still be seen, display his ability and judgment, such as those of Prince Doria, Alfonso, Duke of Ferrara, Clement VII., the Emperor Charles

[1] *Orlando Furioso*, Canto XX. stanza 2.

V., Cardinal Ippolito de' Medici, Bembo, Ariosto, and other similar personages. Being in Bologna for the coronation of Charles V., he did the decoration for the door of S. Petronio, and won notice for being the first to introduce a good method of making portraits in medallions, so that there was no great man in the court for whom he did not work, to his great advantage. Not content with the fame he won for his works in clay, wax and stucco, he began on marble, and made such progress in some things of no great importance that he was employed to do the tomb of Ramazzotto[1] in S. Michele in Bosco, outside Bologna, which won him a great reputation. After this he did some marble half-reliefs for the predella of the altar, at the shrine of St. Dominic in the same city.[2] For the door of S. Petronio he did some small scenes of the Resurrection of Christ of great beauty, on the left on entering the church.[3] But the Bolognese were most pleased with the Death of Our Lady, in full relief, of strong composition and stucco, in the upper apartment of the hospital of la Vita. Among other things, it contains a remarkable figure of a Jew, leaving his hands fixed to the Virgin's bier. In the public palace of the city he made of the same composition a large Hercules over the slain hydra, in the governor's hall. It was done in competition with Zaccheria da Volterra, whom he far surpassed. For the Madonna del Baracane he did two angels in stucco supporting a canopy, in half-relief, and between two arches in the middle of the nave of S. Giuseppe he did the twelve Apostles in clay in medallions.[4] He also did life-size clay figures of St. Petronius, St. Proculus, St. Francis and St. Dominic, of great beauty and fine style, at the corners of the vaulting of S. Maria del Popolo in the same city. By his hand also are some things in stucco at Castel Bolognese, and others in the company of S. Giovanni at Cesena. Let no one wonder that I have spoken of little but clay, wax and stucco, hardly mentioning marble, for Alfonso was always inclined to such work, past a certain age, and being handsome and of youthful appearance, he practised his art for pleasure and a sort of vain-glory, rather than because he wished to chisel stone. He always wore gold and other trinkets on his arms, neck and clothing, proving himself a vain fellow, not an artist anxious for fame. However suitable such ornaments may be for men of wealth or good blood, they are contemptible in artists and others, who only wear them in order to vie with the wealthy,

[1] i.e. Ramazzotto Scaricalasino, probably about 1526.
[2] Commissioned 1533.   [3] Commissioned 1526.
[4] Now in the Duomo, Ferrara.

though they earn not the praise but the scorn of the judicious. Alfonso, being so enamoured of himself and behaving in a manner not beseeming a talented artist, spoiled all the glory which he had acquired in his profession. One evening, at a wedding in the house of a count of Bologna, he had made love to a noble lady, and was invited by her to a torch dance. As he accompanied her, he gazed at her with eyes full of tenderness, and exclaimed, with a sigh:

S'amor non è, che dunque è quel ch'io sento?[1]

The lady, to make him conscious of his presumption, quickly replied, "It must be a louse." This being heard by many, the phrase spread throughout Bologna, and Andrea became a perpetual laughing-stock. If he had abandoned the vanities of the world and devoted himself to art he would undoubtedly have accomplished marvels, as what he did in spite of all clearly shows.

When Charles V. was in Bologna,[2] Alfonso saw the excellent portrait of him done by Titian of Cador, and he also desired to portray the emperor. As he had no other opening he begged Titian, without disclosing the purpose, to take him into his majesty's presence instead of one of those who carried his paints. Titian, being a great friend and very courteous, as ever, took Alfonso with him into the emperor's room. When Titian sat down to begin, Alfonso got behind him in order not to be seen by the artist who was busy with his work and, taking up a small box in the shape of a medal, drew the emperor in stucco, completing it at the same time as Titian finished his portrait. When the emperor rose, Alfonso shut up the box so that Titian should not see it, and put it in his pocket. But when the emperor said, "Show what you have done," he was obliged to produce the portrait with all humility. After looking at it, the emperor said, "Would you venture to do it in marble?" "Certainly, your majesty," replied Alfonso. "Do so, then," said Charles, "and bring it to me at Genoa." Titian's feelings may well be imagined. He must have thought he had compromised his talents. But the strangest of all was that when his majesty sent 1000 crowns to Titian, he commanded him to give half to Alfonso, keeping the rest for himself, which must have caused him much chagrin. Alfonso, meanwhile, putting forth his best efforts, produced a marble head which was considered remarkable. When he took

---

[1] "What is this sensation if it be not love?"
[2] For his coronation on 24 February, 1530.

it to the emperor he deservedly received another 300 crowns. Having thus achieved renown, Alfonso was taken to Rome by Cardinal Ippolito de' Medici to stay with numerous sculptors and painters, and there he copied a much-admired antique bust of the Emperor Vitellius in marble. Having thereby confirmed the good opinion of the cardinal and all Rome, he was employed by his patron to make a bust of Pope Clement VII., and soon after one of Giuliano de' Medici, the cardinal's father, which, however, was not finished. When these busts were sold in Rome, I bought them at the request of Ottaviano de' Medici the Magnificent, with some paintings now placed by Duke Cosimo in the new rooms of his palace, where I painted the ceiling and walls with the deeds of Leo X. They are over the red marbls doors there, a stone found near Florence, together with the busts of other illustrious members of the Medici house.

To return to Alfonso. He continued to do several sculptures for the cardinal, but being small they are lost. On the death of Clement, Alfonso was engaged by the cardinal to make his tomb and that of Leo X. After preparing a beautiful wax model with figures, from sketches by Michelagnolo, he went to Carrara to purchase marble. But the cardinal dying[1] soon after at Itri, having left Rome for Africa, the work was taken out of Alfonso's hands by the Cardinal Salviati, Ridolfi Pucci, Cibo and Gaddi, the commissioners, and allotted by the favour of Madonna Lucrezia Salviati, daughter of the great Lorenzo de' Medici and sister of Leo, to Baccio Bandinelli, sculptor of Florence, who had made models during Clement's life. Half-distracted at this event, Alfonso determined to return to Bologna. On reaching Florence he gave the Duke Alessandro a fine marble head of the Emperor Charles V., which is now at Carrara, whither it was sent by Cardinal Cibo, who, on the duke's death, took it out of his wardrobe. When Alfonso reached Florence the duke was in the humour to have his portrait taken, for it had been done on medals by Domenico di Polo, the engraver, and Francesco di Girolamo dal Prato, and on money by Benvenuto Cellini, and he had been painted by Giorgio Vasari of Arezzo and Jacopo da Pontormo. After Alfonso had done a fine model in relief, much better than that of Il Danese of Carrara,[2] he was allowed to make the marble reproduction at Bologna, whither he was very anxious to go. After receiving many gifts and favours from Duke Alessandro, Alfonso returned to Bologna, where his grief

[1] He went to Carrara in 1530: Cardinal Ippolito died in 1535.
[2] Danese Cattaneo.

at the death of the cardinal and his chagrin at losing the tomb brought on an incurable eruption, which gradually led to his death at the age of forty-nine. He never ceased to complain that Fortune had deprived him of a generous patron, from whom he had reason to look for the felicity that this life could afford him, and that she ought to have closed his eyes before involving him in such wretchedness. He died in 1536.

Michelagnolo, sculptor of Siena, after spending his best years in Sclavonia with other excellent artists, proceeded to Rome in these circumstances. On the death of Pope Adrian, Cardinal Hincfort, who had been his favourite and was grateful for favours received, resolved to erect a marble tomb to him, and entrusted the work to Baldassarre Peruzzi, painter of Siena, who, after making the model, wished his friend and compatriot Michelagnolo to take up the work. Accordingly he made a life-size figure of Pope Adrian on the sarcophagus, and a bas-relief of the people of Rome coming to meet and adore him on his entry into the city. In four marble niches are the virtues Justice, Fortitude, Peace and Prudence, executed by him with great diligence with Baldassarre's advice. Some parts of the work, however, are by Tribolo, a sculptor of Florence, then quite young, and these were considered the best. Michelagnolo did the minor parts with great delicacy, so that the small figures deserve more praise than all the rest. Among other things there are some compositions beautifully finished, so that Michelagnolo was richly rewarded by the cardinal for his pains, and remained in high favour during his life. Indeed it was merited, for the tomb has given as much celebrity to the cardinal as to the artist.[1] Not long after the completion of this work, Michelagnolo passed to the other life, aged about fifty.

Although Girolamo Santacroce of Naples was cut off in the flower of his age, when better work was expected of him, he proved by his productions at Naples during the few years he spent there what he might have accomplished in a longer life. They were beautifully executed and finished, as might be expected in a youth who aspired to surpass the masters of his art. He did some carved tombs with great diligence in the chapel of the Marquis of Vico, a round building with columns and niches, in S. Giovanni Carbonaro at Naples. The marble half-relief here represents the Magi offering their gifts, and is by a Spaniard. In competition with it Girolamo did a St. John in relief for a niche, so beautiful that he showed himself not

[1] The tomb is in S. Maria de Anima, Rome.

inferior to the Spaniard either in spirit or judgment. Having thus won a name for himself, he competed with Giovanni da Nola, considered the best sculptor of Naples, but then an old man, who had done many things at Naples, where it is the fashion to have chapels and panels of marble. In competition with Giovanni, Girolamo undertook to do a chapel on the left side of the door of the church in Monte Oliveto at Naples, as Giovanni did another opposite of the same order. In his chapel Girolamo made a life-size Madonna in full relief, considered a very beautiful figure, and by the diligence displayed in making the draperies, the hands, and piercing the marble, he was considered to have surpassed all those who had worked in marble there up to that time. The Madonna is between two finely conceived figures of St. John and St. Peter, beautifully finished, as are also some children above them. In the church of Capella belonging to the monks of Monte Oliveto he did two handsome statues in full relief. He next began a statue of the Emperor Charles V. when he returned from Tunis, but it was left a mere sketch, for Fortune, envying the world so much merit, removed him at the age of thirty-five. If he had lived it was expected that Girolamo would surpass all the artists of his day as he had already out-distanced all his countrymen. Thus his death caused great grief to the Neapolitans, especially as, in addition to his great abilities, he was a modest and gentle man, of the highest culture, so that it is no marvel that his acquaintances cannot speak of him without tears. His last sculptures were done in 1537, in which year he was honourably buried at Naples.

Giovanni da Nola still lived on, and was a sculptor of considerable skill, as may be seen by his numerous works at Naples, which, however, are not well designed. Don Pietro da Toledo, Marquis of Villafranca and Viceroy of Naples, employed him to make a marble tomb for himself and his wife, in which Giovanni made scenes of victories gained by the marquis over the Turks, and many single statues, very carefully finished. The tomb was to have been taken to Spain, but as this was not done during the marquis's life, it remained at Naples. Giovanni died at the age of seventy, and was buried at Naples in 1558.

About the time that Heaven gave Ferrara and the world the divine Ludovico Ariosto that city saw the birth of Dosso the painter.[1] Although not so rare a painter as Ariosto was among poets, yet his works were highly valued in Ferrara, and earned him the friendship of the great poet, who has left a memorial

[1] Ariosto was born in 1474, Dosso in 1479.

of him in his celebrated writings. Thus the pen of M. Ludovico has brought Dosso more fame than all the brushes and colours that he ever used. I must confess that I think men so praised to be very fortunate, because the authority of the author compels belief in his praise, though it may not be altogether deserved. Dosso was a great favourite of Alfonso, Duke of Ferrara, both for his qualities as an artist and because he was a very affable and pleasant man, such as the duke loved. In Lombardy Dosso had the reputation of being the best landscape painter in the profession, whether on the wall or in oils or water, particularly when compared with the German style. In the cathedral church of Ferrara he did a panel in oils [1] with figures, considered beautiful, and decorated several apartments in the duke's palace, in conjunction with his brother Battista, [2] for though the two were enemies, they worked together at the duke's desire. In the court of the palace they did stories of Hercules in grisaille, and a number of nudes on the walls. They also did a quantity of panels and frescoes in all Ferrara, and many works by them are in the cardinal's palace at Trent, done in conjunction with other painters, while they did a panel in the Duomo at Modena. [3]

At this time Girolamo Genga, the painter and architect, was decorating the imperial palace above Pesaro [4] for Francesco Maria, Duke of Urbino, as will be related. Among the numerous painters employed on this work, at the duke's order, were Dosso and Battista of Ferrara, chiefly to make landscapes, as some time before several pictures in the palace had been painted by Francesco di Mirozzo of Forli, Raffaello dal Colle of Borgo a Sansepolcro and others. Arrived at Imperiale, Dosso and Battista, following the usual practice of such men, blamed everything which they saw, and promised the duke that they would do much better. Seeing what was likely to happen, Genga, who was an acute man, gave them a room to themselves to show what they could do. Accordingly they made every effort to prove their skill. But, whatever the cause, they never in their lives produced such poor results. It seems usually to be the case that, when men are anxious to do best and have excited great expectations, their judgment is blinded and they do worse than usual. This may arise from their malignity in blaming others, or from wishing to do too much, for it is usually best to let Nature go of herself rather than to force the

[1] Dated 1527. [2] Part of this work was destroyed by fire in 1718.
[3] In 1522. [4] The Villa Imperiale.

intelligence. This is true of all arts, but especially in writing, where overstudy and affectation are only too quickly recognised. These works of the Dossi were so ridiculous that they parted with shame from the duke, who was compelled to destroy all they had done and have it repainted from Genga's design. Later on they did a very fine panel of Christ disputing in the Temple for M. Gio. Battista, knight of the Buosi, surpassing themselves, especially in the portrait of the knight and others. The panel was set up in the Duomo at Faenza in 1536. Dosso attained a good old age, and did not work in his last years, being pensioned by Duke Alfonso. Battista survived him, and did many things by himself, maintaining a good position. Dosso was buried in his native Ferrara.

There flourished at the same time Bernazzano Milanese, who excelled in landscapes, herbs, animals and other earthly things, birds and fishes. As he knew his imperfections in treating figures, he joined hands with Cesare da Sesto, who was skilful in that branch. It is said that Bernazzano did some beautiful landscapes in fresco in a courtyard containing a punnet full of ripe strawberries, so well done that some peacocks, supposing them to be real, frequently turned to peck them and spoiled the painting.

Gio. Antonio Licinio da Pordenone, and other Painters of the Friuli

(1483 – 1539)

As I have contended before, benign Mother Nature seems sometimes to endow certain places with rich gifts, where they had never been known before, and raises up men who, without masters, simply imitate living things and become excellent. It frequently happens that when one begins others arise to compete with him, and by their emulation produce marvellous works without ever having seen Rome, Florence, or other places full of notable paintings. Such was the case in the Friuli, where from such a beginning many excellent painters have arisen in our own day, a thing previously unknown there for many centuries.

When Giovanni Bellini was working in Venice, as already related, and teaching many pupils, there were two rivals among them called Pellegrino da Udine of S. Daniello and Giovanni Martini of Udine. Giovanni always imitated the style of the Bellini, which was so hard and dry that no finishing and diligence could soften it. This was because the lights and shadows are violently contrasted, so that the colouring is always crude and unpleasant, although he studied hard to imitate Nature. His works exist in many places in the Friuli, especially at Udine, the Duomo of which has a panel of his in oils of St. Mark seated and surrounded by many other figures,[1] considered his best effort. Another is in the church of the friars of S. Pier Martire, at the altar of St. Ursula, representing the saint with some of the virgins at her feet, with beautiful faces and expressions.[2] Besides being a meritorious painter, Giovanni was a handsome man of excellent character and of estimable prudence, so that he left his wife much property at his death, having no male heirs. She being as prudent as she was beautiful, as I am informed, succeeded in marrying her two lovely daughters into the richest and noblest houses in Udine.

Pellegrino da S. Daniello, Giovanni's rival, and who surpassed him in painting, was christened Martino. But as Giovanni Bellini concluded that he would become a great artist, he changed the name to Pellegrino. He also changed his country because, being fond of S. Daniello, a place ten miles from Udine, and taking a wife there, he spent most of his time in the place and became known in consequence as Pellegrino da S. Daniello. He did many paintings in Udine, of which we may still see the doors of the old organ, on the outside front of which he represented a deep arch in perspective with a St. Peter seated in the midst of a multitude of figures and giving a pastoral staff to St. Ermagoras, the bishop. Inside he did the four Doctors of the Church at study.[3] For the chapel of St. Joseph he did a panel in oils, designed and coloured with much diligence, representing a St. Joseph standing, of grave appearance, with the little Christ near him and a St. John the Baptist dressed as a shepherd regarding the Christ.[4] The picture is so good that we may believe the story that it was done in competition with Giovanni, and that Pellegrino devoted all his energies to making it superior to his rival's St. Mark. For the house of M. Pre Giovanni, agent of the Lords Della Torre at Udine, Pellegrino did a half-length Judith of great beauty, holding the head of Holofernes in her hand. There is a large oil-painting by him on the high altar of the church of S. Maria at Civitale,[1] eight miles from Udine, containing fine heads of virgins and other figures. In a chapel in S. Antonio at S. Daniello he painted the events of the Passion,[2] well deserving his reward of over 1000 crowns. The Dukes of Ferrara greatly favoured him for his ability, and, in addition to numerous gifts, provided two of his relations with stalls in the Duomo of Udine. Among his numorous pupils, of whom he made considerable use, was a Greek of great ability, possessing a good style in imitation of Pellegrino. Luca Monverde of Udine, a great friend of Pellegrino, would have far surpassed him if he had not been cut off so early, when no more than a youth. He left an oil-painting, his first and last, for the high altar of S. Maria delle Grazie in Udine, containing a Madonna seated with the Child,[3] melting softly into the background, while there are two excellent figures below, showing his great promise.

Another pupil was Bastianello Florigorio, who did a panel for the high altar of S. Giorgio, at Udine, of the Virgin in the air surrounded by a number of cherubs, who in various ways are adoring the Child whom she is holding. Beneath is a very good landscape. There is also a fine St. John and a St. George in armour on horseback, of proud aspect, slaying the serpent, while the damsel at the side thanks God and the Virgin for the succour sent to her. The head of St. George is said to be a portrait of Bastianello. In the refectory of the friars of S. Pier Martire he did two pictures in fresco, one of Christ blessing the bread at Emmaus and the other the death of St. Peter Martyr. In a niche at the corner of the palace of M. Marguando, a learned doctor, he painted in fresco a foreshortened nude figure of St. John, which is considered good. Driven out of Udine by some disputes, he went to live in exile at Civitale. His style was crude and sharp, because he was so fond of drawing things by candlelight. He displayed good invention, and took great pleasure in drawing portraits, producing good likenesses. Among others he did those of M. Raffaello Belgrado and the father of M. Gio. Battista Grassi, an excellent painter and architect, to whose courtesy I owe many particulars of the Friuli artists. Bastianello lived about forty years.

Another pupil, Francesco Floriani of Udine, is still living, and is a very good painter and architect. So also is his younger brother, Antonio Floriani, whose abilities have recommended him to the service of the Emperor Maximilian. Some of Fran-

---

[1] Painted 1529.   [2] In 1522.   [3] Painted 1522.

cesco's paintings were in the emperor's hands two years ago,
when he was king, namely a Judith who has cut off the head
of Holofernes, done with admirable judgment and diligence,
and a book of pen-and-ink drawings full of fine ideas for buildings, theatres, arches, porticos, bridges, palaces and many other
architectural works of utility and beauty. Gensio Liberale,
another pupil of Pellegrino, among other things in his paintings,
is an excellent imitator of every kind of fish. He is now in the
service of Ferdinand, Archduke of Austria, in a deservedly high
rank, because he is an admirable painter.

But the most celebrated of these distinguished painters
of the Friuli is of our own day, for he has far surpassed the
others in invention of scenes, in design, boldness, skill in colouring, fresco-work, speed, great relief, and every other department of our art. This is Gio. Antonio Licinio, called Cuticello
by some. He was born in Pordenone in the Friuli, twenty-five
miles from Udine. Being naturally endowed with a fine genius
and drawn towards painting, he studied natural objects without
a master, imitating the methods of Giorgione of Castelfranco,
whose works he had often seen in Venice, and whose style
attracted him. When he had learned the elements of art, he
was forced to remove in order to avoid an epidemic which
broke out in his native place. Remaining in the country for many
months, he did various works for the rustics, making experiments in colouring upon lime at their expense. This being the
best method of learning, he became skilful and judicious in that
kind of work, and was able to obtain such effects as he desired
with his colours, for when used in a soft state there is a risk that
the whites will ruin all harmonious effects when the lime dries.
Having learned the nature of colours and how to work well in
fresco, by long practice, he returned to Udine, and in the convent
of S. Pier Martire, at the altar of the Annunciation, he did an
oil-painting of the Virgin saluted by the Angel Gabriel, with
God the Father in the air, surrounded by cherubs, sending
forth the Holy Spirit. This work, executed with design, grace,
vivacity and relief is considered his best by competent critics.
In the organ pulpit under the doors painted by Pellegrino, in
the Duomo of the city, he did a story of SS. Ermagoras and
Fortunatus,[1] full of lightness and design. In the same city he
painted the front of the palace of the Lords Tinghi in fresco,
to win their friendship. To show his knowledge of architecture
and fresco-work, he introduced some compartments into this,

[1] In 1527.

with decorations and niches full of figures. In three large spaces in the middle he painted scenes of coloured figures, the middle space being square and the side ones oblong. Here he represented a Corinthian column with its base in the sea, and on the right is a siren supporting the column, and a naked Neptune on the left supporting the other side. Above the capital is a cardinal's hat, said to be for Pompeo Colonna, a great friend of the lords of that palace. The other two spaces contain the giants fulminated by Jove, some finely foreshortened corpses lying on the ground. Opposite is a heaven full of gods, with two giants on the earth about to strike Diana with clubs, while she boldly defends herself and attempts to burn the arm of one of them with a lighted torch. In the large church at Spilimbergo, a village fifteen miles above Udine, he painted the organ desk and the doors. On one he did an Assumption, and inside St. Peter and St. Paul before Nero, regarding Simon Magus in the air. On the other is the Conversion of St. Paul and on the desk the Nativity of Christ.[1] Having become famous by this lovely work and many others, Pordenone was invited to Vicenza, and after doing some things there he proceeded to Mantua, where he painted a façade in fresco for M. Paris, a nobleman of the city, with marvellous grace. Among the fine ideas in this work there is a frieze of ancient letters below the cornice, one and a half braccia high, between which are numerous children in varied and beautiful attitudes. After completing this work with much honour, Pordenone returned to Vicenza, and, in addition to many other things, painted the entire tribune of S. Maria di Campagna,[2] although a part left unfinished at his departure was diligently completed by Maestro Bernardo da Vercelli. He did two chapels in fresco in that church, one with stories of St. Catherine and the other with the Nativity of Christ and the adoration of the Magi, both admirable.[3] In the lovely garden of M. Barnaba dal Pozzo, doctor, he did some poetical subjects, and in the church of Campagna, on the left of the entrance, he did a panel of St. Augustine. All these beautiful works led the noblemen of the city to induce him to take a wife there, and they always entertained the highest respect for him. On going to Venice, where he had previously done some works, he painted a façade in S. Geremia on the Grand Canal. In the Madonna del Orto he did a panel in oils[4] with many figures, notably a St. John the Baptist, on which he expended all his

---

[1] Painted 1524. [2] It should be Piacenza, commissioned 1529.
[3] Done 1529-31. [4] Now Accademia, Venice.

powers. On the front of the house of Martin d' Anna, on the same canal, he did many scenes in fresco, notably a Curtius on horseback, foreshortened, which seems to be in relief, as does a Mercury also, flying through the air, with many other ingenious things. This work gave extraordinary delight to the Venetians, and Pordenone received more praise for it than had previously been accorded to any painter there.

Among other circumstances which induced him to make exceptional efforts was the rivalry of Titian, for he hoped, by continual study and a spirited treatment of fresco - work, to wrest the palm from that great artist, who had won his position by his extraordinary skill, unvarying courtesy and affability, and by habitually associating with great men and putting his hand to everything. This competition was certainly beneficial, because it induced Pordenone to exert himself to the utmost in every work, so that he is worthy of all praise. Thus the masters of S. Rocco gave him the chapel and the entire tribune of that church to paint in fresco. Here he did a God the Father in the tribune, and a number of children coming from Him, in fine and varied attitudes. On the frieze of the tribune he did eight figures of the Old Testament, and in the angles the four Evangelists, and above the high altar the Transfiguration, while the two lunettes at the sides contain the four Doctors of the Church. There are two large pictures by him in the middle of the church, one of Christ healing a number of sick, very well done; and the other a St. Christopher with Christ on His shoulders. In the wooden tabernacle of the church, where the silver is kept, he did a St. Martin on horseback, with beggars offering their vows. This work, which was very admirable and brought him honour and advantage, won him the friendship of M. Jacopo Soranzo, who obtained for him a commission to do the hall of the Pregai in competition with Titian. There he did many pictures of fine figures, foreshortened from beneath. He also did a frieze of marine monsters, worked in oils, about this room, for which the senate voted him a provision for life. As he was always anxious to be painting where Titian had worked, he did a St. John the Almoner giving money to the poor in S. Giovanni di Rialto. In another he did St. Sebastian, St. Roch and other saints,[1] a beautiful work, but not equal to Titian's, although many praise it chiefly through malice. In the cloister of S. Stefano he did a number of scenes from the Old Testament in fresco, and one from the New, with various Virtues between

[1] About 1530.

them,[1] and here he displayed marvellous foreshortening This was what he loved, and he sought to introduce very difficult examples into every composition, succeeding better than any other painter.

At Genoa Prince Doria had built a palace on the sea-front,[2] and employed Perino del Vaga, a renowned painter, to decorate the rooms and ante-chambers in oils and fresco. The beauty and richness of the paintings is marvellous; but, as Perino was not devoting much attention to the work just then, the prince, to spur him by competition to exertions which he would not other-wise make, sent for Pordenone, who began an open terrace, where he did in his usual style a frieze of children unloading a bark full of merchandise, and moving in beautiful attitudes. He also did a large scene of Jason asking his uncle's permission to go for the golden fleece. But when the prince saw the difference between the work of Perino and that of Pordenone, he dismissed the latter, and sent for Domenico Beccafumi of Siena, a more excellent master. This artist did not hesitate to leave his native Siena, where his marvellous works abound, to serve so great a prince, but he only did one scene there, for in the end Perino completed everything by himself.

When Gio. Antonio reached Venice, he learned how Ercole, Duke of Ferrara, had brought a great number of masters from Germany, and set them to make silk, gold, flax and woollen cloth as he desired, but there was no good designer of figures in Ferrara, Girolamo da Ferrara [3] being better at portraits and single things than at striking scenes demanding artistic power and design. Anxious to win fame and riches, Pordenone set out from Venice, and on reaching Ferrara was warmly received by the duke. But being soon after seized with severe pains in the chest, he lay half-dead in bed, and in three days expired at the age of fifty-six. It was a great blow to the duke, and to his friends, especially as many believed he had been poisoned. The body was honourably buried, the news of his death causing great grief to many, especially at Venice.

Gio. Antonio was ready-witted and a general favourite; he loved music, and having studied Latin literature he displayed quickness and grace in conversation. He always made his figures large, being very rich in invention, doing everything well. In fresco in particular he was bold and resolute.

Pomponio Amalteo of S. Vito, a pupil of his, became his son-in-law owing to his good qualities, for he executed all his

[1] After 1532.   [2] At Fassuolo.   [3] Girolamo da Carpi.

works well, following in his master's footsteps. We see this by the new organ doors painted in oils, the outside containing Christ driving out the money-changers, and the inside the story of the Pool of Bethesda, with the resurrection of Lazarus.[1] The church of S. Francesco in that city possesses an oil-painting by the same hand of St. Francis receiving the stigmata. This work contains some fine landscapes, the rays of the rising sun obscuring the seraphic moon, and piercing the hands, feet and side of St. Francis, who receives them devoutly on his knees, while his companion, a foreshortened figure, stands in amazement. Pomponio also painted in fresco Christ between the two disciples at Emmaus, at the head of the refectory of the friars of la Vigna. In his native village of S. Vito, twenty miles from Udine, he painted in fresco the chapel of the Madonna in the church of S. Maria,[2] in so fine a style and to the general satisfaction that he was admitted to the nobility of the place by Cardinal Maria [3] Grimani, patriarch of Aquileia and lord of S. Vito.

I have noticed these excellent artists of Friuli in Pordenone's Life because their abilities deserve it, and in order that the much greater excellence of those who followed may be recognised, as will be shown in the Life of Giovanni Ricamatori of Udine, to whom our age is much indebted for his stuccoes and grotesques. But to return to Pordenone. His works in Venice were in the time of the most serene Gritti, and he died as related in 1540. He was amongst the foremost men of our age, his figures seeming to start out from the walls on which they are painted, so that he may be enumerated among those who have contributed to the progress of the arts to the general advantage.

GIO. ANTONIO SOGLIANI, Painter of Florence
(1492 – 1544)

IN letters and in the superior manual arts it is often observed that the melancholy are the most assiduous students and support labour with the most patience. Men of this temperament rarely fail to succeed in such professions, and Gio. Antonio Sogliani was no exception, his cold aspect making him look like melancholy itself. This was so strong in him that, apart from his art, he thought of little but family cares, which were a great burden

Painted 1555.   [2] Begun 1535.   [3] *Rectius* Marino.

to him, although he might easily have escaped them. He remained with Lorenzo di Credi for twenty-four years, painting, living with him, and honouring and serving him. Having thus become an excellent painter, he showed himself a faithful pupil and imitator of his master, as we see by his first paintings in the church of the Osservanza on the hill of S. Miniato outside Florence, where he did a panel copied from the one done by Lorenzo for the nuns of S. Chiara, containing a Nativity,[1] not inferior to his original. After leaving his master, he did in oils a St. Martin dressed as a bishop for the art of the vintners in S. Michele in Orto, which won him the reputation of a good painter. As he cherished a great admiration for the works and style of Frà Bartolommeo of S. Marco, he endeavoured to imitate his colouring, as we see by an unfinished panel, left incomplete because it did not please him. He kept it in his house as worthless, but after his death it was sold to Sinibaldo Gaddi, who gave it to Santi Titi dal Borgo, then a youth, to finish, and put it in his chapel in the church of S. Domenico at Fiesole. It represents the Adoration of the Magi, with a good portrait of the artist at the side. For Madonna Alfonsina, wife of Piero de' Medici, he did a panel which was placed as a votive offering over the altar of the Chapel of the Martyrs in the church of the Camaldoli at Florence. It represents St. Arcadio crucified and other martyrs holding the cross, two half-figures draped, the rest nude and kneeling, the crosses on the ground. In the air are some cherubs with palms in their hands. The picture was executed with much diligence and judgment in the colouring, the heads being very life-like. Owing to the siege of Florence the monastery was taken from the fathers and subsequently given to the nuns of S. Giovannino of the order of the knights of Jerusalem. The monastery being at length destroyed, Duke Cosimo had the picture set up in one of the chapels of the Medici in S. Lorenzo, as being one of Sogliani's best works. For the nuns of la Crocetta he did a Last Supper in oils, then much admired, and in a tabernacle in the via de' Ginori he painted in fresco for Taddeo Taddei a Crucifixion with the Virgin and St. John, and some weeping angels in the air. This is a much-admired and excellent fresco. In the refectory of the abbey of the black monks at Florence he did a crucifix with graceful angels, flying and weeping, while beneath are the Virgin, St. John, St. Benedict, St. Scolastica and others. For the nuns of Spirito Santo, on the hill of S. Giorgio, he painted two pictures of St. Francis and St. Elizabeth, Queen of Hungary,

[1] Berlin Gallery.

a sister of the order. He designed a fine processio.al banner for the company of the Ceppo, representing the Visitation on the front and on the back St. Nicholas the bishop with two children dressed as flagellants, one holding the book and the other the three gold balls. In S. Jacopo sopr' Arno he did a Trinity, with countless cherubs, St.Mary Magdalene kneeling, St.Catherine and St. James.[1] At the sides are two upright figures in fresco of Jerome in penitence and St. John. In the predella he ordered his pupil Sandrino del Calzolaio to do three scenes, which earned considerable praise. For Anghiari, at the end of an oratory, he did a Last Supper in oils on a panel, with life-size figures, and at the side Christ washing the Apostles' feet, and a servant bringing two ewers of water.[2] The work is held in great veneration there, as it is of great value, and brought Sogliani much honour and profit. A Judith of his with Holofernes' head was sent to Hungary as a thing of great beauty, and a Decollation of St. John the Baptist with a perspective representing the exterior of the chapter-house of the Pazzi, in the first cloister of S. Croce, was sent to Naples by Paolo da Terrarossa, who had it done. For one of the Bernardi Sogliani did two other pictures which were placed in the church of the Osservanza on S. Miniato, in a chapel containing two life-size figures in oil of St. John the Baptist and St. Anthony of Padua. But he was so dilatory over the middle picture that the donor died in the meantime, for Andrea was naturally slow and easy-going. Thus the picture was left incomplete; it represented the dead Christ in His Mother's lap.

When Perino del Vaga, after having fallen out with Prince Doria, had left Genoa and was working at Pisa, Stagio, a sculptor of Pietrasanta, had begun a row of new marble chapels in the last aisle of the Duomo, and the sacristy behind the high altar; it was ordained that Perino and other masters should decorate these with paintings. But Perino being recalled to Genoa, Gio. Antonio was instructed to begin to fill the niches behind the high altar.[3] Here he treated of the sacrifices of the Old Testament as symbolic of the Most Holy Sacrament. He began with the sacrifice of Noah and his sons when they came out of the ark, then those of Cain and Abel, which were all much admired, but especially that of Noah, because it contained such fine heads and figures. The one of Abel contains a pretty landscape, and the youth's head is goodness personified, the clouded face of Cain being the

---

[1] Now in S. Marco.
[2] In S. Maria del Fosso, commissioned 1531.
[3] He was at work on this 1531-40.

exact contrary. If Sogliani had been quick, and not so easy-going, he might have done all the work of the Duomo for the warden, who was very pleased with his style, but as it was he only did one picture in addition to those in the chapel where Perino had begun to work. He finished this at Florence and greatly delighted the Pisans. It contains the Virgin, St. John the Baptist, St. George, St. Mary Magdalene, St. Margaret, and other saints. The warden being very pleased gave him three other pictures, which he began, but did not finish during the warden's life. Bastiano della Seta being subsequently elected to that position, and finding the work to be progressing very slowly, gave the part behind the high altar to Domenico Becca-fumi of Siena, who quickly finished a panel, as will be said in his Life, while the remainder was done by other painters. Gio. Antonio meanwhile completed two other panels at his ease, representing a Virgin and saints in each. At length he went to Pisa and did the fourth and last, which was worse than the others, owing to age, the competition with Beccafumi, or some other cause. But the warden, tired of Sogliani's slowness, gave the other three panels to Giorgio Vasari of Arezzo, who finished the two beside the door of the façade. In the one nearest the Campo Santo are a Virgin and Child, caressed by St. Martha, while St. Cecilia, St. Augustine, St. Joseph and St. Guido the hermit are kneeling, and a nude St. Jerome and St. Luke the Evangelist stand in front with cherubs, some raising a curtain and some holding flowers. In the other, in conformity with the warden's wish, he did another Madonna and Child, St. James Intercisus, St. Matthew, St. Silvester the Pope and St .Turpin, knight. In order not to repeat the ideas of the others, he repre-sented the Madonna holding the dead Christ, and the saints as if surrounding a Deposition from the Cross. In the background are the naked bodies of the two crucified thieves, with horses, executioners, Joseph, Nicodemus and the Maries about, done at the request of the warden, who desired that all the saints of the old, dismantled chapels should be introduced. They lacked one panel, which was made by Bronzino, representing a nude Christ and eight saints. Thus was the whole work completed, and Gio. Antonio might have done it all had he not been so slow. As he was in great favour with the Pisans, he was employed after the death of Andrea del Sarto to finish a panel for the company of St. Francesco, sketched by Andrea. It is now in the company on the piazza of S. Francesco at Pisa. For the opera of the Duomo he made some rows of hangings, and others at Florence, as such work pleased him, especially when aided by his friend Tommaso di Stefano, painter of Florence. Being requested by the friars of S. Marco at Florence to do a fresco at the top of their refectory at the cost of Friar de' Molletti, who had possessed a large property, he proposed to represent the Feeding of the Five Thousand, and indeed he made a drawing containing women and children and a confused multitude of persons; but the friars would not have it, preferring something positive, ordinary and simple. To please them he did St. Dominic with his friars miracu- lously fed by two angels in human form bringing them bread.[1] In this he painted the portraits of several of the friars, who are very life-like, especially the donor, who is serving at the table. In a lunette above the table he did St. Dominic at the foot of the cross, and the Virgin and St. John the Evangelist weeping. At the sides are St. Catherine of Siena and St. Antonino, Archbishop of Florence, of that order. This work in fresco was done with great care and finish. But Sogliani would have succeeded far better if he had followed his first design, because painters express their own ideas better than those of others. On the other hand, it is only right to please those who bear the cost. The design referred to is in the possession of Bartolommeo Gondi, who has many others by the same hand, as well as a large picture, obtained from Sogliani's wife, after his death, as she was a friend of his. There are some others of great beauty in our book. For Giovanni Serristori Sogliani began a large panel, to be put in S. Francesco dell' Osservanza outside the S. Miniato gate, with a great number of figures, some of the heads being the best he ever did. But it was left unfinished at the death of Giovanni Serristori. However, as Sogliani had been paid, he gradually finished it, and gave it to M. Alamanno di Jacopo Salviati, Giovanni's son-in-law and heir, who presented it with an ornamentation to the nuns of S. Luca, who still have it at their high altar in the via di S. Gallo. Sogliani did other things in Florence, some of which are in private houses, while some were sent abroad. However, I need not mention them, as I have spoken of the principal ones. He was a worthy and very religious man, minding his own affairs without meddling with other artists. Sandrino del Calzolaio was his pupil, and made the tabernacle at the corner of the Murate, and a St. John the Baptist teaching the duty of giving shelter to the poor, at the hospital of the Temple. He would have produced still more good work if he had not died young. Other pupils were Michele, who afterwards went to Ridolfo Ghirlandajo, from

[1] In 1536.

whom he took his name; Benedetto, who went to France with Antonio Mini, pupil of Michelagnolo Buonarroti, where he did many beautiful works; and lastly Zanobi di Poggino, who did several things for the city. After suffering a long while of the stone, Gio. Antonio finally rendered his soul to God at the age of fifty-two. His death caused great sorrow, because of his goodness and his pleasing style in expressions and colouring, very delightful to those who, without caring for the labours of art, love what is straightforward, easy, soft and graceful. The post-mortem disclosed three large stones, each the size of an egg, but he would never consent to be operated upon, or listen to reason.

GIROLAMO DA TREVIGI, Painter

(1497-1544)

It rarely happens when men persevere at work in their native place that they are raised by Fortune to the rank their ability deserves, and if they are finally recognised, it comes late. Very often, indeed, when they attain the reward of their labours, they are prevented by death from enjoying them for long, and this was the fate of Girolamo da Trevigi, who was reputed a good master. Although not skilful in design, he coloured prettily in oils and fresco, imitating the methods of Raphael of Urbino. He did a good deal in his native Treviso, and many works in Venice, notably the façade of the house of Andrea Udone [1] in fresco, some friezes of children inside the court, and an upper room. He did not do them in grisaille, because the Venetians prefer colours. On the front is a large scene of Juno flying with the moon on her head, enveloped in clouds, her arms above her head, one holding a vase and the other a cup. He also made a fat, rubicund Bacchus, overturning a vase, holding Ceres by the hand, and several ears of corn. There are the Graces and five cherubs flying down to confer plenty upon the house of the Udoni. To show that it was the home of the wise, he made Apollo on one side and Pallas on the other. The work was done very freshly, and brought Girolamo much honour and advantage. For the chapel of the Madonna at S. Petronio he did a picture in competition with some Bolognese artists, as I shall have occasion to say. While in

[1] Odoni.

Bologna he did several paintings, and in the chapel of St. Anthony of Padua in S. Petronio he painted the saint's life with judgment, grace and excellent finish. At S. Salvatore he did a panel of the Virgin mounting the steps with some saints, and another of the Madonna in the air with children and St. Jerome and St. Catherine at her feet, the feeblest of his productions at Bologna. Over a large door there he did in fresco a Crucifixion, the Virgin and St. John, which are admirable. In S. Domenico, at Bologna, he did a Virgin and saints, his best work, near the choir on the steps up to the shrine of St. Dominic, with a portrait of the donor.[1] He also coloured, for Count Gio. Battista Bentivogli, from a cartoon of Baldassarre of Siena, representing the story of the Magi, doing the work with great skill, although there are more than a hundred figures. Bologna contains many other paintings of his in houses and churches, and in Galiera there is a façade in grisaille of the Teofamini, and one behind the houses of the Dolfi, pronounced by some to be his best work in the city. Proceeding to Trent, he painted the palace of the old cardinal[1] in conjunction with other painters, by which he won great fame. Returning to Bologna, he devoted himself to works already begun. It was proposed then to have a picture for the Hospital della Morte. Various competitors' designs were presented, and some being helped by friends rather than by merit, Girolamo was left out. Feeling offended, he soon after left Bologna, whereby the envy of others raised him higher than he had ever dreamed, for if he had obtained the work it would have prevented his enjoying the advantages which Fortune had prepared for him. Proceeding to England,[3] he was presented to King Henry by some of his friends, and entered his service, not as a painter, but as an engineer. Having shown ingenious examples of buildings taken from others in Tuscany and Italy, he was thought a wonder by the king, who richly rewarded him, ordaining a provision of 400 crowns a year, and affording him facilities to erect a noble house at the king's cost. Having thus risen from the depths of misfortune to this height, Girolamo lived happy and contented, giving thanks to God and to fortune for bringing him to a country so favourable to his peculiar abilities. But this unaccustomed happiness could not last long. The war between the French and English was still going on, and Girolamo directed the making of bastions and forts for the artillery and camp.

---

[1] Now in the National Gallery, London, as is the cartoon next mentioned
[1] Bernardo Clesio Cardinal, Archbishop of Trent 1514-39.
[3] In 1542.

One day during the bombardment of Boulogne, in Picardy, he was cut in two by a cannon ball, thus losing his life and all his newly-won honours at the age of thirty-six in 1544.

POLIDORO DA CARAVAGGIO and MATURINO FLORENTINO, Painters

(ob. 1543; ob. c. 1528)

IN the last golden age, as we may call that of Leo X., among the noblest spirits of the time was Polidoro da Caravaggio of Lombardy, a painter, not as the result of long study, but by Nature. Coming to Rome at the time when Pope Leo was building the loggias of his palace, under Raphael's direction, he fetched lime for the builders until he was eighteen; but when Giovanni da Udine began to paint there, the inclinations of Polidoro were turned towards painting, and he lost no time in making himself an artist, associating with the young men of ability to see their methods and study design. Among the others he chose Maturino Florentino as a companion, he being in the Pope's chapel, and considered a good designer of antiquities. He made such progress that in a few months he produced works that astonished those who had known him in his former condition. As the loggia went on, he boldly associated himself with the young painters skilful in the art, so that when he left the work he was the noblest and finest genius of them all. The mutual affection of Polidoro and Maturino was so much increased by this that they determined to live and die together like brothers. They made common their desires, money and works, and lived in perfect agreement. As there were many in Rome who employed brilliant colouring, and as they had seen some façades of houses done in grisaille by Baldassarre of Siena, they resolved to imitate that method, and did so from that time. They therefore began one at Montecavallo, opposite S. Silvestro, in the company of Pellegrino da Modena, and, encouraged by this to go on, they did another on the side door of S. Salvatore dal Lauro, and a scene on the side door of the Minerva, with yet another, a frieze of six monsters, above S. Rocco a Ripetta. They did others of lesser excellence in every part of Rome, which I need not describe, because they produced better work later on. Still further encouraged, they began to study the antiquities of Rome, copying marble antiques in their grisaille, so that there was not a vase, statue, sarcophagus, relief, or any other thing, whether whole or broken, which they did not design or make use of. By this means they both acquired the ancient style, and their work, like their purpose, was very similar, expressing the same knowledge. And although Maturino did not possess as much natural ability as Polidoro, yet he copied his companion's style so carefully that it was not possible to distinguish the work of the one from that of the other. They did a façade on the piazza of Capranica on the way to Colonna, with the theological Virtues, and, in a frieze under the windows, a draped Rome, as Faith, holding the chalice and host, and receiving tribute from all the nations of the world, while the Turks are destroying the tomb of Mahommed, concluding with the saying of Scripture, "There shall be one fold and one shepherd." For invention they had no equals, as is shown by the quantities of clothes, garments, shoes and curiosities wondrously executed. Their works are continually copied by all foreign painters, so that, by their good style and facility, they have done more to benefit painting than all the others together, from Cimabue onwards. All draughtsmen in Rome turn more readily to their works than to any other modern paintings. In the Borgo Nuovo they did a façade in sgraffito, and another at the corner of la Pace, and yet another, a little way off, on the house of the Spinoli going to Parioni, representing ancient wrestling, and sacrifices and the death of Tarpeia. Near Torre di Nona, towards the S. Angelo bridge, is a small façade with the Triumph of Camillus and an ancient sacrifice. On the way leading to the Madonna del Ponte is a beautiful façade with the story of Perillus put into the bronze bull made by himself, remarkable for the vigour of those who are putting him in, and his terror at the approach of the unusual death. Here is Phalaris, I believe, giving orders with imperious gesture to punish the cruel inventor who wished to kill men with greater torture, as well as a beautiful frieze of children painted like bronze, with other figures. Above this he did another wall of the same house, with what is reputed to be a figure of the Bridge, dressed in the ancient Roman habit, and more scenes. On the piazza of the custom-house at S. Eustachio they did a façade of battles. On the right-hand, on entering the church, is a chapel with figures painted by Polidoro. Above Farnese they did another façade of the Cepperelli, and one behind the Minerva, in the street leading to Maddaleni, representing a scene from Roman history. Among other beautiful things in it is a frieze of rejoicing children, in imitation of bronze, executed with the utmost grace and beauty. On the wall of Boniauguri, near the Minerva, are some fine scenes of Romulus tracing the site of his city with the plough, the crows flying above, with most realistic imitations of the costumes and persons of the ancients. Indeed, no one ever displayed such mastery in this art, nor such design, style, skill or dexterity, so that all artists were filled with wonder that Nature should have produced men in this age capable of producing such miracles. Under Corte Savella, in the house bought by Signora Costanza, they did the Rape of the Sabine women, showing the lust and determination of the Romans, and the misery of the poor women, carried off by the soldiers on horseback, and in other ways. Others contain like ideas, such as the stories of Mutius and Horatius, and the flight of Porsenna, King of Tusculum. In the garden of M. Stefano dal Bufalo, near the fountain of Trevi, they did some beautiful scenes of the fountain of Parnassus, making grotesques and small coloured figures. In the house of Baldassino da S. Agostino they did sgraffiti scenes, and heads of emperors over the windows of the court. In Montecavallo, near S. Agata, they did a façade with scenes of the Vestal Tutia carrying water from the Tiber to the Temple in a sieve, Claudia drawing a ship with her girdle, and the rout caused by Camillus as Brennus is weighing the gold. At the other façade beyond the corner they did Romulus and Remus suckled by the wolf, the terrible fight of Horatius defending the bridge alone against a thousand, with many figures behind him anxiously cutting the bridge. There also is Mutius Scævola burning his hand, which had killed the king's servant, before Porsenna, who displays his wrath and desire for vengeance; while inside the house they did several landscapes. They decorated the front of S. Pietro ad Vincola with stories of St. Peter and some colossal prophets. Their fame was spread abroad by their numerous works, which brought them great praise in their lives, and have been freely imitated after their deaths. They decorated a wall behind Naona, on the piazza where the Medici palace stands, with the triumphs of Paulus Emilius and several other Roman stories. At S. Silvestro di Montecavallo they did some small things for the house and garden of Frà Mariano, and painted his chapel, and two coloured scenes of St. Mary Magdalene, containing beautiful portions of landscapes, Polidoro excelling all others in such work, and in trees and stones, being the originator of the present facile methods. They further painted in colour several rooms and friezes for many houses in Rome with frescoes and tempera, done as an experiment, because they could not obtain the same beauty with colours as they did with grisaille, bronze or earths. This is seen in the house of the cardinal of Volterra da Torre Sanguigna,[1] where they decorated a wall beautifully in grisaille, introducing some coloured figures, so badly done that they detract from the excellence of the rest. It is the more noticeable because hard-by are the arms of Pope Leo X., with nudes by Gio. Francesco Vetraio,[2] who would have achieved great things had he not been cut off by death. Persisting in their foolish policy, they did some coloured children at the altar of the Martelli, where Jacopo Sansovino did a marble Madonna, these figures looking like the first efforts of foolish beginners instead of famous masters. But where the canopy covers the altar Polidoro did a dead Christ with the Maries, a most beautiful thing, showing their true strength. Returning to their usual style, they did two fine façades in Campo Marzio, one with stories of Ancus Martius, and the other the Saturnalia celebrated there, with the pair and four-horse chariots racing round the obelisks, the whole being very finely designed and a truthful representation of the spectacle. At the corner of la Chiavica, leading to Corte Savella, they did a façade of surpassing beauty, with the story of the maidens crossing the Tiber, and near the door is a sacrifice done with wonderful industry and art, showing that they had studied all the necessary implements and ancient customs connected with such sacrifices. Below S. Jacopo degli Incurabili they did a façade with stories of Alexander the Great, containing figures of the ancient Nile and Tiber, copied from the Belvedere. At S. Simeone they did the façade of the Gaddi, marvellous for the numerous costumes, the quantity of antiquities, buskins and boats richly decorated, the product of a refined imagination. The memory staggers under the weight of its numerous beauties in the representation of ancient methods, statues of the great and lovely women, containing as it does all the various ways of sacrificing, the embarkation of an army, the fighting with various weapons and arms, executed with such grace and skill that the eye is confounded by the quantity of fine ideas. Opposite is another façade, unequalled for its beauty and wealth, containing the story of Niobe in a frieze, the people bringing her various gifts, and adoring her, the work being so replete with novelty, delicacy, art, genius and relief that it is impossible to describe it adequately. Then follows

---

[1] Francesco Soderini.   [2] Gio. Fr. Bembo, called Vetraio.

the wrath of Latona and the dire revenge upon the proud woman's children, slaughtered by the arrows of Phœbus and Diana, containing a quantity of bronzes that look like metal, not paint. Above are other scenes, containing gold vases so curiously wrought that it would be hard to find anything more beautiful or novel, together with Etruscan helmets and so many other curious inventions that the brain reels at the multiplicity and profusion of their inventions. These works have been imitated times without number. They also did the court of the house, as well as the decoration of the loggia with small grotesques of great beauty. Indeed they endowed everything which they touched with divine grace. I could fill a book with the performances of these two alone, as there is no apartment, palace, garden or country-house which does not contain their work.

While they were thus engaged in embellishing Rome, and looking forward to the reward of their toil, envious Fortune sent Bourbon to sack the city in 1527. By this means Polidoro and Maturino were separated, like many thousands of friends and relations who had been accustomed to share each other's bread. Maturino took to flight, and is supposed at Rome to have died of the plague soon after, brought on by the terrors of the sack. He was buried in S. Eustachio. Polidoro took the road to Naples, where he nearly died of hunger, as the nobles cared little for art. While working for some painters he did a St. Peter in the principal chapel of S. Maria della Grazia, helping them in many things, to eke out a living. But his ability becoming known, he did a vault in tempera for the court of . . . and the walls, which is considered very beautiful. He also did the courtyard of Sig. . . . and some loggias full of decoration, beauty and good work. In S. Angelo, by the fish-market of Naples, he did a small panel in oils of the Virgin and some nude souls in torment, considered beautiful for its design rather than its colouring. In the same style he did some single figures for the high altar.

Seeing his talents were so little appreciated at Naples, Polidoro determined to leave a place where they prefer a horse that jumps well to a clever painter. Accordingly he took ship for Messina, and finding himself better appreciated there, he began to colour with skill, doing several works, which are scattered about in various places, and, studying architecture, he proved his knowledge in several things which he did. When Charles V. passed through Messina on returning from his victory at Tunis,[1] Polidoro made him some fine triumphal arches, for which he won

[1] In 1535.

great fame and reward. Desiring once again to see Rome, which always calls to those who have lived there for many years, he did as a final performance an oil-painting of Christ bearing the Cross,[1] of great excellence and beautiful colouring, a number of figures accompanying the Christ, soldiers, Pharisees, horses, women, children, the thieves in front, being so excellent that Nature seemed to have summoned her strength for a supreme effort to realise such a scene. After this he made several attempts to leave the country, although he was well treated there, but he was detained by the prayers and caresses of a lady whom he had loved for many years. At length he tore himself away, overcome by his desire to see Rome and his friends, taking from the bank a good sum of money which he had deposited there. He had for some time employed a boy of the country who was more fond of Polidoro's money than of his master. While the money was in the bank the boy was helpless, but the night after it was taken out he planned with some friends to kill Polidoro as he slept, and to share the money with them. While Polidoro was in his first sleep they strangled him, and after giving him some wounds they left him dead. To make it appear that they had not done it they carried the body to the door of his mistress, pretending that the relations or others in the house had killed him. The boy gave his rascally companions their share of the money and sent them away. On the following morning he went weeping to the house of a count, a friend of Polidoro, and told him his story. But in spite of diligent search, nothing came to light. However, by God's will, and the wrath of Nature and virtue at such a stroke of fortune, some unprejudiced person was inspired to say that no one but the boy could have assassinated Polidoro. The count therefore had him put to the torture, upon which he confessed his crime, and was condemned to be hanged, after being tortured with red-hot pincers and quartered. This, however, did not restore Polidoro to life or to the art he had so much adorned, so that there had been no one like him for centuries. If his inventions had died with him, then invention, grace, vigour in figures would have perished. Happy were the nature and ability that formed him, and cruel the fate which cut him off, but though he lost his life, his name will remain. His burial took place with solemn obsequies in the cathedral church of Messina in 1543, amid the grief of all the city. Artists, indeed, owe a great debt to him for enriching painting with qualities of various and curious costumes and ornaments, and endowing

[1] Now in the Naples Museum.

his works with grace, making all manner of figures, animals, buildings, grotesques and landscapes, so that all who have aspired to be universal have imitated him. But the instability of Fortune is well illustrated in his career; for after raising him to such a pitch of excellence she brought him to a wretched end at the moment when he hoped to enjoy the fruit of his labours and in such a terrible way as to startle pity, outrage virtue, and convert benefits into ingratitude. His painting must be praised even as his evil fortune in bringing him to a sad and unexpected end is to be lamented.

Rosso, Painter of Florence
(1494–1541)

ABLE men who devote all their efforts to improving their gifts are often, when least expected, raised to the greatest honours in the sight of the world. This occurred to the Florentine painter Rosso, for if he could not obtain satisfactory recognition in Rome and Florence, he proved more fortunate in France, where the glory he acquired would have satiated the most ambitious artist. Indeed, he could not rise higher, being so favoured and esteemed by so great a monarch as the King of France. His merits were indeed such that if Fortune had treated him otherwise she would have done him a great wrong. Besides his skill in painting, Rosso possessed a handsome presence, was gracious and grave in speech, an accomplished musician and a well-versed philosopher, while more important than all were his poetical fancy in the composition of figures, his bold and solid design, light style, beautiful composition and the forcefulness of his grotesques. Excellent as an architect, he was rich in spirit and grandeur, though poor in pocket. Thus those who follow in his steps will always be praised, as his works are; for they have no equal in force and ease, being entirely devoid of that circumstance with which so many endeavour to endow their nothings with importance. In his youth, Rosso drew from the cartoon of Michelagnolo. He would not bind himself to any master, as he had an opinion of his own in opposition to their styles. We may observe this in a tabernacle at Marignolle, outside the S. Pier Gattolini gate at Florence, done in fresco for Piero Bartoli, representing a dead Christ, in which we see the first signs of his desire for a bold and grandiose style beyond others, with lightness of touch and wonderful.

As a beardless youth, when Lorenzo Pucci was created cardinal by Pope Leo,[1] Rosso did the arms of the Pucci over the door of S. Sebastiano of the Servites, with two figures, which then excited the wonder of artists who did not expect success from him. Thus encouraged, and after doing a half-length Madonna with the head of St. John the Evangelist for Maestro Giacopo, a Servite friar who studied poetry, he did an Assumption at the friar's instigation, beside the Visitation of Giacopo da Pontormo, with a heaven full of naked child angels dancing about the Virgin. Their graceful outlines are beautifully foreshortened, and if the colouring had shown the same maturity that he afterwards acquired, he would have far surpassed the other scenes there, for he equalled them in grandeur and good design. The Apostles are laden with draperies, the folds being too ample, but their attitudes and some of the heads are more than divine. The master of the hospital of S. Maria Novella employed Rosso to do a panel, but as he understood little of art, when he saw the sketch he thought the saints were devils, as Rosso usually made his figures harsh at first, softening them after. Accordingly the master rushed out of the house and refused to take the picture, saying that he had been deceived. Over another door leading into the cloister of the convent of the Servites Rosso painted the arms of Pope Leo, with two children, now destroyed, and did several paintings and portraits for private houses. When Pope Leo came to Florence he did a fine arch at the corner of the Bischeri. He next did a beautiful dead Christ[2] for the lord of Piombino, as well as a chapel, while at Volterra he painted a fine Deposition from the Cross.[3] Having thus increased in reputation he did the picture of the Gods at S. Spirito in Florence,[4] which had been allotted to Raphael, who left it for the work at Rome. Rosso executed it with grace and design and with brilliant colouring. No work seems to possess more power or shows to greater advantage at a distance for the boldness of the figures and the ease of the attitudes. As it differed from the work of others it was considered eccentric, but although it was not much admired at the time, men have since gradually come to recognise its merits, for it would be impossible to improve upon the harmony of the colours, the clear lights above merging into the medium lights and then into the shadows with such softness and harmony

---

[1] In 1513.   [2] Doubtfully identified with the Pietà in the Louvre.
[3] Pinacoteca, Volterra.   [4] The three Fates of the Pitti Gallery.

that the figures stand in relief on each other. Indeed, Rosso may be said to have produced a work which, for judgment and mastery, may be compared with the efforts of any other master. In S. Lorenzo he did a panel for Carlo Ginori of the Marriage of Our Lady, considered very beautiful. No one has ever surpassed or even approached him in his facility of production, his colouring being soft, the draperies falling gracefully, so that he is always admirable. Everyone who sees his work must acknowledge the truth of what I say, for his nudes are very fine, showing a thorough knowledge of anatomy. His women are very graceful, their draperies being curious and fanciful. His old men's heads are curious, while those of women and children are sweet and pleasant. He showed such rich invention that he never had any superfluous spaces in his pictures, and he did everything with marvellous facility and grace. For Gio. Bandini he did a picture of some beautiful nudes in a scene of Moses slaying the Egyptian,[1] containing praiseworthy things. I think it was sent to France. He did another for Gio. Cavalcanti, which went to England, of Jacob giving drink to the women at the well, considered divine, seeing that it contained most graceful nudes and women, for whom he loved to make delicate draperies, coiffures and garments. While engaged upon this work Rosso inhabited the Borgo de' Tintori, the rooms of which opened on to the gardens of the friars of S. Croce.

He took a great fancy for a baboon, which was more like a man than an animal, loving it like himself, and as the creature was marvellously intelligent, he employed it on several services. This baboon happened to become very fond of a handsome apprentice called Battistino, divining by signs all that he wished. At the back of the rooms, which led into the friar's garden, there was a vine of the keeper's full of very large *sancolumbane* grapes, and as it was a long way off the window, the apprentices sent the baboon with a rope to gather grapes. The keeper, finding that his grapes were disappearing with no apparent cause, suspected mice and set a watch. When he discovered the culprit to be Rosso's baboon he was filled with rage, and seizing a stick went to beat him. The animal seeing he would be caught whether he climbed up or stayed where he was, began to jump enough to ruin the pergola, and as if moved to throw himself upon the friar he seized the outside cross pieces of the trellis with both hands. Meanwhile the friar arrived with his stick, whereupon the baboon shook with fear to such an extent that he broke the uprights and

[1] Uffizi.

the whole pergola with the baboon collapsed upon the friar's head. The friar cried for mercy, and Battista and the others pulled the rope and brought the baboon back to their room. The keeper picked himself up and going to a small terrace made remarks not to be found in the mass, and went off in a rage to the office of the Eight, a much-dreaded magistracy in Florence. Here he lodged his plaint; Rosso was summoned, and the baboon was condemned to have a weight fastened to his leg, so that he could not leap on to the vine. Rosso made a ring, with an iron weight attached, for him, so that he was able to run about the house, but could not go outside. The creature seemed to know that the friar was the cause of his punishment, and he practised jumping every day, holding the weight in his paws, and so at length achieved his purpose. One day he jumped from roof to roof, at the hour when the keeper was singing vespers, until he reached the roof of his room, and there he let the weight fall and amused himself for half an hour to such purpose that not a tile was left unbroken. Three days afterwards a heavy rain fell, and the keeper was heard to complain bitterly.

When Rosso had completed his works, he went away to Rome with Battista and the baboon. His works were much in request, as some of his designs had preceded him and were considered marvellous, for he drew divinely, with great finish. Above Raphael's work in the Pace he did one of his worst performances.[1] I do not know why, but all suffer in this way, and it is a curious fact that a change of country produces a change of nature, ability and habits, so that men are rendered different and stupid. The air of Rome might have affected him, while the stupendous works of architecture and sculpture, and the paintings and statues of Michelagnolo, may have overcome him. Such considerations induced Frà Bartolommeo and Andrea del Sarto to fly from Rome without leaving any work there. Whatever the cause, Rosso never did worse, and it is unfortunate it should have been next to Raphael's work. At this time he did a dead Christ supported by two angels for his friend the Bishop Torna-buoni, which is now in the hands of the heirs of Monsignor della Casa, and is a beautiful thing. For Il Baviera he designed all the gods afterwards engraved by Jacopo Caraglio, including Saturn changed into a horse and the rape of Proserpine by Pluto. He did a sketch of the Decollation of St. John the Baptist, now in a church on the Piazza de' Salviati at Rome. On the sack of Rome Rosso was taken prisoner by the Germans, and very badly

[1] In 1524.

treated, being stripped and made to carry weights, removing in this way almost the entire stock of a cheesemonger. He dragged himself to Perugia, where he was welcomed and clothed by the painter Domenico di Paris. For him Rosso did a cartoon for a picture of the Magi, a beautiful thing, still in his possession. He did not remain there long, for learning that the Bishop de' Tornabuoni, another refugee from the sack, had arrived at the Borgo, he proceeded thither to meet his friend.

At that time Raffaello dal Colle, painter and pupil of Giulio Romano, was living there. He had undertaken to do a panel cheaply for S. Croce, an oratory of Flagellants, but gave up the task in a friendly spirit to Rosso, that the latter might leave a memorial of himself in the city. The company objected, but the bishop intervened in his favour. When the panel was completed it brought him much renown, and was set up in S. Croce. It represents a Deposition from the Cross of rare beauty, the colouring showing the darkness of the eclipse which took place at Christ's death, and the work displaying great diligence. At Città di Castello he was commissioned to paint a panel,[1] but the roof falling in while he was doing the gesso completely destroyed it, and he caught a fever which brought him to death's door, so that he was carried from Castello to the Borgo. When quartan fever followed this attack he proceeded to the Pieve of S. Stefano to obtain a change of air, and finally to Arezzo, where he was entertained by Benedetto Spadari. He and Gio. Antonio Lappoli of Arezzo and their relations and friends succeeded in securing for him the painting in fresco of a vault in the Madonna delle Lagrime,[2] already allotted to Niccolo Soggi, painter, agreeing to pay him 300 gold crowns to the end that he might leave a memorial of himself in the city. Rosso began the cartoons in a room provided for him in a place called Murello, finishing four. One represents our first parents bound to the tree of sin, and the Virgin taking the sin, represented by the apple, out of their mouths. At their feet lies the serpent, and in the air are Phœbus and Diana, to show that Our Lady was clothed with the sun and moon. In the second, where the ark of the covenant is borne by Moses, he represented the Virgin surrounded by five Virtues. In another is the throne of Solomon, with the same represention. Vows are offered to show that people come to Our Lady for favours, and there are other curious fancies devised by M. Gio. Pollastra of Arezzo, a friend of Rosso, to please whom Rosso made a fine model of the whole work, now in our house at Arezzo. He drew a study of nudes for the work of rare beauty, so that it is a pity it is incomplete, because if he had done it in oils instead of fresco it would have been a miracle. But he always disliked working in fresco, and frittered away his time in making cartoons to be finished by Raffaello dal Borgo and others. Being a courteous man, he at the same time did many designs in Arezzo and elsewhere for paintings and buildings, as, for example, that of a chapel for the rectors of the Fraternity at the foot of the piazza where the Volto Santo now is, for whom he had designed a panel of Our Lady with the people under her mantle, to be put in this place. This design is on our book, with many other fine ones by him.

But to return to the work he was to do in the Madonna delle Lagrime. His trusty friend Gio. Antonio Lappoli was bail for him, for he left no means untried of rendering Rosso a service. But during the siege of Florence in 1530, the Aretines, being liberated from all restraint owing to the imprudence of Papo Altoviti, captured and destroyed the citadel. As the people disliked the Florentines Rosso would not trust them, and went to Borgo S. Sepolcro, leaving his cartoons and drawings shut up in the citadel. Those of Castello who had allotted the panel to him desired him to finish it, and because of the troubles which he had experienced there he would not return, so he finished the panel at Borgo, and would never allow them the pleasure of seeing it. He represented a crowd of people, and Christ in the air adored by four figures, introducing Moors, gipsies, and the strangest figures in the world, though perfectly beautiful, the whole composition being adapted to everything except the purpose for which it was required. At this same time he disinterred the dead in the Vescovado, where he was staying, and made magnificent anatomical studies. In truth Rosso was a diligent student of art, and few days passed when he did not draw some nude from life.

He always hoped to end his days in France, and thus escape the misery and poverty to which, so he said, those who work in Tuscany and in their native places are exposed, and so he determined to go there. To make himself universal he learned Latin, when an event occurred which hastened his departure. One Holy Thursday, during evening service, an Aretine youth and pupil of his was making sparks and flames with a lighted match and some pitch and as they were reciting the *Tenebrae*, the boy was reprimanded by some priests and struck slightly. Rosso, who was seated beside the boy, angrily struck the priest in the face, at which a disturbance arose, and men who knew nothing of the circumstances drew their swords on poor Rosso, who was struggling with the priests. So Rosso fled and fortunately reached his quarters without injury. But considering himself dishonoured by this, he finished his Castello panel, and without thinking of his work at Arezzo or the harm he was doing his surety Gio. Antonio, for he had received more than 150 crowns on account, he departed by night, and, taking the Pesaro road, reached Venice. Here he was received by M. Pietro Aretino, and drew for him a sleeping Mars, with Venus, Cupids and Graces undressing him and trailing about his cuirass. It was afterwards engraved. From Venice Rosso went to France,[1] where he was heartily welcomed by the Florentines. Having painted some pictures, which were afterwards put in the gallery at Fontainebleau, he gave them to King Francis, who was greatly delighted. The monarch was even more pleased with Rosso's bearing, conversation and habits (his ruddy complexion suiting his name), his grave, serious manner and great judgment. After granting him a provision of 400 crowns and giving him a house in Paris, which Rosso used little, spending most of his time in Fontainebleau, where he had apartments and lived like a lord, the king made him chief of all structures, paintings and other ornaments of that place. Here Rosso began a gallery over the lower court, not vaulting it, but making a flat roof with open beams, beautifully partitioned. The sides he decorated with stucco and curious and fantastic panels, with several kinds of cornices carved with life-size figures, the lower part being adorned with rich festoons in stucco, others with paintings of fruit and every sort of verdure. In a large space he had about 25 scenes painted in fresco from his design, if I am rightly informed, of the deeds of Alexander the Great, the designs being water-colours done in grisaille. At the two ends of the gallery are two oil-paintings by him, executed with such perfection that few better can be seen. One contains a Bacchus, the other represents Venus, done with marvellous art and judgment. The Bacchus is a naked youth, tender, delicate and soft, the flesh seeming to palpitate; about him are vessels of gold, silver, crystal and various precious stones of such extraordinary nature that they astound the beholder. Among other things is a satyr, raising part of a canopy, his head with his strange goat's horn being of marvellous beauty, while he seems to smile with delight at seeing such a beautiful youth. There is a child riding a bear, of great beauty, with many other

[1] About 1530.

graceful and beautiful ornaments. The other design contains
Cupid, Venus and other beautiful figures. But the figure to which
Rosso devoted the most pains was the Cupid, represented as a
boy of twelve but possessing greater powers, and beautiful in
every part. When the king saw these works he was greatly
pleased, and took Rosso into high favour, giving him soon
after a stall in Notre Dame at Paris and other revenues, so that
he lived like a lord with his servants and horses, giving banquets
to his friends and acquaintances, especially to the Italians who
came there. For the top-most hall, called the pavilion from its
shape, Rosso did decorations in stucco and figures in relief at
regular intervals, from the floor to the beams, with children,
festoons and various sorts of animals, and a seated figure in
fresco on the level, representing gods and goddesses of the ancients
in great numbers. Over the windows is a rich stucco frieze without
paintings. For the other rooms he did stuccos and paintings,
copies of which have been printed and circulated. They are of
great beauty and grace, as are his designs for salt-cellars, vases,
basins and other curious things which the king had executed in
silver, and which are too numerous to describe. Suffice it to say
that he designed all the vessels for a chamber of the king, and
all the things for horses, masques, triumphs and other events
with a curious and whimsical fancy. When the Emperor Charles
V. came to Fontainebleau in 1540, with only twelve men, trusting
himself to King Francis, Rosso and Francesco Primaticcio of
Bologna between them arranged the tournaments instituted
by the king in honour of his guest. But Rosso's arches, colossi
and such-like things were, it was said, the most stupendous ever
made. A great deal of his work at Fontainebleau has since been
destroyed by Francesco Primaticcio, who has made a new and
larger building there. In these things Rosso was assisted by
his favourites Lorenzo Naldino of Florence, Maestro Francesco
of Orleans, Maestro Simone of Paris and Maestro Claudio,
also of Paris, by Maestro Lorenzo of Picardy, and many
others. But the best of them was Domenico del Barbieri, an
excellent painter and master of stucco, and an extraordinary
designer, as his engraved works show, which may be considered
among the best extant. The painters whom Rosso employed
at Fontainebleau were Luca Penni, brother of Gio. Francesco,
called Il Fattore, a pupil of Raphael, Leonardo Fiammingo, a
very able painter who beautifully coloured Rosso's designs,
Bartolommeo Miniati of Florence, Francesco Caccianimici and
Gio. Battista da Bagnacavallo. They all served him while

Francesco Primaticcio went to Rome by the king's order to make bronze casts of the Laocoon, the Apollo and other rare antiquities. I do not mention the carvers, wood-workers and others without number of whom he made use, because it is unnecessary to speak of all, though many of them produced admirable work. Besides the things mentioned, Rosso did a remarkable St. Michael, and a dead Christ on a panel for the Constable, a rare work, sent to Ecouen. He also did some fine miniatures for the king. He further did a book of anatomy to be printed in France, some portions of which are in our book of designs. After his death two beautiful cartoons were found among his things, one a Leda, the other of the Tiburtine Sibyl showing the glorious Virgin and Christ to the Emperor Octavian. Into this he introduced King Francis and his queen, the guard and the people, with such a quantity of fine figures that it may be accounted one of his best works. The king favoured him so greatly that shortly before his death he possessed an income of 1000 crowns, besides his very considerable gains from his works. He lived more like a prince than a painter, with numerous servants and horses, his house furnished with tapestries, silver and other valuable furniture. But Fortune, who rarely or never allows those who trust too much to her to retain their high degree long, caused his fall in the strangest possible manner. Francesco di Pellegrino, a Florentine, who was fond of painting and a friend of Rosso, associated with him, when the latter was robbed of 100 ducats. Rosso suspected Francesco, and had him removed from court and rigorously examined. Being found innocent and released, Francesco was moved with the greatest indignation against Rosso for the false charge made against him, and attacked his former friend in such a way that Rosso was in a quandary, being unable to defend himself, seeing that he had not only accused his friend falsely, but stained his own honour, proclaiming himself a bad and disloyal man. Accordingly he determined to kill himself. One day, when the king was at Fontainebleau, he sent a peasant to Paris for a poisonous liquor, saying that he wanted it for varnish. The peasant returned with the poison, but such was the nature of the liquid that it had almost destroyed the finger with which he stopped the phial, though it was sealed with wax. Soon afterwards Rosso took this poison and so died. When the news was brought to the king he was much grieved, feeling that in Rosso he had lost the best artist of the day. In order that the work might not suffer, he entrusted it to Francesco Primaticcio of Bologna, who had

already done several works, giving him a good abbey, just as
he had given a canonry to Rosso. The latter died in 1541,
having shown artists what an advantage it is in dealing with
a prince to be universal, courteous and gentle in bearing.
Indeed, he deserves admiration for many reasons as being
truly excellent.

BARTOLOMMEO DA BAGNACAVALLO [1] and other Painters of the Romagna

(1484-1542)

EMULATION in art is generally most desirable, but if pride and
vain-glory are excited by competition, genius is obscured, for
it is hard for men to rise to eminence when they do not know
their own faults or fear the works of others. Success more often
comes to modest students who honour the works of the best
masters and imitate them, than to those whose heads are filled
with empty pride, as were those of the painters Bartolommeo
da Bagnacavallo, Amico Bolognese,[2] Girolamo da Codignuola
and Innocenzio da Imola. They all lived at Bologna at the same
time, and were very jealous of each other, while their pride and
vain-glory, which were not justified by their works, diverted them
from the true way where men strive rather to produce good
work than to crush their rivals. Thus they did not attain to
their expected goal and, presuming to be masters, they were
far removed from excellence. Bartolommeo had gone to Rome
in Raphael's time, hoping to attain to perfection. He had won
a reputation in Bologna as a youth, and was therefore given work
on the first chapel on the right on entering the Pace at Rome,
above the chapel of Baldassare Peruzzi of Siena. But not succeeding so well as was expected, he returned to Bologna, where
he and the others named above each did in competition a scene
from the life of Christ and the Virgin for the chapel of the
Madonna, at the front door on the right-hand in entering S.
Petronio. There is little difference in merit between these works,
Bartolommeo winning fame for his softer and more confident
style. Amico has introduced some strange things into his Resurrection, the soldiers being in distorted postures, and several of
them are struck by the stones of the tomb. Yet Bartolommeo's
was more praised by artists as being of more harmonious design

[1] Bartolommeo Ramenghi.   [2] Amico Aspertini.

and colouring. This led to his subsequent association with Biagio Bolognese,[1] who possessed more skill than genius, and they did a refectory in company in S. Salvatore for the Scopetini friars, partly in fresco and partly *a secco*, representing the Feeding of the Five Thousand. On a wall of the library they did the dispute of St. Augustine, with a meritorious perspective. These masters, from seeing the works of Raphael and from associating with him, possessed some characteristics of merit, but they did not achieve individuality in art. However, as Bologna did not then possess better artists, they were considered the best masters in Italy by the governors and people of the city. There are some medallions in fresco by Bartolommeo under the vaulting of the Podestà palace, and opposite the palace of the Fantucci in S. Vitale there is a Visitation, while the Servites at Bologna have an Annunciation painted in oils, surrounded by some saints in fresco done by Innocenzio da Imola. In S. Michele in Bosco, Bartolommeo painted in fresco the chapel of Ramazzotto, a party chief in Romagna. In a chapel of S. Stefano he painted in fresco two saints with cherubs of great beauty, and decorated a chapel in S. Jacopo for M. Annibale del Corello, representing the Circumcision, with several figures. In a lunette above he did Abraham sacrificing Isaac. This work was really skilfully executed in good style. In the Misericordia outside Bologna he painted the Madonna and some saints in tempera, as well as several pictures and other works in the hands of various people.

Bartolommeo was a man of considerable merit for his good life and his works, possessing better design and invention than the others, as is shown by a drawing in our book of Christ disputing with the doctors in the Temple, the building showing good judgment and composition. He died at the age of fifty-eight, having experienced the jealousy of Amico Bolognese, a fanciful, strange man, whose mad, fantastic figures are all over Italy, but especially in Bologna, where he lived for some time. Indeed, had he worked systematically and not casually, Amico might possibly have surpassed many whom we consider highly. But even as it is, we find good and admirable work among the quantity he produced, for example a façade in grisaille on the Piazza de' Marsigli containing several scenes and a frieze of fighting animals, which is among his best productions. He painted another façade at the S. Mammolo gate, and did a frieze about the principal chapel of S. Salvadore, so full of follies that it would excite the most melancholy to laughter. In

[1] Biagio Pupini.

fine, there is not a church nor a street in Bologna that he has not daubed. He also painted a good deal at Rome, and decorated a chapel in S. Friano [1] at Lucca, containing strange fancies but some admirable things, such as the stories of the Cross and of St. Augustine, containing countless portraits of the noted men of the city. Indeed, this was one of Amico's best works in colours in fresco. At the altar of St. Nicholas in S. Jacopo at Bologna he did some stories of the saint, and a frieze below with perspectives deserving of praise. When the Emperor Charles V. came to Bologna Amico made a triumphal arch at the palace gate, for which Alfonso Lombardi did statues in relief. It is no wonder that Amico produced more than the others, because, being an eccentric and unsociable man, he went through Italy drawing and copying every painting and relief, the good with the bad. He thus became a sort of expert inventor, and he pressed every thing into his service, while he destroyed those which were of no use to him, and thus he formed his curious and fantastic style. At the age of seventy he became actually insane, and M. Francesco Guicciardino, a notable Florentine and the truthful historian of his times, being then governor of Bologna,[2] derived considerable amusement from him, as did all the city. Some believe, however, that his folly was not unmixed with cunning, because, having sold some goods for a small price, and being in extreme need, he wanted them back, and obtained them again upon certain conditions, saying that he had sold them when out of his wits; at least so I have often heard tell. He also studied sculpture, and did a dead Christ supported by Nicodemus in marble on the right on entering S. Petronio,[3] to the best of his ability and in the same style as his paintings. He painted with both hands at once, holding the light brush in one hand and the dark in the other, but it was more laughable to see his belt filled with colours, so that he was like the devil of St. Macaire [4] with all his phials. As he worked in his spectacles he would have made stones laugh, especially if he began to chat, because he would say the strangest things. He would never speak a good

---

[1] i.e. S. Frediano, done after 1506.
[2] From 1531 to 1534.   [3] In 1526.
[4] St. Macaire once saw the devil in the shape of a man in a ragged dress, from the holes of which hung several small bottles. "Where are you going?" asked the saint. "To fuddle the friars," he replied. On his return the saint inquired how he had succeeded. "Badly," said the devil, "they are all saints but one, who yielded." Macaire at once sought the erring friar and brought him to repentance. Soon after he saw the devil again, who replied that the monks were all saints, and he had lost the only one he had, who had become the most holy of all.

word of anyone, however good or skilful or whatever merits they owed to Nature or Fortune. He was so eager to pick up news that one evening a painter of Bologna, who had bought cabbages on the piazza, met Amico, who was full of his news so that the poor man could not shake him off, but was detained under the loggia of the Podestà till the next morning, when Amico said, "Go and boil your cabbage, as time flies." He played many jokes which I must not mention, because I wish to speak of Girolamo da Codignuola,[1] who did many portraits from life in Bologna, and two very fine ones in the house of the Vinacci. He drew the dead body of Gaston de Foix, slain at the rout of Ravenna, and not long after he drew the portrait of Massimiliano Sforza. He did a much-admired panel in S. Giuseppe, and another in oils at S. Michele in Bosco, which is in the chapel of St. Benedict. It led to his being employed with Biagio of Bologna to do all the scenes about the church in fresco, executed *a secco*. They display considerable skill, as I said in speaking of Biagio's style. In St. Colomba at Rimini he painted an altar-picture in competition with Benedetto da Ferrara and Lattanzio of St. Lucy, rather voluptuous than beautiful, and a Coronation of the Virgin in the principal tribune with the twelve Apostles and four Evangelists, shameful caricatures with large heads. Returning to Bologna, he did not remain long there, but went to Rome, where he painted the portraits of several nobles and one of Pope Paul III. Seeing that the place was not made for him, and that he could hardly obtain name and fame among so many noble painters, he went to Naples, where he was taken up by some friends, notably M. Tommaso Cambi, a Florentine merchant who was very fond of marble antiquities and paintings, and who provided for all his needs. So he set to work, and in Monte Oliveto he did a panel of the Magi in the chapel of one Antonello, bishop of some place. In S. Aniello he did another panel in oils of the Virgin, St. Paul and St. John the Baptist, with several portraits of nobles. Being well advanced in years, and wishing to husband his resources, for he was very poor, he soon left Naples, where he had little more to do, and returned to Rome. Some friends there, learning that he had saved a few crowns, persuaded him that he ought to take a wife. He allowed himself to be so beguiled by them for their advantage that he was united to a prostitute of whom they were procurers, and this so afflicted the poor old man that he died in a few weeks at the age of sixty-nine.

[1] Girolamo Marchesi.

Innocenzio da Imola,[1] to say something of him, remained for many years with Mariotto Albertinelli in Florence, and returning afterwards to Imola he did numerous works in the district. At the instance of Count Gio. Battista Bentivogli he went to live at Bologna, where he began by copying a picture of Raphael, done for Signor Lionello da Carpi.[2] For the monks of S. Michele in Bosco he did the Death of the Virgin and the Resurrection of Christ in fresco in the chapter-house. This work was executed [3] with great skill and diligence. He did the high-altar picture for the church there, the upper part being in good style. For the Servites of Bologna he did an Annunciation, painted a crucifix in S. Salvatore, and executed several paintings in the city. At la Viola he did three loggias in fresco for Cardinal Ivrea,[4] two coloured scenes in each, from designs by other painters, but diligently executed. In S. Jacopo he did a chapel in fresco and an oil-painting for Madonna Benozza of considerable merit. He drew the portrait of Cardinal Francesco Alidosio, which I have seen at Imola, with the portrait of Bernardino Carvaial, both of considerable beauty. Innocenzio was a modest and good man, so that he avoided the society of those painters of Bologna whose disposition was the exact opposite. He overworked himself and fell sick of a pestilential fever, which ultimately killed him at the age of fifty-six. He had only just begun a work outside Bologna, but it was completed by Prospero Fontana, a painter of Bologna, according to his instructions given before his death. The works of all the painters named were executed between 1506 and 1542; our book contains drawings by all of them.

FRANCIABIGIO,[5] Painter of Florence
(1482-1525)

THE efforts made by men to raise themselves from poverty, and enable them to help their relations as well as themselves, convert their toil and sweat into pleasure, thereby affording encouragement to others, so that a beneficent Providence, looking down upon a life admirably ordered and devoted to the study

---

[1] Innocenzio Francucci.
[2] The Madonna del Pesce, now in the Prado, Madrid.
[3] In 1517.
[4] Philibert Ferrerio, cardinal, bishop of Ivrea, 1518-50.
[5] Francesco di Cristofano.

of the sciences is constrained to show them more than usual favour. Thus it was with Francia, painter of Florence, who studied painting not so much from lust of fame as to help his poor relations and to raise himself, because his parents were humble artisans. The competition of Andrea del Sarto, then his companion, did much to spur him on, as they kept shop and lived together, the association proving of great advantage to both. Francia learned the principles of art in his youth from his stay of some months with Mariotto Albertinelli, and being drawn to perspective, which he studied incessantly from his love of it, he won a considerable reputation in Florence in his youth. His first works were done in S. Brancazio, a church opposite his house, where he painted St. Bernard in fresco, and a St. Catherine of Siena on a pilaster in the Rucellai Chapel, which gave a taste of his artistic abilities. But far better was a Madonna and Child,[1] in a chapel in S. Pier Maggiore, where a little St. John is playing with Jesus. He did an excellent St. Job in a tabernacle in a corner of S. Giobbe behind the Servites at Florence, where he did an excellent Visitation, the Madonna displaying benignity and Elizabeth reverence. St. Job is represented as poor and leprous, as well as rich and in health. The painting brought Francia credit and reputation. So the captain of the church and company gave him the high-altar picture, where he did much better, painting himself as St. John the Baptist and doing a Virgin and St. Job in poverty.[2] At that time the chapel of St. Nicholas was being built in S. Spirito at Florence, a statue of the saint being carved for it in wood from a model by Jacopo Sansovino. Francia painted two little angels on either side, which were praised, and did an Annunciation in a circle with the miracles of St. Nicholas in the predella in small figures, very carefully finished. On the right-hand on entering S. Pier Maggiore he did an Annunciation,[3] the angel still flying in the air while the Virgin kneels in a most graceful attitude to receive the salutation. It contains a much-admired and ingenious building in perspective. Indeed, although Francia's style was somewhat feeble owing to his laborious workmanship, yet he showed constraint and diligence in his treatment of figures. In the court in front of the church of the Servites he was set to paint a scene in competition with Andrea del Sarto.[4] He did a Marriage of the Virgin, showing the great faith of Joseph in taking her,

---

[1] The Madonna del Pozzo in the Uffizi, which has been attributed to Raphael.
[2] Uffizi.   [3] Turin Gallery.   [4] In 1513.

his face expressing as much fear as joy. A man is giving him a blow, as a reminder, a modern custom at marriages. A nude figure admirably expresses rage and desire in breaking his rod which did not flower. The drawing for this, with many others, is in our book. Surrounding the Virgin are beautiful women with fine coiffures, in which he always delighted; indeed, the scene contains nothing but what is excellent. A woman carrying a child is entering a house, and has cuffed another child which sits down crying and refusing to move, holding one hand to its face very prettily. Into every detail of the picture he has put the greatest diligence, spurred and encouraged to show artists and others how he approached the difficulties of art and overcame them.

The friars being anxious one feast day to uncover the scenes of Andrea and Francia together, rashly uncovered that of Francia on the night that he had finished it, thinking in their ignorance that he would not retouch the figures or do anything else. The news was brought to Francia the next morning, and he was like to die of vexation. Enraged against the friars for their presumption and want of consideration, he went to the work, and jumping on to a part of the scaffolding which had not been removed, he seized a hammer and smashed some female heads, the Madonna and a nude, leaving the wall thus disfigured. The friars hurried in at the noise, and some seculars held his hands to prevent him doing more, but though they offered him double payment, he was so incensed against them that he refused to repair the damage, and out of reverence for him other painters have not cared to finish the picture, and it has remained in the same state until now. It is beautifully executed in fresco with diligence and freshness, so that Francia may be styled the best worker in that medium of his day. In retouching he improved his frescoes, harmonising and shading them, and deserves high praise. At Rovezzano, outside the S. Croce gate, he did a tabernacle with a Crucifixion and saints, and for S. Giovannino, at the S. Pier Gattolino gate, he did a Last Supper in fresco. Not long after Andrea del Sarto went to France. In the company of the Scalzo at Florence he had begun to paint a court in grisaille, doing stories of St. John the Baptist, and as the men wanted it finished they took Francia as an imitator of Andrea's style. In this way he did the ornamental border on one side and completed two scenes, St. John leaving his father Zacharias to go into the desert, and the meeting of Christ and St. John, while Joseph and Mary stand by and see

them embrace.[1] He went no farther, because Andrea returned
to finish what he had begun.

With Ridolfo Ghirlandai, Francia made a fine apparatus for
the wedding of Duke Lorenzo, with two perspectives for the
comedies then presented, done with masterly judgment and
grace, which brought him into favour with the prince. This
led to his employment to gild the vaulting of the hall of Poggio
a Caiano [2] together with Andrea di Cosimo. He began a wall
there in competition with Andrea del Sarto and Jacopo da
Pontormo, of Cicero borne in triumph by the Roman citizens,
a work begun by Pope Leo in memory of Lorenzo, his father,
who had built the place and decorated it with paintings of
antique subjects selected by him. These were assigned to Andrea
del Sarto, Jacopo da Pontormo and Franciabigio by the learned
historian M. Paolo Giovio, bishop of Nocera, then the favourite
of Cardinal Giulio de' Medici, in order that they might show
their skill. Ottaviano de' Medici had given to each artist 30
crowns a month. In his part Francia did a fine scene with
some buildings well measured in perspective. But the work
was interrupted by Leo's death. It was then taken up again
in 1532 by order of Duke Alessandro de' Medici, who employed
Jacopo da Pontormo, but he proved so slow that the work
remained incomplete at the duke's death.

But to return to Francia. He was so enamoured of art that
not a day passed but he drew some nude as a study in his shop,
keeping men paid for the purpose. In S. Maria Nuova he did an
anatomical study at the request of Maestro Andrea Pasquale,
an excellent physician of Florence, which helped him greatly
in his painting. In a lunette over the library door in the convent
of S. Maria Novella he did a St. Thomas confounding heretics,
very carefully finished and in a good style. Among other details
there are two children holding a coat of arms, of great beauty
and grace, produced in the most charming style. He further did
a picture of small figures for Gio. Maria Benintendi in competition with Jacopo da Pontormo, who did a similar one of
the Magi, and Francesco d'Albertino [3] did two others. Francia,
in his, represented David watching Bathsheba in her bath,[4]
with some women, in too soft a manner, and a building in perspective, where David is ordering couriers to go to the camp
to procure the death of Uriah the Hittite. Under the loggia he

---

[1] Painted 1518 and 1519.   [2] In 1521.
[3] Francesco Ubertini called Il Bachiacca.
[4] Painted 1523; now in Dresden Gallery.

represented a royal feast. The work added much to Francia's fame. He did the large figures finely, but the little ones better still. He also did many fine portraits, one in particular of his close friend Matteo Sofferroni,[1] and a life-like one of an agent of Pier Francesco de' Medici [2] at the palace of S. Girolamo, Fiesole. He put his hand to everything that was given him, without shame, and besides many other base works he did a lovely *Noli me tangere* for Arcangelo, the cloth-weaver, at Porta Rossa, on a tower serving as a terrace, and countless other small things which I need not mention, as he was good-natured, easy-going and obliging. He loved his quiet, and so would never take a wife, quoting the trite proverb that "He who has a wife endures pain and sorrow." He would never leave Florence, because he had seen some things of Raphael, and recognising his inferiority to that artist and many others, he refused to compete with them. Indeed, a man's prudence and wisdom can go no farther than to know his own limitations. After having made much profit by his work, though he was not naturally endowed with much invention or any powers which he had not acquired by long study, Francia died in 1524, aged forty-two. Agnolo his brother studied under him, but died after doing a frieze in the cloister of S. Brancazio and a few other things. For Ciano, an eccentric and famous perfumer, Andrea did a shop sign of a gipsy telling a lady's fortune, a curious idea.

Antonio di Donnino Mazzieri studied painting under the same master. He was a bold draughtsman, with invention in dealing with horses and landscapes. He painted in grisaille the cloister of S. Agostino at Monte Sansovino, with scenes from the Old Testament which were much admired. In the Vescovado of Arezzo he did the chapel of St. Matthew, comprising the baptism of a king, and the life-like portrait of a German. For Francesco del Giocondo he did the legends of the Martyrs in a chapel behind the church of the Servites at Florence. But having exhausted his credit he was forced to accept everything.

Francia also taught a youth called Visino, who would have become excellent if he had not died young, and had many other pupils whom I need not mention. He was buried by the company of St. Giobbe in S. Brancazio, opposite his house, in 1525, amid the grief of good artists, for he had been an ingenious and skilful master, modest in all his actions.

[1] Possibly the portrait in the Berlin Gallery, signed and dated 1522.
[2] Now at Windsor Castle.

CONTENTS OF VOLUME THREE

PART III—*continued*

CONTENTS OF VOLUME FOUR

PART III—*continued*